History & Women, Culture & Faith
Volume 3

History and Women, Culture and Faith:
Selected Writings of Elizabeth Fox-Genovese
General Editor, David Moltke-Hansen

Volume 1
Women Past and Present
Edited by Deborah A. Symonds

Volume 2
Ghosts and Memories: White and Black Southern Women's Lives and Writings
Edited by Kibibi Mack-Shelton and Christina Bieber Lake

Volume 3
Intersections: History, Culture, Ideology
Edited by David Moltke-Hansen

Volume 4
Explorations and Commitments: Religion, Faith, and Culture
Edited by Ann Hartle and Sheila O'Connor-Ambrose

Volume 5
Unbought Grace: An Elizabeth Fox-Genovese Reader
Edited by Rebecca Fox and Robert L. Paquette

History & Women
Culture & Faith

Selected Writings of
Elizabeth Fox-Genovese
David Moltke-Hansen, General Editor

Volume 3
Intersections: History, Culture, Ideology
Edited by David Moltke-Hansen
Foreword by Thomas L. Pangle

The University of South Carolina Press

© 2011 University of South Carolina

Published by the University of South Carolina Press
Columbia, South Carolina 29208

www.sc.edu/uscpress

Manufactured in the United States of America

20 19 18 17 16 15 14 13 12 11   10 9 8 7 6 5 4 3 2 1

Library of Congress Cataloging-in-Publication Data
Fox-Genovese, Elizabeth, 1941–2007.
 History and women, culture and faith : selected writings of Elizabeth Fox-Genovese / David Moltke-Hansen, general editor.
  p. cm.
 Includes bibliographical references and index.
 ISBN 978-1-57003-990-4 (cloth : alk. paper) — ISBN 978-1-57003-991-1 (cloth : alk. paper) — **ISBN 978-1-57003-992-8** (cloth : alk. paper) — ISBN 978-1-57003-993-5 (cloth : alk. paper) — ISBN 978-1-57003-994-2 (cloth : alk. paper) 1. Women—History. 2. Culture. 3. Feminism. 4. Fox-Genovese, Elizabeth, 1941–2007. I. Moltke-Hansen, David. II. Title.
 HQ1121.F64 2011
 305.409—dc22
                                   2010048764

Publication of *History & Women, Culture & Faith* is made possible in part by the generous support of the Watson-Brown Foundation.

This book was printed on Glatfelter Natures, a recycled paper with 30 percent postconsumer waste content.

Contents

General Editorial Note *vii*

Foreword: Marxist Social and Political Theory, Americanized *ix*
Thomas L. Pangle

Introduction: Elizabeth Fox-Genovese as Essayist *xix*
David Moltke-Hansen

Part 1 Reviewing and Thinking Historically

   One The Many Faces of Moral Economy: A Contribution to a Debate *3*

   Two The Physiocratic Model and the Transition from Feudalism to Capitalism *11*

   Three Physiocracy and the Overthrow of the Ancien Régime *25*

   Four Psychohistory versus Psychodeterminism: The Case of Rogin's Jackson *36*

   Five The Personal Is Not Political Enough *51*

   Six The Crisis of Our Culture and the Teaching of History *69*

   Seven Gender, Class, and Power: Some Theoretical Considerations *82*

   Eight The Fettered Mind: Time, Place, and the Literary Imagination of the Old South *102*

   Nine The Anxiety of History: The Southern Confrontation with Modernity *124*

Part 2 Challenging and Deploying Cultural Analysis

   Ten The Claims of a Common Culture: Gender, Race, Class, and the Canon *145*

Eleven The Great Tradition and Its Orphans, or, Why the Defense of the Traditional Curriculum Requires the Restoration of Those It Excluded   *156*

Twelve The Empress's New Clothes: The Politics of Fashion   *173*

Thirteen Literary Criticism and the Politics of the New Historicism   *194*

Fourteen Between Individualism and Fragmentation: American Culture and the New Literary Studies of Race and Gender   *207*

Fifteen Beyond Transgression: Toward a Free Market in Morality   *233*

Sixteen Between Elitism and Populism: Whither Comparative Literature?   *255*

Seventeen Of Sin and Horses: The Compelling World of Dick Francis's Mysteries   *264*

Eighteen Multiculturalism in History: Ideologies and Realities   *271*

Selected Bibliography of Works by Elizabeth Fox-Genovese   *281*
Compiled by Ehren K. Foley

Index   *287*

General Editorial Note

This is one of five volumes of the selected essays and reflections of Elizabeth Fox-Genovese. First conceived a week after Fox-Genovese's funeral service, the project received generous support from the Watson-Brown Foundation, on whose Hickory Hill Forum advisory board Fox-Genovese served. Also making this edition possible was the collaboration of a dozen of her former colleagues and students, as well as her sister. Helping this diverse group keep on schedule, the Institute for Southern Studies of the University of South Carolina provided administrative support and the superb assistance of history graduate student Ehren K. Foley, compiler of the selected bibliographies for the first four of the five volumes of the edition.

Because the essays and chapters included were published in some seventy-five different venues, spelling and punctuation vary. No effort was made to standardize either these things or the forms of citation. English spellings are not as common as American but do occur. The editors did correct an occasional, obvious error silently or did insert in brackets missing words or elements of citations. In addition they put all original notes at the ends of pieces. The few editors' notes are placed as footnotes.

Each volume stands on its own, covering an area of Fox-Genovese's long-term scholarly and intellectual involvements. The fifth volume, the reader, is drawn largely from the others to give a broad sampling of the range of her work. It does, nevertheless, also include a couple of items by Fox-Genovese not found in the first four volumes, together with a number of remembrances of her.

The decisions about the contents of individual volumes were the responsibility of the editor or editors of each volume. The editors of the first four volumes nominated items for inclusion in the reader. They were guided in the selections for their own volumes by principles to which they all subscribed at the outset or, in a couple of cases, when joining the project a bit later on. Selections from the books Fox-Genovese wrote, co-wrote, and saw through publication are excluded. These titles are widely known and available. The editors also generally tried to choose more substantial over more popular pieces and limited each volume to a little over one hundred thousand words of her writings and some thirty thousand words of apparatus, including notes and bibliography. These decisions necessitated exclusion of at least a third of her fugitive writings. As a result the present edition includes no more than roughly 20 percent of her total published work.

For background to these materials and for related correspondence, readers are directed to the Southern Historical Collection of the University of North Carolina at Chapel Hill, repository of Elizabeth Fox-Genovese's papers. A finding aid to the papers is currently available at http://www.lib.unc.edu/mss/inv/f/Fox-Genovese,Elizabeth.html.

Foreword
Marxist Social and Political Theory, Americanized

Thomas L. Pangle

The chief theoretical basis for the essays in this volume is an identifiably American Marxism, modified by, and modifying, late-twentieth-century American feminism. From Marxist theory comes, first and foremost, Elizabeth Fox-Genovese's distinguishing insistence on the political structure of all history. The vocation of the historian—even or especially the social historian—is to show that "history as structure is political." Here *politics* is understood in a way that is "at once more modestly and more inclusively political than the defense of a specific political position." Politics is the struggle among economically defined classes to win the power to forge lasting "structured relations of superordination and subordination."[1] These structures are hegemonic in the sense that, if they are to have staying power, they must include compellingly rich ideological justifications—"ideology in the broad sense as worldview rather than as partisan propaganda"; "ideology as a matter of participation rather than . . . manipulation"; in short, ideology as conceived by Antonio Gramsci rather than "in the narrow sense influentially expounded by Karl Mannheim."[2] Hence, in the political struggle so conceived, texts themselves are more than "products of and interventions in the inescapably political nature of human existence." Philosophic and literary "texts enjoy a privileged position in the continuing process of fashioning and refashioning consciousness, of defining possibilities of action, of shaping destinies, and of shaping visions of justice."[3]

Marxism largely defines the way Betsey understood what she specified to be the "abiding concern" that "grounded [her] own work and teaching, which have ranged over a broad spectrum of fields, topics, and historical periods." That abiding concern is "modern individualism," its "emergence, consolidation, and consequences."[4] The enlightening prism of neo-Marxist analysis reveals modern individualism to be simultaneously liberating and incapacitating.

On the one hand, there are "the values of Liberalism": "the twin notions of individual freedom and individual responsibility," along with the "right to self-betterment" and the "opportunity for political participation."[5] Because of the rise of these values, "the industrial worker can rightly claim a view of himself denied to his labouring predecessors."[6] It is true, Betsey continued, "that bourgeois practice defined individualism in unacceptably narrow terms"—identifying it with "the triumph of particular ethnic groups, a particular sex, and a particular class," as well as the "narrow vision" of "preferred epistemological and analytic modes, including classical political economy, utilitarianism, and pragmatism."[7] But none of this (contrary to Karl Marx) necessarily justifies individualism's overthrow.

On the other hand, the possessive individualism of free market capitalism is ever more deeply corrosive of the human spirit, and this advancing corrosion now affects women more dramatically than men. Alienation—the pervasive "divorce of the laborer from his or her labor"—"carr[ies] commodity fetishism into the innermost crannies of our beings." We not only "know how it feels to 'need' things we do not really want." None of us is free from "the true horror of consumerism—the dependence on commodities for a sense of self worth," the "agonizing anxiety of compulsively seeking a reassurance that offers no substitute for love or respect, and that, worse, never satiates the need but rather fuels it for even more panicky demands." In the workplace, while "some women have made gains with respect to employment and financial independence, . . . their independence has tended to release them from the oppressive custodianship of individual men only to throw them into the arms of the corporations and the federal government." More generally "recent economic developments portend the collapse of the traditional professional and propertied middle class to the benefit of affluent, salaried technocrats." Those "bourgeois institutions that had encoded the partial independence of civil society and critical judgment, such as the universities" and "even family businesses, have given way to the government and the multinationals." Ironically the fact that "the new dominant institutions can afford a much greater measure of personal idiosyncrasy" is not a sign of freedom; instead it "portends a terrifying oppressiveness," for it "suggests . . . a world in which personal perceptions and individual behavior are of so little social consequence." At the same time, nonmarket intimate relations among individuals—especially the bonds that unite the nuclear family constituted by immature capitalism out of the ruins of feudal patriarchy— are being steadily dissolved, not only by the acid of market demands for ever intensified commodity production and consumption, but also by the increasing recognition of the specific exploitation of women (not least, through "motherhood") that has been the insidiously veiled function of the bourgeois family.[8]

Thus Marxism focused, clarified, and heightened, if it did not solely inspire, Betsey's moral and civic urgency, her sense of gripping and even desperate responsibility in the confrontation with an age and culture in spiritual crisis. That late-twentieth-century crisis became acutely self-conscious in the "culture wars" in the universities. The attack on the teaching of "Western civilization" and the "Great Tradition" or the "canon" expressed the abashed confession on the part of bourgeois high culture that these organizing concepts of supposedly "liberal" education represent a falsifying ideological construction. "The canon was developed" in the last couple of centuries, first "as a weapon in the struggle against" previous "hierarchy, dependence, and particularism" and then as a way of hegemonically reinterpreting the history of the West so as to make it all appear to progress toward and culminate in bourgeois individualism as the true humanism. This cat is now out of the bag. But the "academic establishment's" reaction to its repellent self-discovery signaled the moral and intellectual bankruptcy of liberal ideology. For the reaction was to abandon the canon, as opposed to undertaking the complex task of "a revision of its contents and the transformation of its teaching." Our intelligentsia's recoil manifests the typically bourgeois-individualist failure to appreciate that "the existence of some canon offers our best guarantee of some common culture"—as opposed to individualist fragmentation and anomic collapse into ethnic and autobiographical narcissism that only intensifies the disintegrative dynamic of advanced capitalism. "The teaching of the canon," given its true intellectual quality, diversity, and pervasive intrinsic controversy and contestation, Betsey argued, "offers the best possible way to expose the limitations of the ideals of individualism on which so much of our public life is based, and the best possible way to introduce some notion of collective standards and values."[9] The pathetic failure on the part of today's "bourgeois" intellectuals —except for the "conservatives" such as Allan Bloom—to accept "political accountability" by facing this cultural crisis; the fact that Bloom's *Closing of the American Mind*, with its philosophically sophisticated defense of the study of the great books, was met with "outraged dismissal rather than serious debate": all this proves that, "by the grace of bourgeois culture in decline, Marxism has emerged as the last bastion of critical thinking."[10] Whereas the "'radical' critics of the purportedly irrelevant canon have sacrificed the ideal of collective identity that constituted its most laudable feature" and, in "settl[ing] for education as personal autobiography or identity," are "tacitly [willing] to accept the worst forms of political domination," the Marxist-feminist critical theorist opposes right, left, and center by seeking to rescue the canon, in its yet unrealized potential as the beacon of true collective humanism: "The challenge is not to condemn quality as anti-democratic (a sure formula for defeat), but to reclaim it for a reinvigorated national democracy."[11]

It goes without saying that Betsey's Marxism was not Soviet, or even Communist Party affiliated.[12] But the most profound, and ultimately fraught, dimension of her unorthodoxy needs to be limned. This dimension becomes evident if one compares the essays in the present volume to key relevant works of Marx and Engels, or of Georg Lukacs. Then one sees at once that, while Betsey deployed class and class-consciousness as a revelatory category of critical analysis and as a call to action, she was conspicuously silent on the foundational, normative status of the class consciousness and praxis of the proletariat in its uniquely revolutionary world-historical role.

The abandonment of this central pillar of original Marxism liberated Betsey's historical craft and cultural criticism. In her hands the revised or neo-Marxist framework became more open, flexible, and exploratory—without losing what was truly penetrating and illuminating in the stricter version. We have indicated how Betsey's versatile Marxism defined her distinctively constructive intervention in the campus culture wars. Let us now consider some similarly distinguishing features of her Marxist historical scholarship and her Marxist feminism, as they come into sight in the writings collected in this volume.

Betsey's first major scholarly achievement was her interpretation of the political theory of the Physiocrats, above all François Quesnay. The leitmotif that sets her approach apart is made clear in her sympathetically critical review of her European Marxist colleague Marguerite Kuczynski, whose work "marks the culmination of a distinguished Marxist tradition of physiocratic studies." In this tradition the focus is on Quesnay's "fundamental contribution to the analysis of capitalist production which extends from him through the English school to Marx." But in this focus Betsey descries a scotoma: "This perspective entails dismissing the traditional, or 'feudal,' aspects of Quesnay's thought as situational or accidental rather than seeing them as integrally related to his central concerns"; this "ignores Mirabeau's important contributions to the formulation of physiocracy" through the intervention of the deep influence of his metaphysical thinking on Quesnay. At the heart of Quesnay's thought was a deep, religiously rooted distrust of modern individualism that was not merely a feudal remnant, but that also was more authentically interpreted as a basic element in a creative, if historically limited, attempt at a distinct synthesis: "Quesnay's failure to develop a thorough analysis of bourgeois social and political relations did not simply reflect a passive acceptance of his historical context; it also represented an attempt to restrain the free play of individual interest and an attempt to create a socially ordered capitalism suitable to the French experience." Quesnay "did see the marketplace as the central arena of economic development," but he "never quite trusted the market to determine social and political relations." His vision "did not entail open-ended growth." Quesnay anticipated Marx not only inasmuch as Quesnay prepared the English school of economics, but also—against the English school—in doubting "the eternal validity of unbridled possessive individualism." Although "his position can be read as a blend of the traditional and the modern, more specifically as the modern, or bourgeois, breaking out of the mold of the traditional, or feudal, . . . it can also be read as an alternate vision of modernity—one that insists that society requires an authority that transcends the immediate struggle." Thus "Quesnay's political economy was, in the full sense of the word, political," involving an "uncompromising defence of legal despotism." Yet Quesnay stood radically apart from Marx inasmuch as Quesnay "sought the realization of the divine plan that existed in nature" and held that ultimately "men do not create wealth; they develop and exploit existing potential wealth." This underlies his "belief in the unique productivity of agriculture," his worry that merchant capital is becoming a drain upon true productivity, his unease at the production of luxuries, and his "insistence upon the good price and his opposition to interest."[13]

Betsey's later achievement in the interpretation of southern social and cultural (especially literary) history exhibits the same fruitful capaciousness of nuanced interpretive understanding. She criticized both the view of the Old South as embodying some "reversion to a medieval social order" or worldview (Allen Tate) and the "reading [of] antebellum slavery through the lens of postbellum racism" (Faulkner, Louis Rubin): instead she argued that "proslavery thought was attempting to develop an alternate vision" with "an ideology, an emerging world view" in confrontation with modernity.[14] It is to the sympathetic if ultimately critical articulation of that emerging alternative—the "distinctiveness of Southern conservatism"—that Betsey bent her labors, especially through literary interpretation and the study of the self-expression of southern women in private letters and journals.[15]

When we turn to Betsey's more political essays, we find a Marxism that is enlarged by feminism, even as it tries to teach feminism some unpalatable political truths. Her feminist enrichment of Marxist cultural criticism is on display in the essay titled "The Empress's New Clothes: The Politics of Fashion." There she argued that fashion—to be sharply distinguished from "innocent" costume and uniform—has become "the premier example of what Marx called 'the fetishism of commodities.'" Precapitalist fashion not only "did not fully engage the lower classes in its web," but among the upper classes existed more as a "display of opulence" than as an ever-mutating form of display that required and promoted a ceaseless acquisition and discarding of clothing commodities. As capitalism matured, "fashion as a system" increasingly "consolidated its hold on the female imagination and increasingly defined its mission as shaping female consciousness and commanding female purchasing power." Men "did not entirely escape its hold, but, as a general rule, it spared them its worst excesses." But for that reason, men are less capable of becoming conscious of the depth of the perversion that modern fashion represents. Especially for women, fashion has been the leading force in making "the ability to buy" become "an ever more important measure of success and worth." Still more insidiously, fashion has become "the medium for self-expression"—for an alienated self, expressing itself through a rapid succession of temporarily rigid patterns of appearance.[16]

One might superficially suppose that as women enjoyed progressively greater freedoms, fashion should have become more expressive of distinct individualities. "In fact, the fashion with which we live is, in its own way, even more dictatorial than the fashion of a century or even a half-century ago." Women today, Betsey claimed, are "hostage to a ceaseless obligation to define and redefine ourselves," to be "in fashion";[17] otherwise the system "will identify us as lacking the money, or the time, or the taste, or the interest to have bought other clothes."[18] And "this process extends throughout society," for "the upper echelons of the fashion industry do establish the styles for the rest of society." The "accelerating accessibility of fashion as commodity, particularly in ready-to-wear clothing and standardized printed dress patterns, and at rapidly falling prices," has brought "at least facsimiles of fashionable dress" to "growing numbers."[19] The herald and coryphaeus of this process is of course advertising. The message of fashion advertising is stark: "without those wares we are nothing." These fashion commodities do not sate desire but fuel it: "we are . . . condemned to experience an escalating sense of need."[20]

Meanwhile the actual labor-intensive production of fashion commodities is carried out less by men than by women—a class of women whose salaries do not allow them even to work seriously toward actual ownership of the more splendid adornments they produce. Yet, paradoxically and ironically, this leaves these producer women decisively less alienated than their faraway consumer sisters. For at least the toiling women producers know who they are and where they stand. For the consumers the acceptance of fashion commodities as the articulation of the self "leads many women, and perhaps men, to focus their efforts on the acquisition of clothing that will somehow transform them, make their dreams come true, make them feel like the leisured, privileged women who represent femininity."[21] But the allure of the fantasy only intensifies the reality of the alienated loss of even the access to truly creative selfhood.

Betsey's Marxist-inspired admonition to feminism centers on the deep political ambiguities in the "sisterhood" that is the "companion" with which, "from its origins[,] American feminism has remained deeply intertwined." For all of its marvelous power to afford a countervailing rallying point for women who seek allies and support in their pilgrimage of liberation, sisterhood carries some substantial risks that need to be averted. Historically sisterhood has "referred particularly to the common experience of oppression and to a nurturing, loving, mutually supporting network born of shared oppression." But sisterhood "must be understood to harbor all the ambiguities of the complex system of family relations from which it derives." Those (bourgeois) family relations have with considerable success sought to "swindle" basically exploited women with "the mirage of the familial haven" as the private sphere uncontaminated by the public sphere of "competing individuals."[22] This bourgeois myth of the family continues to encourage women to see their important relationships—and in particular their feminine sisterhood—as personal rather than political. "Sisterhood essentially identified itself as the egalitarian distribution of powerlessness."[23] "Tragically, the language is in a determining, if not total, measure a structural reversal of the language of oppression"; it can "contribute to an internal transformation of capitalism that will afford yet more humiliating oppression for most."[24]

This language of the personal obscures the need for revolutionary political solidarity and collective political action that is "directed toward the kind of social transformation that will provide social justice for all human beings." The cult of the personal allows even the essential political gains that feminism has made—property rights, the vote, education, and so forth—to strengthen women's middle-class identification and individualism, thus "reinforc[ing] the ideology of the dominant class, especially in the United States." Given the historical configuration of the bourgeois family myth or swindle, "personal politics, including the nature and role of sisterhood, lie on a narrow margin between the commitment to socialism and an inadvertent succor to advanced capitalism." Betsey concluded that "only a strong Marxist-Feminist position, which includes alliances with male comrades, can provide an adequate foundation for the securing of female equality."[25]

Yet looming over all the essays in this volume is the problematic that haunts the entire matrix of late Marxism. We have already spotlighted Betsey's abandonment of the central pillar of original Marxism: the class consciousness and praxis of the proletariat. She at one point remarked with what I think is deceptive complacency that "neo-Marxists have succeeded in divorcing their work from its political moorings."[26] But her thought, and life, as a whole testifies that she could not leave it at this. How could a thinker who saw so clearly the need for political moorings live with their loss or absence? Marx could proclaim that communism is the riddle of history solved; Engels could announce himself and Marx the voices of "scientific socialism"; Lukacs could claim to be the expression of authentic, unreified "wholeness"—and condemn all non-Marxist thought as "reified" abstraction—on what basis? Because they could all conceive themselves as nothing more and nothing less than the articulate vehicles of the consciousness of an existing, world-historical class that they believed they saw actually undertaking the unique transfiguration of human existence everywhere and for all time. This seemed "empirical"; this seemed undeniably real; this seemed foundational. But no serious person, and certainly not Betsey, could put faith or find completion in this anymore. Nothing about the proletariat in its actual historical praxis has turned out to provide any nonvague answer to the question: what exactly does it mean to be unalienated, unreified, whole? What does it mean to exist in the truly just society, to which we are driven to aspire in our revulsion at past and present historical injustice? Plato and Cicero in their *Republics* and their *Laws*, Aristotle in his *Politics*, Alfarabi in his *Political Regime*, Averroës in his *Commentary on Plato's "Republic,"* Sir Thomas More in his *Utopia*, Sir Francis Bacon in his *New Atlantis*, Jean-Jacques Rousseau in his *Social Contract*, G. W. F. Hegel in his *Philosophy of Right*, Friedrich Nietzsche in *The Antichrist* gave elaborate and specific, vigorously competing, answers—with which one can agree or disagree. In Marx or later Marxism—be it in the hands of Lukacs or C. B. Macpherson or Jean-Paul Sartre or Louis Althusser or the Frankfurt School—when did the proletariat, with clarity and precision and without fulmination, elaborate anything close to an answer? When and where did it even enter the great debate?

One may surmise that the evermore honest confrontation with this intellectual vacuum on the left was a major ingredient in what slowly but surely prepared Betsey to embrace—better put, to be graced by the capacity to put her faith in—the response given in the New Testament. For the scripture responds: there is not yet available, on this earth, an answer to the question of the good and just society, because of the humanly insuperable force of radical, even cosmic evil, together with its expression in the more pedestrian but pervasive sin within us all. These dark forces, the recognition of which Betsey came to understand as essential to any adequate, nonnaive comprehension of our human condition, can be effectively countered only by grace—the anticipation of which is seen in a "Christian image of manliness" (and, one surmises, of womanliness).[27] These terms and categories (radical evil, sin, grace, Christian manliness) play no role in any of the writings in this volume, with a single exception—the book review titled "Of Sin and Horses." There and there alone do we catch a glimpse of the dramatically new trajectory of Betsey's theoretical reflections in her last years. This momentous final stage in her spiritual journey is of course not explained—it is at most only adumbrated—by the writings in this volume. The foreshadowing is present, it seems to me, from the start. I find it visible in her respect for Quesnay's rootedness in eternal nature as the divine mind. I see it continuing in Betsey's deep sympathy for the character Beulah, the heroine of Augusta Jane Evans's best-selling novel by that name, who "represents the Southern triumph over the seductions of modernity through an acceptance of faith, limits, and ordained social roles." In *Beulah,* Evans "attacks the perils of individualism—the besetting temptations of pride and independence." Where other feminist critics "view the novel as yet another instance of the suppression of female intellect and ambition," Betsey insisted that such an "interpretation fails to acknowledge that Beulah's ultimate submission is not to man, but to God, much less that in the end her greatest triumph is over misguided men—the male intellectuals who have led her astray."[28] Betsey's final stand was foreshadowed more subtly, but no less powerfully, when she conceded in passing that "eternal human nature has its place in philosophy and literature" even though it cannot be reconciled with "historical process";[29] and when, in declaring that "no story . . . tells it like it always will be, presents human affairs from the perspective of eternity," she felt impelled explicitly to "grant exception to the fundamental religious texts."[30]

Eternity: the dim, primordial, but perduring awareness that our humanity is constituted by our directedness to eternity—an eternity not found in, but transcending, history—does not cease its gentle but insistent knocking on the portal of our modern souls. Finally, decisively, with her whole heart, Betsey gathered herself and flung open the door.

Notes

1. Elizabeth Fox-Genovese, "Literary Criticism and the Politics of the New Historicism," in *The New Historicism,* ed. H. Aram Veeser (New York: Routledge, Chapman & Hall, 1989), 221, 221, 222; article reprinted in this volume, pp. 194–206.

2. Elizabeth Fox-Genovese, "Multiculturalism in History: Ideologies and Realities," *Orbis: A Journal of World Affairs* 43 (Fall 1999): 532, 532, 531; article reprinted in this volume, pp. 271–80.

3. Fox-Genovese, "Literary Criticism," 221, 222.

4. Elizabeth Fox-Genovese, "Liberal Education in the University: Prospects and Pitfalls," *Journal of Education* 183, no. 3 (2002): 41–42.

5. Elizabeth Fox-Genovese, "The Many Faces of Moral Economy: A Contribution to a Debate," *Past and Present* 58 (February 1973): 168 (article reprinted in this volume, pp. 3–10); Elizabeth Fox-Genovese, "The Crisis of Our Culture and the Teaching of

History," *History Teacher* 13 (November 1979): 95 (article reprinted in this volume, pp. 69–81); Fox-Genovese, "Many Faces," 168, 168.

6. Fox-Genovese, "Many Faces," 168.

7. Fox-Genovese, "Crisis of Our Culture," 95.

8. Elizabeth Fox-Genovese, "The Personal Is Not Political Enough," *Marxist Perspectives* 2 (Winter 1979): 103–4, 108–10; article reprinted in this volume, pp. 51–68.

9. Elizabeth Fox-Genovese, "The Claims of a Common Culture: Gender, Race, Class, and the Canon," *Salmagundi* 72 (Fall 1986): 132, 136; article reprinted in this volume, pp. 145–55.

10. Fox-Genovese, "Literary Criticism," 220.

11. Fox-Genovese, "Claims of a Common Culture," 133, 143.

12. Fox-Genovese, "Literary Criticism," 220n19.

13. Elizabeth Fox-Genovese, "The Physiocratic Model and the Transition from Feudalism to Capitalism," *Journal of European Economic History* 4, no. 3 (1975), 725, 727, 729, 733, 736–37; article reprinted in this volume, pp. 11–24.

14. Elizabeth Fox-Genovese, "The Fettered Mind: Time, Place, and the Literary Imagination of the Old South," *Georgia Historical Quarterly* 76 (Winter 1990): 628, 636, 636, 630; article reprinted in this volume, pp. 102–23.

15. Elizabeth Fox-Genovese, "The Anxiety of History: The Southern Confrontation with Modernity," *Southern Cultures*, inaugural issue (1993): 65; article reprinted in this volume, pp. 124–42.

16. Elizabeth Fox-Genovese, "The Empress's New Clothes: The Politics of Fashion," *Socialist Review* 17 (January/February 1987): 7–30; article reprinted in this volume, pp. 173–93.

17. Ibid., 20.

18. Ibid., 25.

19. Ibid., 18–19.

20. Ibid., 25, 26.

21. Ibid., 26.

22. Fox-Genovese, "Not Political Enough," 97.

23. Ibid., 103.

24. Ibid., 109

25. Ibid., 112, 97, 96, 96.

26. Fox-Genovese, "Literary Criticism," 220.

27. Elizabeth Fox-Genovese, "Of Sin and Horses: The Compelling World of Dick Francis's Mysteries." *Books and Culture: A Christian Review*, January/February 1998, 43; article reprinted in this volume, pp. 264–70.

28. Fox-Genovese, "Anxiety of History," 75.

29. Fox-Genovese, "Crisis of Our Culture," 101.

30. Elizabeth Fox-Genovese, "The Great Tradition and Its Orphans, or, Why the Defense of the Traditional Curriculum Requires the Restoration of Those It Has Excluded," in *The Rights of Memory: Essays on History, Science, and American Culture*, ed. Taylor Littleton (University: University of Alabama Press, 1986), 192; article reprinted in this volume, pp. 156–72.

Introduction
Elizabeth Fox-Genovese as Essayist

David Moltke-Hansen

Elizabeth Fox-Genovese engaged in and wrote on a remarkable array of topics. Making that patent are the eighty essays, introductions, afterwords, chapters, and talks, together with the spiritual reflections, collected in this and the other volumes in the selected edition of her nonbook writings. The first of the five volumes examines women outside of the American South and reflects the continuities and changes in Betsey's treatment of women and gender relations in history, politics, and culture. The second, on white and black southern women and their writings, demonstrates Betsey's understandings of the interplay of race, gender, and class in the South, of the ways to read literary and other texts in such historically charged contexts, and of the role of the literary canon. Volume 3 concentrates on what Betsey viewed as critical historical and cultural issues beyond these previous volumes' women's studies topics and the religious thought and experience that are the subjects of volume 4. This fourth volume shows both Betsey's scholarly study of religion, especially in American women's lives, and her own evolving religious thinking and its implications. Volume 5, the reader drawn from all Betsey's essays, does not give an overview so much as a broad sampling of her work and influence. It includes only a couple of items not found in the other volumes.

Despite their diversity, these essays and essayistic pieces are not encyclopedic in their range but instead are quite focused. To what ends? With what consequences? What are the connections among these many and diverse pieces? Why was the essay genre important to Betsey, and why did she give so much time and energy to writing essays?

To call attention to the essay genre in this fashion requires explanation. After all, it was primarily through the books that she wrote or cowrote over three decades that Betsey earned both professional acclaim and fierce antagonism. Yet the editors of the volumes of Betsey's essays early agreed not to draw from the books. Instead they decided that, in the case of the titles published during her lifetime, they would not even include essays that became parts of books for which she was a principal author. Most of those books are widely known and widely available. Not so the great majority of her essays, including introductions to and chapters in books either edited by or contributed to, but not written or cowritten by, Betsey.

In making their selections, the editors chose from among a much larger body of fugitive work. Perhaps this work would be better known, at least in part, had Betsey made collections out of portions of it, in the fashion of C. Vann Woodward's *The Burden of Southern History*. She did not, although she included, in more or less revised and extended form, individual essays in such works as her and Gene Genovese's *Fruits of Merchant Capital: Slavery and Bourgeois Property in the Rise and Expansion of Capitalism* (1983). She also intended to draw on her writings on African American women writers for a volume that never appeared.

It is not only this failure to collect more of her essays, however, that has hidden Betsey's work in the essay genre in plain view. The staggering quantity and diversity of the work also offer a partial explanation. In addition to being author of five books, Betsey was coauthor of seven more (three published posthumously). She also contributed ten times as many essays, introductions, and chapters, not to mention interviews, letters to the editor, and (in manuscript) lectures, talks, and spiritual reflections. Of her total printed oeuvre, the selected edition contains perhaps 20 percent, some 450,000 words, exclusive of notes.

Given this crude estimate, it appears that, on average, Betsey wrote or cowrote for eventual publication close to six thousand words a month—more or less seventy thousand words a year—over thirty-three years. Had she been a writer of fiction, composing out of her imagination and experience, this volume would have been impressive, but she was instead a scholar and a professor. Just the research underpinning much of her production was hugely time consuming. The intellectual demands of framing, shaping, and honing arguments added significantly to the time required. Yet Betsey researched and wrote in the midst of other, wide-ranging activities and commitments.

First published while a doctoral student in early modern European history at Harvard, she did not stop studying when she got her degree. She learned statistics, trained as a Freudian psychoanalyst, and moved into women's studies, then into literary, American, and African American studies, and finally from Marxism to Roman Catholicism and, many judged, away from feminism. With each step she studied intensively. At the same time, she taught both undergraduates and, ultimately, dozens of doctoral students in

Introduction xxi

a half-dozen fields. At different times, too, she ran an education project for the Organization of American Historians, served as international editor of the journal *Marxist Perspectives* (edited by her husband), founded and directed the women's studies program at Emory, helped launch the St. George Tucker Society (an interdisciplinary southern studies organization), helped found the Historical Society, launched and edited the society's journal, and served on the council of the National Endowment for the Humanities. For six months each year as well, she avidly followed her favorite baseball team, the Yankees. In between times she taught herself to cook the Italian foods her husband loved, read widely outside of as well as within her various scholarly fields, doted on her cats and dogs, and welcomed a seemingly endless stream of visits from current and former students, as well as colleagues, family, and friends.

If Betsey's productivity makes knowing the range of her work difficult, scholarly presuppositions and specialization compound the problem. The historical profession values books—written, not edited—over other scholarly productions. The various other humanities disciplines in which Betsey worked also are oriented to books. Women's, American, and African American studies are, as are literature and religion. Moreover, given Betsey's roles in and contributions to each of these fields and the transatlantic scope of her historical scholarship, few scholars have had reason or been equipped to read across the range of her writings.

Her books represent better the foci than the range of Betsey's work. To get an adequate sense of the range, one needs to consider instead the essays. While impressive and daunting, even bemusing, their variety and number are, in several senses, misleading. Underlying and shaping the diversity in subjects treated and issues engaged are both the historical unities and cultural functions of the essay genre and the centripetal preoccupations that informed most of Betsey's essays, early and late.

As Betsey well understood, the genre developed as an expression and a vehicle of bourgeois individualism and culture, the hegemony of which she spent her life both studying and resisting. At the same time, however, the essay became a vehicle for the assertion of the importance of a broadly shared culture and its analysis, and Betsey believed profoundly in both. Further it evolved as a locus of civic society and civil discourse. To understand these developments and their implications for Betsey's career as an essayist, it is important first to review their history.

The first great essayist, Montaigne, son of a wealthy merchant, already understood the value of the genre for the exercise and expression of individualism. His *Essais*, written in the latter half of the sixteenth century, were faulted then for their personal tone and language. It was precisely those individualizing qualities, however, that appealed to Joseph Addison and Richard Steele. The two men's early-eighteenth-century occasional essays, in the *Tatler* and the *Spectator*, had as their explicit purpose the reformation of manners and morals. Reason, moderation, and modesty—values of the growing middle class of professionals, merchants, and officials—were set against the extravagant excesses, conspicuous consumption, and intemperance of the aristocracy and the boorishness, brutality, and mawkishness of the lower classes. Too, the glancing, humorous, and elegantly casual treatment of books, ideas, and mores promoted aesthetic values and good taste. In the process Addison and Steele both defined what it meant to be cultured and exemplified how to exercise one's critical faculties and discernment. By treating culture as an attainment and a pursuit rather than as a birthright, a privilege, or a condition, they made it at once a democratic and an elitist accomplishment.

At the same time, Addison and Steele advocated separate spheres for men and women as well as polite venues and occasions for heterosociability. Men shared the newly popular public sphere of the coffeehouse for conversation about literature, politics, and the commonweal. Women shared the private and sober elegance of the domestic sphere, where they cultivated manners, morals, and refinement in addition to the domestic arts. Musical performances, the theater, the dinner table, and the garden became places of decorous mingling and, as such, healthy and moral alternatives to the endless whirl of aristocratic balls, games of whist, and fashionable preening and amorous competition.

Following, adapting, and building on Addison's and Steele's examples, Samuel Johnson, Oliver Goldsmith, and many others—both in England and on the Continent—wrote occasional essays for the cultural journals that multiplied after the mid–eighteenth century. These continued variously to foster the reform program, build the audiences, and assert the values promoted in the *Tatler* and the *Spectator*. Moreover they began to frame an emerging consensus about what modern vernacular as well as ancient classical works belonged in the canon and about the role of the canon in shaping common understandings and values through shared knowledge, references, and perspectives.

Polite letters, however, were not the only pursuit. In the course of the eighteenth century, an increasing number and variety of learned societies published journals that reflected specialized antiquarian, scientific, economic, and social improvement agendas and discourses. Eventually the review essay drew on this tradition as well as on that of the occasional essay in the cultural journals. Initially, however, the proliferation of journals, interests, and

Introduction xxiii

discourses seemed to threaten the common culture envisioned and evoked by the occasional essayists. The question became: how can one keep up with, gain perspective on, and intellectually integrate the burgeoning literary, philosophical, scientific, historical, and other output of the Enlightenment then sweeping Europe?

Part of the answer was suggested in 1728, when Ephraim Chambers's *Cyclopaedia, or Universal Dictionary of Arts and Letters* first appeared. Denis Diderot's *Encyclopédie* (1751–72) began as a project to translate a later, expanded edition of Chambers before being transformed into a new and much more ambitious work, a summa of Enlightenment thought. In reaction to this French summation, several Scots in Edinburgh joined together to commission and publish William Smellie's *Encyclopaedia Britannica* (1st ed., 1768–71). Dramatically expanded in the third edition (1797) and supplement (1801), the *Britannica* reached twenty volumes by multiple hands.

Yet the expansion did not address adequately the question of how to keep up and keep current. People could not afford to buy a new encyclopedia every few years, and adding supplements was both inelegant and inadequate. Having just participated in the joint publication of the expanded *Britannica*'s 1801 supplement, Archibald Constable agreed to publish a new venture that promised to address the problem in a novel way. The *Edinburgh Review* first appeared in October 1802, begun by two young Scottish lawyers and Speculative Society members, Francis (later Lord) Jeffrey and Henry (later Lord) Brougham, and by an English cleric, Sidney Smith, who then was preaching to great acclaim while studying in the Scottish capital.

Unlike other British reviews, which primarily served as publishers' organs, and unlike the occasional essay journals of the prior century that were the products of at most a few individuals, this new journal, like the expanded *Britannica*, sought contributions from numerous leading writers of the day. These writers, moreover, were both well paid and given the space and freedom to treat subjects of interest to them. From the outset the ritual starting point for many of the essays was one or more books, generally recently published. The resulting essays were, however, at once more and less than just reviews. They might or might not appraise the books under consideration, but they almost invariably used those titles as starting points for broad discussions of aspects of the books' subjects.

These discussions differed from the eighteenth-century models on which they drew. Unlike Addisonian essays, they were extended. Unlike the contributions to the journals of learned societies, they were addressed to general audiences of educated readers rather than to members with specialized interests. Collectively they also ranged across discursive realms, treating not only the social, moral, and cultural ones of Addison and Steele, but also the scientific, economic, and historical ones of the learned societies. To these, moreover, they added the political of Daniel Defoe, Johnson, and others.

The *Edinburgh Review* was founded by Whigs, though Tories such as Sir Walter Scott contributed in the early years. When in October 1808, however, Jeffrey and Brougham attacked the Tory government's handling of the Iberian campaign against Napoleon, Scott withdrew, urging the creation of a rival journal. Within months George Canning, the foreign minister, had recruited William Gifford to edit the *Quarterly Review* in London. So the age of the review journal and of its characteristic contribution, the review essay, was born.

While eventually divided among conservatives, liberals, and radicals (on both the right and the left), the authors and readers of review essays and journals shared fundamental expectations, orientations, and beliefs. Requiring more or less wide interests, broad learning, and serious as well as extended attention to contemporary debates, emergent trends, and pathbreaking work in varied arenas, the review journal both fostered cultured elitism and exalted intellectual discourse. Further the review journal promoted integration of intellectual, artistic, political, and social concerns, encouraged cosmopolitanism, and assumed a shared, canonical, Western culture as the basis upon which to view and engage the world and to develop critical stances on issues and cultural productions.

This Western culture was not static, but dynamic. The review journal emerged and then spread with the development of democratic institutions, reform politics, and nationalism. It grew, too, with urban-industrialism, the bourgeoisie, and class conflict. Moreover it developed with romanticism and flourished as science and higher learning expanded and as the West extended its imperial sway over large portions of the globe not conquered by it in the sixteenth century, when the personal, occasional essay first appeared. Finally it increased its audiences and roles in the course of the spiraling conflict over gendered, racial, and cultural natures and hierarchies. In the pages of review journals, all of these developments became foci of ongoing discussion and debate.

Betsey knew this history intimately. She early read what the Physiocrats and, later, Marx had read. Included were the works of the members of her beloved Scottish Historical School, the last generation of which filled the pages of *Britannica*'s third edition and also of the *Edinburgh Review* in its early years. The southern planters, about whom she came to write in the 1980s, were in numerous instances consumers of review journals. In some cases they also were contributors. Although they may have been noncapitalists in

Introduction xxv

Betsey's initial understanding, the reviews they read at once articulated, advanced, and thereby drew them into the ambit of emergent, hegemonic, bourgeois individualism and canonical culture.

The founding presumption of the review journals—that individuals' reflections could build (by examining) this common culture—got to the center of many of Betsey's concerns and aspirations. Betsey shared as well the ambition of many review essayists to address large issues for diverse readers. Again and again she did just that. Also making reviews vital in her eyes was their historical role as centers of partisan debate on fundamental social, cultural, and economic, as well as political, issues. Partisanship mattered, because politics do. Moreover the necessity of forceful argument helped one at once comprehend and undercut one's opponents' positions as well as advance one's own and one's allies'.

Her first essays already suggest some of her abiding concerns. Although she eventually stopped considering herself a Marxist, Betsey continued to read class and other power relations as critical to historical understanding, points she made in her 1973 essay "The Many Faces of Moral Economy." From the outset, too, she conceived of political economy as having a moral dimension—of necessity, not just in the thought of the Physiocrats, the pre-Revolutionary French economic reformers on whom she wrote her dissertation and first book. Economic and political policies and choices have necessarily always had moral implications and consequences. Generally the decisions have reflected, in the distant as well as the immediate past, the class or other interests, orientations, and self-justifications that need to be uncovered and scrutinized. The assertion of moral presuppositions and aims did not and does not free people from the consequences of their actions. Nevertheless Betsey agreed with the Scottish school philosophers on whom the Physiocrats drew: morality and the moral sense are at once a reflection and a function of human beings' social natures and relations.

Teasing out the interplay of moral and power relations became another of Betsey's abiding concerns. Indeed she judged that "all of the humanities address problems of values and human relations, problems of authority and freedom in society."[1] She conceived and pursued these fundamental problems in theoretically informed and demanding ways. In part she agreed with the Hungarian sociologist of knowledge Karl Mannheim that each class has its own worldview, shaped by its interests, values, and beliefs, articulated as ideology, and pursued as ends framed as a utopian vision. Yet Betsey went beyond, and in the process challenged, Mannheim's analysis in *Ideology and Utopia* (1929). She had a more historical, cultural, and linguistic sense of how social classes come to and maintain effective dominance in the face of divisions within their ranks and also within the broader society.

Her focus on the rise of the bourgeoisie, combined with her literary and linguistic sensibilities, led Betsey to concur with aspects of the analysis of Mikhail Bakhtin, a thinker whom she deeply admired. Language, she understood, is inescapably ideological and also social. That is why interrelations precede and condition individual awareness, perceptions, and articulations. It is also why individuals share worldviews as well as language and society. Such worldviews need not be monolithic—indeed in many ways must be created, expressed, and channeled through dialogue among a culture's multiple shapers and carriers. Yet individual classes and other social groups end up developing, speaking, and enacting common views that limit as well as form individual views. Groups do this in ways that inform every aspect of members' divergent thought and expression. Members' dialogues become the means of at once venting or confronting and resolving or channeling social, cultural, and political tensions.

Not all participants in dialogues are equal, however, and neither are all dialogues. The inequalities determine in some degree which discourses are most heard, how, and by whom. As Craig Brandist observed in "Gramsci, Bakhtin and the Semiotics of Hegemony," his 1996 *New Left Review* article, "a discourse becomes hegemonic when one social class's worldview is accepted as kindred by other social classes. This does not mean the struggle for hegemony consists merely of a conflict between two performed ideologies but a conflict of *hegemonic principles*. Discourses seek to bind other discourses to themselves according to two basic principles: either by establishing a relation of authority between the enclosing and target discourses or by facilitating the further advancement of the target discourse *through* the enclosing discourse."[2]

Trained as a historical linguist, Antonio Gramsci drew on some of the same thinkers as Bakhtin. Writing in the 1920s and 1930s, Gramsci argued that the bourgeoisie achieved economic and political dominance not simply through the progressive acquisition and development of the means of production or through the accretion of power and deployment of force, but also through the development, reproduction, and promotion of cultural norms and expectations—encoded and conveyed in language, as through other means. Rather than resist, many of the have-nots came to aspire to the middle class and absorbed bourgeois values and expectations. In the process bourgeois culture gained and maintained hegemonic control over ever wider parts of the West and its world empires. This was so even in the face of the growing conviction that the working class would have to engineer cultural change to gain fair access to the means of production and appropriate compensation for members' productive labor.

Introduction xxvii

Betsey used this understanding of cultural hegemony by dominant classes not just in treating the bourgeoisie, but in treating what she considered noncapitalist elites in seventeenth-century England, in eighteenth-century France, or in the nineteenth-century American South. She applied it as well in her analysis of gender roles and relations, insisting that most women most of the time did not and could not escape the class norms and cultural presuppositions that framed their own and others' expectations of them.

This emphasis on elites stemmed from Betsey's concern with the ways in which most people's lives were distorted and directed by dominant classes through their hegemonic cultural hold on society. The dispossessed were always in the forefront of her thinking, even when she wrote about ruling classes. This was true when she treated the plantation household as a center of hegemonic cultural production and reproduction. It also was true when she described and assessed the planter worldview. It was true as well when she wrote about what she came increasingly to consider the hegemonic dominance of bourgeois individualism among feminist elites out of touch with the concerns and priorities of the majority of women.

While recognizing "that bourgeois individualism, with all its injustices and failings, provided the firmest cornerstone for individual freedom the world has yet known," Betsey also insisted that the "individualist bias reinforces the ideology of the dominant class, especially in the United States, where propertied individualism has afforded the historical and social basis for freedom and equality."[3] Hegemonic cultural norms, she judged, did more than shape the environment in which people acted and thought. They deeply influenced thought and action as well as people's perceptions of themselves and others.

Consequently, even when reading nonelites, Betsey argued, one needs to keep elite culture in view. This is one reason, she reasoned, to respect and teach the canon, while also expanding it. Not to do so would be to lose sight of how hegemonic cultures have ranked and favored some over others and the reasons why. It also would be to lose sight of the identities shaping states and regions and, in the process, uniting classes into nations, faiths, and other larger groupings.

The collective matters. Betsey always was clear on that point. Radical individualism, postmodernist subjectivism, and ideological (as opposed to demographic) multiculturalism, she came to insist, all deracinate and dehistoricize texts written, and subjects living, in specific historical contexts. At the same time, they have helped in the discovery and consideration of historically marginalized and deracinated or orientalized people and their texts. Yet these people and texts also need to be understood as operating under particular conditions and circumstances in specific historical contexts. In the end, Betsey argued consistently, history has to be about how and to what ends people deploy power, not just on the individual or in a text, but also on and through communities, populations, and bodies of texts.

Experiences of the consequences of such deployments are fundamental to who people are as individuals and also as members of communities. What people share in many ways defines them. If history in a sense is a collective autobiography, it is the overlaps in people's self-accountings that open windows on historical conditions, continuities, and changes. Betsey put the point succinctly early in her career, in the title to her essay "The Personal Is Not Political Enough." The training she pursued in psychoanalysis helped her to look for and understand the implications of the commonalities undergirding personal trauma and other individual experience. These she read in Freudian terms. Religion, too, gave her a domain in which to examine the commonalities structuring the meanings and implications of individuals' faith journeys and experiences, including ultimately her own.

Unlike Gramsci or Marx before him, Betsey never reduced religion analytically to a form of hegemonic control or an opiate for the masses. Even before her study of medieval history at Harvard, though a nonbeliever at the time, she understood and valued religion as a dimension of both personhood and community, as an aspirational and a morally critical force, and as a powerful historical phenomenon and a serious intellectual as well as cultural vector. Her grandmother, she remembered, "turned to religion to give meaning and purpose to a life that was frequently difficult."[4] Betsey also appreciated that throughout history "the promise of spiritual equality at some level, or at least hereafter, has constituted one of the premier attractions of Christianity in general and a variety of radical or reforming Christian sects in particular."[5] Further, she maintained, religion offers "a meaningful story about . . . [one's] identity" and provides "a higher standard by which . . . [to] judge others."[6]

The questions—what should we do and why—seemed to Betsey fundamental. This was especially so because people too easily assert self-interest as the basis for the common good. Her early Marxism and her late Roman Catholicism alike were ways of embodying and pursuing goals that took her far beyond her privileged, bourgeois childhood to the address of social wrongs, cultural brutalities, and historical inequalities. Distrusting people's habits of self-regard, self-interest, and self-deception, she sought systematic perspectives on, and methods of pursuing, the collective good. She used her early reading of Marx, of the Scottish school, of Aquinas, and of Freud all to this end. Late in life this same potent mix—albeit with shifting proportions and new admixtures—continued to direct Betsey's search for systemic and systematic address of the issues facing the powerless and the dispossessed.

Betsey always was political, rejecting "the final capitalist mystification—that politics is irrelevant to the real business of life." She acknowledged that "politics may not solve the problems of sexual, racial, and economic injustice." Nevertheless, she insisted, "politics provides the terrain on which those problems can be addressed and the language and the practice whereby those problems can be externalized and, therefore, recognized and solved." The motivation for her politics continued to be to bridge "the gap between the particular and the general and [to construct] a nexus through which need may be translated into justice." That is why she decided, at least by 1979, that "sexual liberation and narrowly personal selfhood may not be the freedom of the people, but their new opiate."[7]

Marxism early and Roman Catholicism late each not only accommodated, but also reinforced and framed Betsey's commitment to the kind of justice she sought. Both emphasized the collective over the individual and resisted what they saw as the atomizing and narcissistic tendencies of bourgeois individualism. Moreover both accepted and promoted doctrinal authority in the face of democratic, antiauthoritarian impulses. Both appeared to many to be culturally and intellectually conservative as well, again in the face of various challenges from within and without. Both self-consciously resisted the pursuit of transitory fashion, though not evolutionary change. Politically both sought to institutionalize their transformative or revolutionary values, objectives, and roles. Both also sought to use the state to these ends, albeit in different ways. Both further believed in educating and guiding as well as policing their rank and file. And finally both were fundamentally, in Betsey's understanding, antiliberal, despite the vagrant tendencies of some adherents.

Betsey saw these similarities long before her conversion. Consequently she long entertained the question: to what extent do the communitarian left and the corporatist right share essential characteristics and values? She decided that in many ways they mirrored each other. Similarly at the other end of the spectrum, the anarchistic left and the radically libertarian right mirrored each other. This did not mean, however, that the right and the left could come together except to agree to disagree. When Gene and Betsey invited prominent intellectuals of the American far left and far right to their Atlanta home in the early 1990s to see if they could effect at least an alliance of convenience, they found that the commonalities of the radical right and left could not overcome histories of deep suspicion, habits of vehement opposition, and convictions of fundamental difference.

Further, when Betsey converted to Roman Catholicism in the mid-1990s, following her shift on abortion from a reluctantly but realistically pro-choice to a vigorously pro-life position, she found herself a pariah among many of her former leftist colleagues. Few understood or accepted Betsey's continued search for a basis for personal morality, social justice, and the collective definition and pursuit of the good. Yet in the wake of the fall of Communism, the failure of populist revolutions, the resurgence of ethnic and other atavisms, and the continued, largely unchallenged, roughshod progress of capitalism, there were many Marxists who paused to rethink—if not always in the end to change—their views. Given her lifelong antiliberal orientation, it was not surprising in this process that Betsey refused to compromise with bourgeois individualism. Neither was she alone in rejecting "a free market in morality," as she put it in the subtitle of her essay "Beyond Transgression." Nor, on the other hand, was she alone in continuing to deploy Marxist perspectives and concepts in her scholarly work and political analysis while seeking another historical, institutional, intellectual, and moral basis for her continued commitments.

Betsey always used but never limited herself to such perspectives. Instead she drew variously on theoretically rigorous work from diverse sources to define and gain insight into what she regarded as critical problems. So equipped, she found even fashion an avenue to the political, going beyond, though using, Marx's analysis of the fetishism of commodities. "We must remember," she wrote, "that politics ultimately consists in the formal and informal relations of domination and subordination that govern the distribution of resources, opportunities, and respect within a society—i.e., the distribution and ends of power." In her eyes "fashion constitutes an important dimension of politics in this precise sense." Moreover "it also constitutes a representation of the social relations and values that some are imposing and others are accepting, or at least failing to challenge." These impositions reflect not just the "politics of gender," but also "the politics of class."[8]

Betsey understood fashion to be fundamentally about something different than its ostensible matters—clothes, shoes, and personal accessories. She also understood fashion and the habit of its pursuit to operate in many realms, including the intellectual and artistic. In these arenas, too, she felt compelled to analyze the political. "The new literary studies of race and gender," she argued, "have, in general, insisted upon the claims of a myriad of subjective experiences and upon the cultural distinctiveness of marginalized or oppressed communities." The problem was that "for all their insistence on community, they have not decisively challenged the commitment to individualism advanced by the dominant culture." It was folly, in her view, to repudiate "the very notion of power in favor of a radical democratization."

Introduction xxxi

This was because "the incalculable advantage of the dominant culture [in the United States] has been its ability . . . to define the individual as not black and not female."[9]

This historical negation needs continuous address, Betsey concluded. It should not be lost to view in the celebration of diversity or in the discovery of new voices and experiences. As valuable and necessary as those efforts are, they do not help in the formulation or consideration of the challenges that have confronted subaltern and marginalized populations throughout history. She also believed it wrong and irresponsible in effect to deny, as postmodernists often have, that one not only can, but must, critically research, report, and assess such historical challenges and their consequences. She could make this argument because she did not accept that all individual historical texts and accounts are so motivated and compromised by their subjectivity as to be essentially worthless as data or reportage or analysis.

Betsey's critique of this line of reasoning was at once clear and complex. Not all texts are created equal, she noted. Many do reflect the personal, true. Yet that does not mean that they are worthless as clues to and windows on wider experiences and understandings. Many other texts (the bulk of government records, for instance) report the transactional, using shared conventions and measures, and provide data in series that invite analysis. Still other texts sum up shared, if not always stable, understandings.

Seeking to escape the problem of the subjectivity of perceptions and knowledge, the commonsense theorists of the Scottish Enlightenment argued that such shared views reflect if not unmediated reality, then the experience of reality by and in a community or population. Betsey's stance was more skeptical. Such common sense, she held, of course requires rigorous interrogation. It nevertheless also provides important data that the historian can use to gain perspective on historical conditions, continuities, and changes and on the ways in which these phenomena have been at once perceived and experienced, accepted and resisted, deployed and enacted.

Essays can become parts of books, but they have fundamentally different functions. Their relative brevity requires the distillation rather than the elaboration of arguments and the use of illustrative examples rather than the marshaling of evidence. Clarity through concision is different from the precision of a carefully developed monograph or the magisterial ambition of a big book. In effect, therefore, the essay serves as the summing up of an argument that is not presented.

One reason review essayists often have begun with consideration of one or more books is that the books included the quantities and kinds of detail beyond the essayists' scope but essential to the essayists' arguments. Betsey early and often wrote review essays. Rarely was this just to summarize and then challenge or concur with the arguments advanced. She might agree or disagree with these arguments, but it was in the course of the consideration of the implications of these arguments for fundamental questions that she was pursuing. When, for example, assessing Michael Paul Rogin's study of Andrew Jackson, first published in 1975, Betsey used her essay, inter alia, to ask: when and how is it appropriate for historians to pursue psychological analysis of dead historical subjects? That Rogin in her view seriously overstepped the bounds of judiciousness mattered less than that his having done so gave her the occasion to formulate her thinking on a critical issue facing historians in an age of widespread, often ill-informed, facile, and reckless psychologizing.[10]

It was just a decade earlier, after all, that the American Psychiatric Association had had to issue the so-called Goldwater Rule, "which defines as unethical the expression of an opinion about a person who has not been examined."[11] This was in the wake of many APA members having expressed generally negative opinions about Barry Goldwater's psychological fitness for the presidency during his campaign. Historians, Betsey understood, could not examine their dead subjects, but historians could draw on evidence in archives often not available to analysts. What historians should not do is go beyond the limits of that evidence. Silences may speak, but often not clearly. They should be heard, but not overinterpreted.

Beyond her desire to address critical issues, Betsey also had other motives for writing essays. She tried as much as possible to respond positively to requests for scholarly contributions from friends and colleagues, because she thought it an important responsibility to participate in the ongoing discussions and life of the professional communities with which she was involved. On occasion, too, she wanted to introduce authors or issues to wider consideration. She took opportunities to address nonhistorians, because she thought it important to bring historical perspective to bear in literary, cultural, racial, gender, and religious analyses. She welcomed occasions to address nonacademic audiences, because she believed intellectuals should have public roles, bringing their training and expertise to bear as citizens. Then, too, she wanted to share her enthusiasms—for instance for the works of mystery novelist Dick Francis. In doing so, however, she did not just express pleasure and her reasons for it. Instead she probed the implications of works often treated merely as popular fiction. Given her Bakhtinian perspective, such attitudes were barriers to overcome in the pursuit of understanding a culture's deep values and dynamics. Early and late as well, she felt it important to speak out on issues of the day. Occasionally, though not often, she as well sought to share personal experiences. Usually this was in an aside. In the wake of her conversion to Roman Catholicism, however, she told her conversion story in print on more than one occasion.

The fruit of these varied impulses are the sum and substance of the five volumes of Betsey's selected essays and reflections. Few scholars have given as much time to the genre. Few have ranged more widely in doing so. Few have broached as many critical intellectual and public issues of the last quarter of the twentieth century in the process.

In the new age of blogs and social networks, the essay no longer may have the salience it had for the three centuries following the *Spectator* and the *Tatler*. Indeed Betsey's childhood and early adulthood, in the thirty or so years after World War II, were arguably the last great era of the review journal. Since then the erosion of the belief in and commitment to canonical, common culture has undercut an original reason for the review journals. The fragmentation of readerships according to racial, ethnic, and gendered identities challenges the ideas of the public sphere and civic culture that review journals of very different political orientations long shared in promoting. The current, nearly instant resort to apocalyptic political and religious violence and extremism challenges the value and even the possibility of discourse about contested ideas, beliefs, and interests that the review journals long represented and advocated.

Betsey fought against these tendencies even as she sought to overturn the hegemonic power of bourgeois individualism and liberalism. By contributing essays to numerous review journals and elsewhere, she was taking her campaign to the intellectual bastions of that hegemony, but she also was supporting the public sphere, civic culture, and civil discourse, all of which she thought critical. The irony is that many of her colleagues from her days as a feminist on the left did not want to accord her the hearing she continued to want to give others. Their individualism could not brook her dissent. Even if review journals no longer have the presence and role they once did, the hegemonic impulses they have represented continue.

Notes

1. Elizabeth Fox-Genovese, "The Claims of a Common Culture: Gender, Race, Class, and the Canon," *Salmagundi* 72 (Fall 1986): 136; article reprinted in this volume, pp. 145–55.

2. Craig Brandist, "Gramsci, Bakhtin and the Semiotics of Hegemony," *New Left Review* 216 (1996): 103.

3. Elizabeth Fox-Genovese, "The Personal Is Not Political Enough," *Marxist Perspectives* 2 (Winter 1979): 109, 97; article reprinted in this volume, pp. 51–68.

4. Elizabeth Fox-Genovese, "Religion and Women in America," in *World Religions in America: An Introduction*, ed. Jacob Neusner (Louisville: Westminster / John Knox, 1994), 259.

5. Elizabeth Fox-Genovese, "Two Steps Forward, One Step Back: New Questions and Old Models in the Religious History of American Women," *Journal of the American Academy of Religion* 53 (1985): 468.

6. Fox-Genovese, "Religion and Women," 261.

7. Fox-Genovese, "Personal Is Not Political," 111, 112; Elizabeth Fox-Genovese, "The Crisis of Our Culture and the Teaching of History," *History Teacher* 13 (November 1979): 93; article reprinted in this volume, pp. 69–81.

8. Elizabeth Fox-Genovese, "The Empress's New Clothes: The Politics of Fashion," *Socialist Review* 17 (January/February 1987): 8, 10; article reprinted in this volume, pp. 173–93.

9. Elizabeth Fox-Genovese, "Between Individualism and Fragmentation: American Culture and the New Literary Studies of Race and Gender," *American Quarterly* 42 (March 1990): 27, 28; article reprinted in this volume, pp. 207–32.

10. Elizabeth Fox-Genovese, "Psychohistory versus Psychodeterminism: The Case of Rogin's Jackson," *Reviews in American History* 3, no. 4 (1975): 407–18; article reprinted in this volume, pp. 36–50.

11. Henry Pinkser, "'Goldwater Rule' History," *Psychiatric News*, August 3, 2007, 33.

The young Elizabeth Fox, a decade before her marriage to Eugene Genovese. Courtesy of Eugene D. Genovese

Part One

*Reviewing and
Thinking Historically*

One

The Many Faces of Moral Economy
A Contribution to a Debate

In the February 1972 issue of *Past and Present*, Mr. Coats defends the classical economists against charges he finds directed at them in Mr. E. P. Thompson's "Moral Economy of the English Crowd in the Eighteenth Century." He begins by disputing Mr. Thompson's contention that the free market model invariably worked against the poor. After granting that such models are at best "ideal types," he argues that the mechanisms of the market itself discouraged farmers, and even middlemen, from extensive tampering with prices at the expense of the consumer.[1] Yet in no way does he directly refute Mr. Thompson's wealth of evidence documenting the consciousness or fear of dearth on the part of the consumer. To say that the free market worked is not to dispel the reality of the bread riot. Mr. Thompson, on his side, suggests that the traditional model better assured the provisioning of the common people. But that contention does not dispel the very real evidence of misery, or at least an extremely low standard of living among most pre-industrial peoples.

It seems to me that the problem lies less in the validity of the two models—let alone in the intentions of their creators—than in the complexity of eighteenth-century realities. For the transition from traditional to classical economic theory mirrors a real shift in the social rôle of economic activity.[2] And eighteenth-century Englishmen experienced the original occurrence of this particular transition: by the end of the century, it was becoming clear that economic organization would revolve not around the provisioning of a structurally limited population, but around the accumulation of seemingly infinitely expanding capital. This shift marks the transition from preindustrial to industrial society. Mr. Thompson suggests as much when he writes, "the market-place was as much an arena of class war as the factory and mine became in the industrial revolution . . . ,"[3] although he never fully develops the insight. He consistently implies that industrial society emerged directly from traditional society and fails to identify explicitly the outstanding characteristic of eighteenth-century England: namely, that it was a capitalist society—industrial not yet, but capitalist definitely. And the intrusion of capitalism into the fundamental relations of production changes a society.

In pre-capitalist traditional society, the corn market derived its commanding importance from inherent limitations upon corn production within that society. Production could be temporarily increased by expanding the area of land under cultivation, but, without the introduction of qualitative changes, this temporary expedient did not yield permanent gains.[4] In such a situation, under normal conditions, production served only to support population. The surplus, such as it was, was appropriated by the ruling class for military, judicial, religious and artistic purposes. Furthermore, bulky agricultural products could be transported from one region to another only at practically prohibitive cost. By the nature of things, the market was local and closed. In any particular region, the available food supply had to be parcelled out among a given number of individuals. Hence its overwhelming social significance, so correctly stressed by Mr. Thompson.[5] Hence the rôle of the sovereign, and secondarily his magistrates, in assuring the provisioning of the poor. The closed market demanded a certain amount of manipulation to assure its minimal functioning. But where these conditions obtained, there was, to all intents and purposes, no national market. The very emergence of such a market suggests the erosion of traditional society. And Mr. Thompson has presented us with a market-place fully enough developed to be "an arena of class warfare."

What confuses the issue is that Mr. Thompson's England was, in fact, no longer traditional. Without going into the momentous changes introduced by the development of merchant capital in domestic industry and overseas commerce, we can see the transformation occasioned by the revolution in agricultural production. According to Eric Kerridge, "The agricultural revolution dominated the period between 1560 and 1767" and "all its main achievements fell before 1720, most of them before 1673, and many of them earlier still."[6] The changes in farming practice introduced during these years resulted in the doubling, if not trebling, of the gross output of English farms.[7] Thus, for the first time in European history, the Malthusian population-production scissors had been overcome. As early as the 1620s, there is evidence that the English people had forsaken rye for wheat, that marketing at home had increased and that the opposition to exports could be put aside. In a word, "the danger of dearth had vanished."[8]

These changes were not, however, accompanied by a true industrial revolution and its attendant wholesale transfer of population from agriculture to industry. Between 1540 and 1700, the population doubled, but the increase was in large measure absorbed into rural areas and fed by the growing home production. The agricultural depression of 1720–50, together with the levelling off of population growth in those years, would seem to have contributed to a high standard of living for the English worker and an expanding home market for English industry.[9] It is as if the country stopped to draw breath on the eve of its great push. Here, indeed, is the golden age. The food riots analysed by Mr. Thompson, as well as their particular "moral economy," must be seen against this backdrop. The formulation of the traditional morality of provisioning was not a product of the middle ages—of true traditional society. The *Book of Orders* dates from 1587, in other words from the period of agricultural revolution and increased marketing.[10] It dates from a period of Tudor enclosures and population growth. Because the fruits of the new agriculture proved so bounteous, the implications of these changes were not immediately realized. Throughout the first half of the eighteenth century a kind of equilibrium prevailed. Increased production fed the increasing population. The agricultural progress itself demanded labour on the land and in related industries. Enclosure did not result in total expropriation and frequently even entailed an increase in rural population. The standard of living of the common people rose.

It is hard, however, to shake the impression that structural changes had occurred. If enclosure did not destroy the yeomanry, it did promote an increase in smaller and larger holdings at the expense of middling farms. If the agricultural revolution did not transfer the working force from agriculture to industry, it did promote a partial dependence upon wages and an increased dependence upon the market.[11] And, above all, it exhausted the opportunities for agricultural improvement. When, after 1750, the population again started to grow, and most acutely when the harvests were bad, the price of food rose while that of labour declined. And instead of the automatic elimination of surplus population which would have occurred in a purely traditional society, there occurred the tremendous hardship of industrial revolution. Increasingly, and at an accelerating rate, the livelihood of the working population depended less upon the local distribution of corn and more upon the national employment of labour. In describing the close of the eighteenth century, Mr. Thompson refers to this trend: "We are coming to the end of one tradition, and the new tradition has scarcely emerged.

In these years the alternative form of economic pressure—pressure upon wages—is becoming more vigorous. . . ."[12]

Without for one moment minimizing the agonies experienced by the individuals subjected to this process, one must at least recognize that for the first time a society faced with a crisis of subsistence enjoyed a choice. In the eighteenth century, England could no longer look forward to an agricultural revolution which would increase production at home. As Kerridge says, "the wheel had turned full circle and was never to turn more."[13] What it could do, however, was to increase industrial production in order to buy grain from others. It enjoyed this option precisely because of the capitalist nature of its agricultural society. This is what Mr. Thompson fails to make clear. For the moral economy his crowd defends, perhaps represents, nothing so much as an attempt to forestall changes that had already taken place. To be sure, much of the grain produced locally was locally consumed, but the structure for a national market did exist. In times of plenty, the market had handled primarily surplus: its activity had been directed towards industrial consumption of agricultural produce in, for instance, the brewing industry. Only in a period of relative scarcity, such as that which began to prevail after 1750, did it become clear that the market would handle everyone's daily bread.[14] But the other side of the process was that the working population would have to command a wage adequate to the buying of that bread. And in the late eighteenth century it was not yet perfectly clear that the size of the wage would be the deciding factor in popular well-being. Mr. Thompson cites a telling example from East Anglia in 1816 where the labourers "do not only set the prices, they also demand a minimum wage and an end to Speenhamland relief."[15] This convergence of rising union mentality with declining *taxation populaire* says much about popular perception of the changing situation.

When Mr. Coats chides Mr. Thompson for switching back and forth between micro- and macro-economics,[16] he has a point—not, however, a point that validates the Smithian model, any more than Mr. Thompson validated the traditional model, of which more in a moment. Mr. Coats, of course, sees the confusion between micro- and macro-economics on the level of economic analysis, but Mr. Thompson is primarily concerned with a historical process and introduces economic analysis more to support his historical judgement than for its own sake—a procedure that does result in some confusion. Let me suggest, however, that the real confusion lies in the conflict between two economic systems and the relationship between reality and the contending models. Economics itself, in the eighteenth century, was moving from micro to macro concerns. In other words, although traditional economics spoke with the national tongue, its centre of attention was directed to a series of local (micro) grain markets—"The economy of the poor was still local and regional, derivative from a subsistence economy"[17]—while the classical school was concerned primarily with a national (macro) labour and capital market. The confusion between micro- and macro-economic analysis reflects the confusion of the eighteenth century itself. The confusion became particularly acute in the second half of the century when a crisis of subsistence called for positive action. The conflicting economics, on the basis on their respective analyses of economic reality, prescribed different solutions.[18]

Which brings me to what I understand to be the other point at issue between these two scholars: namely, the relative merits of traditional and classical economics. Any economics, of course, is nothing if not an ideology—*pace* the scientists. On this basis, Mr. Coats is clearly correct in emphasizing the normative basis of Adam Smith's economics.[19] Mr. Thompson is no less correct in emphasizing the "moral" intent of traditional economics.[20] Neither traditional paternalism nor classical liberalism could plausibly have maintained their respective hegemonies for so long without a plausible moral base. But let us not forget that they were both part of larger ruling class ideologies and, as such, instruments of class rule. They both represented interests distinct from the interests of the ruled. For Mr. Thompson, despite his tremendous sympathy and respect for the lower classes, leans toward a romantic view of the traditionalists. Time and again, he lumps the paternalists and the crowd against the new market practices. "By the notion of legitimation I mean that the men and women in the crowd were informed by the belief that they were defending traditional rights or customs; and, in general, that they were supported by the wider consensus of the community";[21] "Hence the paternalist model had an ideal existence, and also a very fragmentary real existence."[22] By contrast the repeal of the legislation against forestalling in 1772 represented a victory for *laissez-faire* which "signified less a new model than an anti-model . . . ,"[23] one against which "Paternalists and the poor continued to complain . . .";[24] "Indeed, one may suggest that if the rioting or price setting crowd acted according to any consistent theoretical model, then this model was a selective reconstruction of the paternalist one. . . ."[25]

Mr. Thompson does, most certainly, acknowledge some divergence of interest: ". . . in one respect the moral economy of the crowd broke decisively with that of the paternalists: for the popular ethic sanctioned direct action by the crowd, whereas the values of order underpinning the paternalist model emphatically did not."[26] But it is fair to say that, by focusing so closely on the moral economy of grain, he minimizes the more profound conflicts between paternalist and popular interests. For, in traditional society, it was ultimately in the interest of the rulers to assure a minimum subsistence to at least the "honest" poor. When it came to work practices, forms of land tenure, access to political life, etc., the paternalists were less generous.

If we take France as an even more extreme case as regards notions of paternalist responsibility in the matter of provisioning, we can see that the self-same king, who attended so punctiliously to the regulations governing the bread supply of his *peuple*, was the first strike-breaker of the kingdom, accorded patents of nobility to those who hired women and children at the expense of able-bodied men, and remained the bulwark of the system of seigneurial privilege—until he lost his head for his intransigence. The first seigneur of his realm was seigneur indeed! In this perspective, toleration for the "moral economy of the crowd" begins to look more like the prudence of the magistrates than pure, disinterested social conscience.

It would be grossly unfair, I insist, to suggest that Mr. Thompson fails to appreciate the conflicts in the traditional model—after all, his work is overwhelmingly devoted to a learned and sympathetic portrayal of working people's consciousness—but, alert as he is to the horrors of early industrial society, he inclines to favour the paternalists, whom he sees as spokesmen for a more harmonious and responsible social order, over the classicists. And in this he may be wrong. For Mr. Coats is right in defending the moral intentions of the classicists. If the rise of a market society brought indisputable horrors, it also brought an emphasis on individual freedom of choice, the right to self-betterment, eventually the opportunity for political participation. The values of Liberalism should not be reduced to nought simply because their practice has historically been so shoddy. The industrial worker can rightly claim a view of himself denied to his labouring predecessors, and he can claim it by virtue of the classical ideal type. This is no little gain. Nor, of course, is it the workers' own economics. That came later, with Marx.

Traditional economics and classical economics both represented the views of the "haves" as against the "have-nots." Both also spoke to genuine aspirations of the "have-nots"—and even claimed to answer a genuine sense of rights: the right to bread in the one case and the right to work in the other. That neither, in practice, delivered on its promises is responsible for the growth of yet another economics which portrayed the social relations of production from the working people's own perspective.

Notes

1. A. W. Coats, "Contrary Moralities: Plebs, Paternalists and Political Economists," *Past and Present*, no. 54 (Feb. 1972), pp. 130–1; E. P. Thompson, "The Moral Economy of the English Crowd in the Eighteenth Century," *Past and Present*, no. 50 (Feb. 1971), pp. 76–136.

The Many Faces of Moral Economy 9

2. The use of the terms "traditional economics" and "classical economics" as practised by both Mr. Thompson and Mr. Coats requires some comment: the terms are not strictly parallel. While there can be little question that the classical school refers to Adam Smith and his followers, there is room to question who is included in the designation traditional school. The classicists were academic economists and their historical predecessors in academic economics were the mercantilists; yet neither Mr. Thompson nor Mr. Coats refers directly to a mercantilist of major stature. Rather they refer to a body of traditional legislation. Economic legislation is not the same thing as economic theory. If we were dealing directly with mercantilist theorists, it would considerably complicate the debate.

3. Thompson, *op. cit.*, p. 120.

4. Eric Kerridge, *The Agricultural Revolution* (London, 1967), p. 332.

5. Thompson, *op. cit.*, p. 135.

6. Kerridge, *op. cit.*, p. 328.

7. Ibid., p. 334.

8. Ibid., p. 345.

9. Ibid., pp. 332–4. A. H. John, "Aspects of English Economic Growth in the First Half of the Eighteenth Century," in E. M. Carus-Wilson (ed.), *Essays in Economic History*, vol. ii (London, 1962), *passim*.

10. Alan Everitt, "The Marketing of Agricultural Produce," in Joan Thirsk (ed.), *The Agrarian History of England and Wales*, vol. iv, *1500–1640* (Cambridge, 1967), pp. 581–2.

11. E. L. Jones, "Editor's Introduction," in E. L. Jones (ed.), *Agricultural Revolution and Economic Growth in England 1650–1815* (London, 1967), pp. 21–5.

12. Thompson, *op. cit.*, p. 128.

13. Kerridge, *op. cit.*, p. 338.

14. Everitt, *op. cit.*, p. 548. It may be that the second half of the eighteenth century, and the beginning of the nineteenth—the period from which Mr. Thompson's examples are mainly drawn—witnessed a recrudescence of bread riots because retail purchase of grain was falling under the purveyance of wholesale operations. From the later sixteenth century to the mid-eighteenth, the market had handled predominantly wholesale commerce. As the labouring poor began to buy more of their bread in the form of ready-made loaves and the market became increasingly directed to supplying the immediate needs of home consumers—as opposed to export or brewing, both of which declined—the consumers undoubtedly perceived themselves as subject to its operations in a direct fashion. This new resentment of the market itself may have been stronger than previously.

15. Thompson, *op. cit.*, p. 128.

16. Coats, *op. cit.*, p. 131.

17. Thompson, *op. cit.*, p. 98.

18. Any economic analysis intends to describe reality, but its vision of reality necessarily entails a vision of optimum future reality and a judgement of how best to attain desired goals. Traditional economics saw reality as essentially unchanging and decreed that in hard times existing resources were to be allocated among the members of society in order to ensure maximum survival. Classical economics saw wealth as potentially growing over time—linear progression as opposed to cyclical swings—and judged that resources should be allocated to advance production in society as a whole on the grounds that such growth would provide a higher standard of living for all in the future. In the eighteenth century,

in other words, the optimal social allocation of economic resources became a subject for debate. Both sides in the debate could claim equally genuine concern with social morality.
19. Coats, *op. cit.*, p. 133.
20. Thompson, *op. cit.*, p. 90.
21. Ibid., p. 78.
22. Ibid., p. 88.
23. Ibid., p. 89.
24. Ibid., p. 86.
25. Ibid., p. 98.
26. Ibid.

Two

The Physiocratic Model and the Transition from Feudalism to Capitalism

Marguerite Kuczynski, by her discovery and publication of the third edition of François Quesnay's *Tableau économique*, has long since established her claims to rank among the foremost scholars of physiocracy in our time. The first volume of her edition, François Quesnay, *Ökonomische Schriften*, which covers the period 1756–1759, surpasses her own previous efforts and all other editions of Quesnay's writings.* Her masterful and learned work is, moreover, intelligent—which cannot be said of all masterful and learned work. It marks the culmination of a distinguished Marxist tradition of physiocratic studies. Kuczynski remains faithful to the essentials of that tradition, particularly to the path-breaking work of Marx himself and to the more recent and equally sophisticated studies by Ronald Meek; but in her erudition and her thorough consideration of a wide range of questions, she contributes brilliant insights and thereby creates a new synthesis that exceeds the sum of its parts.[1]

Kuczynski, as her title suggests, restricts her focus to Quesnay's writings, and to his specifically economic writings. The present volume, to be followed

---

"The Physiocratic Model and the Transition from Feudalism to Capitalism." *Journal of European Economic History* 4, no. 3 (1975): 725–37. Copyright 1975 by the *Journal of European Economic History*. All rights reserved. Used by permission of UniCredit Group.

*François Quesnay, *Ökonomische Schriften*, in zwei Bänden, Band I., 1756–1759, ed. and trans., Marguerite Kuczynski (Berlin: Akademic-Verlag, 1971), 2 vols., V–XCI, 3–833 pp.

by a second, carries the development of Quesnay's economic thought to the first publication of the *Tableau économique* in the sixth part of Mirabeau's enlarged edition of *L'ami des hommes* in 1760. The edition includes Quesnay's four economic articles for the *Encyclopédie: Fermiers, Grains, Impôts* and the first three "editions" of *Tableau*. As supporting material, Kuczynski also presents two letters from Quesnay to Forbonnais, two from Quesnay to Mirabeau, a piece of ten paragraphs on grain production, grain trade, and population, and a selected list of books from Quesnay's library.

Kuczynski's edition constitutes the most extensive body of scholarship ever published on Quesnay. Her most dramatic contributions lie in her demonstration, through the manuscript at the Bibliothèque de l'Arsenal, of Quesnay's contribution to Mirabeau's *Explication du Tableau économique* (which she does not include, nor project for her second volume), and her argument that *Impôts* precedes *Hommes* in the forging of Quesnay's thought, of which more later. Both these contributions transcend mere scholarly curiosity and force substantial revisions in any interpretation of Quesnay's thought, although not necessarily the ones Kuczynski proposes. Less flashily, but no less substantially, she traces all references in correspondence and ancillary works such as Patullo's *Essai sur l'amélioration des terres* (which has long been recognized as a *bona fide* guide to aspects of Quesnay's thought, but never fully exploited in this regard). She makes full use of the recent work of French scholars, such as Jacqueline Hecht's discovery of Quesnay's letters to Forbonnais (although she significantly excludes Hecht's equally important uncovering of a letter to Le Blanc, the translator of Hume) and Jules Conan's discovery of the ten paragraph "demographic fantasy."[2] Her use of the inventory of Quesnay's library far outdistances that of Félix Lorin, the only other scholar to have attempted deciphering that intractable document, although it too bears the mark of her interpretative preferences.[3]

Any student of physiocracy, of the history of economic thought, or of the French ancien régime must celebrate the appearance of this superlative edition, but must also be permitted a sigh of regret at Kuczynski's modesty. Under the guise of the editorial role—reminiscent of Quesnay's own description of the *Tableau* as a small book of household accounts—she has developed a major interpretation of Quesnay's thought, including a revised periodization of the unfolding of that thought. She has also provided the most accurate published versions of two of his articles, *Impôts* and *Hommes*, available in any language, including the "definitive" INED edition.[4] Kuczynski's analysis, developed in a lengthy general introduction, individual introductions to each selection, and substantial notes to the text, which appropriately receive a volume to themselves (*Halbband* 2), constitutes an independent treatment of the forging of physiocratic economics. It also constitutes the clearest and most heavily documented example of a venerable, but never before adequately supported, reading of the nature of Quesnay's economic thought. The reading emphasizes Quesnay's primary focus on the dynamics of capitalist production within the context of a still seigneurial ancien régime; it stresses Quesnay's materialism; and it implicitly divorces him, to the extent possible, from the physiocrats who lobbied in his name.

Kuczynski has already presented the outlines of her interpretation in her monumental editorial contribution to her and Ronald Meek's *Quesnay's Tableau économique*.[5] Her present effort buttresses and extends her previous work. Although her argument emerges clearly from the introductions and notes, it is a pity to have to piece together a discussion that would have more than justified a separate book. As Kuczynski indicates in her opening quotation from Marx and Engels's *The German Ideology*, she assumes that an understanding of Quesnay's economics contributes to an understanding of modern economic science. For, "through the [work of the] physiocrats, the economy was first raised to a discrete science, and has since then been treated as such." Kuczynski, in other words, emphasizes, through her choice of texts and her commentary on them, Quesnay's fundamental contribution to the analysis of capitalist production which extends from him through the English classical school to Marx. This perspective entails dismissing the traditional, or "feudal," aspects of Quesnay's thought as situational or accidental rather than seeing them as integrally related to his central concerns. In my opinion, it slights some of the complexity of Quesnay's thought and assuredly ignores Mirabeau's important contributions to the formulation of physiocracy (which I should distinguish from Quesnay's pre-physiocratic economic articles), but it rests upon breath-taking learning and years of considered judgement. It not only represents the most complete investigation of physiocracy as agrarian capitalism and materialist economics yet presented by the many scholars of all ideological persuasions; it also represents a serious assessment of the transition, in the theoretical realm, from feudalism to capitalism.[6]

Kuczynski situates Quesnay's economics, as have so many scholars from Marx to Pierre Goubert, in the context of the ancien régime. She follows Marx closely in describing Quesnay's system as a bourgeois representation of the feudal system (xxviii), and in ascribing Quesnay's grasp of the nature of property in land as an absolute or individual right to the experience of Law's system in which so much land changed hands (xlviii–xlix). She also suggests, without elaboration, that Quesnay relied heavily on an analysis of the English agricultural revolution in developing his own model; but, she notes, he did so without taking account of the English political revolution of the seventeenth century and thus ended by trying to reconcile English-style economic progress with the existing French social system. In other words, she argues that Quesnay discovered the nature of capitalist production without understanding its inseparability from bourgeois social relations: His understanding of capitalist production "naturally did not mean" that he had "worked out and defined" the "essential economic categories of capitalism" (lxxix). Quesnay's commanding importance, in her view, lies in his having discovered the centrality of the economy to human life and social relations: He falls into "the category of realistically thinking investigators for whom the primary needs and the way of satisfying them are the basis of human society" (xiii).

Kuczynski's analysis of Quesnay's economics thus contains a contradiction as disturbing as that in the economics itself. The economics, by its realism and material determinism, implicitly foreshadows Marx's own economics, yet it remains colored by its historical context and by certain non-economic values of its progenitor. Kuczynski never slips into anachronism on these questions. She knows the ancien régime well and has great admiration for Quesnay as ex-peasant, scientist, courtier, and man of character. She never reproaches him for not having been what he could not have been. By concentrating exclusively upon his economics, however, she bypasses exactly that dimension of his thought which helps to explain the puzzling silences at the heart of his work. Thus, although she never falls into the ahistoricism of some of the recent econometric commentators on the *Tableau* (whose work she does not mention), she does fall into some of the same methodological traps, particularly that of ignoring the deep ideological and psychological roots of Quesnay's seemingly extraneous "feudal" residues.[7] For this reason, although Kuczynski's edition is the best in any language for those texts it includes, it does not entirely supersede the other two classic editions, Onken's of 1888 and INED's of 1958, both of which include some of Quesnay's metaphysical work, especially the article *Evidence*, which appeared, like *Fermiers*, in 1756, in volume VI of the *Encyclopédie*.[8] *Evidence*, particularly when examined in the context of Quesnay's later medical works (excerpts of which are included in the Onken edition, but not the INED), establishes the metaphysical and epistemological context for Quesnay's economics. Most important, it demonstrates that Quesnay's attitude toward the ancien régime is both deeper and more complex than the simple acceptance of its social and political manifestations.

Quesnay never unilaterally accepted the philosophic premises that we can retroactively read into his economic analysis. Quesnay's economic analysis, by its emphasis on capitalist production and its reliance upon possessive individualism and market relations, suggests a throughly modern individualism, such as that underlying classical political economy. Quesnay, however, never trusted unbridled individualism. He did not expect men necessarily to follow their own best economic interest. He retained a deep religious commitment in which God figured as the necessary guarantor of human intelligence. He did not believe that the dictates of nature or of the material natural order would necessarily triumph over human stupidity. He was not, in any normal sense of the word, an economic determinist. He did believe that nature embodied the divine plan, but he also believed that men must realize this plan and that nothing predetermined their success or failure. Quesnay's failure to develop a thorough analysis of bourgeois social and political relations did not simply reflect a passive acceptance of his historical context; it also represented an attempt to restrain the free play of individual interest and an attempt to create a socially ordered capitalism suitable to the French experience. Quesnay did see the marketplace as the central arena of economic development, but he never quite trusted the market to determine social and political relations. He always insisted upon the necessity for a central authority to guarantee the workings of the market.

Karl Polanyi has argued that the free market of the nineteenth century constituted an aberration in human affairs. Normally, he claimed, the market—or the exchange of goods and services—is embedded within the larger context of human relations, which determine its functioning.[9] For Polanyi, the great originality (and crime) of nineteenth-century classical liberalism was to disengage the market from the larger human network and to assign such preponderance to market activities that they came to determine social and political relations. First human subsistence and then human labor become commodities, and, ultimately, the fetishism of commodities—to recall Marx's term—comes to dominate notions of justice and optimum human good. Quesnay discovered the market through his observation of English economic power and his reading of other economists, notably Richard Cantillon. He always stressed market relations—including wage labor—as the necessary path to economic development. He never, however, accepted the market as an adequate model for society as a whole, particularly not for political relations. Quesnay's economic thought remains colored by his conviction that men had first to create the market—which nature, unassisted, could not do—and then to restrict its influence to the proper sphere. The economics make little sense when divorced from his metaphysical dualism.

Kuczynski does not raise these problems in the form in which I have presented them. Furthermore, the interpretation that emerges from her choice of texts and her editorial comments intentionally relegates them to a position of peripheral importance. Nevertheless, her discussion of Quesnay's economics—even within her chosen perspective—does raise them implicitly and brilliantly. Unfortunately, by remaining so close to the economic terrain, her analysis of the discrete aspects of Quesnay's complexity does not lead her to a more ambitious reevaluation of his thought. By avoiding the integral links between Quesnay's economic thought and physiocratic social and political thought, by avoiding Quesnay's collaborative work, and, above all, by avoiding an explicit discussion of the relationship between Quesnay's early work and physiocracy, she obscures the thorny problems of periodization, and thus obscures the relationship between Quesnay's economic analysis and his political economy which is correctly—*pace*, Madame Kuczynski—known as physiocracy. The materialist economics runs like a silver thread from the statist (not to say mercantilist) *Fermiers, Grains,* and *Impôts*, through the exploratory *Hommes* and early *Tableaux,* to the Spartan third "edition," and on to the *Dialogues* and other late pieces that will appear in the second volume. Significantly, Kuczynski discusses the general problems of Quesnay's economic analysis in her introduction without reference to shifts in his thought over time. Her brilliant treatment of chronology—particularly the reordering of *Impôts* and *Hommes*—must be dug out of the individual introductions and the notes. She uses that reordering to support her interpretation of the economics, specifically to tie the writing of *Hommes* to the elaboration of the first *Tableau,* but does so without integrating it into the problems of the economics.

In her introduction, Kuczynski presents a brief, but uncommonly sensitive discussion of Quesnay's theory of value in which she shows that Quesnay possessed both a use and an exchange theory of value (lxxx–lxxxi). She seems to assume that because of the feudal context in which he worked Quesnay could not be expected to have developed a labor theory of value. She finds it understandable, moreover, that, given the agricultural society of the ancien régime, he should see use value primarily in terms of agricultural products understood as subsistence goods. The influence of "feudal thought" more than accounts for his seeing that "production is natural production, is production of use value" (lxxx). She then turns to Quesnay's concept of venal value, which she breaks down into two component parts—exchange value and market value—and argues that since Quesnay assumed that exchange would take place between equivalent values, the price of a good would not only accurately reflect its market value but also its intrinsic value: "the price is the value." She then extends the discussion to rent and to the net product, which she equates to surplus value, and discusses the thorny problem of the farmer's putative profit.

In her discussion of value, Kuczynski essentially argues that the net product appropriated by the proprietors (including the sovereign and the tithe holders) reflects the prevailing feudal system and that the farmer's "profit" obeys the dictates of a capitalist system and constitutes part of the differential rent. Her discussion does not follow the tortuous development of Quesnay's thought on these questions, nor does it resolve the problem of value as she originally presented it. She merely asserts that Quesnay himself never fully defined the word; he observed its appearance as the results of market transactions (xxxi). She also suggests, however, that his single term, value, carried several meanings and thus reflected a thought in transition (not so much within itself, as between feudalism and capitalism). At the end of her introductory note to *Hommes*, moreover, she draws attention to the glimmer of a labor theory of value that indubitably does figure in that article. She further asserts that traces of such a value theory recur throughout his later work, but never crystalize into a systematic statement (238). Kuczynski thus lucidly indicates all the elements that contribute to Quesnay's value theory, but, in her ultimate acceptance of a "transitional" reading for the thought as a unity, begs the key developmental questions and does less than justice to the rigor of Quesnay's physiocratic thought.

Quesnay firmly grasped the essentials of a use theory and a labor theory of value as he worked through them in the early articles. And he rejected them both. Use alone had no value: The subsistence economy of *petite culture* and peasant misery rested upon use value. The whole point of Quesnay's economics is to break out of that cycle of impoverishment by conferring a monetary—or market—value upon all commodities and all human labor. The market, to Quesnay, linked all members of society on a new and more advanced basis than had been possible under subsistence production. Yet Quesnay's commitment to economic modernity did not lead him to espouse that labor theory of value to which his work so frequently seemed to point. He well understood that such a premise led to the social and political divisiveness of rampant individualism—as indeed it did until Marx's reformulation. Quesnay's conception of market value, however unsatisfactory it may appear to modern economists, mirrored in the economic sphere his conception of legal despotism in the political: it simultaneously assured the escape from "feudal" stagnation and barred the way to bourgeois liberalism.

Kuczynski is right: Quesnay did predicate his discussion of venal (market/exchange) value upon the assumption that value exchanged for equal value. She is wrong, however, in dismissing the exchange component. In so doing, she is reacting, as she states, to modern economic controversies, specifically to the Schumpeter/Keynes emphasis upon the role of exchange (the primacy of demand) in economic development. Quesnay preceded those debates and was no party to them. For him, the emergence of market relations both testified to and embodied economic development. Such relations required ascribing a monetary value to commodities. For all agricultural commodities to have a monetary value, labor had to be divorced from the land in order to constitute a market for agricultural products that heretofore had been valueless. The market supplanted traditional notions of social justice as the determinant of social relations; it could not, however, in Quesnay's view, give free rein to individual interest (which might be uneconomic). The market, in Quesnay's thought, came to supply a new standard of social justice, but one no less authoritarian than the old.

Quesnay's notion of the "good" price illustrates the problem. Rhetorically, in the reverential emphasis it received in physiocratic writings, the good price carried an aura comparable to that previously endowed upon the just price, which embodied the notion that social decency required curtailing strict economic advantage. In contradistinction, the good price reflected what appear to be purely economic concerns. The good price had to cover the costs of the farmer and assure him a return of one hundred percent on his investment to finance taxation and to promote further growth. That price was not, however, in the first instance, a market price; it did not represent the supply/demand equilibrium. It represented the needs of economic development and political order. Quesnay assuredly understood that it should be a market price, hence the impassioned physiocratic pleas for free trade in grain. That concern with free trade, however, in some measure obscured Quesnay's deeper intent. Physiocratic opponents, such as Galiani, argued tellingly that the impediments to free circulation in France were such that the national market was a physiocratic fantasy. Quesnay implicitly recognized the problem when he fell back on the contention that the international market would produce the good price. Even in the international context, however, the actual workings of supply and demand figure less importantly than the compelling need of an adequate return to the farmers. The international price represented a kind of *deus ex machina,* or more accurately, a vision in the mind of God. Rather than an economically determined price, the international price was the price necessary to the creation of the market economy. Quesnay, who did understand the role that the market should play in a developed economy, read the miraculous institution into a premarket context.

Scholars have occasionally used the less-than-modern aspects of physiocracy—particularly Quesnay's opposition to interest—to argue that, under the guise of market economics, Quesnay sought to restore a medieval society.[10] My criticism of Kuczynski has nothing in common with this viewpoint. The brilliance and modernity of Quesnay's economic analysis cannot be dismissed so cheaply. Nevertheless, Quesnay did not espouse unlimited growth any more than he espoused unfettered possessive individualism. Quesnay sought to promote his vision of a full-market society. His dream entailed a qualitative revolution in French relations of production, including not only a market in grain but also one in labor-power. But it did not entail open-ended growth, which he neither foresaw nor desired. Here lies the core of Quesnay's belief in the unique productivity of agriculture. Quesnay did understand industry or manufacture within the context of his own society as the product of merchant capital and therefore a drain upon the productive life of society. He also, however, understood the value of the division of labor. Even when he advocated the advantages of the production of boots and nails (as opposed to luxury goods), he continued to insist on the primacy of agriculture. His recalcitrance on this question rested not only on his analysis of manufacture under the ancien régime, but also on his conviction that manufacture serves to realize the full potential of given material resources. Men do not create wealth; they develop and exploit existing potential wealth to its full extent. Quesnay sought the realization of the divine plan that existed in nature. The potential for the market society based on agricultural capitalism existed in nature, which for him also meant in the mind of God, but it had to be implemented by human choice. His insistence upon the good price and his opposition to interest formed parts of a coherent political economy and world view. Quesnay understood that if eighteenth-century Frenchmen were left to pursue their own interests, as they understood them, the resulting free market would strengthen seigneurial relations in agriculture at the expense of capitalist, and would strengthen merchant and finance capital at the expense of productive capital.

Quesnay's political economy was, in the full sense of the word, political. The first of the natural law, scientific economists built a programme for change into the heart of his "value free" economics. His *Tableau économique* which Kuczynski, the leading authority on the subjects, handles so brilliantly embodies exactly the same contradictions as the political economy it crowns. Kuczynski concurs with Marx in portraying the *Tableau* as "a notion of the highest genius, of incontestably the highest genius to which political economy has heretofore been indebted" (xix). Like so many subsequent economists, she remains awe-struck before that small diagram which, in the middle of the eighteenth century, could depict the entire process of the reproduction and circulation of wealth. Furthermore, both implicitly and explicitly, she links Quesnay's invention of the *Tableau* with his writing of the economic articles. She maintains, I think correctly, that he probably conceived the notion of a diagram in 1757 while at work on *Hommes* (233ff. and 342). In addition, her grouping of the economic articles with the *Tableau* in its early forms constitutes an interpretative statement. This reading, which emphasizes Quesnay's analysis of capitalist production to the exclusion of his political economy, presents no problems in respect to *Fermiers* and *Grains*, which establish the micro-economic analysis of capitalist production in a single firm to which Quesnay remained faithful for the rest of his life. Room for respectful controversy emerges, however, in the direct linking of *Fermiers, Hommes,* and the *Tableau.* Like Kuczynski, I see *Hommes* as pivotal, but not in quite the same way, and I should also accord Mirabeau a larger role, as influence if not as author, in all Quesnay's post-1757 works, especially in the formulation of the *Explication* which differs in important respects from the earlier *Tableaux.*

Kuczynski's reading rests on the assumption that Quesnay consistently focussed on his discovery of capitalist production and that the apparent distortions of his analysis of capitalism can be written off to the intractability of his socio-political environment, or to the meddling of his disciples. Quesnay's determination to implement agricultural capitalism as the basis of the life of the nation and the treasury of the sovereign cannot be gainsaid. In *Fermiers, Grains,* and *Impôts,* he openly presents his programme as a means of increasing royal revenues and diverges from previous mercantilist programme less in goals than in method. Nevertheless, in the period in which he wrote *Hommes* and elaborated the first two *Tableaux,* he developed another preoccupation as well: In 1757, he shifted from his preoccupation with micro-economic analysis to a preoccupation with macro-economic analysis. For the purposes of production, his method was simple. He extended his micro-economics to the entire kingdom, which he treated as a single firm. Thus, in analytic terms, the taxes which accrue to the sovereign differ not at all from the rent that accrues to a single proprietor. Quesnay, however, introduced an entirely new concept, which he never openly acknowledged, when he turned to the process of circulation and exchange. A close reading of the economic articles suggests that Quesnay must have first read Cantillon's *Essai sur le commerce* in 1757. *Hommes,* by this reading, represents his attempt to come to terms with Cantillon.[11] And the first *Tableau,* quite explicitly, embodies Quesnay's attempt to depict graphically Cantillon's argument that an increase in the velocity of circulation produces the same effect as an increase in the money in circulation—it permits an increase in the population that can survive on a finite revenue. Quesnay rapidly turned to integrating his own analysis of production into the macro-economic model. Over time, the textual commentaries that accompanied each *Tableau* increased in volume—by the *Explication* the text has swallowed the diagramme which now serves to illustrate a theoretical discussion—and Quesnay placed increasing emphasis on the division of labor that results from agricultural capitalism (which helps to account for his interest in the labor theory of value in *Hommes*) as well as on the miraculous powers of the market. But he never changed the form of his diagram that had been designed to illustrate Cantillon's premise from the perspective of royal finances.

Kuczynski understands the dual nature of Quesnay's thought perfectly: She counterposes its modern, capitalist content with its traditional form. Furthermore, through an analysis of Quesnay's ambiguous vocabulary, she comes to the conclusion that although he understood the phenomenon, he avoided the terminology of capitalism (lxxxvi). She thus shows that his choice of vocabulary manifested the ambiguity of his historical context. By extension, the same argument could be made about the *Tableau*, which also seems to contain a revolutionary content in a traditional form. The *Tableau*, however, more clearly even than the vocabulary, illustrates the complexity of Quesnay's thought. For the *Tableau* does not actually contain the revolutionary content. It does not depict the productive sector; it depicts the social and political network of exchange and presupposes capitalist reproduction. Quesnay never succeeded in fully integrating his micro- and his macro-economic analyses. If he had done so on the basis of capitalist production, the agricultural capitalists, rather than the proprietors and the sovereign, would have been the centerpoint of the diagram. Nor did Quesnay ever decide between the primacy of supply and that of demand in spurring economic growth. Ultimately, he was less concerned with economic growth than he was with economic revolution. Growth within the existing system would not produce capitalist agriculture or a market society. Growth within a fully developed capitalist system (which he did not equate with an as yet non-existent industrial capitalist system) would not be necessary.

Quesnay probably understood the revolutionary implications of his thought, but he always became outraged at the notion that he was promoting social or political revolution. His protestations of innocence on that count were not hypocritical. Just as many of the philosophes genuinely supported a degree of social, intellectual, or political individualism and rejected economic individualism as an anti-social horror, so did Quesnay genuinely promote economic individualism even as he rejected its social and political implications. His position can be read as a blend of the traditional and the modern, more specifically as the modern, or bourgeois, breaking out of the mold of the traditional, or feudal, but it can also be read as an alternate vision of modernity—one that insists that society requires an authority that transcends the immediate struggle (Quesnay, unlike Smith, would not have said harmony) of individual interests. The hegemony of English political economy, carried as it was on the wave of English industrial success, has led scholars to see necessity in the Anglo-Saxon model of modern society. It has been assumed that an industrial triumph that commanded world emulation did indeed represent the realization of a natural law.

Quesnay surely did not foresee that industrial production would carry the economic division of labor to world hegemony. But even if he had understood the economic potential of industrial capitalism, I doubt that he would have regarded it as the necessary outcome of a given material potential. Quesnay knew that economic development, justice, and social order depend upon human choice, which in turn depends upon human beings overcoming their material condition—in his mind through divine assistance—rather than realizing it. Quesnay has much in common with Marx, beginning with economic genius, but only one of the links between them lies through the development of an analysis of capitalist production via the English political economists. The English experience, and the English interpretations of that experience, remain germane to the physiocracy and the Marxism that bracket the first onset of industrial revolution. Both Quesnay and Marx, however, doubted the eternal validity of unbridled possessive individualism.

In her systematic exclusion of Mirabeau from the formulation of Quesnay's economic thought, Kuczynski rejects one of the most important aspects of that thought, for Mirabeau, his bombastic rhetoric and intransigent "feudalism" notwithstanding, taught Quesnay much. Quesnay, prior to his association with Mirabeau, had addressed himself overwhelmingly to the economic mechanism. Mirabeau introduced him to the importance of the social system in which the mechanism is embedded. Physiocracy, including the third "edition" of the *Tableau* and the *Explication*, reflects this debt. In this connection, it is to be regretted that Kuczynski did not include Mirabeau's *Mémoire pour la Société d'Agriculture de Berne* on which Quesnay and Mirabeau collaborated at the same time that Quesnay was working on the third and fourth versions of the *Tableau*. The economic analysis in the *Mémoire* belongs almost entirely to Quesnay, and Quesnay himself deemed it a worthy, if partial, introduction to the *Tableau*. The *Mémoire* moves Quesnay's economics from the realm of mechanism into a full-fledged political economy and contains some of the most explicit statements ever formulated about physiocracy. It brings to a close the exploratory period that opened with *Hommes* and forms an integral part of the Quesnay-Mirabeau collaboration that separates the economic articles from the unmistakeable physiocracy of *Philosophie rurale*.[12]

Kuczynski, however, seems intent upon rescuing Quesnay's accomplishment from the mire of physiocracy. This intention, if indeed she harbors it, as her almost total avoidance of the term suggests, is understandable. Quesnay's staunchest and most acute admirers have regularly sought to free him from that confusing association. But it is misguided. Quesnay can no more be separated from physiocracy than his economics can be separated from his dualistic metaphysics. The transition from the traditional to the modern, from feudalism to capitalism, is as yet but poorly understood. Each thinker, as each society, which bridged that gap did so on the basis of a specific historical context. The general models are useful—indeed necessary to fruitful comparison—but must not obscure the differences in various responses to theoretical and social problems. Each revolutionary theory, like each revolutionized society, carries aspects of the past into the present and the program for the future. Over-emphasizing the persistence of older typologies in too general terms—feudalism, artisans, and so forth—can lead, as with so much recent social history, to the implication that nothing really changes, that, for example, workers do not espouse political goals because they are really caught up in immediate problems. Conversely, overemphasizing the radical explosion of new typologies—capitalism, socialism, and so forth—can lead to exaggerating the rate of change in human culture. Different men, like different societies, select from their inherited experience the values or forms they most wish to preserve and carry their essence to new commitments. The process varies from case to case, but the different solutions should not be evaluated merely as aberrations from the norm of the abstract model. Physiocracy embodies Quesnay's brilliant economic analysis just as it embodies his commitment to social order and to political authority. Its uncompromising defence of absolute property shows how little it passively accepted the residual feudal system; its equally uncompromising defence of legal despotism shows how little it accepted the intrusion of possessive individualism into the social and political spheres. The physiocratic model, which so clearly bears Quesnay's imprint, elaborates a particular French vision of the transition from feudalism to capitalism, not a compromise between the two, much less a lapse from some Anglo-Saxon liberal norm.

Notes

1. Karl Marx, *Theories of Surplus Value*, Part I (Moscow, 1963); Ronald Meek, *The Economics of Physiocracy* (Cambridge, Mass., 1963).
2. All published in *François Quesnay et la Physiocratie*, 2 vols. (Paris, 1958). Henceforth, INED.
3. Félix Lorin, "Mémoire sur la fortune de François Quesnay," repr. from *Bulletin des Sciences économiques et sociales du Comité des travaux historiques et scientifiques* (Paris, 1897). Hecht, "Vie," INED, I, 279, also mentions the library but does not describe its contents at all. Cf. A. D. Yvelines, *Etude Huber de Versailles, Minutes Thibault*, 1774, "Inventaire et liquidation après le décès de M. François Quesnay (29 décembre 1774)." The inventory of the library is an almost impossibly difficult document to use, not only because of misspellings, but also because it contains no indication of date of purchase. It does, however, contain a great deal of history and theology which Kuczynski does not mention. Cf. also Bibliothèque de l'Arsenal, Fonds de la Bastille, Ms. 1201. Quesnay annotated both of Mirabeau's drafts, although sparingly.
4. Meek, *Economics*, 88–101, in his translation of extracts from *Hommes*, also returns to the original manuscript and corrects some of the INED errors.
5. *Quesnay's Tableau Economique*, edited, with new material, translations and notes by Marguerite Kuczynski and Ronald L. Meek (London and New York, 1972). Kuczynski

had previously edited the *Tableau économique von François Quesnay* (Berlin, 1965), also based on her discovery of the third "edition."

6. E.g. Bert F. Hoselitz, "Agrarian Capitalism, the Natural Order of Things: François Quesnay," *Kyklos*, XXI (1968), 637–64.

7. E.g. Robert V. Eagley, "A Physiocratic Model of Dynamic Equilibrium," *Journal of Political Economy*, LXXVII (1969), 66–84, and his *The Structure of Classical Economic Theory* (New York and London, 1974); Izumi Hishiyama, "The Tableau Economique of François Quesnay—Its Analysis, Reconstruction, and Application," *Kyoto University Economic Review*, XXX (1960), 1–45.

8. Auguste Onken, ed., *Oeuvres économiques et philosophiques de F. Quesnay, fondateur du système physiocratique* . . . (Frankfurt-am-Main and Paris, 1888).

9. Karl Polanyi, *The Great Transformation* (Boston, 1957 [1944]), esp. 33–76.

10. E.g. Max Beer, *An Inquiry into Physiocracy* (New York, 1966 [1939]).

11. The problems of the relationship between the early articles are extremely complex and I shall treat them in a separate article. There is only one reference to Cantillon in *Grains* and that is in a note that may well have been added in 1757, after the article was written and just before it went to press.

12. My view of these and related questions is developed in *The Origins of Physiocracy: Economic Revolution and Social Order in Eighteenth-Century France* (Ithaca: Cornell University Press, 1976).

Three

Physiocracy and the Overthrow of the Ancien Régime

After almost two centuries, the origins of the French Revolution, or the causes of the overthrow or collapse of the ancien régime, remain as subject to debate as at the time of the event itself. In particular, the intellectual and ideological origins pose staggering problems for historians concerned with a modicum of scientific accuracy or at least convincing proof. The censorship practices of the eighteenth-century monarchy suggest that the crown periodically recognized some danger in the new enlightened thought with its message of rational criticism and its attention to many facets of individualism. And since 1789, any number of historians have been willing to discuss the intellectual origins of the French Revolution and to point to the connections between pre-Revolutionary criticism and post-Revolutionary arrangements. Indeed, on the most general plane, the affiliation is so direct as to defy comment. Nevertheless, the common-sensical wisdom that grasps the obvious link between Enlightenment and Revolution, specifically the results of Revolution, stumbles awkwardly on the uncertain terrain of rational demonstration.

As a general rule, philosophy and Revolution made poor bedfellows. Few of the intellectual luminaries of the ancien régime survived to witness the events of 1789. Of those few who actually participated in Revolutionary events, even fewer wielded great influence much less retained it through the tempest of 1793–1794. But the historical problem of Enlightenment and

"Physiocracy and the Overthrow of the Ancien Régime." In *Proceedings of the Third Annual Meeting of the Western Society for French History*, edited by Brison D. Gooch, 156–64. N.p.: Western Society for French History, 1976. Copyright 1976 by the Western Society for French History. All rights reserved. Used by permission of the Western Society for French History.

Revolution far transcends the pitfalls of the great individual thesis. The central issues turn on the pre-Revolutionary *mentalité*, the diffusion and acceptance of enlightened thought among the population at large. The sociology of enlightenment in this general sense exceeds the scope of my present discussion. Nevertheless, the work of scholars like Daniel Roche and Robert Darnton among many is gradually familiarizing us with the material network of message exchange: how much did books cost, how were they circulated and where, which ideas did provincial academies adopt for discussion.[1] The full emergence of this network will require much more of this painstaking anthropological and sociological attention to the medium of cultural transmission. Yet even a reasonably complete dossier of artifact exchange or even prize competitions will not solve the problems.

Another recent approach to the ties between pre-Revolutionary criticism and Revolutionary events, notably Mackrell's work on the attack on feudalism, tends toward dismissing the problem of affiliation (causation seems to have fallen from mere poor taste to absolute proof of stupidity) altogether.[2] Many intellectuals did criticize feudalism and even faced bookburning for their pains, but peasants did not read and they destroyed feudalism, which survived in any case. The rational attack on the institutions of the ancien régime produced no real effects in the realm of action and expressed little more than a literary sensibility. Furthermore, as Denis Richet and others have argued, aristocrats, or those possessed of legal titles of nobility, provided many of the afficionados of enlightened thought even when its tenets contradicted their immediate interests. The ancien régime generated an elite composed of privileged and non-privileged who willingly discussed the need for rational reform, but viscerally repudiated any notion of violent, or non-violent, Revolution.[3] That final drama played itself out in the Assembly of the Notables in which his majesty's weightiest subjects insisted that he set his house in order without taxing his nobility.

All of these approaches combine to foster the impression that ideas—intellectual life or ideological commitment—cannot have mattered significantly in the overthrow of the ancien régime. And, assuredly, ideas that do not circulate cannot cause political events. Casting the discussion in the stark materialist terms in which it recently has been cast, however, obscures the vast if intractable realm of ideological formulation, the interplay between immediate experience and the creation of a language adequate to the expression of that experience. An understanding of the ideological origins of the French Revolution requires fresh attention to several different levels of human experience. The intellectual tradition itself must be reexamined in the methodological perspective proposed by J. G. A. Pocock, not in terms of unilinear causation but rather in terms of a shift in paradigms.[4] A firmer grasp of the older traditions, with which the theorists were working, will better help us to understand what aspects of material experience the population at large might recast in the new vocabulary. The interplay between public discourse and private grievance cannot be reduced to some neo-Beardean interest theory of historical process. A new vocabulary, imperfectly circulated among an imperfectly literate population, can serve as a major catalyst for legitimizing angers, perceived injustices, time-out-of-mind hostilities, and for directing them toward political action. In a generally inflammatory situation, the words need not mean the same things to all participants. It is the momentary convergence of discrete dissatisfactions upon a common language that provides a political context for private miseries and permits common action among widely disparate individuals. As Kenneth Burke and Clifford Geertz have reminded us, ideology results from a process of symbolic formulation.[5]

The intellectual structure and public career of physiocracy afford a superb illustration of one strand of the forging of a bourgeois or liberal ideology. For generations scholars of widely divergent points of view have identified physiocracy as essentially bourgeois and some have attributed considerable weight to its role in the overthrow of the ancien régime and the formulation of Revolutionary thought. Thus physiocracy has been credited with considerable responsibility for the contours of French liberal thought, particularly ideas of property, and even for the content of the Declaration of the Rights of Man and the Citizen.[6] This view has certain merit, but represents only a first approximation to the underlying tensions of physiocratic public proclamations. Furthermore, the attempt to translate physiocratic thought directly into more modern and unambiguous liberal terminology glosses over the problems with which the physiocrats grappled and, worse, seriously clouds those aspects of their thought to which contemporaries responded.

Physiocracy retains its primary claim upon modern attention because of the revolutionary economic analysis of François Quesnay. The unique productivity of agriculture notwithstanding, Quesnay's economic analysis constitutes the first coherent picture of the circular flow of economic life and as such has survived all the specifics of its progenitor's moral and social commitments. In the second half of the eighteenth century, however, the physiocrats did not stake their claims to thorough-going social scientific truth upon a narrow economic analysis, whatever its merits and however loudly they touted its claims. The physiocrats knew themselves to be the custodians of the science of man in society and included within their purview enlightened justice in all its forms.[7] They began with the insistence that their science would save the monarchy from its financial blunders and went on to claim that observance of their strictures would reestablish the regime on sure socio-economic foundations, in full conformity with the dictates of natural law and without the subversive intrusion of political dissension or fiscal representation. They proposed, in other words, to reform society from above without directly challenging any of the fundamental institutions. In their view, the destruction of the extraneous apparatus of financiers, *traitants*, and tax-farmers would not constitute a serious threat to the crown or to the principles of social order. Whatever their private views, they refrained from direct assaults upon the church and upon the nobility. They reserved their fire for abuses defined merely as manifestations of the corruption of legitimate institutions. Their insistence upon the primacy of agriculture and their espousal of legal despotism self-consciously affirmed their distrust of political meddling or social discord.[8]

The physiocrats, however, rested their entire system upon the sanctity and inviolability of absolute private property. This defense of bourgeois property and an attendant economic individualism accounts for the reading of their thought as liberal and directly revolutionary. Their uncompromising insistence upon the absolute rights of property and upon free trade seems to augur the political individualism of the Revolutionary period. The obvious verisimilitude of this connection, however, misses the complexity of physiocratic liberalism and lends itself to a great-landlords-making-the-Revolution reading that will not stand the test of empirical investigation.

None should doubt the radical thrust of the physiocratic defense of private property. Within the context of the ancien régime that simple proposition represented perhaps the most subversive theoretical or practical stance. For the property the physiocrats had in mind predated society and constituted the only viable rationale for government of any kind. Property, in true Lockean fashion, formed the cornerstone of all social organization and the implicit locus of sovereignty. The implementation of physiocratic notions of property would have required dismantling the entire feudal legal apparatus including the monarchy itself. Right, in the physiocratic view, emanated from the individual parcels of property and brooked no interference of any kind, including misguided notions of social justice. Only the free workings of the market could produce justice. In the interests of property and general well-being, which could derive only from the defense of property, no false ideas of charity could justify interfering with the divinely-sanctioned natural order.

Physiocratic property theory, however revolutionary, did not derive directly from Quesnay's early economic work. It resulted from the collaboration between Quesnay and that unreconstituted *feudataire*, Mirabeau, particularly on their unpublished manuscript, "Le Traité de la Monarchie."[9] Mirabeau introduced Quesnay to the importance of the social system upon which the monarchy rested and within which any economics must be embedded. In a prolonged interchange, the two men privately fought out the confrontation between the statist (or absolutist) and the feudal views of the monarchy current in eighteenth-century France. From their interchange, they gradually developed physiocracy. In the course of their dialogue, Quesnay's economic discovery of the net product, or social surplus, increasingly assumed the role of standard for social and political performance. The distressing conclusions which emerged from their discussion of the history and current behavior of the monarchy discouraged them from publishing the results of their inquiry. They accordingly abstracted from their historical and theoretical work a set of superficially timeless or arbitrary principles which comprise what gradually became known as physiocracy.

The true novelty of physiocracy lay in grounding the science of man in economics, and that apparent depersonalization of human social relations accounts for much of the contemporaneous and subsequent misunderstanding of physiocracy. As much as the physiocrats proclaimed the virtues of economic individualism, so did they denounce the contentious influence of political individualism. A close analysis of their own society fully convinced them that the pursuit of individual self-interest does not result in the general good: Manifestly, it results in the pursuit of anti-social privilege. All the physiocrats, even the noted fellow-traveller Turgot, repudiated political representation.[10] Nature, not fallible humans, determines the level of taxation. Political discussion has no place in the natural order. The physiocrats did, indisputably, advocate a market in labor-power and thus might seem to have opened their theoretical model to the evils of class conflict. Not at all. In the physiocratic view, while men in the manufacturing sector might best be described as machines, men engaged in agriculture are our fathers, our brothers, our sons.[11] They thus project the instrumental or exploitive aspects of individualism onto a functional division of social groups and retain the concept of one big family to characterize the world of agricultural production. And they buttress this ideological commitment with an economic analysis that argues that wages will automatically rise with rising prices so that class conflict between the producers and the consumer/employees can never arise. With the different classes of society in such complete harmony, political discussion has no place. Once the natural order of absolute private property has been instituted no divergence of interest can occur.

The summary discussion to which I am restricted here cannot begin to do justice to the complexity of physiocratic thought. I should nonetheless like to underscore a few key points. Modern individualism triumphed pretty much of a piece in Anglo-Saxon countries and came to dominate not only practice, but also social science theory. Subsequent commentators on physiocracy, themselves immersed in individualism triumphant, found it easy to ascribe greater homogeneity of purpose or modernity to physiocracy than it in fact contained. Physiocratic thought assuredly challenged the ideological foundations of the ancien régime and contributed to the Revolution. But it did not do so directly, nor can physiocracy alone explain post-Revolutionary France. The physiocrats, working within the same intellectual paradigm as Diderot, Rousseau, Galiani, Necker, and a host of others, reformulated aspects of that tradition in a profoundly but only partially individualistic, modern, or liberal perspective. By isolating economics as a new language of discourse, they were able to accomplish two major, but in many respects contradictory breakthroughs. They succeeded, at least in their own eyes, in defining a new absolute standard that would command the obedience of sovereigns and thus force recasting the ancien régime along suspiciously bourgeois lines in conformity with the dictates of economic production and the absolute property that alone could guarantee the workings of the market. They succeeded simultaneously in banishing all political individualism or negotiated social decision-making from the brave new world of economic individualism. Self-interest in physiocracy reduces essentially to obedience to the law of nature with no intervention of choice, no difference of opinion, and above all no divergence of interests. Physiocracy has no room for social contracts, much less representative institutions or popular assemblies that aspire to an active role in the political process.

Specific physiocratic programs under the ancien régime rapidly served to expose the historical and political limits of the purportedly struggle-free ideology. The conflict over free trade in grain set them at passionate variance with those responsible for urban tranquility, not to mention those dependent upon wages. Furthermore, even their own supporters among the landholders proved much more enthusiastic about free export and the appropriation of commons than about abolishing residual seigneurial rights. Those enlightened administrators, most notably Turgot, who attempted to implement physiocratic policy as a matter of royal engineering, rapidly discovered that freedom to work, to buy, to sell constituted explosive political issues and that proclamations about natural law and common interest would not suffice to convince those threatened in their more immediate interests.[12] In the absence of a functioning national market, the relationship between producers and consumers looked more like warfare than harmonious cooperation. And, as the events of the Revolution would prove, some of the most virulent defenders of private property, the peasants, would turn out to be totally uneconomic in their approach to economic interconnectedness.

Neither in theory nor in practice can the liberalism of physiocracy be cast as clearly Revolutionary or unambiguously liberal or bourgeois. Physiocracy can, however, help to elucidate the problems of pre-Revolutionary ideological formulation. Like many others working from different perspectives, the physiocrats subjected certain aspects of the ancien régime to searching criticism and shaped their findings into a program for change. No more than Diderot, for example, did they mount an open assault upon the ancien régime. Nor did their ideas find a coherent and disaffected social class (the mythical bourgeoisie) that could carry them to triumph. The physiocrats contributed to a liberal critique of the ancien régime, but did so indirectly. To take only their defense of property: Formally their language could seem to echo that of Jean Bodin; they never stopped to explain that their concept of property was absolutely incompatible with existing arrangements; nor did they ever choose to admit that it might require a revolution to implement it. They lobbied vigorously for free trade in grain and tried to rally support for their program among administrators and landlords, yet they never constituted a political party in the modern sense.

But that is, after all, the point. The ancien régime had no room for a modern political life. It normally experienced a profound disjuncture between theoretical criticism and daily experience. Furthermore those who agreed on such general principles as individual freedom or the sanctity of property disagreed entirely upon the practical consequences of their views. In a situation in which reactionary *parlementaires* presented themselves as the foremost champions of liberty, political issues might well appear confused. Nevertheless, the range of intellectuals and interested groups did debate a series of issues that gradually permeated more and more of society. The peasants doubtless did not read the physiocrats. Nevertheless, the agricultural societies did. And in some regions the members of the agricultural societies questioned the peasants in a vocabulary derived from physiocratic writings. Thus the society of Brittany interrogated and subsequently reported that Brittany contained peasants who left their fields fallow because, they claimed, without free trade—absolute property—they could reap no profit.[13] Who knows how much physiocratic theory the peasant ever acquired, or how much he needed? He had always known that he would prefer unburdened possession of his land. To be able to identify lack of interference as a principled defense of property permitted him, when the occasion arose, to form a groping identification with those who for quite other reasons were defending such notions in a political context. One need only think of the *Feuille villageoise,* or even Gambetta, to grasp the potential of an intersection between eternal peasant misery and an emerging political nation.

The investigation of such linkages, of the diffusion, the use, and the abuse of an emerging vocabulary could and should be carried on at length.

I have found innumerable examples in a wide range of administrative and other sources. The same kind of work must also be pursued for other bodies of thought. What, for example, should we make of pre-Girondist individualism in the form of the writing of romantic poetry? The culturally sanctioned assertion of self and the self-conscious investigation of all aspects of human experience carry a revolutionary potential so profound as to render trivial the unilateral search for strains of material self-interest.

The varied and conflicting strands of liberal thought in pre-Revolutionary France do not lend themselves to easy synthesis. In one general area, however, they do seem to converge. Many subjects of His Most Christian Majesty were groping toward some alternate concept of social identity than subservience to throne and altar. In the *Social Contract*, Rousseau discusses the political body "which is called by its members *State* when it is passive, *Sovereign* when it is active." Quesnay, in his edition, noted in the margin that Rousseau was at his best in his distinction between the notion of sovereign and that of government, which constituted an important aspect of political economy. Quesnay, characteristically, then added that this discussion affords Rousseau's only useful contribution. For Quesnay opposed all Rousseau's political and republican concerns as firmly as he did urban notions of moral economy and the economic claims of merchant capital. He nevertheless shared with Rousseau a profound concern about the locus of sovereignty. Quesnay had begun his career in economics in an essentially mercantilist framework. Mirabeau had introduced him to the pitfalls of such statism. Working through Mirabeau's commitment to community in the organic, hierarchical sense had brought both men to a concept of what the Revolutionaries would call the nation. It is this sense of society as the locus of sovereignty and of government as an administrative agent that Quesnay admires in Rousseau. Rousseau, however, remained deeply impregnated with the classical republican tradition which Quesnay and Mirabeau repudiated entirely. The physiocratic concept of nationhood placed far more emphasis on economic foundations. Humans, indisputably, should hold those absolute property rights that alone could provide for the optimal functioning of the natural economic mechanism, but as property holders they remained more willing agents of the natural law than active political beings. Quesnay believed deeply in the freedom of the human will and in human responsibility, but he implicitly restricted that freedom to conformity with or distortion of the process of natural law. The physiocratic language of economics would prove a major contribution to French liberal ideology, but only when that language meshed with the emerging political vocabulary of the other philosophes and crystallized in the political events of the Revolution would its liberal thrust be severed from its residual traditional moorings. That the still essentially un-market and un-liberal aspects of French society against which the physiocrats tried to guard would also flourish in the Revolution and emerge in the nineteenth century as discernible factors in the new nation capable of pursuing anti-economic self-interest remains a disturbing irony of liberal natural law and a problem for another occasion.

Physiocratic contributions to the undermining of the ancien régime ranged from the most purely theoretical to the most eminently practical. On all levels, however, physiocracy contributed to the politicization of French society. Urban grain supply, for example, which had traditionally failed because of an act of God, the negligence of the monarch, or the activities of essentially extra-social hoarders, now could be perceived to fail because of a matter of public policy. The conflicting interests that pitted towns against the countryside, producers against consumers, cannot be reduced to some neat class confrontation. It can, however, be understood as fostering the notion that subsistence might be subject to the political decisions of humans. Similarly, on the theoretical plane, physiocracy transformed economics from its traditional role as management of the social household to the science of humans in society and thus, despite the physiocrats' intentions to the contrary, paved the way for the politicization of social organization. The physiocrats remained as deeply committed as any divine-right-absolutist to the notion of a divine order that governed collective social life. Nonetheless, by transferring the locus of authority from the summit of a hierarchy to the individual embodiments of the economic process, they effected a major theoretical revolution. In their thought, the traditional community reemerged, at least potentially, as the sovereign nation. The political language and practice introduced during the Revolution would set the final seal on their legacy.

Notes

1. Daniel Roche, "Encyclopédistes et académiciens. Essai sur la diffusion sociale des lumières," in F. Furet, ed., *Livre et société dans la France du XVIIIe siècle,* II (Paris and The Hague, 1970), 73–89, and his "Milieux académiques provinciaux et société des lumières," in *Livre et société dans la France du XVIIIe siècle* (Paris and The Hague, 1965); Robert Darnton, "Le livre francais à la fin de l'ancien régime," *Annales E.S.C.,* XXVIII (1973), 735–44, and his "The Encyclopédie Wars of Prerevolutionary France," *American Historical Review,* 78 (1973), 1331–52.

2. J. Q. C. Mackrell, *The Attack on Feudalism in Eighteenth-Century France* (London and Toronto, 1973), esp. 163–92.

3. Denis Richet, "Autour des origines lointaines de la révolution française: Elites et despotisme," *Annales E.S.C.,* XXIV (1969), 1–23; Marcel Reinhard, "Elite et noblesse dans la seconde moitié du XVIIIe siècle," *Revue d'histoire moderne et contemporaine,* III

(1956), 1–37; Michel Vovelle, "L'élite ou le mensonge des mots," *Annales E.S.C.*, XXIX (1974), 49–72.

4. J. G. A. Pocock, *Politics, Language, and Time* (New York, 1971), and his *The Machiavellian Moment: Florentine Political Thought and the Atlantic Republican Tradition* (Princeton, N.J., 1975).

5. Clifford Geertz, "Ideology as a Cultural System," *Ideology and Discontent*, ed. D. Apter (New York, 1964); Kenneth Burke, *The Philosophy of Literary Form*, 2nd ed. (Baton Rouge, La., 1967).

6. V. Marcaggi, *Les origines de la Déclaration des droits de l'homme de 1789*, 2nd ed. (Paris, 1912); Eugene Daire, "La doctrine des physiocrates," *Journal des économistes*, XXVII (1847), 349–75, and XXVIII (1847), 113–40; Michel Bernard, *Introduction à une sociologie des doctrines économiques des Physiocrates à Stuart Mill* (Paris and The Hague, 1963); Lucien Goldman, *Sciences humaines et philosophie* (Paris, 1952); Ernst Hinrichs, "Produit Net, Propriétaire, Cultivateur. Aspekte des sozialen Wandels bei den Physiockraten und Turgot," *Festschrift für Herman Heimpel zum 70. Geburtstag am 19. September 1971*, I (Göttingen, 1971), 473–510; Ronald Meek, *The Economics of Physiocracy* (Cambridge, Mass., 1963); Marguerite Kuczynski, ed., François Quesnay, *Ökonomische Schriften* (Berlin, 1971); Giorgio Rebuffa, *Origine della ricchezza e diritto di proprietà: Quesnay e Turgot* (Milan, 1974); Bert F. Hoselitz, "Agrarian Capitalism, the Natural Order of Things: François Quesnay," *Kyklos*, XXI (1968), 637–64.

7. P. S. du Pont de Nemours to J.-B. Say, letter of 22 April 1815, in Eugene Daire, ed., *Physiocratie*, 2 vols. (Paris, 1846), I, 397. See also, among many, G.-F. Le Trosne, *De l'intérêt social* (Paris, 1777); P. P. F. J. H. Le Mercier de la Rivière, *L'ordre naturel et essentiel des sociétés politiques (1769)*, ed. Edgar Depître (Paris, 1910) and his *De l'intérêt général de l'Etat . . .* (Amsterdam and Paris, 1770); Victor Riqueti, marquis de Mirabeau, *Elémens de la philosophie rurale* (The Hague, 1767), his *Lettres sur la législation . . .* , 3 vols. (Berne, 1775), and his *La science ou les droits et les devoirs de l'homme* (Lausanne, 1774).

8. François Quesnay, "Le droit naturel des hommes réunis en société," *Journal de l'agriculture* (1765); Victor Riqueti, marquis de Mirabeau, *Philosophie rurale . . .* (Amsterdam, 1763); Nicolas Baudeau, *Exposition de la loi naturelle* (Amsterdam and Paris, 1767).

9. *Archives nationales*, M 778.

10. A. R. J. Turgot, *Oeuvres de Turgot*, 5 vols., ed. Gustave Schelle (Paris, 1913–23), IV, "Mémoire sur les municipalités," esp. 576 ff. See also, P. S. du Pont to Count Scheffer in 1773, Eleutherian Mills Historical Library, Winterthur Mss., Group 2, series A; A. Esmein, "L'assemblée nationale proposée par les physiocrates," *Revue des séances et travaux de l'académie des sciences morales et politiques*, CLXII (1904), 397–420; Gerald Cavanaugh, "Turgot: The Rejection of Enlightened Despotism," *French Historical Studies*, VI (1969), 31–58; Luigi Einaudi, "The Physiocratic Theory of Taxation," *Economic Essays in Honor of Gustav Cassel* (London, 1933), 129–42; Keith Baker, *Condorcet. From Natural Philosophy to Social Mathematics* (Chicago, 1975), esp. 214–25.

11. Victor Riqueti, marquis de Mirabeau, *L'ami des hommes*, 5th ed. (n.p., 1760), II, 38.

12. Edgar Faure, *La disgrace de Turgot* (Paris, 1961). See also Charles Henry, ed., *Correspondance inédite de Condorcet et de Turgot* (1883; repr. Geneva, 1973); Carl Knies, ed., *Carl Friedrichs von Baden brieflicher Verkehr mit Mirabeau und Dupont*, 2 vols.

(Heidelberg, 1892), esp. II; [J. A. Caritat, marquis de Condorcet], *Vie de M. Turgot* (Londres, 1786).

13. L. P. Abeille and J. Montaudoin de la Touche, *Corps d'observations de la société d'agriculture, de commerce, et des arts, établie par les Etats de Bretagne* (Rennes, 1760; Paris, 1772). See also *Archives nationales,* F^{10} 222 and 252–53, F^{11} 223, 264, and 265, F^{12} 149, 713, and 715, H 1501–10.

Four

Psychohistory versus Psychodeterminism
The Case of Rogin's Jackson

Michael Paul Rogin's *Fathers and Children* is unlikely to revolutionize the study of Jacksonian America, provide an abiding model of the emergence and nature of "liberal" or "market" society in the United States, or provoke mass conversion to psychohistory. It does not contribute significantly to an explanation of the rise of American capitalism, does not establish the relationship between family patterns of authority and the emergence of modern political life, does not adequately relate the changing social and political positions of Indians, slaves, women, workers, regions, or classes in the early nineteenth century. Nor does it contribute much to the theoretical or comparative framework within which such questions must be analyzed, much less develop a framework that integrates new historical questions—social, cultural, psychohistorical—into the fabric of political and economic history.

But, the charitable might demur, what single book can do so much? Rogin, however, invites the most sweeping reproaches precisely because of the breadth of his attempt and theoretical claims. *Fathers and Children* fails not because of its questions or its scope, but because of its answers and theoretical confusions. Rogin should not be criticized in the interests of returning to a good honest (and quantified) history of the railroads in western

"Psychohistory Versus Psychodeterminism: The Case of Rogin's Jackson." *Reviews in American History* 3, no. 4 (1975): 407–18. Copyright 1975 by the Johns Hopkins University Press. All rights reserved. Used by permission of the Johns Hopkins University Press.

Pennsylvania in any given two-year period; he should, nevertheless, be questioned by those committed to his attempt who believe that he got it wrong.

Stripped of larger theoretical pretensions, *Fathers and Children* constitutes a study of Andrew Jackson in his time and an attempt to elucidate the mainsprings of Jacksonian democracy. Rogin's tripartite division groups "Whites," "Whites and Indians," and "Jacksonian Democracy." The development proceeds from the legacy of the "Revolutionary Fathers" to the early life of Andrew Jackson and then on to the Indians, frontier warfare, and Indian removal. The final part considers "the market revolution and the reconstruction of paternal authority" and touches briefly upon the bank war ("The Mother Bank") and manifest destiny. The treatment of Indian removal per se rests at the core of the work and offers its freshest and probably most enduring contribution. Rogin's sensitivity to the nuances of language discloses a strong component of what he calls "familial" language in Jackson's official discussion of removal. Hence the fathers and children of the title reflect the centrality of a paternalist ethos to the justification of dispossession.

Rogin does not, however, restrict himself to a simple reappraisal of Andrew Jackson and Indian removal. He offers Jackson as a key to understanding the transition from customary to market society in the United States; he offers Indian removal as the American experience of "primitive accumulation"; and he offers Jacksonian democracy as a unique formulation of nineteenth-century liberalism. He claims to explain the fundamental psychological underpinnings of American politics, which must be seen as different not only in specifics but also in theoretical dynamics from European politics.

The confusion between specifics—the individual variations of time, place, experience—and theoretical dynamics—the model or system of explanation by which varying experiences are ordered and understood—pervades Rogin's work and flaws his attempt to move from Andrew Jackson, Indians, and early nineteenth-century America to a new model of historical process. Rogin's United States represents not a special case of the emergence of modern society, but a case so special as to require a rupture of the theoretical problematic itself. The unadorned core of Rogin's argument demands some translation, but might be stated as follows: possessive individualism and industrial capitalism grew from European historical experience; in Europe (he implies) their triumph and ultimate contours depended at least in part on class struggle; America had no class struggle—he does not use the words—worthy of mention; American development rested on psychodynamics; *ergo*, Freud, not Marx, provides the only viable theoretical guide to the formation of Jacksonian—and modern—America. For in Rogin's terms Americans did not confront other social classes; they confronted Indians. This white/Indian conflict embodied more than some simple clash between cultures, much less social groups; it embodied white men's confrontation with "their own fantasies, longings, and fears" (pp. 11, 12). Thus, the intrapsychic struggles of whites replace the social struggle between classes or civilizations; fantasy replaces historical process.

Despite a luxuriant use of terms such as "liberalism" and "capitalism" that suggest general, as opposed to narrowly American, historical problems, Rogin cannot relinquish the Turnerian legacy of American uniqueness. That primal vision, combined with his ultimate reliance upon Freud at the expense of Marx (or Weber, or Adam Smith, or Robertson, or Macaulay), costs him dearly.[1] Rogin seems to conceive his principal mission as restoring "acts of force and fraud" (p. 3) to their rightful place at the center of American history, particularly the transformation of "liberal America . . . during Jackson's lifetime" (p. 12). Indian relations provide the operative experience of force and fraud. Other historians, by failing to place Indians at the center of Jackson's life, have "interpreted the Age of Jackson from every perspective but Indian destruction, the one from which it actually developed historically" (p. 4). But Rogin, by disproportionately stressing the psychic dimension of white/Indian relations, misleadingly differentiates the American experience of force and fraud from the garden-variety force and fraud that characterize the relations between most rulers and ruled.

Rogin apparently recognizes that the Indians posed an actual barrier to the demographic and economic expansion of white American society, which, in the simplest terms, coveted the land occupied by Indian tribes. He proudly rejects, however, the simple-minded explanations of pragmatists, behaviorists, and materialists, who "violate the perceptions of men who mattered in Indian policy" (p. 12). He allows that the Indians had to be destroyed, but insists that their destruction had to be reconciled with "the American self-image" (p. 4). In other words, as Mary Young has so admirably demonstrated in *Redskins, Ruffleshirts, and Rednecks* (1961), the development of the western states "depended upon cessions of land by Indian tribes," and the process of dispossession "confronted the Jacksonians with a practical and moral dilemma." For, Young continues, if the Jacksonians "were avaricious, they were also 'all honorable men.' They recognized . . . that the Indians had some claim on the lands they occupied and that they should be divested of this claim only by a 'free contract.'" Yet, as she points out, "the lands must be obtained. It is not easy to reconcile avarice with honor or force with voluntarism, but the Jacksonians tried it" (Young, p. 3).

Justification, the reconciling of avarice with honor, of force with voluntarism, constitutes the time-honored quest of individuals and ruling classes. When successful, it permits the effective operation of the individual ego and the unchallenged sway of the ruling class. The deepest dynamics of dominion, of legitimate power, of authority seem to be reasonably constant over time and space. The specifics, however, vary tremendously. The problems of individual autonomy and class rule can only be resolved in time and space. Antonio Gramsci called the successful, or morally accepted, dominion of one class over others "hegemony."

The American quest for hegemony, according to Rogin, focused on the Indians; and the American/Indian struggle, again according to Rogin, resists a class analysis. (If you finish the syllogism, American history resists a class—or even a sociological—analysis.) Did not American rhetoric fill the "white-Indian tie with intimate symbolic meaning"? Did it not cast the Indians as "our 'friends and brothers'"? Did it not designate "'our red brethren'" as the "'voice of nature' in the 'human family'" (p. 5)? Brotherhood could not, of course, be allowed to interfere with white possession of Indian land—even fratricidal quarrels may have some fragmentary material base. To achieve their purpose, "whites must take Indian land." "The fraternal conflict of Indians and whites contained no moral resolution" (p. 6). And, strange to say, conflicts between the strong and the weak over possession—be it of land, of labor-power, of women, of political power—rarely do. Even stranger, until very recently, most justifications for rule—consider Southern slaveholders or Russian boyars—have drawn upon Rogin's "familial language" to justify their authority.

American whites, further, "developed, as they took Indian land, a powerful, legitimating cultural myth," which portrayed white progress across the continent as a reproduction of "the historical evolution of mankind." The relative development of human societies from savagery to civilization paralleled the "evolution of individual men" (p. 6). This reading comfortably cast the Indian as the child of the human race and reinforced his identity as the child of nature. Pushing back the Indians could thus be accepted as assuring the triumph of civilization over barbarism, as mastering the chaos of nature, the regressive appeal of childhood. Mastering nature entailed killing Indians whose "destruction symbolized the American experience" (p. 7). Come now: symbolized? or constituted the essence of? or determined? Americans hardly had a monopoly of the rhetoric of stages of civilization and of the civilized triumph over savagery. It received eloquent formulation by Macaulay and has served most imperialists from the Spanish in the Americas through the British in India to the French in Algeria and beyond. But the American whites also confronted the wilderness, which, by the time the Jacksonians set out to dispossess the Indians, European intellectuals had already identified with nature, with innocence, with lost paradise.[2] The "aggressive expansionism" that fueled the modernist mastery of nature, therefore, remained haunted by the integrally related "regressive inner disposition" that informed the images of the noble savage and a lost paradise. "In America 'aggressive expansionism' encountered the regressive impulse as a 'political reality'" (p. 8).

Presumably, Rogin means that the political reality of the regressive impulse in American life radically differentiates the American transition from customary to market society from the European. In Europe, he contends, liberalism "encountered resistance . . . first from feudalism and then from revolutionary socialism." Americans, however, "confronted . . . no alternatives to liberal uniformity save the psychically charged presences of 'the black race within our bosom . . . [and] the red on our borders'" (p. 7). Rogin's wild oscillation between people and forces, human beings and isms reveals much. European liberalism confronted feudalism and socialism, while Americans confronted black men and red men. At the risk of underlining the obvious, I submit that "feudalism" disguises and anesthetizes nobles (human beings), that "socialism" depersonalizes working men and women, and that black men and red men can respectively be grouped analytically as slaves (a social class) or slavery (an institution) and as Indians (a tribal social group) or "savagery" (a stage of development). Admittedly, the further one gets from the European experience, the harder it becomes to translate social groups into European categories. The difficulties attendant upon analyzing the clash between civilizations or societies cannot, however, obscure the simple truth that all societies consist of human beings and that the struggle for dominion among human beings, whether within or between societies, always occurs in the realm of human action. Thus, if we observe Rogin's strictures about the importance of language, and listen attentively when Jackson says "children," may we not also listen when Calhoun says "no tariff"? Conversely, may we not take European industrialists' references to their workers as "children" as seriously as we do their political polemics against the "red menace"? The sensitivity to both conscious and unconscious meaning must be held constant in the study of all societies, just as in the analysis of human beings.

Rogin apparently thinks differently. America may have undergone "subculture conflict and historical change," but it "lacked the historical bases for political alternatives to liberalism, and radical historians who search for such alternatives mistake the American experience. Liberalism reached everywhere in white America; the resistance it encountered came from within" (p. 7). So much for class, status, or regional struggle; so much for the clash between slave and free societies. In the United States, the move from customary to modern society, the collective experience of reordering external and internal worlds, followed a unique development which found its ultimate exponent in the person of Andrew Jackson.

Jackson and his political cronies freed "Indian land for the commodity economy, [and] initiated a market revolution." Their destruction of the Indians "defines for America the stage of primitive accumulation." Jackson's motives, however, in contradistinction to those of ordinary men, cannot be reduced to economic considerations. Those "economic motives of ordinary men" which, according to Rogin, "feed the market once it has established its sway," were, in the United States (does he mean that Europe was different?), "unequal to primitive accumulation." Jackson, rather than following some economic imperative, transformed "his problems into national political solutions." Jackson defeated "those demons which, in bad moments, overwhelm ordinary men." By mastering the "regressive appeal" of childhood, nature, and Indians, he "infused American politics with regenerated paternal authority." In the place of the actual household order, which could not survive the force of his "ubiquitous rage," Jackson constructed "a familial politics purified of the temptations to conflict, dependence, and vice, purified of the power of women" (p. 15).

Rogin's distinction between the motives ("economic") of ordinary men and those (psychological) of Jackson remains suspect. If intrapsychic conflict should be accepted as an important feature of historical process—and I believe that it should—then, surely, it must rest its claim upon universality. The psychological mainsprings of Jackson's remarkable achievement must be what he holds in common with other men, not what differentiates him from them. At the risk of some overschematization, one might propose that the significant difference lies in political genius. Jackson's life affords a fascinating example of the modern political leader who, unlike his premodern counterpart, cannot rely on divine sanction to justify his exercise of power. Rogin senses the different problems of authority in customary and modern societies, but his exaggerated emphasis on Jackson's psychodynamics weakens his specific historical case and unnecessarily opens his Freudianism to attack. For Rogin not only slights the political dimension of Jackson's career, he misses the novelty and the significance of the political dimension in American, and, for that matter, in European history.

Rogin knows that the emergence of possessive individualism so cogently expressed in Lockean political theory represents a fundamental shift in the nature of human social relations. "Lockean liberalism shifted conflict from the public to the private realm. Contractual authority sought to protect private property from political interference. It depoliticized society" (p. 88). Then what does he mean by political? He argues that as men relinquished traditional "claims to paternal political power over an entire society," they "gained in return 'despotic dominion' (Blackstone) over their own estates" (p. 88).

Rogin seems to have confused paternal power with political power. Politics is not new to human affairs: Aristotle identified it in ancient Greece. Medieval Christians, particularly feudal monarchs, did not, however, talk about it very much—and certainly not in front of the barons. When Machiavelli rediscovered its *sui generis* claims, polite company conspired to ignore him. No one doubted that "th' murderous Machiavel" threatened organic order. In desperation, Jean Bodin and his party—significantly named *Les Politiques*—dared to advance the political as a possible solution to fratricide and national chaos promoted in the name of God. God's acquisition of a second party acting in the name of His immutable order had done more to undermine that order than any upstart Italian ever could. Even Bodin, however, could not arrive at a satisfactory definition of sovereignty. Property, being still largely feudal, itself depended upon monarchical sanction and could not provide a basis for autonomy. Hobbes, who like Euclid looked on beauty bare, grasped the fundamental logic of the market revolution that, together with religious dissent, offered the promise of possessive individualism. He, however, banished the political to the state of nature: only men's relinquishing of the political identity inherent in their absolute possession, or bourgeois property, could guarantee any kind of social order. And then came Locke, and with him, *pace* Mr. Rogin, the triumph of the political.

Politics, after all, transpires among sovereign beings. For much of early modern history, Europeans used the word mainly to describe the relations between states. Men, in acquiring absolute property in themselves and their land, acquired, as Rogin says, a kind of despotic dominion—but not over others who held equally sovereign rights. The politics comes in when they must negotiate with each other. The necessity for creating social order and national harmony out of innumerable parcels of sovereignty forced a profound revolution in human affairs. Furthermore, it required a new vocabulary, new institutions, and new conceptions of legitimate authority. England, France, and the United States all confronted the task in the first half of the nineteenth century.

Not surprisingly, the new full-fledged members of political society sought to restrict its access as much as possible. First, settling differences and guaranteeing government presented enough problems even to white, male property-holders. Second, no one wanted to relinquish the virtues of the customary order altogether. Women, slaves, and even industrial workers were cast, when possible, in traditional roles.

In customary society, paternal authority had been, to the extent possible, embedded in all social relations. The rise of Western capitalism and individualism can be read, on one level, as the gradual disengaging of classes and individuals from that web—as the politicization of the social household. But this politicization undermined the household's paternal foundations. If the oedipal bases of authority survive the advent of civil society as the legacy of the private family to the larger community, they do not always find unmediated political expression.[3] The political life of the ideal-type liberal society rests on the assumption that the family remains at home. That ideal-type may rarely, or never, occur; yet even its imperfectly realized tendencies may lie at the root of the cultural and political crisis of the modern Western world. But we shall not solve the crisis by mistaking the assumptions upon which liberal society rests. The repressed indeed returns, but modern politics, in contradistinction to traditional paternal authority, forces it into indirect channels.

The erosion, not to mention the violent overthrow, of the traditional repositories of paternal authority forced the creation of a political life and an attendant vocabulary. According to Rogin, the "problems which the Revolution failed to solve—problems of power, sexuality, family authority, and worldly materialism—reveal themselves in the materials of fantasy. These were the problems, shaped by the Revolution and revolutionary language, which returned to face Andrew Jackson" (p. 29). We might ask: What revolutions have ever solved the problems of the human condition? And how could they? The Revolution, however, did bequeath the problem of creating a politics.

The revolutionary fathers, operating from their mercantile and slaveholding bases in a Lockean framework of contractual obligation based on the responsibility of the propertied, in the context of merchant capital, managed reasonably well. They designed a constitution to fit their needs. Responsible, white men would govern the country together while remaining free to keep order at home individually. So long as their domestic problems did not intrude upon the national political arena, all went well. But, as William Freehling has brilliantly demonstrated in *Prelude to Civil War* (1966), the moment their domestic concerns pushed them to seek the action of the federal government, or were threatened by some action of the federal government, they disturbed the fragile liberal balance upon which their as yet limited political life rested. The accelerating pace of economic transformation, the pressure of demographic expansion, and the politicization of familial responsibilities triggered intensified national political debate and increased repression of the remaining family members. The roughly simultaneous emergence of the proslavery argument, the cult of true womanhood, and the asylum can hardly be written off as coincidental. The unitary "liberal" America depicted by Rogin, had it ever existed, assuredly succumbed to the advent of the nineteenth century. For with the further erosion of the household order came the emergence of a spectrum of political preferences among political men. Regional and class differences could less easily be masked as more people, with different interests, began to speak, lobby, and act in their name. Rogin's liberal America may not have included nobles or serfs but it did include Southern planters, merchants, farmers, artisans, wage laborers, entrepreneurs. While all may have been committed possessive individualists as concerned themselves, not all extended their enthusiasm to others, much less saw eye to eye on the problems that wracked the nation. A general ideological uniformity does not entail a specific political consensus.

Rogin has, in effect, taken the Hartz model of the liberal tradition and enlivened it with a psychoanalytic interpretation designed to explain the peculiarities of American political life. Rogin's liberal tradition, however, bears an unfamiliarly grim stamp; and its political implementation derives from Jackson's black vision of a "barren landscape where repressive superego warred with chaotic id" (p. 278). Jackson's self-mastery established his claim to represent "the undisciplined classes of the community"; but "Jacksonian paternalism failed to attach men to new institutions with powerful emotional bonds. It failed to relieve them of the punitive feelings engendered by competitive individualism" (p. 279).

Rogin's psychohistorical method requires appraisal on three levels: his psychoanalytic treatment of Jackson's personality; his assessment of the psychodynamic dimension of Jacksonian political authority; and his claims for the role of psychological conflict in historical process. Rogin deserves respect for trying to build on such plausible assumptions as that human beings must be understood as psychological tinderboxes; that human language must be examined for hidden as well as overt meaning; and that the interaction between human beings, including political leaders and their followers, contains an important psychological component that can, in some measure, be apprehended and analyzed. Rogin, in his attempt to incorporate historical change within a psychohistorical interpretation, moves well beyond the more reductionist recent psychohistorical work. To this extent, his residual historical materialism (it would be misleading to label his analysis Marxist, Marxian terminology notwithstanding) serves him well. Unfortunately, he fails to develop a dialectical relationship between the historical process and individual psychodynamics. In failing to bridge the chasm between social experience and politics, between experience and consciousness, he neglects a remarkably promising terrain not only for uniting traditional and psychohistory but for convincing skeptics of the validity of a psychohistorical approach. His failure can only sadden historians who, like myself, are Freudians and sympathize with his efforts.

Rogin's psychoanalytic reading of Jackson's personality rests on slender evidence. In particular, he lacks any direct testimony pertaining to Jackson's earliest and—for Freudians as for Jesuits—critical years. He nevertheless draws upon later accounts to argue that Jackson remained dominated by oral conflicts, that he lacked a sense of basic trust, and that his relations with his mother remained central to his development. He also points out that Jackson, as a posthumous child, grew up with the special problems of a boy who must resolve his oedipal conflicts with an imaginary, and hence larger than life, father. In this sense, Jackson created himself. Nevertheless, fathers played "an intimate and obsessive role in Jackson's imagination and in Jacksonian culture as well" (p. 53). The juxtaposition of Jackson's imagination with Jacksonian culture exemplifies an important aspect of Rogin's psychoanalytic method. Lacking a fully documented case study, he fills in lacunae or merely strengthens his own fragmentary evidence with material drawn from contemporaneous cultural patterns. Similarly, he draws upon what Freudian theory or modern clinical work has discovered about characteristic patterns of psychological development. He further supports the strength of Jackson's maternal tie with the *hoc post facto* argument that Jackson had moods of "manic omnipotence, paranoid rage, and occasional deep depression. Such moods are common in personalities which remain dominated by the early maternal relationship" (p. 45).

Rogin, in other words, has not presented a thorough analytic case study of Jackson: he could not do so, and, wisely, he did not try. Among psychohistory's heaviest crosses, it bears that of the goal of clinical precision. In point of fact, no psychohistorian (whatever his or her fantasies) is a practicing analyst; the subjects of psychohistorical analysis, being dead, speak only indirectly through writing, song, story, etc.; they cannot free-associate, nor can they be cured. The mere proliferation of technical terminology does not strengthen a sensitive and literate reading of a human personality. In this respect, Rogin has tried a refreshing method. His discussion of Jackson's early life does not differ as much from John Clive's beautiful treatment of Macaulay (1973) as those put off by the intrusion of technical language might think. The fundamental soundness of this method, however, does not exempt Rogin, any more than a traditional biographer, from questions about his reading. Nor can it save him from criticism of his too facile picture of the cultural context of Jackson's childhood. For if psychohistorical interpretations can be freed to draw upon social and generational experience as legitimate evidence, they must be held to very rigorous standards in the formulation of that evidence. Psychosocial and psychocultural studies have yet to develop precise tools of analysis. Historians, if they insist upon scrupulous sensitivity to the particulars of time, place, and historical process, can help. They will, however, help neither themselves, nor general understanding, if they continue to rely upon vast patterns of the decline of stem families and the rise of "the imperial self."

Let me take a couple of examples, the first hypothetical, the second specific. Rogin deals much more convincingly with Jackson's feelings about his mother than with those about his father. Yet the crux of Rogin's larger argument turns exclusively upon Jackson's willingness to assume and to exercise paternal authority. Here, unquestionably, additional evidence would help. How did Jackson's father's death affect his mother? Did she see her son as a final gift from her husband, or a final burden? Did she present herself, or her dead husband, as the model for that self-reliance she attempted to inculcate in her son? That is, rhetoric does not always present a direct outlet for feelings: an existing rhetoric, such as that of the revolutionary fathers, can present a fairly rigid mold into which quite different feelings must be channeled if they are to find outlet at all. Thus Jackson's mature paternalism may have reflected his ultimate assumption of his mother's, not his father's, role, or some combination of the two. Rogin's evidence permits such speculation, although it provides no answers. Perhaps the answer does not matter. Certainly, given the present overly generalized formulae about the nature of the American family, American culture, American violence, and so forth, we have no historical context into which such an answer might be fitted. A deeper understanding of the historical specifics of cultural and social change might, however, provide a setting in which such a reading about the confusion between maternal and paternal authority in the United States might shed light upon the role of women in this country, or the relative absence of an American culture and intelligentsia in the European sense.

The second example moves closer to the historical specifics. Rogin, like other students of the Jacksonian administration, deals with the Peggy Eaton affair, which he relates to Jackson's grief at the loss of Rachel, and thus to Jackson's earliest experience of women, his mother. No doubt, the death of a loved one induces mourning and, quite plausibly, regression to earlier emotional conflicts. But the old emotions operate in new environmental circumstances. In the Peggy Eaton affair, Jackson confronted women who would not only snub women of questionable marital status and sexual purity, but who would also snub women of debatable social standing—lower class, for the cruder of us. Lo and behold, Calhoun's regional, slave-holding, aspiring-aristocratic—in a word, class—politics returns through the psychoanalytic back door. Intrapsychic conflict, together with a Nashville rather than

Charleston background, reinforces a real political battle. The class question, of course, never surfaces in the political rhetoric. After all, Jackson thought that he, being white, male, and free, not to mention self-reliant, was Calhoun's equal by virtue of the legacy of the revolutionary fathers. Just because he discovered that he was not, he can hardly be expected to have proclaimed his own inferiority or to have translated his rage into a direct proclamation of class struggle—the issue being further confused by his own status as a slave-holding planter. Rather, he would infinitely prefer to beat Calhoun on higher, and formally egalitarian, ideological grounds. He denied his own class background and, in the best hegemonic tradition, elaborated a political language that emphasized the dignity of his constituents, who were, after all, free men and aspiring planters and capitalists (that is, as Hofstadter has argued, farmers not peasants), even if they were not Calhouns or Adamses.[4]

But before Calhoun came the Indians. According to Rogin, "liberalism attacked paternal political power in theory; capitalism weakened it in practice. But market liberalism also engendered longings for paternal authority, and Indian removal gave these longings their historic task" (p. 168). European and American history both bear evidence of Rogin's argument that the erosion of or revolt against embedded paternalism, whether social, governmental, or religious, engendered regressive longings for paternal, or organic, authority. Rogin misses, however, an important historical dimension of such regression: normally it occurred in domestic (family, plantation, etc.) institutions rather than in the newly liberated public domain. Nevertheless, those who led the public revolt against embedded paternalism more often than not legitimized their insubordination, their declarations of autonomy, in the name of a higher paternal authority. Luther revolted against the church in the name of God. The Enlightenment deified nature. The liberal theorists from Locke through the Scottish historical school demonstrated that the individual, rather than the collectivity, embodied the divine purpose. The reinforced practice of domestic paternalism and the public rhetoric of legitimizing paternalism constitute two separate legacies of the breakdown of traditional authority. Rogin has combined them. He thus presents Jackson as creating a "paternal state." As the mushrooming body of monographs on political parties amply demonstrates, Jackson operated in the context of an emerging political state: he merely justified it with a paternalist rhetoric.

This distinction profoundly influences the nuances with which one reads the practice and language of Indian removal. Jackson, according to Rogin, used slavery as the model of paternalism in Indian removal. "But the slave model of paternalism, appropriate enough to Indian removal, contained force and violence at its core. Indian removal exposed the sadistic underside of American expansion and the difficulties of building from liberal assumptions a structure of legitimate public authority" (p. 169). Later, Rogin concedes that Jackson had idiosyncratic notions of paternalism as military rather than familial: "Jackson, anticipating the spokesmen for plantation, asylum, and factory, offered the army itself as the model for the new family" (p. 275). Rogin grasps that a basic common denominator underlies the exercise of paternal authority over women and children, over slaves, over Indians. He does not, however, grasp the nature of that common denominator, much less the fundamental differences cloaked by the model. Jackson probably did see the plantation in military terms; Calhoun undoubtedly did not. Once again, a limited rhetoric derived from a more unitary historical past obscures shifting historical patterns. And Rogin's translation of that vocabulary into Jackson's psychological perceptions does not help.

Lockean theory carried within it the seeds not merely of theoretical, but also of thorough-going practical individualism. The exclusion of any human being from full social participation required some explanation. The discrete languages of antifeminism, the proslavery argument, and Indian removal share an emphasis on organic, in contradistinction to political, bonds. I cannot deal with the relations between women and society here. But slaves, it might be worth noting, were objects of white desire for labor, whereas Indians were objects of white desire for land. Both cases involved conflict of cultures and interests but in the one the goal was limited social integration, in the other, obliteration. As the blacks dramatically reproduced themselves and expanded, the Indians declined.

Ruling class dominion can run a gamut from hegemony to genocide, and usually settles someplace between the two. The Southern planters, a pervasive climate of fearful violence notwithstanding, strove for hegemony. Furthermore, they strove for it while asking only that the state (that is, federal government) not interfere. Speculators and farmers moving westward came closer to genocide. They needed the federal government not only for troops, but for legitimization. Indian removal may not so much have "exposed" their sadism as mobilized it in the service of an economic goal they deemed necessary even at the price of a clear conscience. As a student of Freud, Rogin knows that every man has sadistic impulses, normally controlled. But, then, their "exposure" says little, whereas their political mobilization says a good deal about the social context.

We remain far from understanding the dynamism of Euro-American capitalism. We do know, however, that its expansionary tendencies have extended around the world and that each new "frontier" has brought it into direct conflict with other civilizations. The North and South American continents differed from India, Madagascar, or Algeria primarily in their relatively large tracts of sparsely inhabited, but climatically and ecologically attractive, land and the relatively primitive culture of their indigenous inhabitants. Western capitalism transformed the most organic, and apparently immutable, bases of human existence, labor and land, into commodities. That revolution undoubtedly entailed an enormous concomitant psychological upheaval. Once it had begun to occur, however, these commodities became desirable as commodities: they had passed from the world of fantasy to that of reality. One might have to mobilize one's sadism in order to do what had to be done to acquire them, but one had to acquire them in order to provide a living for one's family, to exercise political authority, to attain adult autonomy in those given historical conditions. What did Freud call the refusal to wish to survive? *Thanatos.* How did he describe women who preserved traditional values in a market world? Masochistic. Therefore, one may stand Rogin on his Freudian head and compliment the white frontiersmen for resisting the death instinct and masochistic passivity in favor of a healthy, if unpleasant, adjustment to the hard reality of a white and increasingly bourgeois world.

Indian removal involved a clash between two civilizations, not between two societies within a common civilization, much less between two classes within a common society. Paternalist rhetoric provided the white removers with a means of explaining their actions to themselves. That they saw the paternal relation as permitting authority and entailing responsibility, but excluding equal participation, is of considerable importance. That they could use it as a cloak for the perpetration of violence which they could not formulate in a class or political language should make historians thoughtful. Indian removal, slavery, racism all distinguish the American experience from the European—not because the Europeans did not experience these things, but because they did not experience them at home as readily as they experienced class and national war. Octave Mannoni's *Prospero and Caliban* (1956) has shed light on overseas colonialism, but we have yet to grasp fully the significance of a colonial experience built into the forging of a modern political (bourgeois) society.

Freudian theory has more to offer on this intermediate plane of cultural dynamics than rival theories do. It can sharpen our perceptions about the nature of authority, paternal and political, wielded and accepted. It should be able to help us understand the foundations of modern political charisma. It certainly can force us to ask why some internalize injustice as guilt, and others project guilt as righteous power. It cannot, however, substitute intrapsychic conflicts for the hard questions about historical process. Ironically, in relation to recent theories of psychogenetic determinism, it can extend historical frontiers only in direct proportion to the understanding of historical process on the conscious and institutional and political level. The entire

Western world experienced a monumental transformation in the eighteenth and early nineteenth centuries. The capitalist civilization and the possessive individualist ideology (Rogin's liberalism) that it engendered have profoundly altered the bases of human life, the relations between human beings, and human perceptions of the human condition. Freud's theoretical work, like that of Marx, belongs to the upheaval. American history, like European, constitutes part of the attempt to build an individualistic, capitalist society. Precisely because of its divergences from Europe, America, in many respects, constitutes the theoretical and actual problem confronting historians and social theorists. But in the long, or psychohistorical, perspective, American problems remain mainly, if not exclusively, European problems. The variables of frontier, absence of a nobility, Indians, and resident slaves remain variables in the deeper problems of world-view and legitimate authority among free, propertied individuals. David Brion Davis has elegantly offered a framework for an analysis of these problems in his recent book, *The Problem of Slavery in the Age of Revolution* (1975). In such a context, Freud can be seen as an indispensable "also," but hardly as an "instead."

Notes

1. Although, as a Marxist, I bristle at Rogin's use of Marxist terminology drained of all Marxist content (his use of "primitive accumulation" alone justifies an essay), as a historian with a commitment to the material bases of historical process, I cannot forgive his total disregard of the Scottish historical school.

2. Richard Slotkin deals admirably with both the European origins and the American tradition in *Regeneration through Violence* (Middletown, Conn., Wesleyan University Press, 1973).

3. Cf. Sigmund Freud, *Group Psychology and the Analysis of the Ego* (1921), in *Standard Edition of the Complete Psychological Works of Sigmund Freud*, trans. James Strachey, vol. 18 (London: Hogarth Press, 1955). Freud does not take up this question per se in *Group Psychology*, but his picture of the psychodynamics of mass psychology in modern political movements differs considerably from the picture of adult autonomy presented elsewhere in his work. I intend to treat the problem in a separate piece.

4. Rogin apparently does not understand the difference between farmers and peasants. See *Fathers and Children*, p. 278, where he uses Marx's well-known description of peasant political behavior in *The Eighteenth Brumaire* to describe the political behavior of American farmers ("Farmers, he [Marx] wrote . . ."), without mentioning that Marx meant peasants—in the traditional European sense so radically different from farmers.

Five

The Personal Is Not Political Enough

Advanced capitalist society has stripped away the veils of neutral, natural-rights politics. The personal is political. The family, that sacred haven, itself has a politics. Hierarchy and domination obtain in the most intimate relationships—as if they had not always—which consequently demand political responses. The discovery comes as no great surprise to women, who have always, singly or collectively, consciously or unconsciously, understood as much. The new climate has, however, contributed something to the prominence of sisterhood as a metaphor of female solidarity and struggle. Sisterhood, as a daily practice and as a cultural representation, has existed throughout capitalist society, and before. But the metaphor acquired particular meanings from the specific productive and reproductive configurations of capitalism, just as its meanings and implications are subtly changing with the transformations in capitalism itself. Since the great bourgeois revolutions sisterhood has been intimately tied to feminism—the historically specific attempts to insure full social participation for women.

Although the struggle for woman's place in man's world covers the entire spectrum of human experience, it is always specific to particular social relations of production and reproduction. In some measure, forms of resistance and combat are inevitably shaped by their historical conditions. Similarly, the language in which goals and aspirations are formulated derives, in part, from the prevailing social representations of collective life. No politics remains

"The Personal Is Not Political Enough." *Marxist Perspectives* 2 (Winter 1979): 94–113. Copyright 1979 by *Marxist Perspectives*. All rights reserved. Used by permission of the Radical Society, Ltd.

innocent of that which it contests. The politics of the contemporary women's movement, like Marxist politics, remains at least marginally hostage to the social and political relations, culture, and ideology of advanced capitalist society. Recognition of our historical mortgages need not entail resignation or complacency. Rather, it should sharpen our political determination and strategy. The women's movement, in particular, requires a delicate balance between independence and alliance. I take the defense of the independent movement as the bottom line, but submit that obtaining lasting structural change will depend upon strong political alliances. The movement requires a lively sensitivity to the pitfalls inherent in the politics of the personal and must remain alert to the possible, unintended results of a personal politics that lacks some external anchor. A politics of the personal, in other words, requires consolidation in alliances with other social groups whose personal politics may differ, but who share a commitment to radical social and political transformation.

The special notion of power and authority that has characterized capitalist society has depended heavily upon the proclaimed separation of the public and private spheres. Never as absolute as its formulators claimed, that separation functioned as a norm which in fact helped to obscure the intense interdependence of production and reproduction. The notion of the two spheres also contributed to mystifying class relations. Particularly in the United States, where democratic individualism has attained its most advanced form, the conception of the sexual division of labor tended to replace other forms of political and social hierarchy as the perceived foundation of social order. Obviously, I am not referring to the reality of class relations, but to their ideological recognition. (Racism played a similar role but cannot be discussed here). The general emphasis accorded the sexual division of labor made it particularly tempting for women to consider their special oppression in terms of women as a discrete class and thus, with varying degrees of intention, to deny the importance of prevailing class relations in the political/productive sphere. Psychologically, this strategy appealed to many women courageous enough to recognize the full coercion under which they lived, but, socially, it tended to favor the objective interests of those women with adequate economic resources to participate fully in middle-class prerogatives. In an apparently devastating confirmation of the analysis, socialist women who accepted the primacy of class exploitation frequently found their feminism, if not repudiated, at least sacrificed to more pressing concerns by the very male comrades they supported.

The relationship between capitalism and patriarchy defies facile analysis, just as it challenges resourceful opposition. In the recent past, theorists from Juliet Mitchell to Joan Kelly-Gadol have substantially advanced our understanding of the special role of feminism in any viable Marxist theory. Their work draws upon, even as it contributes to, the growing body of feminist theory generated by the contemporary women's movement. I am indebted to that work and associate myself with its general thrust. I remain, however, concerned with the complexity of the struggle in which we are engaged. In my judgment, only a strong Marxist-Feminist position, which includes alliances with male comrades, can provide an adequate foundation for the securing of female equality.

We face a conjuncture in which only the independent women's movement can force the claims of feminism within political groupings, as well as struggle for those claims on a daily basis in the larger society. But the women's movement itself contains conflicting internal tendencies that risk severing privileged women from their less fortunate sisters. The feminist claim must be universal. But, paradoxically, to realize its universal aspirations, it must be Marxist. Without social and economic conditions capable of insuring decent lives for all people, the rights of women collapse into privilege for the few and exploitation for the many. The distinction between the public and private spheres may now be recognized as a bourgeois swindle, but it throws a long shadow on our present estimates of our situation, our personal psychologies, our political possibilities, and, hence, on the allocation of our energies. In that configuration personal politics, including the nature and role of sisterhood, lie on a narrow margin between the commitment to socialism and an inadvertent succor to advanced capitalism.

Historically, the politics of feminism necessarily derived from the special place of women within the public and private spheres. In capitalist society women of all social groups have shared systematic exclusion from the public world and more or less violent containment within the home. Feminism, in its various manifestations, has thus encompassed women's rights and women's liberation at home as well as in the public arena. By and large, victorious feminist struggles have succeeded in advancing the entry of women into rights and activities previously reserved to men. Property rights, the vote, education, and some improvement in employment and credit possibilities spring readily to mind. Child custody rights constitute a special case because so readily assimilated to the special image of nurturant womanhood, but their normal ascription to women constituted a significant political recognition in time and place—and are now being challenged again.

Ironically, these essential political gains have frequently resulted in the fragmentation of a collective movement into class or even individual entities. This decomposition of female solidarity tends overwhelmingly both to strengthen individual women's class identification at the expense of their identification with other women and to strengthen their commitment to individualism. This individualist bias reinforces the ideology of the dominant class, especially in the United States, where propertied individualism has afforded the historical and social basis for freedom and equality. Those women most prepared to profit from the new opportunities of uniform access normally come from the middle class, or they rapidly join it by virtue of earning and enjoying the income necessary to support themselves as individuals.

From its origins American feminism has remained deeply intertwined with its companion, sisterhood. In a general way sisterhood captured the enduring relations between women bound together in a subordination that transcended class lines. Sisterhood referred particularly to the common experience of oppression and to a nurturing, loving, mutually supporting network born of shared oppression. Significantly, the term sisterhood derives from those familial relations which provided the nexus of identification that transformed women from vulnerable and dangerous sexual beings into acceptable, if constrained, social beings.

The formidable limitations on freedom that many women experienced at home and in the world gave genuine power to the negative or threatening features of the myth of the separate spheres. The myth may, therefore, have penetrated the self-image of many women who did not even benefit from the romantic and chivalric treatment promised by the social representation. As custodians of the mirage of the familial haven, middle-class women found themselves cast as the softening antidote to dominant class relations depicted as the impersonal interaction of competing individuals. Lower-class women may more often have escaped these illusions. But the mere existence of the illusions was taken to license special forms of male aggression and even violence against those who transgressed their bounds. Sisterhood, as a metaphor, must be understood to harbor all the ambiguities of the complex system of family relations from which it derives.

In itself, sisterhood has entailed no special political positions, although it has made a decisive contribution to every feminist upsurge and, recently, to both the independent women's movement and to female separatism. Because of its universal appeal, it has, moreover, periodically offered aid and comfort to a pervasive cultural feminism that, at its most mystifying, merely elaborates a universal ideology appropriate to easing the passage of a few middle-class women into the public sphere. Such highly differential feminist victories can actually result in the sharpening of class lines by pushing lower-class and minority women, as well as their men, even further down the socio-economic scale.

Nothing inherently opposes sisterhood to feminism. Indeed, they have frequently meshed, as with the domestic feminism of the nineteenth century, various campaigns for women's rights, and specific labor struggles. They can and do join on both ends of the political spectrum, as the history and fate of the ERA amply testifies. Originating as a bourgeois-feminist measure, strongly laced with the sisterly glow of the revived women's movement, the ERA has now become a genuinely Marxist-Feminist issue, necessarily drawing upon feminist and sisterly currents. In the course of its recent history, however, the struggle for the ERA intersected with the split in NOW that seemed to juxtapose a political bourgeois feminism against a radical, separatist sisterhood. In the wake of that split, sisterhood has again been invoked in defense of individual female privilege. Neither the separatist nor the bourgeois readings of sisterhood suffice. Bourgeois feminism may come to rely more and more heavily on the notion of sisterhood as the socio-economic prospects for an inclusive feminism diminish while the political and individual careers of bourgeois feminists require a general female solidarity.

The contemporary ideas of sisterhood and feminism both have their roots in the great bourgeois revolutions of the seventeenth and eighteenth centuries. Sisterhood perpetuates the struggle within the familial metaphor of politics that those revolutions repudiated in theory; feminism demands the realization of the democratic potential that the revolutions have thus far failed to deliver in practice. The triumph of capitalist social relations of production replaced, at least in a particular public discourse, time-honored notions of patriarchy and dependency with the notion of bourgeois individualism. Like any representation of social relations, bourgeois individualism did not so much transform a dense and intractable social system as reformulate it with respect to both theoretical preference and political practice. Paradoxically, the advent of capitalism at once offered women a greater hope of full social participation than any previous social system had and raised more systematic barriers to their social integration and self-respect.

I do not need to rehearse that contradictory and deceptive history here. Suffice it to say that individualism, rationalism, and universalism were all interpreted in strictly male terms. Worse, they all, in some measure, rested upon a more or less explicit repudiation of women as simultaneously the opposite of the desired male norm and the emotional anchor necessary to the functioning of that norm under conditions of intense competition. Having rejected dependency in favor of autonomy, the dominant male culture nonetheless itself depended, in the lives of individual men, upon a repressed domestic sphere represented as custodian of all the qualities the public sphere could not tolerate.

Throughout the nineteenth and twentieth centuries sisterhood and feminism constituted the two tendencies within successive strategies. Sometimes in conflict, sometimes in concord, they both helped to identify the decisive features of female weakness and to build foundations for female strength. Sisterhood, moreover, flourished, in ways we are only beginning to appreciate among women who remained uninterested in, when not openly opposed to, feminism. It also flourished among feminists, union women, and women who were just working to survive. Frequently unnamed as such, sisterhood provided both the model for and the substance of those bonds through which women nurtured, supported, sustained, and enjoyed each other. Over time, the behavior and values of the private sphere—the world of women—came to offer an alternate model to that of striving, competitive capitalism. The world of women became a world of reproduction in the broadest sense, including not only the reproduction of the species but the reproduction of its values and level of civilization. Almost invariably, however, the spectrum of female activities, from charity and social work through the education of children and the support of culture, remained dissociated from, or in sufferance to, the world of men, understood as the world of real power.

The perceived cleavage between the male and female modes of being and understanding remained so broad that many strong self-reliant women could, in good conscience, oppose feminism as either irrelevant or corrosive of women's special contribution. Feminists, of course, did not concur. To them the conquest of the vote and of access to a full political life remained of critical, if not unique, importance. Even more than political equality, human equality preoccupied both male and female feminists of the late nineteenth century. Accepting the distinct characteristics of female being, they nonetheless favored a model of human being not dissimilar to what today is known as androgyny. In this sense they can be seen as integrationists not merely on the level of access to the public sphere but on the level of human consciousness as well. Attractive as their position frequently appears—see especially the forthcoming work of William Leach—it obscured the tragic and conflict-ridden dimension of all relations between the sexes. In making their case for female equality, they in some measure fashioned a vision of human nature that repudiated the notion of power.

Seen in retrospect, the women's movement or movements of the bourgeois world can be understood as confronting a complex range of problems. Women faced the inherent struggle with men that derives from the intractable differences between the sexes. They faced a particular struggle with paternalism and with the anxious patriarchy relegated from the public to the private sphere. Confronting not the socially and politically embedded patriarchs of the distant past, nor even the relatively secure pseudo-patriarchs of the Filmerian model, but their increasingly market-dependent heirs, women had to deal with a male authority that depended for its very existence upon female internalization of a particular female role. Hierarchy, banished from the public sphere, was transplanted to the domestic sphere and the individual psyche. To be sure, it did not survive intact: Social relations do not outlive their social base, even when their forms and rhetoric may evoke a reassuring continuity.[1] Hence the anxiety and "nervous diseases" that plagued both men and women. Hence the particular kinds of violence that savaged domestic life and barred women's free access to the public world.

Discouragements notwithstanding, women embraced the struggle for equal access to the public sphere, including the vote, legal equality, and employment. They struggled for respect for themselves and other women and for the recognition and implementation of female values throughout society. In the most difficult instances they struggled with other women to insure the triumph of their commitments. In almost all instances they struggled against male complacency, condescension, idealization, disdain, and abuse. In all instances they struggled against themselves—against the ingrained contradictions between the positive and negative views of themselves in which they had been reared, not to mention the contradictions within the good and bad views respectively.

The confusion between the public and private roles of women remained paramount: Women's private roles—the natural privacy of the appropriate female role—were taken to have a public function. Female aspiration to a public role was taken to violate female nature itself. The feminization of the public sphere threatened the irreparable corruption of femininity as a public representation. Yet, how were female goals to be realized without the activity of women? How indeed were women to act publicly if they did not succeed in changing their self and social representations?

Such doubts plagued women as well as men, but they must be recognized as deeply colored by an official—i.e., predominantly male—view of the appropriate female role. I raise these contradictions less out of historical curiosity than out of the conviction that the tensions they betray still characterize all assessments of female political activity. Without doubt, we are more directly the heirs of our predecessors than we usually acknowledge: The historical development of their struggles, complete with victories, failures, and compromises, binds us, just as the historical development of the social relations and attitudes we oppose binds our opponents. Beyond that historical bond, however, lie the very dynamics and structure of the movement for female equality within capitalist social relations of production. And that legacy, with its present manifestations, itself raises the specter of social transformation as the prerequisite for female emancipation.

Any feminist struggle draws much of its impetus from the inescapable conflict between men and women. As social facts, male strength and female reproductive power pit the sexes against each other in a conflict rendered only more poignant by the attraction that locks mortal enemies in each other's embrace. Female self-definition, like female self-determination, remains informed by the basic rage against the eternal possibility of rape and violent subjugation. The motive force of feminism can never entirely be divorced from that psychological mainspring. And it only appears the more decisive when its institutionalization within the family is taken into account. But if feminist motivation reaches back to the intrapsychic depths, feminist meaning remains unavoidably historical in its formulations. The language adopted by feminism corresponds to the available political language, including its various transformations and negations. The prevailing social relations of production and their political institutionalization establish the conditions—and, therefore, the forms—of feminism.

The relationship between feminism proper and the dominant political language appears obvious. The quest for the realization of equal rights for all individuals regardless of sex or race draws immediately upon common political themes and addresses existing juro-legal, social, and economic structures. The relationship between sisterhood and that political configuration appears less clear.

The bonds of sisterhood that entwined women throughout the nineteenth century are only beginning to surface under the painstaking scrutiny of historians. Their extent and strength, as depicted in the work of Nancy Cott, Sarah Elbert, Keith Melder, Carroll Smith-Rosenberg, and others, provided a network of reinforcement for innumerable women going about the daily business of ordinary lives. Frequently, the sustenance they proffered remained largely defensive, serving to organize and inform the domestic space. In this respect, they must be understood in the context of that voluntary motherhood so thoughtfully evoked by Linda Gordon. The bonds of sisterhood thus appropriated for women areas of love, mutual respect, and personal choices. They even contributed to a sense of appropriate female power, which carried over into the public sphere.

But the public translation of private female norms betrayed a tension that would continue to haunt feminist goals and successes. For female power conflicted decisively with capitalist norms, to the extent that these norms had been defined as male. Thus, women who entered the public sphere normally faced the alternatives of doing so as individuals fitted into prefabricated male slots, or doing so on the basis of a special female mission that challenged the very normative foundations of a masculine world. And many women never feared to do precisely that. In the name of a higher—female—ethic, they set about purifying the world. Members of reform societies, WCTUers, pacifists, settlement house workers, tackled male corruption head-on. The full story of their activities and beliefs remains to be told, although a good start has been made, and political evaluation of their work may long remain difficult, independent of our respect for their courage and our estimate of the value of the discrete reforms they accomplished.

Female reformers, formalizing a radical social housekeeping along female norms, occasionally secured conservative allies and even contributed to a conservative political climate. And their very conception of female power and female values derived from the same social system that had produced the male behavior they abhorred. We cannot afford to build a politics on this confusion.

A society that generates a particular model of masculinity generates a complementary model of femininity. Even those self-declared female values that constitute as much a reaction against the artificial model of femininity as against misused male supremacy remain hostage to the social relations from which they emerge. In attempting to substitute female for male norms, the sisterhood for the brotherhood, women have risked perpetuating polarized conceptions of human values—specific in their articulation, if more general in their underlying logic—engendered by capitalist social relations.

The women's movement of the 1960s and early 1970s extended the meaning and claims of sisterhood further yet. Sisterhood, claimed Robin Morgan, is powerful. Powerful because the personal is political. And it therefore follows that personal relations should be brought to bear against bankrupt political relations.

Sisterhood, in the sense that it came to be used, functioned as a sign or code word for a vast panoply of ideas. In perhaps its most important meaning, sisterhood evoked an image of nonauthoritarian binding among female peers. Like the notion of brotherhood, which it paralleled, sisterhood drew its meaning from the familial metaphor of politics. In this respect, it suggested the antipatriarchal egalitarianism of the brother band's revolt against the father. Like brotherhood, it proposed an alternate model of appropriate political relations. Like brotherhood also, it invoked bonds that transcended the interest-group coalitions and competitive struggles associated with market-determined relations.

Sisterhood thus sought to retain notions of attachment and loyalty associated with familial relations. In some measure, its model for relations within the capitalist world embedded a fundamental opposition to the principles of that world. But where brotherhood seemed to imply a redistribution of patriarchy—that internalization so vividly evoked by Freud's picture of eating the father—sisterhood contained the seeds of a more radical repudiation of patriarchy. In rejecting the law of the father, sisterhood rejected the domination of the male. Despite occasional attempts to resuscitate a myth of matriarchy, female goddesses, or other prototypes of female power, sisterhood essentially identified itself as the egalitarian distribution of powerlessness. For just as brotherhood proposes the antidote to fatherhood, so must sisterhood be understood to propose the antidote to motherhood. The frequently silent term must be restored to the syllogism before we can proceed to consider sisterhood relative to patriarchy itself.

I cannot explore here the psychological complexities of sisterhood and motherhood in bourgeois culture. The cultural immediacy of the problem can best be testified to by the spate of recent books on mothers, mothering, and motherhood. Dorothy Dinnerstein and Nancy Chodorow have most recently and most cogently called attention to the reproduction of mothering in capitalist society, and to the terrifying price it extracts from male as well as female children. Motherhood has entailed a kind of power, but one that has gone largely unacknowledged. The emphasis on love and nurture in some measure has marked the ambiguity of a power the major responsibility of which has lain in teaching sons to free themselves from maternal bonds—and values—and in teaching daughters to internalize constraints—and repress angers—against which the powerful mother herself has had no recourse. The question deserves extended treatment, but for the moment I merely wish to suggest that sisterhood as a model of being and of relating should not be divorced from the familial nexus from which it derives.

As a familial metaphor, sisterhood invokes nonpolitical relations, while it claims to unite political and personal relations in a single struggle. The call to understand the personal as political apparently demands the intrusion of competitive and conflictive relations into the purportedly nonconflictive personal realm. This call itself demands the recognition that beneath myths of harmony and innate characteristics lay buried an intense political struggle. In this respect, the notion of sisterhood implicitly affirms a continuum between private and public relations. It also tends to affirm the primacy of the personal struggle, understood as the struggle between men and women, over conventional political struggles, understood as the war games of boys.

At the core of the notion of sisterhood lies the affirmation of the solidarity and similarity of all women. As it unfolded in the consciousness-raising groups of the 1960s and early 1970s, this understanding became one of the most powerful weapons of the women's movement. The groups themselves forged a practice of sisterhood by providing psychological space within which women could come to know themselves through knowing each other. Late capitalist society had contributed a particularly bitter twist to the centuries of female oppression. Consumerism, suburban residence patterns, declining family size, increased male occupational mobility, increased female education, declining parental control over children and their marriage choices, rising divorce rates, and a host of other changes had interwoven in a dense network of isolation and anxiety for many women. Not all these changes were *eo ipso* bad for women. But what rising female individualism and opportunity had given with one hand, they had often taken away with the other. Stripping away the barriers that had simultaneously oppressed and sheltered women, and lightening the burdens of childbirth, physical labor, and employment, they had failed to provide viable alternatives. And they had decisively encouraged greater competition among women to get and keep husbands, to consume with style, and generally to cultivate an appearance of perfection according to prevailing styles. In a general way, the traditional world of women was dismantled without substitution and without sufficient access for women to the world of men. That the appearance of greater female freedom provoked an increase in more or less veiled male hostility and violence hardly helped.

Sisterhood helped women to break out of those walls of silence erected by the suburban home and the media's message of female success. Sisterhood permitted women to forge a common language with which to express their hostility to men, to their lives, even to their children. That language provided a new vocabulary for female anger and, thus, at least opened paths through which women might turn natural aggression outward rather than upon themselves. Sisterhood also, and miraculously, allowed the expression of women's jealousy of each other. The privately nurtured inadequacies, guilts, and fears broke out in an orgy of recognition. Suddenly none of us was unique. One of the major traps of modern culture had been exploded: Strength lay not in being different—always presented as being best—it lay in being similar, even, or especially, if that meant being no better than. We were wasting our energies and talents on the wrong things. Dupes of our need to please men, we had become unable to like ourselves, to like our sisters, to like anything.

Sisterhood has thus afforded a network of mutual support—a fund of collective strength and affection from which women could draw in their still private battles in the home or on the job. At its most extreme, it has flirted with proclamations of self-sufficiency. Learning to love and respect each other, women could do completely without men. Practically and emotionally, this position seems to be proving unrealistic for most women. But its mere existence has encouraged women to a new independence and to a new understanding of differences in sexual preference or style of life as variations on the shared identity of being women. The gains, to which I have briefly alluded, have been innumerable. Each of us has her own memory of the decisive click—the moment of recognition. For me it came at a party in the late 1960s when I recognized that I was more interested in talking to the women guests than to the men.

Whenever or wherever that click has occurred, it flicked on a light that has chased the shadows from years of training to mold our beings to please socially dominant males. With the illumination came an uncomfortable vision of the past, which, like all visions, remains partial. Commonly, the molding to please men had not included much liking of men. The crux of the exercise lay in persuading men to like us, usually for reasons recognized as artificial and artificially cultivated. That psychological environment had, moreover, pitted us in deadly competition with our peers, even as we imposed on their friendship to underscore their—and our own—secondary status. A plan to do something with other girls could always be pushed aside if something better—read, date—came up. And even success brought little genuine sense of worth. Rather, it confirmed an anxious narcissism almost schizophrenically divided from an incubating sense of a whole self. The sudden recognition that other women were not merely okay but important opened a new path to that long stifled sense of our own self.

In recent years sisterhood has made it possible for women to like and respect other women. The rising self-awareness has brought many to confront how much of the early anger, presumably related to male oppressors, derived in fact from our early relations with our mothers. And having learned to hate our mothers, we have come again to love them, as we have come to love the children against whom we had never been free to rage. Recognizing and repossessing our own anger has gradually freed many of us to function as whole human beings in the larger world. In this respect, sisterhood has provided the critical ingredient in women's political coming-of-age.

Sisterhood has thus contributed to the creation of political female beings, by freeing women from the continual replay of the familial psychological drama—by freeing women from the necessity of continually reproducing their own childhoods and their own narcissism. So understood, sisterhood might be described as political. Common struggle against individual demons identifies those demons as social rather than personal. The struggle with an individual husband, mother, or child can be understood as the struggle with the reproductive system attendant upon the prevailing social relations of production. It behooves us, however, not to neutralize too much. The struggle would lack immediacy and conviction without the deepest feelings of rage that derive from fundamental oppositions between men and women and between generations. Nor can those eternal polarities be apprehended as removed archetypes. For each of us they exist as personal histories. We hate not categories but people—frequently the very people we most love. The familial struggle remains personal whatever its political implications.

But, some will counter, the personal is political: Only by fighting on that terrain can we hope to effect lasting change, for the struggle is for human minds. To be sure. But if minds can only be won in the here-and-now of daily life, daily life moves within constraints established by massive political forces. Bourgeois society, in diffusing patriarchal authority from the monarch to the paterfamilias, even as it exposed that minor potentate to the agonizing pressures of capitalist competition, diffused potential opposition to its reign.

With the further erosion and displacement of paternalism from the individual bourgeois male to the massive corporations and institutions of contemporary society, opposition becomes all the more difficult. Domestic paternalism may be seen as the preferred form of female oppression generated by classical bourgeois society or capitalist social relations of production. Women caught in the tentacles of such domestic paternalism may understandably have experienced it through the prism of the legacy of centuries of older patriarchal modes. But in essence, it has remained a preponderantly bourgeois phenomenon. Its characteristics have included a partial rather than central reliance upon religious ideology; an emphasis on the material, especially economic, bases of social participation; and a tendency to foster the fragmentation rather than the collectivization of personal experience. The positive contributions of domestic paternalism, in contradistinction to older modes, have included a preference for universalism as against particularism—for the production of a single image of woman taken to prevail over class differences; for an invocation of science as the explanation of presumably female traits; for a language of individualism that has not necessarily excluded women; and for a technology that has both permitted effective contraception and grounded socially productive labor in something other than brute force.

To be sure, the image of domestic paternalism has always deviated widely from the experience of most women. Class and racial differences have had a tremendous impact on women's lives and have generated discrete versions of sisterhood that have promoted a range of sexually specific struggles. The list includes welfare strikes, rent strikes, and day care strikes, among others. The power of women in such circumstances has indeed led to "the subversion of the community." And contemporary struggles have their prototypes in, for example, the roles played by women in bread riots in England, in France, in the South during the Civil War. But the image has acquired a certain social existence of its own and, like any component of a hegemonic culture, it has obscured deviations from its norm, denied alternatives to its vision, and suppressed challenges to its authority.

Not surprisingly, the opposition to the specifically bourgeois oppression of women has arisen within the structures of capitalist social relations themselves.

Consider the standard criticism of the nineteenth-century suffrage movement. From the struggles themselves to retrospective accounts of them, critics have insisted that the fight for the vote gained women nothing, distracted their energies from more important battles, and generally proved them dupes of prevailing male power structures. It has also commonly been noted that once women acquired the vote they tended to use it not in defense of feminism, or even of other women, but in defense of the class and ethnic positions that bound them more closely to their men than to their sisters. Ellen DuBois has recently advanced a refreshing dissent from this received wisdom, but we need to extend her analysis to address female political activity in the contemporary setting.

Those proponents of sisterhood who emphasize cultural or separatist strategies tend to minimize the importance of concerted political action. They tend, moreover, to see in sisterhood a genuine alternative to bourgeois oppression of women—an alternative that can bind women of different races and classes in single struggle against their common dominators.

In my judgment, this assessment is mistaken. The perception that the personal is political derives directly from the general collapse of classical bourgeois society. The mystification of public politics, the social diffusion of authority, has proceeded so far that we have trouble discerning our enemies. I do not wish for one moment to suggest that women should not struggle for equality and respect on every level, including and perhaps especially in their daily lives, and against both the degradation and the idealization of women by whatever regime. Women have a persisting need to struggle with their lovers, husbands, brothers, fathers, and comrades for full equality in any social or political movement. I do not, however, believe that that struggle will ever be won independent of an alliance with progressive men in the political arena.

Proverbially, capitalist social relations of production have taken their greatest toll in their mystification of the proper object of action and desire. The divorce of the laborer from his or her labor provides the material foundations of alienation. That alienation infiltrates the lives and consciousness of all members of capitalist society. In its metaphoric extension, a pervasive sense of alienation clouds our inter- and intrapersonal relations, carrying commodity fetishism into the innermost crannies of our beings. We know how it feels to "need" things we do not really want. Which of us is free from the true horror of consumerism—the dependence on commodities for a sense of self worth? Which of us has not experienced the agonizing anxiety of compulsively seeking a reassurance that offers no substitute for love or respect, and that, worse, never satiates the need but rather fuels it for even more panicky demands? We grope through the world without ever knowing the object of our desire.

For those many women lucky enough to have experienced the effects of sisterhood, it has offered the most powerful antidote to that neediness. It has helped many of us to name our oppressors, including our own unconscious object worlds, and to construct a phenomenological description of our prison. It has been an invaluable experience of naming. And since that naming has been collectively undertaken, it has helped us to forge ties of mutual respect and, yes, nurture. But it has not—and, in my estimate, cannot [have]—given us tools adequate to the naming of the conditions of our oppression. Tragically, the language is in a determining, if not total, measure a structural reversal of the language of oppression itself. Born of the capitalist split between the domestic and public spheres, it can inadvertently contribute to an internal transformation of capitalism that will afford yet more humiliating oppression for most, if not all, women.

Late capitalism is assuring its reinvigorated domination by turning upon its own progeny. The legally and economically structured nuclear family, characteristic of capitalist society, is, for all practical purposes, a thing of the past. I do not join those who bemoan its passing. Romanticization of a past that existed primarily in the privileges of oppressors or the fantasies of their anxious heirs has no place in our vision of the future. We must, however, recognize that bourgeois individualism, with all its injustices and failings, provided the firmest cornerstone for individual freedom the world has yet known. And the personal liberation that is emerging from the ruins of bourgeois society may not do as well, for its success will depend upon its political articulation.

The possibilities of even the most generous and inclusive sisterhood cannot extend much beyond dominant social conditions. And we are currently experiencing something less than an optimal situation. Some women have made gains with respect to employment and financial independence, but their independence has tended to release them from the oppressive custodianship of individual men only to throw them into the arms of the corporations and the federal government. And even that pitiful independence is available to only a small group. Recent economic developments portend the collapse of the traditional professional and propertied middle class to the benefit of affluent, salaried technocrats. The bourgeois institutions that had encoded the partial independence of civil society and critical judgment, such as the universities, cultural institutions, the professions, and even family businesses, have given way to the government and the multinationals. Ironically, the new dominant institutions can afford a much greater measure of personal idiosyncrasy than their bourgeois predecessors could. Internalization of values appears increasingly peripheral to the smooth functioning of the social system. Far from signaling the explosion of immediacy, however, this development portends a terrifying oppressiveness. It suggests, in fact, a world in which personal perceptions and individual behavior are of so little social consequence that innumerable varieties can be tolerated. For we lack conduits to channel personal expression into public will.

This emerging system falls far short of realizing the universal claims of sisterhood. If the upper echelons can now indiscriminately employ men, women, blacks, then the lower echelons can, with equal arbitrariness, employ fewer workers of any gender or race. The first result of the new patterns would appear to be a widening and ominous gap between social classes. Among the new rich, financial security depends upon two salaries. Among the new poor, women's work, when it can be obtained with adequate remuneration, cannot cover the costs of decent childcare, much less education for children and household help for the woman. The woman's work thus jeopardizes the reproduction of the standard of living and culture in the next generation. If the woman does not work, the family confronts a declining standard of living. I must here pass over the devastating psychological consequences of contemporary life on the relations between men and women in our culture as a whole. Suffice it to note the rising rate of violence against women, the pornographic explosion, and related cultural manifestations. Even more devastating are the new barriers that emerge between women. The critical distinctions are multiple. For example, the break between the employed and the unemployed, between the employed with benefits and pensions and those without, between those who can afford the $300–$600 a month for full childcare and those who cannot.

In this perspective, the ERA cannot be dismissed as a bourgeois swindle or a meaningless political gesture. It constitutes the indispensable political arm of sisterhood: Without it—i.e., without society's formal recognition of women's right to full economic and political equality—sisterhood will collapse into the debilitating sibling rivalry within which bourgeois culture had sought to contain it. And withal, the ERA alone will certainly not be enough. For equal rights, indispensable though they may be, derive from that democratic tradition which has never been able to come to terms with the psychological, social, and economic foundations of any meaningful right. Political rights have remained susceptible to all the abuses we know.

The point is not to defend a simple application of individual political rights, which come to us trailing their clouds of racism, sexism, and economic exploitation. We must subject them to the most searching criticism and implement them in a spirit of transformation. But implement them we must.

To forsake them now is to fall prey to the final capitalist mystification—that politics is irrelevant to the real business of life. Politics may not solve the problems of sexual, racial, and economic injustice. But politics provides the terrain on which those problems can be addressed and the language and the practice whereby those problems can be externalized and, therefore, recognized and solved.

Only within a political context can we grasp the meaning of sisterhood and defend its aspirations. For sisterhood without politics exposes us to the political destruction of sisterhood itself. The women's movement has taught us that a viable politics must incorporate the personal experience of all members of society. It has taught us that men cannot be left to speak for the interests of women, much less to use and oppress women within political coalitions. It has taught us that transforming the conditions of production will remain an empty shell unless the conditions of reproduction are transformed as well. More, the women's movement has taught us not to be apologetic or defensive in these claims. It has given us that pride in ourselves which can only come from our respect for our sisters.

Through our struggles we have learned that no politics worthy of allegiance can hope to succeed without full attention to the claims of women. We bring to our potential political allies not merely our productive and reproductive power but the decisive understanding that may permit a breaking-free from the political modes of our enemies. No more than our male comrades, however, can we hope to do the job alone. If we misunderstand the political scope of sisterhood, we will fall victim to the very mystifications we seek to oppose. We too will mistake the object of our attack and, once more, pass beside the main chance.

Sisterhood has helped us, as it helped so many of our predecessors, to forge ourselves as political beings. Sisterhood has mobilized our loyalty to each other and hence to ourselves. It has given form to a dream of genuine equality for all women. But without a broader politics directed toward the kind of social transformation that will provide social justice for all human beings, it will, in a poignant irony, result in our dropping each other by the wayside as we compete with rising desperation for crumbs. The worst nightmare women must face is that in a decade or two the women's movement may be seen as having done the dirty work of monopoly capital—of having eroded those older bourgeois structures that block the road to a new bourgeois despotism.

In complex ways any serious politics must forge a language and a practice that permits an objectification of social and personal relations. Politics bridges the gap between the particular and the general and constructs a nexus through which need may be translated into justice. By transforming the subjective impetus into an objective standard, politics permits the grouping of individual experiences into general goals. The process can be likened to Marx's transformation of alienation from a subjective response into an economic law. In our society, law—the universal category—has had a distinct class and male cast. The political struggle addresses the cast of that law and the social relations of production and reproduction that inform and support it. The independent women's movement constitutes a major force in the struggle, even as it radically changes its terms and extends its scope. But the movement cannot effect its goals without allies. Hence, for example, the disagreeable necessity of working with the Law Enforcement Assistance Administration in the prosecution of rape. A series of such tactical alliances, while discretely justifiable, can contribute to the strengthening of the state at the expense of civil society.

One can imagine a certain egalitarianism in a totalitarian state—a kind of institutional uniformity that would have scant use for sexual hierarchy. But assuredly, it bodes as ill for a vibrant sisterhood as it does for other substantive and intimate personal relations. Capitalist society, which has generated our specific experience of sisterhood, has already proved unable to endow its ideals with adequate substance. In this context, sisterhood flourishes as a defensive posture and as the foundation of political engagement, but also as a rationale for political cooptation. In a crazy reversal, the politicization of the personal can become the personalization of the political, with individual successes and arbitrary choices justified in the name of sisterhood. The individual thus appropriates the being of others by claiming individual preferment as the realization of collective purpose. Such an individual identification with a manifestation of collective purpose can only be tolerated if differential opportunities are so comparable as to leave the difference truly a reflection of individual capabilities—in contradistinction to social privilege.

Only an autonomous women's movement in alliance with a strong socialist movement can implement the claims of women and provide the context for that full realization of sisterhood which will broaden its substantive meaning, even as sisterhood itself helps to shape the theory and practice of Marxism. In such a perspective, sisterhood must be claimed as an essential part of our—and our male allies'—politics. But not, in itself, as a political position.

Note

1. See Gayle Rubin, "The Traffic in Women," in Rayna R. Reiter, ed., *Toward an Anthropology of Women* (New York, 1975), and my "Property and Patriarchy in Classical Bourgeois Political Theory," *Radical History Review* (1977), 36–59.

Six

The Crisis of Our Culture and the Teaching of History

Until very recently, history enjoyed a privileged position in the liberal arts curriculum. An educated individual could be expected to possess a general familiarity not merely with the history of the United States, but with that of Western Civilization as well. Formal requirements confirmed and protected the status of history, which itself was taken to provide an indispensable introduction to political culture and the responsibilities of citizenship. The collapse of the entire structure of requirements in recent decades has exposed history courses, including the basic surveys, to fierce competition. But the broader cultural and political crisis, of which the abolition of requirements constitutes merely a symptom, challenges the very core of history as a discipline and a profession. Thus the current move, in some institutions, to restore requirements does not necessarily address the internal problems of historical writing and teaching any more than it reinvigorates the fragile relationship between academic history and the general culture.

Nationally, history, like other humanities, finds itself very much on the defensive. The decline in enrollments can best be described as a collapse. To be sure, the growing concern with illiteracy—or at least precipitously declining SAT verbal scores—affects other disciplines as well. But English departments retain their monopoly of basic writing courses, which they can flesh out with courses in speech.

Across the board—in public and private, two-year and four-year, large and small institutions—teachers of history struggle to fill classes with enough

"The Crisis of Our Culture and the Teaching of History." *History Teacher* 13 (November 1979): 89–101. Copyright 1979 by the Society for History Education. All rights reserved. Used by permission of the Society for History Education.

bodies to justify their being scheduled at all—not to mention to justify the salaries and respect to which teachers of history believe themselves entitled. Pious homilies about the virtues of small classes, personalized instruction, and faculty-student contact cannot cloak the painful truth. Students are not much interested in history. Or at least they do not know that they might or should be interested in history. Symptomatically, the survey courses appear to be in a state of disarray.

Many individuals and departments have reacted with a kind of defensive panic: around the country, history departments sponsor a bewildering smörgasbord of courses in film, women, witchcraft, rock and roll, oral history, great individuals, folk traditions, what-have-you. The tactic, which seems to rest on the assumption that if you cannot beat them, you can at least join them, includes some excellent and imaginative teaching as well as genuine contributions to the range and immediacy of historical understanding. But as a defense of history as a cornerstone of the curriculum, the tactic has failed to work. The rhythm of change in contemporary fads runs directly counter to the very notion of history. In large measure, moreover, these innovations owe their success to their appeal to the subjective experience of students and thus rest upon a profound de-politicization of historical process.

The proper issue is not the inclusion within history of the experience and perspectives of social groups frequently excluded from the conventional narrative. That inclusion has been long overdue and should be enthusiastically welcomed by all responsible historians. The proper issue is rather the terms of the inclusion. No present-minded, fragmented, pseudo-historical sociology can do justice to those neglected by the conventional political history, nor to history as the unfolding process of collective life. In succumbing to the blackmail of our "now/me/self" culture, historians may be signing their professional death-sentence.

The current plight of history derives in some measure from the general assault on requirements and the espousal of relevance that characterized the 1960s, and in some measure from the growing crisis of appropriate subject matter and method within our discipline. It also reflects the pressures of the job market upon students, as well as the increase in the numbers of students who must secure a degree in order to confront the job market at all. Other factors have contributed to the relative decline of our discipline, but for present purposes I shall stand on the blanket assertion that the crisis in the teaching of history remains inseparable from the crisis in our culture as a whole.

I do not raise this spectre of general crisis in a spirit of defeatism or mindless condemnation of change, but rather in a spirit of contention and struggle. As historians, we possess the indispensable tools for critical reflection upon our own position and therefore for a collective defense of the integrity and political centrality of our discipline.

Some may be surprised at my imputing our present woes to the progressive events of the 1960s and to the attendant concern with social inclusiveness and pedagogical immediacy. Others may discern a call for the arbitrary restoration of standards and orthodox curricula. Let me be clear on both points: I am neither damning the claims of the '60s nor advocating a return to the *status quo ante*. I do, however, submit that the realization of the legitimate claims of the '60s requires fidelity to the purpose and practice of history, which I take to be the construction of a narrative. I also wish to suggest that the road back is blocked: the defense of standards now requires coming to terms with the proliferation of contemporary and historical voices.

The problem of an appropriate narrative remains troublesome and plagues other fields as well. Complex notions of time, a general retreat from simple models of causation, and the new ordering of facts permitted by statistical methods and computer technology all challenge older, more or less teleological visions of historical process and the structure of historical accounts. A full exploration of this problem far transcends the present context. Nonetheless, a narrative—even if profoundly renovated and internally transfigured—remains central to our discipline. Thus, for the moment, by narrative I mean no more than an internally ordered, sequential structure that takes account of change over time and human motivation. I should further assert that narrative in this sense requires serious attention to the political dimension of social life. But Eugene D. Genovese and I have begun developing this theme in our essay, "The Political Crisis of Social History," and are currently pursuing it in other work.[1]

In this perspective, the '60s challenged the received historical narrative, even as they challenged dominant institutions, by producing a panoply of social movements that gave voice to the discontents and aspirations of groups which had been excluded from the institutionalization of the ideals of democracy and freedom in this country. In one sense, the black movement, the women's movement, the anti-war movement, the agricultural and service workers' union movements can all be understood as strands in a broad movement for civil rights for all Americans.

In different ways, however, these movements intersected with a cultural aspiration for personal liberation that derived from a long-percolating rebellion against the repressive values of the dominant middle-class culture, and that frequently appeared as the most radical demand of all. To the extent that the goals of the various movements merged in a general attack on the authority of fathers, presidents, governments, and other custodians of power, they shared an opposition to what were increasingly perceived as artificial constraints on individual freedom. The insistent demand for participation or direct democracy in all spheres encoded this suspicion of authority. It required the economic difficulties of the '70s to demonstrate how deeply the goals of the various groups might come into conflict under conditions of scarce resources and a declining growth rate. As an economy of affluence gives way to one of scarcity and energy shortage, the political and ethical problems of choice—and the authority to implement choice—will inevitably reassert themselves.

But even before the conflicting claims of various social groups had become apparent, the confusion between liberation and freedom had been ensconced at the center of the pervasive anti-authoritarianism. This confusion lies at the core of the fragile position of history in the curriculum and in the culture.

As historians, we have learned to recognize the complex institutionalization of authority in different societies. We have also learned to recognize that historical movements frequently mistake their proper target. Direct action can assault an apparent agent of oppression, only to clear the way for a worse oppression. We also know that there can be structural relationships between the preferred forms of opposition to a class or a regime and the nature of the class or the regime itself.

It is now becoming clear that throughout the twentieth century, but particularly since the Second World War, the most dynamic and ominous custodians of power have been institutions—particularly the great corporations—rather than individuals. Nonetheless, the shadow of a more classical bourgeois authority hung on. Opposition to the Dow Chemical Company or the military-industrial complex notwithstanding, much of the deeper impetus to revolt in the '60s, especially among the students, remained fixated on the spectre of the bourgeois father and entrepreneur in his various guises. Hence, reaction against oppression took the form of opposition to restraints in the classroom, in the curriculum, in sexual practice, in personal life. To the extent that participatory and community movements of various kinds succeeded in organizing pockets of individuals or bits of turf, they nonetheless failed decisively to modify dominant political and corporate structures.

Perhaps we should have been more suspicious of the speed with which the vestiges of bourgeois culture collapsed. In retrospect, it is easy to understand that the erosion had been proceeding apace. But the cultural representations of normality had retained such vigor that their collapse appeared dramatic and was dramatically captured in such phrases as "sexual revolution."

Similarly, Watergate and the resignation of Richard Nixon carried all the drama of a regicide—or at the very least a patricide. But instead of catharsis, we got the Ford pardon and the publication of *All the President's Men*. Behind the surface events, the system grinds on.

The message could not have been clearer. But rather than linking the deceptiveness of authority in the public sphere with its possible deceptiveness in the private sphere, the commitment to personal liberation persisted. We have yet to hear probing and progressive questioning of the accepted equation of absolute freedom of choice in personal matters with social freedom. To be sure, we have Phyllis Schlafly, Anita Bryant, and the New Right. But reaction is not what I had in mind. The foundations of the world they wish to restore have been irreparably undermined, as have those of Christopher Lasch's fantasy of domestic patriarchy. What we badly need are voices to suggest that sexual liberation and narrowly personal selfhood may not be the freedom of the people, but their new opiate. Which brings me to the teaching of history.

The general crisis impinges both upon the conditions within which we work and upon our subject. Moreover, it remains difficult to separate the conditions and the subject completely. Having benefited from the constraints imposed by traditional requirements, history has suffered from their demise. Opening the curriculum to the free play of student choice was initially taken to be a progressive step. And as long as the relative politicization of the '60s persisted, history did not do too badly, particularly not in the areas of the new social history that seemed to echo the concerns of vital social movements. Black history and the history of women did especially well, but labor history also improved its position. And many of the more traditional historians had their own doubts about mainstream political history and the surveys.

With the perspective of a decade, however, free choice in course selection has not done all that well by history. College administrators can be quick to suggest that declining history enrollments should be blamed on the failure of history teachers. Presumably, their teaching is not good enough, or their courses are not sexy enough. Hence the smörgasbord. This harsh judgment does not, however, really speak to the problem. We may well have our own self-criticism to undertake, but no amount of soul-searching and renovation will suffice to solve the deeper problem.

The market has intruded into academic life more decisively than the simple free selection of courses reveals. For the selection process itself transpires under serious constraints. The rising cost of even public education and the ominous job market push students towards very early professional or vocational specialization. Pre-med and business majors swamp the campuses. The competition in these areas has become so intense that students feel compelled to devote whatever energy they are willing to devote to any academic matters to their professional or vocational courses. At the same time, they require the highest possible cumulative average. Obviously, the courses they take outside their major must demand no work and promise A's or at least B's.

Teachers of history face the same market conditions as their students do. Salaries, sizes of departments, and perquisites depend on proven usefulness—read: number of student bodies. The conjunction of these two trends places unbearable strains on the teaching of history. To meet the objective conditions of our existence we must make unacceptable concessions in subject matter and intellectual standards. Nor is it simply a question of handing out high grades in the traditional courses. Students must be persuaded to take the courses—i.e., they must be convinced of their entertainment value.

Here, we must pass over such ancillary problems as the apparently declining rate of literacy. But I assume that most teachers have encountered the difficulty of teaching students who cannot or will not read very much or with very great comprehension. And beyond the reading problem lies the writing problem. These are major difficulties that challenge us all. To the extent that they reflect the general reaction against discipline, structure, and authority, they are systematically related to the crisis within our subject. But they can be partially bracketed as technical problems the resolution of which would not necessarily solve the special problems confronting historians.

The place of history within the curriculum cannot be understood independently of the place of history within the culture. As one of the cornerstones of the modern bourgeois conception of a liberal education, history as we know it is intimately tied to the complex of bourgeois values captured in the notions of liberalism and individualism. From the great bourgeois revolutions of the mid-seventeenth and late eighteenth centuries until the very recent past, history has enjoyed a privileged place in the dominant culture. Western, individualist societies embraced one or another variant of the Whig interpretation of history as the official record of their own progress to merited world dominance. To be sure, they identified that progress with the triumph of particular ethnic groups, a particular sex, and a particular class. In addition, they identified it with preferred epistemological and analytic modes, including classical political economy, utilitarianism, and pragmatism. Few today would try to defend their narrow vision—and certainly not I.

But however narrow and self-serving their political, social, and cultural ideals proved in execution, the principles on which they rested potentially promised more than was delivered. And those ideals rested squarely on the twin notions of individual freedom and individual responsibility. That bourgeois practice defined individualism in unacceptably narrow terms challenges the implementation of the ideal, but does not necessarily justify its overthrow. The rising attacks upon the hypocrisy of bourgeois self-interest and authoritarianism have clouded the relationship between the foundations of individual freedom and a particular conception of history.

One fruitful, if simplified, way of understanding history is as collective memory. The historiographical and philosophical debates that rage over the nature of historical understanding, the problem of historical causation, and the production of a historical discourse are important and interesting, but can easily obscure the main point. Within bourgeois, individualist society, history has provided a narrative of origins, development, and ends. As memory, it has recorded the sequence of moments in the past that served as indispensable reference points for identity and action in the present. Never an innocent process, the selection of the relevant moments privileged the class formation and rise to cultural and political dominance of the bourgeoisie itself—presented, to be sure, as the logical unfolding of a natural law, helped along by the virtuous and exemplary actions of outstanding male individuals. With the rise of a mass/corporate society and the emergence of the pressing claims of those excluded from this saga, the special claims of the self-representation of this dominant group were called into question. More ominously, the very conception of history was called into question as well.

Bourgeois history had indeed appropriated collective memory to the exclusive profit of one social type—the purposeful, white, male individual. I need hardly underscore the inherent cultural oppression, not to say outright theft. As collective memory, history must keep faith with all the social groups that enacted our past. But the demand that history be true to its agents—living, struggling human beings—should not be surrendered to the easier and politically suicidal rejection of all history as an authoritarian bourgeois swindle.

Not that a massive rejection of history *per se* occurred in this precise form. Many committed practitioners of engaged social history did reject the conventional accounts as unresponsive to the experience and needs of working people, black people, and women. But they continued to write and teach history. They also became less and less interested in the standard courses, in particular the survey courses. And the falling interest of many of the most vital members of our profession in the basic courses coincided with the abolition of requirements. As political and social involvement gave way to mounting cynicism, even the interest in engaged social history waned.

Both black history and the history of women have, all *caveats* aside, displayed genuine vitality during the past decade. Whatever the criticisms that may be leveled, both have commanded a broad popular appeal. Publishers still shudder and talk about the female mafia. But they accept it, because it sells books. And the block-busting success of *Roots*—followed by *Roots II*—more than testifies to popular response.

But for all their vigor, black history and the history of women have suffered reverses as well. For both have tended to be identified with Black Studies and Women's Studies programs respectively. Or, when offered in regular history departments, they have been compartmentalized. Thus, a department may offer one or two courses in the history of women or in the history of the black experience, but continue to exclude both subjects from their national and political history offerings. This ghettoization harms both the excluded and the excluders.

The process of compartmentalization tends to label courses in black history or the history of women as "ideological." The very engagement with contemporary struggles that helps to account for their vitality is turned against them—as if commitment were *ipso facto* proof of intellectual dishonesty. Because students in such courses are so frequently in search of direct contact with their own past as members of a particular group, slighting the validity of the courses simultaneously slights a living involvement with history. This implicit—or explicit—denigration reinforces the more general notion of a deep cleavage between subjective identity and objective social and political processes. It also creates a climate in which those engaged in the history of women or black history may be tempted to turn more towards myth than history. Because both groups experienced oppression—albeit in different forms and to different degrees—both can be drawn towards explanations of their history that exaggerate either the totality of the oppression or the heroic resistance to oppression. Either myth discourages a genuine understanding of how the oppressed members of any society struggle on a daily basis to assure themselves some living space under unfavorable conditions. The institutional ghettoization of black history or the history of women tends to erode the vital tension between the consciousness and actions of the oppressed and the historical conditions of their oppression.

I have emphasized these dangers with special reference to the history of women or black history, because my sympathies lie with them. But it ought to be obvious that the exclusion of these groups from mainstream history reduces that history to an impoverished shell. And, to give credit where credit is due, on some level the establishment understands as much.

Social history, including the history of women, of blacks, of workers, has not been totally barred from the mainstream of the academy. Its inclusion, however, has in large measure been based on its neutralization by massive infusions of social science. Thus, the history of women appears as the history—most frequently the demographic history—of the family. The oppression and exploitation of working and black people wash out in studies of economic growth or social mobility. Careful case studies, normally in the form of doctoral dissertations, permit machine-readable comparisons of marvelous nuggets of data. And we all know how easy it is to mesmerize a class of sluggish freshmen with a shower of demographic data.

I am being unfair, but with malice aforethought. I do not oppose quantitative history, any more than I oppose theoretical sophistication or the highest possible standards of historical accuracy. High-principled opposition to quantification amounts to reactionary stupidity or simple blindness. Quantification constitutes an invaluable tool—provided it is recognized as no more than a tool and used as such. Thus, I contest only the subsumption of history under the categories of social science, in the same spirit with which I deplore the widening gap between scholarship and teaching, between scholarship and the general culture.

Subsuming history under social science involves succumbing to a kind of technological blackmail. There are moments in cultures—normally when people have nothing of any importance to say—when wisdom is sacrificed to a false conception of intellectual sophistication that rests upon proving yourself yet more arcane than your colleagues. Today, in fields as disparate as economics and literary criticism, we see similar kinds of production of theory on the basis of theory. The game is to construct ever more complex models regardless of whether the models bear any relationship to what they purport to describe or explain.

These tendencies within scholarship undercut the sense of history as process or as change over time. They point in the direction of using history as a data bank designed to illustrate one or another model. In so doing, they not merely minimize the process of historical development, but minimize the particular historical features of various periods. In these respects, as in others, current scholarship often sets itself apart from the teaching of history. And the gap between teaching and scholarship sharply reinforces an artificial professional hierarchy.

Much in the contemporary academic scene contributes to the hierarchy within our profession. Even the relatively wealthy research universities are bringing cost-effectiveness analyses to bear on teachers of history. As a general rule, the number of teaching hours is rising, the number of books and serials in the libraries is declining, salaries are crumbling under inflation. Research money is ever more dependent upon the federal government and the large foundations, and university-paid leaves are ever more rare. But life in these institutions is a picnic compared to what prevails in smaller schools and community colleges. And the initial advantages and disadvantages are self-reinforcing. So that the person teaching in the less wealthy school teaches more hours, deals with less well-prepared students, has a poorer library, faces no prospect of paid leave, and rarely if ever has the time or means to design the kind of research project that might receive outside funding. We may expect that a continually shrinking professional elite will obtain a growing proportion of available research funds, while an expanding army of social custodians—by ironic courtesy known as teachers—entertain, to the best of their ability, unwilling adolescents.

The economic and social conditions which favor such a development require an appropriate opposition. But historians, even within their uncomfortable contours in an inclusive profession, can do more than they have done so far to oppose the forces that threaten to rend the profession. It may be inevitable that, whether by inclination, opportunity, or talent, some do more teaching and some do more research. It is by no means inevitable that teaching and research point in radically different directions. The best defense against that internal fragmentation must lie in the defense of history itself. The divorce between subjective experience and the objectification of social process extends well beyond our discipline. But our discipline may constitute the most important potential bulwark against that collective schizophrenia.

Consider the basic survey courses. The design of the surveys dates from a period in which a nodding acquaintance with the contours of American history and the history of Western Civilization was taken to be an essential accouterment of enlightened citizenship—which in those days normally meant being a gentleman. Constructed around a political narrative—commonly presented as a "rise"—the surveys constituted a bridge between undergraduate education and the general culture. Their preferred outline of progress served as a general context for adult reading, political judgments, and social views. They offered a core identity: the basis of class responsibility for the college-educated, the basis of national loyalty in their popular or public-school variants. Today, the crisis of authority—i.e., of falling confidence in the "rise"—and the findings of new research, especially in social history, have challenged their plausibility. Moreover, the overdue responsibility to deal seriously with the twentieth century demands a rethinking of the internal structure of the entire survey course.

Our first order of business must be to reappropriate the surveys. From the conventional surveys we must take the preoccupation with narrative—with a chronological sequence that addresses change over time and attempts to grapple with the reasons for change. In so doing, we must retain some notion of political process—i.e., pay scrupulous attention to the relations of subordination and superordination that obtain in any society, even as we take account of the role of intentionality, of individual human volition. But, retaining so much, we must forcefully reject all presuppositions about the preordained or moral order embodied in the historical record. More important, we must forgo the sanctimonious complacency that ascribes the fundamental human attributes of desire, will, courage, vision, or a conception of justice to one particular group simply because it won.

I am arguing for the overdue incorporation within the narrative itself of the voices of those who did not win. Dominant white males cannot be understood, historically, independent of those whom they have dominated. The historical legacy of oppression and relegation to silence more than justifies the discrete importance of Black Studies and Women's Studies. The needs of those groups for private investigations of their history, status, and prospects command respect. But the persistence of those private inquiries in no way exonerates "mainstream" history from its own responsibility for coming to terms with the opposition to white male hegemony or from assessing the price that oppression exacted from the justice that the oppressor purported to implement.

The integration of the experience of women, blacks, workers, and other minority and excluded groups into the received historical narrative cannot proceed without effort. It cannot merely be a case of tacking on examples. Integration in any meaningful sense entails integration into the process of explanation—into the structure of the narrative itself. Given the tendency of students to read less rather than more, not to mention their tendency to arrive at college less rather than better prepared, the inclusion of new material and new perspectives will force the exclusion of some standard items and the rethinking of others. We may be led to think more of social groups and classes as historical agents and actors and less in terms of the careers of individual leaders.

We shall assuredly have to explore the silences of the older narratives. Where we have accepted the classical and neo-classical models as adequate to explaining economic processes, we shall have to consider productive and reproductive labor which never passed directly through the market nexus and never received a price. Where we have accepted the pronounced intentions of an ideology or a set of dominant cultural representations, we shall have to explore the tensions they defended against. The myth of black docility, like that of black sexual potency, must take their place as features of the real planter hidden behind the cavalier. The myth of female inferiority, like that of innate submissiveness, must be understood as an integral part of the myth of male self-reliance and striving for achievement. And these examples barely scratch the surface. But only in coming to terms with such questions can we hope to write a history appropriate to our epoch.

And I do believe it essential that we write and teach such a history. Certainly, jettisoning the alienating social science model in favor of an unmediated subjective mode will not do. We already have large doses of the history of sexuality, of love, and of other forms of private experience. These topics have the virtue of speaking directly to the personal concerns of our students and whatever readers we retain in the broader culture. But like the social science model, to which they provide the antidote and complement, they ultimately sacrifice the distinctive character of history itself. For without a carefully drawn context, personal experience paradoxically loses its content. Across the ages, all loves become interchangeable. Eternal human nature has its place in philosophy and literature, but to evoke it in lieu of historical process is to reduce historical events to epiphenomena unworthy of serious consideration. In such a perspective the special experiences of blacks and women become merely accidental instances of the general case of oppression—hardly what those groups seek in their attempt to understand their own history. To the contrary, they seek a viable identity that will help to equip them for present struggles. To the extent that their enterprise may occasionally lean towards myth-making, it does so only through the failure to take adequate account of the intentions and possibilities of their oppressors.

History is ultimately a form of self-consciousness: an informed understanding of self in relation to past and present experience, which can only be understood in relation to each other. And any self—the myth of individualism notwithstanding—is a social being, a product of relations with others. Losing the external reference points provided by other independent and willful selves, we collapse into a narcissism from which no purposeful action is possible. Collectively, if we lose the reference points provided by a structured history, we lose the possibility for purposeful action. Such liberation from the past and from the constraints of knowing deprives us of our freedom.

There is a powerful tendency at work in our society that encourages just such oblivion. Our enlightened self-interest should also prompt us to collective action and mutual support. If we accept the divorce of teaching and scholarship, even the relatively privileged among us will one day wake up to find our position irreparably eroded. We may survive personally, but at the price of a higher and deeply debilitating dependency. Without the integrity of our discipline, we will live on sufferance and find ourselves jumping higher and higher at the crack of the whip. Perhaps the defense of our discipline is merely a special case of the defense of academic freedom in general—the defense of some critical distance from the present operations of society. But I tend to think that it is something more. For the defense of history is the defense of a unique critical distance—that self-conscious and questioning relationship to our own past that provides the basis for any meaningful freedom.

Note

1. "The Political Crisis of Social History" appeared in the *Journal of Social History* in Winter 1976. Our next article on the subject, "Social History: Radical Sensibility, Conservative Bias," will appear in *The Insurgent Sociologist*. [Editor's Note: There is no record of this article, or any other authored or coauthored by Fox-Genovese, appearing in the *Insurgent Sociologist* after this date. There also is no record of an article with this title appearing in print elsewhere.]

Seven

Gender, Class, and Power
Some Theoretical Considerations

Gender, class, and power are three abstract nouns that refer to social relations, but whereas gender and class refer to socially specific sets of relations, power—the ability to impose one's will—refers to an ingredient in all such sets. Power can vary from hegemony, perceived as legitimate, to violence or the threat of violence. Class is the relation to the means of production, especially the right of direct access to the fruits of production. Gender has been used to mean the social form of biological sexuality, but is best understood as the relations between men and women. The three together constitute the fundamental social, economic, cultural, and political relations that determine any social system.

Power, the firstborn of historical and social analysis, has long figured as an object of celebration or castigation. Too frequently it has been presented as *sui generis*, as imposed on society and susceptible to analysis independent of social relations as a whole. Marx introduced class as a systematic category and argued that class relations determine the decisive relations of power in society. Recently, feminist politics and scholarship have challenged the primacy of class as an explanation for or even the most prevalent manifestation of power, understood as the domination of the many by the few. Men's domination of women, it is argued, is more ancient and remains more pervasive than class domination. This claim mocks the commonsensical evidence that some women have profited marvelously from class position, even if not as marvelously as the men of their class. Similarly, exclusive attention

"Gender, Class, and Power: Some Theoretical Considerations." *History Teacher* 15 (February 1982): 255–76. Copyright 1982 by the Society for History Education. All rights reserved. Used by permission of the Society for History Education.

to class mocks the evidence of all women's domination by the men of their own class and others. This domination of even the most privileged women has left a crippling legacy. Little is gained by pressing the primary claims of either class or gender, although either may be more important in a given instance, and, ultimately, both must be evaluated in relation to ethnicity or race. The great contribution of the new feminist scholarship has been to insist that gender is social, not biological, and to separate it from what we take to be our instinctive knowledge of sex. The next step is to insist that gender is not merely social, but a social relation that interacts in every conceivable way with class relations.

For most people, it is difficult to separate the sense of one's person or of one's humanity from one's sexuality, broadly construed. Sexuality figures prominently in art and other forms of symbolization. Even when specific forms of culture do not make explicit sexual references, they frequently draw upon an underlying concept of sexuality to encourage identification with or acceptance of their non-sexual messages. Yet no human culture or society rests upon the direct experience or expression of sexuality in the sense of innate biological characteristics. Cultures and societies transform biology into gender. It could, in fact, be argued that the primary responsibility of any society or culture is to perform this transformation in such a way that infants naturally develop as integral members of the community into which they have been born. Cultures and societies must, therefore, simultaneously transform instincts into drives, sexuality into gender, and deny the act of transformation so that members of the community experience their gender as if it were their biology. In short, the social identities of individuals must appear to them as their natural identities. This process of mediation between biology and society may vary considerably from group to group and, especially, may rest upon exhibitionist or inhibitionist attitudes towards sexuality.

At least since Freud called attention to the sexual power struggle that underlay the bourgeois civilization of his day, it has become commonplace to describe bourgeois civilization as sexually repressive. Michel Foucault, in a wondrously provocative if wrong-headed essay, has recently challenged this received wisdom that "repression has indeed been the fundamental link between power, and knowledge, and sexuality since the classical age. . . ."[1] His critical point is stunningly obvious once stated, although it reverses most of what had previously been taken for granted: Bourgeois society did not repress sexual awareness; it brought sexuality to the center of social consciousness. In other words, Foucault claims that the very preoccupation with the repression of sexuality disguised the compulsive elaboration of a dense and variegated sexual discourse. By noisy and repeated denials, bourgeois society managed to spend a lot of time talking about sex. Foucault's insight is keen: not approval or disapproval is at issue, but the amount of time and energy devoted to a subject. But Foucault presses further. The foregrounding of the sexual discourse, in his view, accompanied a radical reformulation of the concept of power, which moved from a model based on law to one based on strategy. And this reformulation gradually influenced relations of power themselves, "which for a long time had found expression in war . . . in the order of political power."[2]

The History of Sexuality, as a whole, constitutes a running argument with—the polite formulation for attack on—Freud. Foucault's thesis rests upon an explicit repudiation of the psychoanalytic view of sexuality as "a stubborn drive, by nature alien and of necessity disobedient. . . ." Sexuality, according to Foucault, "is not the most intractable element in power relations, but rather one of those endowed with greatest instrumentality. . . ."[3] He thus portrays sexuality as an unusually plastic or pliant mediator of power relations, especially in the modern period during which its older custodians, such as families and their systems of alliance, crumble before the growing power of the states. Foucault's apparently unorthodox view of sexuality as plastic, rather than intractable, provides an important contribution to historians who are more comfortable with social forms than biological structures. But here, as elsewhere in his work, he falls short of realizing that contribution because he restricts his attention primarily to the epistemology or discourse of sexuality. Although worthy, Foucault's project does not illuminate the complex relations between sexuality and power that permeate all relations between men and women. For, to link sexuality to the various ways in which established power is wielded, we must also look at the way in which gender wields power and how it acquired its dominance. In other words, it is all very well to look at the power of say, the state, and at the ways in which it manipulates sexuality. But it is not very helpful to leave out the different relations of males and females to power, or the different ways in which male and female sexuality are manipulated. In fact, it is rather like presenting a statistical view of marriage based on the mean of undifferentiated male and female experience. For example, on the average, men married at 28, women at 20, therefore the average age at marriage was 24. And the problems are compounded when power and sexuality are not considered with reference to class differences.

Foucault contributes in fresh and important ways to the rising criticism of the failures of contemporary capitalist society. He finds the power of the state the more alarming for its growing reliance on veiled manipulation and its growing evasion of forthright politics. Yet more significantly, perhaps, he takes sharp issue with the various schools, especially the Reichian, that look to personal, sexual liberation as the glorious future of the peoples. In short, he correctly argues that sexual liberation has no necessary relation to politics, and may even facilitate new and sinister forms of domination. Foucault has long been engaged in developing a new language and method of social analysis that will avoid the rigidities of bourgeois social science and Marxism alike. He has chosen to address primarily epistemological problems. His reflections on power thus question our ability to recognize the true nature and sources of our oppression. He is not alone in regretting what he takes to be a more honest and, ultimately, less oppressive precapitalist world. His arguments about the forms of contemporary power and the misperceptions that inform contemporary resistance are acute. Nonetheless, even in his own framework, his unwillingness to consider seriously the class and gender relations that comprise both old and new forms of power compromises his analysis of power as a whole. The undermining of hierarchical and familial forms of power has surely benefitted many, especially women and working people. Even if they too now confront the dangers of rampant manipulative power, they have little to regret in the older, more honest forms of domination that cast them as natural subordinates.

Foucault primarily wishes to underscore an omnipresent attention to sexuality. He cogently argues that repression does not adequately capture the complex attitudes of bourgeois society toward sexuality. He highlights a series of important questions and forces us to look at familiar assumptions in a fresh perspective. But by not differentiating between genders and classes, he remains silent about the dynamics of power as distinct from its manifestation.

Foucault arbitrarily equates sexuality as stubborn biology to sexuality as the most intractable element in power relations. This equation permits him to dispose unilaterally of innate, or presocial sexuality. For, if he can demonstrate, or merely argue attractively, that sexuality is plastic rather than intractable in power relations he can then assert, with apparent logic, that sexuality is not stubborn biology. In short Freud was wrong. There is no such thing as presocial sexuality. But there is a large practical and theoretical gap between sexuality as innate biology and sexuality as resistance to oppression or power. Gender provides the link between these two very different concepts of sexuality. The sexuality that figures in resistance to or manipulation by power has long since been organized as gender. But the important social component that informs all gender cannot, *ipso facto*, prove that gender itself is not anchored in the body. To the contrary, it is more than likely that the very force of biology accounts for the deep roots of gender identity in individual consciousness and, hence, for the vulnerability of the individual, to the domination of the powerful. For the gender identity and expectations into which a male or female child is reared are themselves systemically linked to the prevailing relations of power. And since gender is presumably so closely tied to the body and to the deepest human identity, violating the relations of power can easily be interpreted as violating the relations of a person.[4]

Sexuality is an individual and essentially biological experience, of which gender is the social organization and representation. Gender provides the epistemology, or language, through which members of society name and experience their sexuality. In this respect, as Gayle Rubin among others has insisted, gender is essentially a social construct. It builds upon the primary experience of sexuality, but cannot be equated with its simple unfolding. Gender, unlike sexuality, is not individual, however personally individuals may interpret it. Nor do social groups simply construct gender in the abstract: They inherit, elaborate, and adapt gender systems.[5]

The concept of gender, like that of its social construction, calls attention to the role of social groups in transforming sexuality into prevailing views of male and female. The concept of gender thus calls into question Foucault's implicit identification of sexuality with social males and females. But even the concept of gender, *per se,* does not adequately emphasize gender as a system of social relations nor the interdependence of genders in all societies and cultures. The gender system as a whole, rather than isolated gender roles or the degree of repression, contributes most directly to an understanding of the relations of power in a society. In this respect, Foucault's insistence on repression, in isolation from gender systems, reveals little about the dynamics of power. For societies can promote general or selective repression: the repression of male and female sexuality or both or neither. And the repression can be associated with the denial or the display of power. In short, the presence or absence of repression may indicate something about the quality of a culture, but it does not necessarily indicate anything about the social and gender relations that the culture articulates.

In classless societies, as anthropologists have insisted, gender or kinship systems provide the fundamental social classification. This basic classification by gender simultaneously provides the rules that govern reproduction and organize the essential cognition and experience of otherness. It thus pervades notions of power and clemency, explanations of natural phenomena, and articulations of hierarchy. Although such systems take sexual difference as the essential raw material of all social representation and classification, they should not be interpreted as necessary extensions of individual biology. They do not, in other words, simply transform female reproductive powers into a female gender role. Rather, they take two genders, the notion of polarity, as the decisive data and attribute characteristics to the genders as a function of the differentiation of the social universe. Power thus functions as a cause of the representation of the gender system, not merely as a consequence of innate biological difference. It is the existence of difference within a community group that is to be explained, not biological or sexual difference that can be assumed to determine the shape of the gender system.[6]

Gender systems thus codify the sexual division that constitutes the primary social organization. In their purest form, in classless societies, such gender systems frequently constitute the public expression of relations of production and of subordination and superordination, which they subsume unto themselves. In this respect gender constitutes a privileged but by no means an exhaustive discourse. Gender merely affords the most visible and convincing language of classification. Since the assumption of a gender identity is, moreover, so directly linked to the individual's earliest social experience of social participation, the attachment to gender identity and the willingness to interpret other social relations through the prism of gender remains strong.

Gender overdetermines the investment of any individual in what he/she takes to be social order precisely because of the tendency to identify personal identity with the social system into which one was inducted. Gender thus links residual biology to ideology in the most encompassing sense. But the core of this personal identity remains charged with a representation of gender as a system. To assume a female gender identity means to repudiate or renounce a male gender identity. To participate in a gender system—to participate in a society and a culture—as a female means to accept the related but differential participation of males in the same system. The sexual division of labor thus does more than encode the systemic differentiation between genders: it actively contributes to the prevailing relations of power.

Understood in this fashion, the sexual division of labor transcends what one might call the division of labor by sex, namely the specific allocation of tasks by gender in specific social formations. However awkward my terms, the distinction remains important to the relations between gender systems and power relations in complex societies. For, with the emergence of classes and states—if not before—a legally structured and militarily enforced hierarchy allows unequal access to resources and prestige as well as class—and state-based command over the labor of others. In all instances such transformations include shifts in the relations of power and dominance between the genders. But the shifts are far from uniform. Normally class-specific, the shifts in the division of labor by sex can range from the relative "liberation" to the quasi-total seclusion of upper-class women and can result in a wide variety of gender-specific allocation of tasks among lower-class women. The performance of various kinds of (productive) labor may correspond more or less closely and positively or negatively to the exercise of power or the ascription of status within the society and within the specific social class. On a spectrum of social labor from child-bearing and infant care on the one end to warfare on the other, the former group of tasks normally accrues to women and the latter to men. And the rule obtains most strictly in societies in which all men and women participate directly in the labor ascribed to their gender group at the appropriate stage in their respective life cycles.[7] (Purchase or command of substitutes for direct participation in social labor, which is common in class societies, introduces significant complications, although with respect to infant care and warfare substitutes are likely to be drawn from the same gender group.) The variations in the division of labor by sex can only coexist in a cohesive society or polity if the normative representations of the sexual division of labor of the constituent social groups or classes are not violated. In other words, the prevailing sexual division of labor—the explicit articulation of the dominant gender system—must not merely be compatible with group-specific practices, but indeed must mediate and facilitate the relations of power that permit ruling classes, or states, to command the labor of others.

From Sumer to ancient China and India, from the classical world to the feudal monarchies, the consolidation of classes and states has normally favored and strengthened male dominance over women, has normally confirmed women's exclusion from warfare and unequal access to the control of basic resources. Dominant religions and, as they appeared, political ideologies, set forth universal principles of the gender system for the various groups within their sway. But within states or other general forms of organization, the patterns of male dominance could vary significantly between classes and groups. The principles of the dominant gender system could encompass considerable variation in the ways component groups allocated tasks by sex and leave considerable ambiguity in the relations between men of one social class and women of another, or between women of different classes. In Europe and elsewhere, formal political organization long remained heavily dependent upon family and lineage, or what Foucault calls alliance-based systems. The men of different social groups frequently exchanged women among families as a way of solidifying their mutual interdependence. In addition, men of the upper classes could proclaim their right—at least symbolically—to the women of lower classes as a means of underscoring their political and economic power over subordinate men. And women of the upper classes could, at least in principle, command the labor, or the fruits of the labor of lower-class men. But normally, both the exercise of and the subjection to power were ascribed not to individuals, but to the appropriate delegates of families. Thus the purported ritual access of lords to serf or peasant women was taken to occur on the woman's wedding night and was, accordingly, a reminder to her husband in a way that the subsequent practice of trifling with servant girls was not. The oppression and degradation of women is common to both cases, but its place in prevailing class relations differs considerably. In both instances, it binds dominance and subordination into a common ideology through respect for shared assumptions about gender relations. There is no question of the right of the upper-class woman to assume a sexually aggressive role with respect to lower-class men.

However much examples could be multiplied and debated, the gender and class systems intersected. And the patriarchalism that characterized both similarly pervaded the dominant political relations of the state. Thus, for example, property was more a title to a bundle of sovereign rights than it was absolute possession in the modern sense. Rights in the land, however partial, entailed rights to the labor to cultivate it. Labor, or work, under these conditions, was an object of command, rather than a confirmation of individualism. And the gender-specific ascription of tasks was not common to the society as a whole. Under these conditions, the prevailing representation of the sexual division was not specifically anchored to the division of labor by sex.

The force of patriarchalism derived from its successful conflation of gender identity, family position, and the right to rule. It enunciated the legitimacy of gender and generational hierarchy. It would appear to have been a particularly successful model when rule included the unmediated command of labor, as in slave societies or in situations of indentured service, prolonged apprenticeship, or other instances of adult males' extended residence in the households or under the control of other adult males designated as superior. By drawing on the status of father as the title to sovereignty, it meshed gender and political dominance and reinforced the legitimacy of political dominance as natural or organic. But the patriarchal model of sovereignty did not perfectly reflect the complexities of class relations. The dominant metaphor of fatherhood, as legitimation of [the] sovereignty it propounded, constituted a form of symbolic action—a figurative binding of the polity to the immediate experience of individuals through analogy. As the father dominated the members of the family or household, so the monarch dominated his subjects. As the authority of fathers was legitimate, so was that of sovereigns. The force of the analogy depended upon the congruence between patterns of gender identity formation and the dominant representation of patriarchy. If public patriarchy closely mirrored the intimate experience of individuals of various social groups it would appear a natural emanation of their own culture and experience. But a public representation of patriarchy could also privilege features of the practices of different groups and, in turn, influence the ways in which those practices developed.[8]

Throughout the early modern period the inescapability of dependence reinforced the plausibility of the metaphor as a general representation of authority. Those who escaped dependence on their own families of origin normally were forced into dependence on others through one or another form of patronage or clientage. This model of patriarchalism, however, coexisted with class relations that promoted more complex models of interdependence between genders and families. With respect to class, patriarchal sovereignty commonly coexisted with explicitly hierarchical and legally structured class relations. Law, as a forthright social classification, identified individuals as members of defined social classes. Within such legally articulated social hierarchies, families retained tremendous importance. In principle, one belonged to a social class by birth as a member of one's family. Membership in the first estate resulted from vocation, but did not include biological reproduction. For other estates and for the sub-classifications organized largely around membership in the complex urban communities, laws were intended to control appropriate modes of dress, permissible occupations and other attributes of class status. For all these groups, family alliances provided an important element of class cohesiveness, especially among the ruling classes which in Europe tended to favor the maximum endogamy tolerated by church and state.

Under these conditions generalized representations of gender roles were seriously constrained. If both Church and patriarchalism favored a concept of male dominance based on masculine superiority, their models of gender relations concerned gender identity in the broadest sense rather than specific attributes of gender role. Thus the common representations of womanhood, as captured in the Virgin Mary, for example, emphasized woman as female of the species—sexuality, reproduction, incomplete man—rather than as social actor. To the extent that women enjoyed public opportunities and status, they did so as delegates of families, hence as members of specific class functions rather than as individuals. In large measure, the same can be said of men. But men were also represented as generic social types: the monarch, the priest, the laborer, the craftsman, or the soldier. Women in fact participated in almost all the functions and occupations conventionally identified as male. Hence, a heated debate has been raging over the purported losses or gains in status by women with the advent of capitalism and industrialization, but the debate has so far missed the intersection of class and gender relations.[9]

Gender systems, however disparate their specific content, constitute the most accessible common denominator of the social and cultural relations of various groups. The function of classes and states, as they developed, was to establish the power of some groups over the political destinies and labor, or its fruits, of others. The patriarchalism that figured so prominently in the formation of Western European states emphasized gender, and seniority within gender, as the legitimation of rule. It encouraged the perception of the state as the mirror of the family and the reverse. In so doing, it attempted to codify a variety of patterns of male dominance in a single authentic ("natural") model. And in the process, it influenced the subsequent development of those patterns of male dominance through forms of inheritance, the necessity of providing labor or paying taxes and other institutions that pressed, at least indirectly, upon subordinate groups. The development of class and state institutions was also hostage to, or influenced by, the variety of prevailing gender systems. By espousing the familial model of authority, patriarchal institutions left much of those gender systems intact, including cultural traditions of male and female space, egalitarian inheritance patterns for male and female children among the peasantry and popular traditions of female strength and malevolence.[10] The patriarchal model invited a minimum degree of identification on the part of all fathers, whatever their class position, but it also permitted an organic differentiation between rulers and ruled: The adult male could, simultaneously, be father at home and "child"— that is, dependent—in the polity. The existence of the family legitimated the privileged position of its head: He was its delegate, its political representative. But, in important respects, even his special prerogatives depended on it and were ultimately subordinate to its interests. He was explicitly the steward, the one who had access to a special role. He did not owe his status to his merits as an individual. The rights he exercised were not individual rights, but special cases of collective rights.

Debates rage over the extent to which this patriarchalism and the feudalism into which it sank its roots penetrated the experience of peasant and servile populations. Alan Macfarlane claims to find individualism at the dawn of English history. But the emergence of class and state formations encouraged hierarchy and relied upon a representation of the father in the family to provide its popular roots. This political strategy contributed as much to the formation of the concept of the family and the generalization of attendant gender identities as it drew from some semipaternal "natural" family. The gender systems proved mutable and important in the formation and transformation of class and state relations.[11]

The primacy of the adult male father in the articulation of political relations and their attendant ideologies did not preclude the existence of other delegates of the family. The very notion of delegation, or representation, the sense of representing the interests of, opened the possibility that a variety of individuals might on given occasions occupy a particular social role. In the English tradition, for example, a woman could succeed to the highest political office in the kingdom, although in France she could not.[12] At lower social levels, it is likely that the concept of delegation merged with common law traditions of partible inheritance to facilitate the succession of women to their husbands' crafts and shops, even to their guild memberships. In addition, the quasi-absence of the idea of work from dominant representations simultaneously reflected the aristocracy's distancing of itself from any work and the extremely variegated patterns of the division of labor by sex among other groups. In principle, work did not afford a source of positive identity or entitlement to privilege for any group of either gender. Participation in sovereignty, the right to command, did, and it was actively identified as male. But the family still took precedence over the male as individual so, failing male delegates, women could and did step into a variety of roles as the delegates of the group. A litmus test here is the frequency with which males from outside the family were adopted in preference to recognizing female heirs. Any thorough analysis would have to take account of the complexities of preferred succession as between nephews and daughters.

The complexities and regional variations themselves testify to the importance of gender systems in shaping concepts of delegation and the predominant definitions of the family. The foundations of patriarchy in legally codified hierarchy and in a strong commitment to the primacy of the family or household could, in regions subject to random waves of high mortality, be more closely identified with the house *per se* than with biological relations.[13] The identification permitted the subordination of qualifications derived from gender to those of group membership. Attitudes towards perpetuating conventional gender systems within groups have remained, but group survival, including the survival of a hierarchical social structure and the hard-won position of specific families, would, at least at the margin, permit women to serve as delegates. This attitude and these strategies largely account for the positions of status occupied by women in precapitalist and pre-industrial societies. As a rule, the evidence of female activity should not be interpreted as evidence of higher status or greater power for women as women or as individuals. Women experienced no golden age before the great bourgeois revolutions or the advent of capitalism or industrialization; neither did women experience improvement in their status with the glorious advent of "modernization."

In precapitalist systems women, in addition to having occasional access to a variety of social roles as delegates, enjoyed a range of powers and status that accrued to them by virtue of their monopoly of, or association with, specific tasks or bodies of knowledge. But the emergence of states had tended to confirm women's unequal access to the control of basic resources and to appropriate or attack many of their customary powers. Whatever the

Gender, Class, and Power 93

variety of custom, the law of the state and the lords favored male heirs. And law and custom concurred in favoring the legal and economic subordination of women to their husbands. A generous share of the paternal inheritance, frequently advanced as a dowery, might permit a girl to marry as well as possible, but it was not intended to set her up on her own with possibly a consort to assist her.

The emergence of capitalism as the dominant mode of production in European and North American society included fundamental if complex and gradual transformations in the relationships among class formations, gender systems, and power. One way to understand individualism, which can be taken as the dominant ideology of capitalism, took shape around the twin poles of the wage and property, linked by the notion of work. Work carries special connotations in capitalist societies. Capitalist cultures have granted the concept of work unusual prestige as a good, practically a moral value in its own right, and as an external manifestation of individual worth. This privileging of work as a positive attribute of the individual roughly accompanied—to borrow loosely from the late Karl Polanyi—the disembedding of the market from social process and the individual from the collectivity. In the process it associated work with the essence of what it is to be an individual and subordinated all the specific activities in which different laborers had engaged to the generic concept. This new generalized notion of work was itself deeply bound to the legitimation of work as property in oneself and, by extension, property in general. Thus the wage and the property could be equated as simply different manifestations of the common attribute of individualism—work.[14]

The emergence of bourgeois individualism as a dominant ideology, like the transformation of the concept of work that was so central to it, coincided with substantive changes in the nature of class relations and the ideological foundations of political authority. In brief, the individual was taken to be the indivisible unit of sovereignty and all legitimate government was taken to emanate from him. The extra-individual, hierarchical organization of classes was swept away first by the great bourgeois revolutions and subsequently by reforms. Class differences were acknowledged in practice, but increasingly denied in principle—especially in the United States—which lacked a genuine aristocratic tradition. Differences in wealth and status were presented more as accidental than as innate and attributed to the failure of individuals to better themselves through work. Obviously this simplistic model distorts the complexities of historical process, but it is faithful enough at the level of generality at which the ideology was promulgated. Capitalist ideology simultaneously raised the sexual division of labor to a governing principle of social order.

The cultural and social trends that encouraged the emergence of work as the foundation for male identity and integrity found echoes in the dawning self-consciousness about women's appropriate gender role. As for men, these early attempts to construct a positive representation of work occurred mainly among the urban middle class and reforming segments of the aristocracy. They were closely tied to changing ideas about family and the household with a new ideology of propertied individualism. They were especially associated with religious and moral questions and with education. The various strands coalesced slowly, but by the end of the eighteenth century they had produced the contours of an ideology of women's proper work that corresponds closely to Linda Kerber's picture of Republican motherhood. The general model integrated the idea of work as a socially necessary contribution and an extension of the individual in a general representation of modest and dutiful womanhood. The referents of such work include solicitous motherhood, orderly domestic economy, tasks for idle hands to keep the devil at bay and education. Some writers even allow for the economic benefit or possible necessity of such work. But by and large, all concur in presenting women's work as the proper organization of the female personality in the service of husband and children.[15]

In fact, during the earliest phases of industrial capitalism women were already working in factories. The early experiments with female factory labor, especially those in France and in the United States, revealed considerable flexibility in such work and the lack of a strong ideological position or an accepted practice with respect to factory employment. Although wage-labor, this early female factory work was not taken to legitimate or provide the economic foundations for female social independence. The experiment with female wage-labor did not alter the dominant representation of the sexual division of labor nor validate a division of labor by sex that would include independent female wage-earners with economic autonomy and an independent identity.[16]

The participation of female labor in early industrialization was most common in societies in which agricultural producers, not yet fully dispossessed, retained some claim on their holdings and therefore still perceived the plot of land as the foundation of the family's resources. Unmarried daughters constituted the most disposable labor force. But with the spread of industrialization and the increasing inability of men to retain a bit of land, the wage gradually came to substitute for the agricultural holding as the basis of the family's resources. Survival for many working class families still required more than the wage of the father alone, but the participation of women and children in wage labor was not officially legitimated. And even where children and young female adults were sent to work, there seems to have been a decided preference to avoid participation of married women in the labor force. Only protracted class struggle and the gradual organization of the working class would produce a genuine family wage adequate to the maintenance not merely of the male worker but of his dependent children and his wife as well, but the ideal preceded the realization.[17]

During the period of early capitalism indentured servitude in various forms gave way to what has been called the "feminization" of domestic service. The combined impact of economic, ideological and political change in Western Europe and the United States discouraged overt servitude for able-bodied men, just as it increasingly discouraged partial rights in the labor of another. Labor, like the land, came increasingly under the aegis of outright ownership, which at least in the early stages meant that slavery could be accepted along with the sale of labor-power, but that partial forms of dependence or control of the life of another free man became ever less acceptable. Similarly, the collapse of the household into the home and the gradual withdrawal of political function and "productive" work from its interstices encouraged the emergence of women as full-time domestic economists and helped to establish the special appropriateness of female servants as their auxiliaries. However complex and protracted, these trends yielded a sexual division of labor that would, by the middle of the nineteenth century, be so firmly ensconced as to look "natural" in the principal capitalist nations.[18]

The new ideology of work, like the new generalized sexual division of labor, reinforced for women precisely that dependency and those notions of personal service they were attempting to repudiate for men. This process, which had firm roots in economic, political and legal institutions, could not be adequately explained by the simple notion that men followed productive work from the home while women remained behind to pick up the pieces. It included a transformation of women's lives as well as those of men. For men, the generalized representation of work was intended to obscure the sharp class lines that characterized the social division of labor and to promote a common identity as a man. For women, the generalized representation of motherhood and housewifery was intended to fulfill a similar function. Capitalism fostered a universalization of the division of labor by sex in such a way as to make it seem a direct extension of innate sexual difference under conditions in which the sexual division of labor was carrying an increasing responsibility for social and moral order in general.

Perhaps this is what Foucault is calling attention to in his insistence on the ubiquity of a sexual discourse in modern society. But Europeans and Americans were obsessed with sexuality in the context of their search for viable class relations and a viable gender system. Smith-Rosenberg has cogently argued that the various reform movements of the Jacksonian period should be interpreted as a manifestation of anxiety with respect to social purity, and indeed social order, threatened by the increased numbers of what Hobbes would have called "masterless" men. She also argues that the forms of behavior celebrated in the Davy Crockett Manuals represented an alternate path of induction into male individualism, appropriate for other circumstances in the same period. It would be possible to place greater emphasis on the class and regional variations in the elaboration of these attitudes and others, but her main point is telling. The anxiety about sexuality betrayed concern with binding individuals to a changing social and symbolic order.[19]

Capitalist class relations and the modern state long cooperated in promoting a universal gender system, based on the identification of gender identity and gender role, or sexual differentiation in general and the gender-specific allocation of tasks in particular. The pervasive sexual discourse to which Foucault has called attention measured the importance attached to the gender system as the custodian of repudiated notions of hierarchy and dependency, and measured the perceived necessity for individuals to internalize universal gender identities that would anchor social order.

Gender, as the primary articulation of differentiation, acquired special importance in capitalist societies. For the general tendency of capitalism was to promote standardization in the production process, rationalism in epistemology and cosmology, and the functional interchangeability of individuals in politics. In other words, those social and ideological relations most explicitly grounded in the dignity and integrity of the individual carried within themselves the potential disavowal of individual difference. The strengthening and generalizing of the forms of male dominance facilitated the long induction of peasant populations and different ethnic groups into the mainstream of industrial capitalism and bourgeois ideology. Labor market segmentation, reinforced by the ideology of domesticity, encouraged the withdrawal of married women from the labor force. Working-class men themselves organized on the basis of excluding women from the most remunerative employment. The interests of bosses and workers converged, whether by agreement or as a result of struggle, to promote the dominance of men over the women of their own group. This solution removed the possible struggle over the same women as yet another cause of discord between men of different classes. The control of women helped to obscure the gulf between classes. The standardization of the gender system mightily strengthened the myth of individual mobility. Class power was not defined to include any rights to the labor or sexuality of the men of lower classes, although relations between the races in the United States present a very painful special case. Even the real power, often brutally exercised, of men over their wives was culturally denied. Marriage was based on love and undertaken by the choice of participants. But gradually capitalism reinforced the economic power of the husband over the wife. The conquest of the male "family wage" finally consolidated the possibility for male survival independent of the family and consigned women to ever greater dependence on the economic power of a man.

The dominant forms of power under capitalism were veiled. Bourgeois individualism originally included an explicit repudiation of upper and lower class violence. Celebrations of male power as the sign of masculinity persisted, especially among military groups and in parts of the United States, but the prevailing current ran towards the denial of power as physical force. Cultural norms and social etiquette favored civility as the governing principle of gender relations. Power became ever more economic, bureaucratic and intellectual. The state, class relations and individual men continued to exercise determining power over the lives of women. But violent manifestations of that power, such as blows, physical abuse and rape, were frowned on in theory, however widespread their practice. If power can be understood as running a gamut from violence to legitimate authority, those who wielded it increasingly preferred authority, depicted as the emanation of individual worth. Science and anthropology contributed much to transforming older, frequently religious, invariably hierarchical views of men and women and the proper relations between the them. But however much they altered the terms in which gender relations were described, they reinforced the commitment to the authority of men over women. Women's unequal access to political life and economic participation provided firm foundations for the ideology of gender difference. The dominant representations of gender relations stressed the naturalness and legitimacy of male authority and minimized the role of coercion. Yet coercion, and frequently its violent manifestation, regularly encouraged women to accept their subordinate status.

Not all women were beaten and raped, although many more may have been than the complacent self-image of bourgeois society would suggest. But even the most self-serving celebrations of the progress of chivalry and civility allowed that the inviolability of women depended upon male protection and female compliance with the prescribed female roles. Violence descended upon women who "asked for it," upon women who lacked male protection, upon women who transgressed on male turf. Male violence against women was accepted as unfortunate perhaps, but nonetheless understandable. And male violence against women who deviated from the accepted path served as a constant, if frequently unspoken, reminder of the risks of deviation. This undercurrent of violence that informed purportedly legitimate male dominance says much about the elements of that legitimacy, even as it helps to explain women's apparent acceptance of male authority.

The obsessive concealment of sexuality like the obsessive discourse about its exhibition are surely related. But they cannot be understood in terms of sexuality alone. Both testify to the centrality of the gender system in the elaboration of the social, economic, and political relations of capitalist society. All societies elaborate gender systems that link intimate experience to collective life, but as a general rule precapitalist class societies spawned a multiplicity of discourses on class and power even as they tolerated the persistence of local variations. Capitalism, with its inherent impulse to generalize and standardize social and economic relations and institutions, placed a disproportionate weight upon the gender system both as custodian of hierarchical and religious values and as agent for forging a viable social and political order.

Notes

1. Michel Foucault, *A History of Sexuality* (New York, 1980), 5. For a feminist critique of Foucault which appeared after this article had been submitted, see Monique Plaza, "Our Damages and Their Compensation—Rape: The 'Will Not to Know' of Michel Foucault," *Feminist Issues*, I, no. 3 (Summer 1981): 25–36.

2. Ibid., 102.

3. Ibid., 103.

4. Ibid., *passim*. See also his, *Les Mots et Les Choses. Une Archeologie des Sciences Humaines* (Paris, 1966).

5. Gayle Rubin, "The Traffic in Women: Notes on the Political Economy of Sex," in Rayna Reiter, ed., *Towards an Anthropology of Women* (New York, 1976).

6. Michelle Rosaldo, "The Use and Abuse of Anthropology: Reflections on Feminism and Cross-cultural Understanding," *Signs* 5, no. 3 (Spring 1980): 389–417, esp. 394. See also, Robin Fox, *Kinship and Marriage* (Baltimore, 1967); Rodney Needham, ed., *Rethinking Kinship and Marriage* (London, 1971); Meyer Fortes, *Kinship and the Social Order* (London, 1969); Jack Goody, *Production and Reproduction* (Cambridge, 1976); Claude Meillassoux, *Maidens, Meal and Money. Capitalism and the Domestic Community* (Cambridge, 1981); Karen Sacks, *Sisters and Wives: The Past and Future of Sexual Equality* (Westport, Conn., 1979).

7. I am using sexual division of labor to designate the prescriptions of the gender system, the normative representations of male and female roles and responsibilities, whereas I am using division of labor by sex to designate the specific allocation of tasks in particular communities: the two need not be isomorphic. Cf. Judith K. Brown, "An Anthropological Perspective on Sex Roles and Subsistence," in Michael S. Teitelbaum, ed., *Sex Differences. Social and Biological Perspectives* (Garden City, N. Y., 1976), 122–37, and her, "A Note on the Division of Labor by Sex," *American Anthropologist* 72 (1970): 1073–78, and "The Subsistence Activities of Women and the Socialization of Children," *Ethos* 1 (1973): 413–23; George Peter Murdock, "Comparative Data on the Division of Labor by Sex," *Social Forces* 15 (1937): 551–53; George P. Murdock and Caterina Provost, "Factors in the Division of Labor by Sex: A Cross-Cultural Analysis," *Ethnology* 12 (1973): 203–25. See also Martin King Whyte, *The Status of Women in Preindustrial Societies* (Princeton, 1978); Peggy Reeves Sanday, *Female Power and Male Dominance: On the Origins of Sexual Inequality* (Cambridge, 1981); Ernestine Friedl, "The Position

of Women: Appearance and Reality," *Anthropological Quarterly* 40 (1967): 97–108; Susan Carol Rogers, "Women's Place: A Critical Review of Anthropological Theory," *Comparative Studies in Society and History* 20, no. 1 (1978): 123–62.

8. Elizabeth Fox-Genovese, "Property and Patriarchy in Classical Bourgeois Political Theory," *Radical History Review* 4, Nos. 2–3 (Spring–Summer 1977): 36–59; Gordon Schochet, *Patriarchalism in Political Thought: The Authoritarian Family and Political Speculation and Attitudes Especially in Seventeenth-Century England* (New York, 1975); Peter Laslett, ed., *Patriarchia and Other Political Works of Sir Robert Filmer* (Oxford, 1949).

9. See, for example, Joan Hoff Wilson, "The Illusion of Change: Women and the American Revolution," in Alfred F. Young, ed., *The American Revolution: Explorations in the History of American Radicalism* (De Kalb, Il., 1976), and the critique by Mary Beth Norton, "American History," *Signs* 5, no. 2 (Winter 1979): 324–37, and her, "'What an Alarming Crisis Is This'": Southern Women and the American Revolution," in Jeffrey J. Crow and Larry Tise, eds., *The Southern Experience in the American Revolution* (Chapel Hill, 1978), 203–34. See also, Marylynn Salmon, "Equality or Submersion? Feme Covert Status in Early Pennsylvania," in Carol Berkin and Mary Beth Norton, eds., *Women of America. A History* (Boston, 1979), 92–113; and her, "'Life, Liberty, and Dower': The Legal Status of Women after the American Revolution," in Carol Berkin and Clara Lovett, eds., *Women, War & Revolution* (New York, 1980), 85–106; Richard T. Vann, "Toward a New Lifestyle: Women in Pre-industrial Capitalism," in Renate Bridenthal and Claudia Koonz, eds., *Becoming Visible: Women in European History* (Boston, 1977), 192–216; Alice Clark, *Working Life of Women in the Seventeenth Century* (London, 1919; repr. 1968); Margaret George, "From 'Goodwife' to 'Mistress': The Transformation of the Female in Bourgeois Culture," *Science and Society* 37 (Summer 1973): 152–77; E. Lousse, *La Société d'ancien régime: organisation et représentation corporatives* I (Louvain, 1952); Gustave Fagniez, *La Femme et la société française dans la premierè moitié du XVIIe siècle* (Paris, 1929); Mervyn James, *Family, Lineage & Civil Society: A Study in the Society, Politics, and Mentality of the Durham Region* (Oxford, 1974); Jean-Louis Flandrin, *Families in Former Times: Kinship, Household and Society*, trans. Richard Southern (Cambridge, 1976); Nicole Castan, "La criminalité familiale dans le ressort du Parlement de Toulouse (1690–1730)," in A. Abbiateci, ed., *Crimes et criminalité en France 17e–18e siècles* (Paris, 1971); Marina Warner, *Alone of All Her Sex: The Myth and Cult of the Virgin Mary* (London, 1976); Geoffrey Ashe, *The Virgin* (London, 1976).

10. Ronald Trumbach, *The Rise of the Egalitarian Family: Aristocratic Kinship and Domestic Relations in Eighteenth-Century England* (New York, 1978); James Traer, *Marriage and the Family in Eighteenth-Century France* (Ithaca, N. Y., 1980), and his, "From Reform to Revolution: The Critical Century in the Development of the French Legal System," *Journal of Modern History* 49, no. 1 (1977): 73–88; Ralph Giesey, "Rules of Inheritance & Strategies of Mobility in Prerevolutionary France," *American Historical Review* 82, no. 2 (1977): 271–89; Janelle Greenburg, "The Legal Status of Women in Early Eighteenth-Century Common Law and Equity," *Studies in Eighteenth-Century Culture* 4 (1975): 171–82; Lawrence Stone, *The Family, Sex and Marriage in England 1500–1800* (New York, 1977); Emmanuel Le Roy Ladurie, "A System of Customary Law: Family Structures and Inheritance Customs in Sixteenth-Century France," in R. Forster & O. Ranum, eds., *Family and Society* (Baltimore, 1976); Jacques Lafon, *Les Époux Bordelais, 1450–1550* (Paris, 1972); Jack Goody, Joan Thirsk, & E. P. Thompson, eds., *Family and Inheritance. Rural Society in Western Europe, 1200–1800* (Cambridge,

1976); Andre Burguière, "De Malthus à Max Weber; le mariage tardif et l'esprit d'entreprise," *Annales E. S. C. 27*, nos. 4–5 (July–October): 1128–38.

11. Alan Macfarlane, *The Origins of English Individualism: The Family, Property and Social Transition* (Oxford, 1978); Eleanor Searle, "Merchet in Medieval England," *Past and Present* 82 (1979): 3–43; Yves Castan, *Honnêteté et relations sociales en languedoc, 1715–1780* (Paris, 1974), esp. 162–251; Roland Mousnier, trans. Brian Pierce, *The Institutions of France Under the Absolute Monarchy: Society and the State* (Chicago, 1979), esp. 48–95.

12. The so-called Salic Law was invented by Medieval French jurists to prevent transmission of the throne through the female line. See Edouard Perroy, trans. W. B. Wells, *The Hundred Years War*, (London, 1959).

13. Nancy Fitch, "The Effects of the Development of Rural Capitalism on the Form of Male Dominance in the Bourbonnais Region of France: Some Analytical Considerations," Paper delivered at the annual meeting of the American Historical Association (Washington, D.C., 1980), and her dissertation in progress, "Paternalism and Power: The Effects of Capitalist Development on the Formulation and Implementation of Class Authority in the Bourbonnais Region of France." See also, Nancy Fitch, "The Demographic and Economic Effects of Seventeenth Century Wars: The Case of the Bourbonnais, France," *Review* 2, no. 2 (Fall 1978): 181–206.

14. Karl Polanyi, *The Great Transformation* (New York, 1944); Ronald Meek, *Studies in the Labor Theory of Value* (London, 1973); J. E. Crowley, *This Sheba, Self: The Conceptualization of Economic Life in Eighteenth-Century America* (Baltimore, 1974); C. B. Macpherson, *The Political Theory of Possessive Individualism from Hobbes to Locke* (Oxford, 1962); E. J. Hundert, "The Making of Homo Faber: John Locke between Ideology and History," *Journal of the History of Ideas* 33 (1973)[: 3–22]; Louis Dumont, *From Mandeville to Marx: The Genesis and Triumph of Economic Ideology* (Chicago, 1977); Daniel T. Rogers, *The Work Ethic in Industrial America 1885–1920* (Chicago, 1974); Edna Lemay, "La Notion du travail à travers la litérature de voyages au XVIIIe siècle," in Roland Mortier & Hervé Hasquin, eds., *Études sur le XVIIIe siècle 3* (Bruxelles, 1976). Cf. John Dunn, *The Political Thought of John Locke* (Cambridge, 1971).

15. Linda K. Kerber, *Women of the Republic: Intellect and Ideology in Revolutionary America* (Chapel Hill, 1980). For early manifestations of this attitude in France, see Carolyn Lougee, *Le Paradis des femmes: Women, Salons, and Social Stratification in Seventeenth-Century France* (Princeton, 1976), esp. 173–208. See also "Ideological Bases of Domestic Economy," in Elizabeth Fox-Genovese and Eugene D. Genovese, *Fruits of Merchant Capital* (New York: Oxford University Press, 1983). The chapter on women in Rogers, *Work Ethic*, does not deal with these questions systematically. See also Barbara Corrado Pope, "Revolution and Retreat: Upper-Class French Women After 1789," in Berkin & Lovett, eds., *Women, War & Revolution*; Mary Wollstonecraft Godwin, *Thoughts on the Education of Daughters* (Clifton, N. J., 1972; 1787); M. G. Jones, *Hannah More* (Cambridge, 1962); Hannah More, *Coelebs in Search of a Wife* (London, 1809); Catherine Hall, "The Early Formation of Victorian Domestic Ideology," in S. Burman, ed., *Fit Work for Women* (New York, 1979); Miriam J. Benkowitz, "Some Observations on Women's Concept of Self in the Eighteenth Century," in Paul Fritz & Richard Morton, eds., *Woman in the 18th Century and Other Essays* (Toronto & Sarasota, 1976); Marilyn Butler, *Jane Austen and the War of Ideas* (Oxford, 1975). For novels that especially embody these notions, see Jane Austen, *Mansfield Park*; Samuel Richardson, *Sir Charles*

Grandison; Maria Edgeworth, *Belinda*; Mme. Gacon Dufour, *De la Nécessité de l'instruction pour les femmes*.

16. Bettina Eileen Berch, *Industrialization and Working Women in the Nineteenth Century: England, France and the United States* (Ann Arbor: University Microfilms, 1976); Yvonne Forado-Cubeno, "Les Ateliers de charité de Paris pendant la révolution française 1789–1791," *La Révolution Française* 86 (1933): 317–42, & 87 (1934): 29–123; Shelby T. McLoy, "Charity Workshops for Women, Paris, 1790–95," *The Social Service Review* 11 (1937): 274–84; Gary B. Nash, "The Failure of Female Factory Labor in Colonial Boston," *Labor History* [20 (Spring 1979): 165–88].

17. Thomas Dublin, *Women at Work* (New York, 1980); James R. Lehning, *The Peasants of Marlhes: Economic Development and Family Organization in Nineteenth Century France* (Chapel Hill, 1980). Cf. Mark Selden, "The Proletariat, Revolutionary Change and the State in China and Japan, 1850–1950," *Fernand Braudel Center Working Papers*, Seminar I (February 1981). See also Louise Tilly and Joan Scott, *Women, Work and Family* (New York, 1977); Léon Abensour, *La Femme et le féminisme avant la Révolution*, repr. (Geneva, 1977), 204–209.

18. Cissie Fairchilds, "Masters and Servants in Eighteenth-Century Toulouse," *Journal of Social History* 12, no. 3 (Spring 1979): 368–93; Richard Cobb, "A View on the Street: Seduction and Pregnancy in Revolutionary Lyon," in his *A Sense of Place* (London, 1975); R. W. Malcolmson, "Infanticide in Eighteenth-Century England," in J. S. Cockburn, ed., *Crime in England* (London, 1976); Theresa McBride, *The Domestic Revolution: The Modernization of Household Service in England and France, 1820–1920* (London, 1976), and her, "The Long Road Home: Women's Work and Industrialization," in Bridenthal & Koonz, eds., *Becoming Visible*; J. Jean Hecht, *The Domestic Servant in Eighteenth-Century England* (London, 1956; repr. 1980); Abel Chatelain, "Migrations et domesticité féminine urbaine en France, XVIIIe siècle," *Revue d'histoire économique et sociale* 17, no. 4 (1969): 506–28; Pierre Guiral & Guy Thullier, *La Vie quotidienne des domestiques en France au XIXe siècle* (Paris, 1978); David Katzman, *Seven Days a Week: Domestic Service in Industrializing America* (New York, 1978).

19. Carroll Smith-Rosenberg, "Sex as Symbol in Victorian Purity: An Ethnological Analysis of Jacksonian America," in John Demos and Sarane Spence Boocock, eds., *Turning Points: Historical and Sociological Essays on the Family* (Chicago, 1978), S212–S247.

Eight

The Fettered Mind

*Time, Place, and the
Literary Imagination of the Old South*

The new historicism in literary studies has, once again, called attention to the rich, if complex and elusive, relations between history and literature. Louis Rubin's *The Edge of the Swamp: A Study in the Literature and Society of the Old South* impressively contributes to our still inadequate understanding of those relations in the Old South. Wisely, Rubin bypasses the more heated theoretical debates over the new historicism, which primarily concern the current state and practice of criticism. Instead, he opens an important and promising line of inquiry.

For historians in particular, this book brings a new dimension to the debates over the nature of antebellum Southern society and culture. Indeed, Rubin seems more interested in the theoretical debates in history than in literature. He devotes almost no attention to the questions of how to read texts, and displays almost no interest in extending the principles of poststructuralist literary criticism to the interpretation of history itself. But he does seriously engage the controversies among historians over the character of Southern slave society, coming down hard on the side of those who see it as essentially of a piece with American society in general. And he does demonstrate that how one understands the nature of that society must influence the ways in which one reads its literature. For this, if no other reason—and other reasons abound—historians have much to learn from his book.

"The Fettered Mind: Time, Place, and the Literary Imagination of the Old South." *Georgia Historical Quarterly* 76 (Winter 1990): 621–51. Copyright 1990 by the Georgia Historical Society. All rights reserved. Used by permission of the Georgia Historical Society.

Antebellum American literary and intellectual history has focused disproportionately on the unfolding of the New England mind. The focus cannot be explained by intellectual quality. Among Southerners, only John C. Calhoun gets an occasional bow. Yet James Henley Thornwell (Presbyterian theologian and ecclesiologist), St. George Tucker and Thomas R. R. Cobb (legal scholars), Alfred Bledsoe (mathematician, theologian, political theorist), Thomas R. Dew (political economist, historian, political theorist), George Tucker (political economist), William Trescot (historian and political theorist), Thomas Ruffin (jurist), Edmund Ruffin (soil scientist) and others deserve to be acknowledged among the leading American minds of their day. That they have fallen into virtual oblivion cannot readily be explained except by ideological bias, for they were men who significantly departed from what we now consider the mainstream of American thought. Almost all defended slavery, not merely as a system of racial subordination but as a superior social system, and they insisted upon the inevitability of hierarchy in civilized life.

The neglect of their literary colleagues poses a special problem. If Nathaniel Beverley Tucker, John Pendleton Kennedy, Augustus Baldwin Longstreet, and William Gilmore Simms have faded from our literary tradition, might it be because of the quality of their writing? No match for Hawthorne and Melville, they may well deserve their fate. And if Edgar Allan Poe has escaped a similar fate, he has also been largely assimilated into the mainstream tradition so that, however ludicrously, his Southernness can be denied or at least minimized.

Why did antebellum Southern literature lag or, in only slightly if significantly different words, why did antebellum Southern writers fail to participate in the American Renaissance? As a Southern-born critic and historian of Southern literature, Louis D. Rubin brings to the problem precisely that "balancing of passionate involvement with notable scholarly rigor" which he admires in others, notably Allen Tate and Lewis P. Simpson (p. 4). And for Rubin, the attempt to understand that failure requires a willingness to accept "the obvious truth that there were crucial factors in the region's social and political life that kept its literary imagination fettered" (p. 5).

In *The Edge of the Swamp*, Rubin attempts to identify the most fettering aspects of antebellum social and political life and to follow their traces in the work of three exemplary Southern writers: William Gilmore Simms, Edgar Allan Poe, and Henry Timrod. In this book, "as always," Rubin insists, "I have written to find out what I thought," by which he means that he has eschewed the temptation to write in the service of some "previously determined conclusion" and has allowed the argument of each chapter to develop as he wrote it (p. 10). Rubin's admirable life's work certainly acquits him of any charge of dogmatism or tunnel vision, but, in a large sense, his claim of agnosticism is called into question by the evidence of his own distinguished career, which embodies a distinct perspective on Southern literature.

Rubin is here returning to the origins of Southern literature in order to shed new light on its trajectory and, indeed, on the Southern mind. The subtitle of his first chapter, "Literature and Society in the Old South," echoing the subtitle of the book, sets the scope of his inquiry. In it, Rubin directly engages the arguments of Lewis P. Simpson, Allen Tate, and Eugene D. Genovese about the character of antebellum Southern society.[1] And, after respectful and thoughtful consideration, he rejects them. In Rubin's view, Simpson, Tate, and Genovese, differences notwithstanding, share a misguided view of the antebellum South as radically different from the rest of the nation.

In wrestling with the arguments of Simpson, Tate, and Genovese, Rubin combines two principal interrelated but nonetheless distinct questions: first, was the antebellum South different; and, second, if so, why? Both questions lead Rubin into a series of contradictions. The discretely rich textual interpretations in this book would strongly support the view that the South, or at least its literature, was, in fact, different. But Rubin is clearly not entirely comfortable with an emphasis on difference. Or rather, if he is willing to attribute difference to Southern literature, he is very edgy about attributing difference to Southern society. Therein lies the heart of the problem. For if Southern writers belonged to a people who were very much like other folks throughout the nation in their fundamentally "middle-class" values, how do we explain their not having matched New England writers in talent and vision? We cannot invoke the West and the frontiers, with their delayed course of development, for the leading writers of the South came precisely from tidewater communities as old as those of New England and were heir to the same trans-Atlantic culture.

Rubin remains suspicious of Simpson's view that the South developed as that rare new thing under the sun, a modern slave society. For Simpson, the antebellum slaveholders, in choosing to base their society on chattel slavery, were also attempting "to establish a lasting hierarchical community" that would enable its men of letters to redeem Western men in general from the thralls of secular materialism and modernism. In Simpson's reading, Southern men of letters differed from their Northeastern counterparts in rejecting the Romantic conception of the alienated artist. They were, so to speak, alienated from the alienation that tormented the writers of trans-Atlantic bourgeois society.

Rubin contrasts Simpson's views, which he considers primarily theological, with those of Eugene D. Genovese, which he considers primarily economic, attributing to Genovese a dialectical opposition between the fundamentally anarchic and exploitative bourgeois society of the North and the fundamentally aristocratic slave society of the South. And he contrasts both with Allen Tate's effort to associate Southern slavery with traditional forms of bondage. But he reproaches all three for sharing the assumption that the Old South featured "a separate and superior class of slaveholders, adhering to a paternalistic code that had little place within it for unrestrained money-grubbing and the naked acquisitiveness of finance capitalism" (p. 29).

No, and again no. The view of the Old South as significantly different, if never entirely divorced, from the rest of the country does not depend upon the existence of an aristocratic slaveholding class—although a slaveholding elite did exist and did, in important ways, influence the cultural values of Southern society. Tellingly, Rubin turns from Tate, Simpson, and Genovese to William Taylor's image of the cavalier as the Southern counterpart to the Northern image of the Yankee.[2] But the various interpretations of Tate, Simpson, and Genovese all depart from Taylor in insisting that Southern culture and values permeated white Southern society, and Rubin might notice that Taylor's *Cavalier and Yankee* contains not a shred of evidence to support its assertions about the nature of Southern society. Their views of Southern society as distinct all emphasize the complex combination of shared assumptions and antagonisms that bound elite and ordinary slaveholders to each other and to the yeomanry.

Rubin allows that he has trouble with the notion that the Old South ever featured a master class that espoused "seigneurial values," disdained the cash nexus, and was "imbued with faith in a 'hierarchical' order based securely and lastingly on the ownership of slave property" (p. 33). Rubin here errs for only Tate and emphatically neither Simpson nor Genovese have ever interpreted Southern slave society and culture as seigneurial. Where, Rubin asks, is the evidence that such a class ever existed? Certainly not in the census. Those facts, he insists, show that throughout the antebellum decades every Southern state manifested a growth in the preponderance of the middle class and a concomitant decline in the significance of large estates; an extension of the franchise to all white males; an elimination in property requirements for voting; and a steady (if admittedly inadequate) increase in expenditure for public education. To crown the absurdity, the Confederate constitution arguably provided for greater popular participation than the federal constitution. According to Rubin, this evidence proves that no master class successfully dominated the South. But to assume that this evidence, which itself may be questioned, proves that the South manifested no distinct culture and values requires the prior assumptions that only a master class could embody them, and that middle class meant the same thing in the slaveholding South as in the nonslaveholding North.[3]

Rubin admits that some Southerners did talk of "a patriarchal ethos and an attitude toward society that was profoundly and qualitatively different from other Southerners or from Americans elsewhere," but dismisses it as, in the main, "only skin-deep in its ideological import" (p. 38). There is, he insists, no need to ascribe the Civil War "to any permanent, irreconcilable social and moral cleavage between North and South" (p. 38). The reality of the antebellum South lay in its being essentially an American community like any other that happened to include a few great planters who had inherited their social position and some others who had recently acquired it, but was mainly composed of citizens of conventional middle-class values, who, like other Americans, were bent upon improving their social and economic position. The Old South "differed from the other American regions principally because it was more abidingly rural in outlook, and because it had in its midst a vast black population, the ownership of which as chattel was accepted both because they could be better controlled and made to work that way and because, since they were black, it was considered no unacceptable abridgement of their humanity for them not to be free" (p. 39).

With this stroke, Rubin simultaneously repudiates the notion that as a slaveholding society the South engendered distinct values and attempts to explain its demonstrable cultural difference from the rest of the country. Racism, a common American failing, replaces slavery as a social system. In defining the South as simply more rural and more racist than the rest of the country, Rubin assimilates it to a general national past in order to argue that the perceived differences merely reflected a slower rate of progress down (or perhaps up) a common path.

Southern men of letters paid the price of this "provincial, ancillary status" in their failure to develop any "intensive imaginative scrutiny of the individual *on the land* as contrasted with the individual as *citizen*" (p. 50). Neither the increasing suppression of any discussion of slavery nor the small size of the intellectual community alone can account for this imaginative failure. The more important cause should be sought in the ideal of the plantation, which, as "the imaginative ideal of the society, the symbol of social and material achievement, *itself involved nature, the life on the land as a central ingredient*" (p. 50).

The American Romantic mind, Rubin argues, found its most important and dynamic theme in the opposition between the freedom of the solitary man in nature and the social imprisonment of man in society. The Southern Romantic mind could not follow that imaginative path, for its vision of life on the land "was inescapably linked *with* human bondage" (p. 51). In effect, Rubin insists, any attempt to explore human freedom on the land led Southern intellectuals back to slavery. And slavery, which blocked the Southern engagement with freedom, more than sufficed "to stifle any kind of sustained dialectic within the literary imagination" (p. 51). Slavery did not, as Simpson suggests, lead Southerners to imagine an alternate social vision based on social hierarchy. Had the South, in fact, "been a reversion to a pre-industrial, medieval-like social order with an assured aristocracy," Rubin proceeds, deceptively slipping from Simpson to Tate, then a classical or neo-classical literary tradition might have served its purposes. But it was not. Hostage to the dominant voice of European and American Romanticism, with which they could not break, Southern writers ended by imagining nature beyond the boundaries of the plantation as a swamp and themselves as standing at its edge.

Rubin's arresting formulation captures an important tension within antebellum Southern letters but forecloses exploration of it. Neither Simpson nor Genovese, in contrast to Tate, is arguing that the antebellum South represented a reversion to a medieval social order, nor a reversion to a medieval world view.[4] Nor if it had would there be any reason to believe that a classical or neo-classical literary tradition would have served its cultural purposes. Southerners did remain very much attached to Dr. Johnson and Alexander Pope and did spawn their own version of the battle over the Ancients and the Moderns. The lingering neo-classical sensibilities of some did not radically differentiate them from many other Americans or western Europeans of their day. The issue is not whether antebellum Southern writers drew upon European and American Romanticism, for they unquestionably did. Borrowing and adapting, they sought to bend words and conventions to fit their own experience and, more important, their own values.[5] They took pride in their association with what they viewed as the finest aspects of European civilization; they took pride in staying abreast of modernity; and they took pride in their own morals and institutions, which they recognized as increasingly in conflict with those of the bourgeois societies.

It is, in Rubin's view, misguided "to approach the views that these men [William Gilmore Simms and James Hammond], and others like them, expressed about the Peculiar Institution principally as ideology, in the sense that any logical and coherent exposition of ideas is what is at issue" (p. 94). Simms, Rubin painstakingly explains, must be understood as quintessentially middle class in his life and career. Only his pursuit of a respected and honored status within the South Carolina slaveholding elite impelled him to a defense of slavery and at that he defended it almost as "an abstract Romantic ideal" (p. 101). Yet Rubin reproaches Simms with his failure in *The Yemassee* and other border novels to depict a hero's self-identification with the forest, his failure to represent the wilderness as a welcome escape from the complexities and hypocrisies of civilized society.[6] Simms saw the plantation as the height of civilization and "like most of his fellow white Southerners of the time he did not see the use of the slave labor that made it possible as importantly marring its perfection" (p. 125).

For Rubin, Simms's "inability to recognize the hideousness of such a blemish and so helping to doom any promise of lasting fulfillment" testified to his complicity in "the common failure of his time and place" (p. 125). But if Simms did not see slavery as a hideous blemish, and if his views indeed derived from his time and place, then why should we not view his defense of slavery as a contribution to a coherent set of ideas, an ideology, an emerging world view?

Rubin credits Simms with a dream of fulfillment "*in* society and history," but refuses to take seriously his vision of society and history. Like other Southern men of letters, including his friend James Hammond, Simms believed that in a modern world, which was being conquered by free labor, slavery alone could guarantee a civilization worthy of the name. He believed, therefore, that hierarchy was a necessary feature of human society. He believed that the pursuit of arts and letters, not to mention the exercise of responsible government, required freedom from manual labor. And he believed that those who would, with or without slavery, inescapably perform that labor were better served by a system that held individual men accountable for their subsistence and protection.

These beliefs were admittedly at odds with the growing commitment to systematic individualism that predominated in the northeast and western Europe, but they were deeply rooted in Western thought and practice, not to mention, as most secular Southern theorists as well as the theologians insisted, in the Bible. Racism notwithstanding, Simms belonged to an intellectual tradition that was defending slavery as a system of social stratification that, in the absence of blacks, would have to be imposed on white labor. Since the tradition ran directly counter to the most dynamic intellectual and literary currents of the day, it may be tempting to dismiss it as a failed and morally flawed version of the current that triumphed. But to do so may miss the point of what Simms was about and, worse, it risks the attribution of his literary weakness to his moral weakness. It is, in short, to assume that he tried but failed to do what Melville or Hawthorne did.

Simms was not trying to do what Melville or Hawthorne were trying to do, although, like them, he was building on the tradition of the romance as developed by Sir Walter Scott and James Fenimore Cooper. Mary Ann Wimsatt, in *The Major Fiction of William Gilmore Simms*, convincingly argues that Simms was not especially interested in realism, but was self-consciously attempting to develop the romance as a genre and was, accordingly, working with conventions and assumptions that were alien to the central developments in fiction in his day.⁷ In the advertisement to *The Yemassee: A Romance of Carolina,* Simms offered his own most coherent statement about the romance:

> Modern romance is the substitute which the people of to-day offer for the ancient epic. Its standards are the same. . . . It invests individuals with an absorbing interest—it hurries them through crowding events in a narrow space of time—it requires the same unities of plan, of purpose, and harmony of parts, and it seeks for its adventures among the wild and wonderful. It does not insist upon what is known, or even what is probable. It grasps at the possible; and, placing a human agent in hitherto untried situations, it exercises its ingenuity in extricating him from them, while describing his feelings and his fortunes in their progress.⁸

Simms, Wimsatt argues, turned to historical and contemporary romance in his fiction about the low country and the Gulf Coast, in which he demonstrated a keen awareness of romance traditions and attempted to convey historical judgments through literary means. His romances endorse his vision of the ideals of a ruling class—the slaveholding class of the colonial and antebellum South—through dramatized conflicts with the forces that threaten them. This conflict, Wimsatt points out, follows the structure of a dialectic, which is resolved by the happy or providential marriage of the hero and heroine, and follows the romance tactic of slanting the dialectic in favor of the side perceived as "right." In these novels, Simms also employs "a framing or an enveloping action that constitutes the public side of the narration and that is grounded in the history of a society and an epoch" (p. 39). This framing action includes an important "time perspective," that of Simms's own day, which permits him to impose "the interpretation of his age upon the events of the past" (p. 39).

According to Wimsatt, a substantial, and largely unacknowledged, accomplishment of Simms's long fiction lay in his blending elements of history and literary tradition so that the cultural traditions of the low country reinforced his use of literary conventions at every turn. Simms used the romance, with its conventionalized plot, to articulate an abstract design that manifested the relation of history to contemporary values. But that very concern with contemporary interpretation also led Simms to modify the romance. Whereas Scott had used the providential marriages to represent the reconciliation of contending social groups, Simms used them to signal the triumph of good social groups over bad. Scott's marriages united erstwhile opponents in the symbolic marriage of the hero and heroine; Simms's marriages, in contrast, signaled the internal strength and future prospects of the victorious group. "The situation in the love story echoes the situation in the framing action where, either actually within a novel or implicitly in its references to history completed, the Southern civilization represented by the lovers has likewise overcome the obstacles confronting it" (pp. 39–40).

Simms may also have followed a similar strategy with individual characters. Rubin believes that in *The Yemassee*, Simms converted his hero, Charles Craven, an English-born royal governor, into Gabriel Harrison, a "middle-class American" and frontier hero, because Simms believed that "what was required to make middle-class American frontiersmen accept someone's right to lead them was not hereditary status but true leadership qualities" (p. 115). Up to a point, the interpretation makes sense, but Rubin presses it too far. For Rubin also argues that the settlers follow Craven/Harrison because "he can perform better than they can in the woods" (p. 115). In truth, Craven/Harrison represents the resolution of a dialectic of skill and nobility that together identify the natural aristocrat, and establish him as the natural leader of men. If, in frontier conditions, no royal warrant or decreed position can substitute for skill, even superior skill cannot alone legitimate him as leader. Simms, like many other Southern men of letters and most Romantics, favored a social system open to talent, but in also believing that superior talent was a sign of natural nobility, he staunchly believed that leadership was for the few, not the many. The ideal has much in common with important currents in Romantic thought in general, but differed in seeing the naturally gifted individual as associated with society rather than opposed to it.

In general, Simms combined the dialectic structure of the romance plot with a close attention to realism in description and cultural content. The South of his fiction abounds with realistic details, ranging from the diversity of social groups to the variations of the South Carolina terrain. And when, in the 1850s, he increasingly turned to comedies of manners and to humor, his realism endowed his critique of the foibles and failings of Southern society with an immediacy that testified to his growing awareness of the internal threats to the Southern garden. Modernity could not be held entirely at bay, nor should it be. But its accelerating incursions directly threatened the precarious balance of the plantation that had been built by a modernity which in turn promised to destroy it. Romance embodied Simms's attempt to contain the symptoms of destruction, which he so clearly recognized.

For Simms, as Rubin insists, the core of Southern civilization did lie in the plantation—in the hierarchical, rural household embedded in nature. And in elaborating his vision of it, Simms contributed to the tradition of the pastoral in Southern romance. But Simms's pastoral plantation vision did not betoken a denial of history or conflict. That harmonious ideal, located within but also unceasingly carved from nature, faced a double threat. In the first instance, it had to be dynamically carved from nature, literally to be conquered from the Yemassee. In the second instance, it had to be defended against the corrosive forces of modernity. The swamp at the edge of which he was perched could stand for either or both threats to the solidity of the ideal, which, like those who cherished it, continually faced the problem of self-reproduction captured in Captain Porgy's failure to marry. The problem was all the more acute for those who, like Simms and his friend Hammond, never denied the claims of progress or, in Simms's word, "doing."[9] Doing had, after all, effected the creation of the civilized plantation in the first place. Doing ushered in the considerable material benefits of modern life. But further doing threatened the stability of the plantation itself.

Rubin's argument that antebellum Southern writers failed to grasp the tension between the individual's freedom in nature and his stifling by urban society rests upon the assumption that Northern and Southern writers shared a common definition of freedom. Yet the pastoral vision of Simms, which had much in common with those of John Pendleton Kennedy, William Caruthers, and John Esten Cooke, whom Rubin does not discuss, did counterpoise the freedom of rural society to the constraints of urban.[10] That vision primarily departed from its Northern variant in viewing rural freedom as social rather than solitary. And, in this respect, it testified to an alternate vision of the possible relations between the individual and society.

The mainstream Romantic imagination envisioned the individual as essentially solitary and isolated, whether in nature or amidst the urban throng. That individual's communion with nature strongly evoked images of an autonomy that severed all binding social ties. Wordsworth's solitude, "I wandered lonely as a cloud," is peopled not by other humans but by a host of golden daffodils, which, upon his return to his study, remains with him in "that inward eye, which is the bliss of solitude." The Southern Romantic tradition, however much indebted to European currents, took a different turn, retaining the aspiration to a pastoral community. The Southern mind saw no contradiction between slavery and that ideal, for it accepted hierarchical interdependence as the condition of freedom.

Rubin argues that Simms's dream "is of fulfillment in society and history" and thus "deprives the antebellum Southern imagination of the dream of natural freedom in the wilderness, the mythic escape from history and society" (p. 126). And he apparently credits the rootedness of Simms's imagination with its literary impoverishment. No doubt, Simms suffered the contradictions that resulted from his simultaneous commitment to the transAtlantic world of Romantic letters, which favored a vision of mythic freedom, and to a Southern society grounded in slavery. But it may be misleading to read his insistent defense of slavery through contemporary eyes as empty rhetoric or, conversely, as testimony to moral impoverishment. Rather, might it not be more illuminating to accept Simms's dream of freedom as grounded in a specific (slave) society and as the product of a specific (American and Southern) history?

Rubin attributes Simms's failure to reach the highest literary rank to his situation as a Southern writer, but denies that Simms sincerely embraced a proslavery ideology that influenced his writing. In his view, Simms fell short of greatness because he was a provincial—in both senses of rural and regional—middle-class writer. But if he differed in no essential respects from his great Northern contemporaries, why not simply attribute his failure to lack of talent? Or, to put it differently, had he lived in Salem would he have written greater novels? The problem arises from Rubin's simultaneous dismissal of the significance of world view for literary craft and insistence upon the influence of society on literary accomplishment. By reducing proslavery thought to middle-class racism, Rubin forecloses a full examination of Simms's intentions. Tellingly, he concludes his discussion of Simms with an evocation of the close of Faulkner's "magnificent novel," *Absalom, Absalom!*, in which "the weeds and thickets of the once-virgin Southern forest reassert their timeless dominion over the fire-gutted ruins of Sutpen's Hundred" (p. 126). But Faulkner, like Rubin, was reading antebellum slavery through the lens of postbellum racism, which indeed constituted a betrayal of the bourgeois ideal of freedom whereas proslavery thought was attempting to develop an alternate vision.

The secular and clerical intellectuals of the Old South were wrestling with many of the same problems as Simms, and confronting many of the same difficulties. Frederick Porcher captured the essence of their dilemma when he wrote, "Our whole fabric of society is based on slave institutions, and yet our conventional language is drawn from scenes totally at variance with those which lie about us."[11] Never indifferent to the intellectual developments of their age, Southern men and women of letters struggled to adapt what they viewed as its indisputable value to their own conception of civilization.

The secular intellectuals, as a group, proved wonderfully successful—up to a point. Assuredly, their commitment to slavery did not hamper the development of their intellectual talent, although it did, sooner or later, impose limits on their willingness to follow the logical development of advanced bourgeois thought. The political economists, notably Thomas Cooper, T. R. Dew, Jacob Cardozo, and especially George Tucker, ranked among the most sophisticated of antebellum economists, but invariably ended in the contradiction between slavery and capitalist development.[12] Similarly, leading jurists and legal scholars such as Thomas Ruffin and Thomas R. R.

Cobb departed from the American mainstream in developing the legal implications of slavery as a social system.[13]

In some respects, the divines, with the brilliant Presbyterian James Henley Thornwell in the lead, had an easier time, if only because they could demonstrate that the Bible sanctioned slavery in particular and social hierarchy in general. In religion, as in secular letters, Southern thought was by the 1850s acquiring a distinct character that combined many aspects of trans-Atlantic bourgeois thought with a defense of slavery as a hierarchical social system that contradicted the central tenets of bourgeois individualism.

In literature, Augusta Jane Evans, whose reputation has suffered even more than that of Simms, probed the implications of those contradictions for women. Her novel, *Beulah,* published in 1859 and immensely popular in time and place, explored individualism's threat to religious faith and social order in the heart and mind of a young woman. Herself immersed in trans-Atlantic bourgeois culture, Evans represented Beulah as wracked by the escalating temptations of social and religious independence. Unlike Simms, she did not dwell on—indeed barely mentioned—slavery as a social system. Yet a commitment to proslavery as an ideology and world view informed and fueled her fierce condemnation of individualism. An exemplary *bildungsroman, Beulah* concludes with Beulah's rejection of the arrogance of Emersonian individualism, her reacceptance of her faith, and her marriage. Evans left her readers no doubt that the evils of individualism threatened the very fabric of Southern society and required the utmost vigilance. Modernity must be embraced only insofar as it did not threaten social and divine order.

Evans combined Simms's concern with time and place with what Rubin calls Edgar Allan Poe's preoccupation with "the inward imagination." There is, Rubin insists, no evidence of Poe's "ever dissenting from the Southern defense of Negro slavery," although it does not figure explicitly in his literary work, which is normally set in distant, frequently urban, places (p. 133). Rubin convincingly defends Poe's identity as a Southern writer, but recognizes it as a problem. Of all the leading writers of his day, Poe seems the most completely urban in sensibility; his people invariably find themselves trapped within cities and buildings; no "escape into nature is ever possible" (p. 137). His protagonists epitomize the deracinated modern man. His work embodies the haunting conviction that the metropolitan masses were here to stay; that "the traditional political, economic, religious, and social forms, restraints, and outlets could never suffice to encompass and regulate their needs" (p. 138); and that no new formulations—"those of science, democracy, leveling, nationalism"—could adequately replace the old (pp. 138–39).

The problem for Rubin, as for others, is that Poe, the least visibly Southern of antebellum Southern writers, is "the single antebellum Southern author whose work has importantly survived its occasion," and made "the sole important contribution of the Old South to the American Renaissance" (p. 146). Rubin, accordingly, devotes much of his chapter on Poe to an ingenious quest for the Southern roots of Poe's imagination. Making much of Poe's personal situation as the orphaned son of actor parents, adopted by a hard-driving, Scottish-born, Richmond tobacco merchant, Rubin stresses his alienation from the social ambitions of his stepfather and the stifling conventions of Richmond. Affecting "a Byronic contempt for mere practicality," Poe led a peripatetic life, mainly in Richmond, New York, Philadelphia, Boston, and Baltimore. He was never able to earn a substantial living from his writings and magazine work and was much given to excessive drinking, from which he died in 1849 at age forty.

Poe, who always, Rubin insists, thought of himself as a Southerner and a Virginian, shared affinities with other Southern writers of his day, notably a preference for lyricism over moralizing in poetry, "a morbid preoccupation with dead female beauty," and a "disapproval of New England transcendentalism as an insight into the nature of reality" (p. 152). Like other Southern writers, he also valued formalism and occasionally inflated rhetoric; like them he refrained from autobiographical self-revelation in print and doubted the perfectibility of man. But he wrote almost nothing about the South—"about living there, or about Southern history and Southern society, or for that matter about any kind of history whatever" (p. 152).

In the end, Rubin finds the Southern roots of Poe's imagination in his personal response to slavery as a sign of blackness and danger. From an ingenious reading of Poe's last tale, "Hop-Frog," Rubin teases out evidence of Poe's resentment of Richmond's philistine indifference to the fate of his mother and her children, intertwined with his attitudes towards slavery. Admitting that Poe's fiction provides little direct evidence of his attitudes towards slavery, Rubin speculates that he must, above all, have associated slavery with fear. "Whatever his thoughts about the rightness or wrongness of the Peculiar Institution, what haunted his imagination were blackness, suffocation, the menace of revolt, the dread of vengeance" (p. 182). It would, nonetheless, be interesting to know what Rubin makes of Jupiter in "The Gold-Bug."

In many respects, Jupiter would not seem out of place in one of Simms's novels. Manumitted by Legrand's family before their financial reverses, Jupiter lives with and takes care of Legrand, and could "be induced, neither by threats nor by promises, to abandon what he considered his right of attendance upon the footsteps of his young 'Massa Will.'" It is, the narrator speculates, more than likely that Legrand's relatives, believing him "to be somewhat unsettled in intellect, had contrived to instill this obstinacy into Jupiter, with a view to the supervision and guardianship of the wanderer."[14] Whatever the reasons for this loyalty, Jupiter has clear notions of his own strengths and limitations. He tells the narrator that he has to keep a very tight eye on Legrand out of fear for his obsession with the gold bug. One day Legrand gives him the slip. "I had a big stick ready cut for to gib him d—d good beating when he did come—but Ise sich a fool dat I hadn't de heart arter all—he look so berry poorly."[15]

The reversal is obvious: Masters whip slaves, not the reverse. But if Jupiter assumes the position of responsibility for Legrand's psychological and physical well-being, as the plot unfolds he increasingly demonstrates his subordinate position with respect to intellect. Jupiter, who represents the good sense of the world in his assessment of Legrand's obsession, does not know his left eye from his right. And when it comes to Legrand that his confusion might account for the failure of the expedition, "he strode up to Jupiter, and seized him by the collar." The ultimate discovery of the gold reveals Legrand's apparent insanity to have been the most unerring rationality and exposes what the narrator calls "Jupiter's stupidity."[16]

This single example proves little except perhaps that Poe was immersed in the Southern paradoxes of hierarchy and dependence, and, on occasion, prepared to use them in his tales. It is not necessary entirely to accept Rubin's psychological explanation for the pervasive current of danger that runs through Poe's tales, to acknowledge its importance nor even to attempt to link it to Poe's Southernness. But even Rubin's customary insightful readings of discrete tales do not substitute for an assessment of the relation between Poe's Southernness and his literary work as a whole. Notwithstanding his discrete Southern literary sensibilities and attitudes, Rubin's Poe remains that puzzling anomaly, an essentially cosmopolitan writer—and the father of the detective story to boot.

If it is difficult to wrap Poe in a neat Southern package, it is possible to identify currents in his work that, however indirectly, derive from the contradictions that plagued all of the leading Southern minds of his day. From one perspective, Poe wrote on the margins of the dominant antebellum Southern discourse. On the surface, nothing could be further from Simms's concern for romance and pastoral than Poe's preoccupation with the irrational and the macabre. Yet taken together, Poe's tales reveal a strange balance between the rational and the irrational. His most compelling interests oscillate between order and disorder, testing the limits of each and, above all, testing the limits of science and the certainty of knowledge. Seen in this perspective, his work embodies one of the most searing cases of the Southern mind's engagement with modernity.

Tales like "The Unparalleled Adventure of One Hans Pfaall," "The Balloon Hoax," and "M.S. Found in a Bottle" move imperceptibly from the most scrupulous concern with scientific accuracy into fantasy, probing the boundaries between the two. The tales on mesmerism do the same. "The Gold-Bug" explores the relation between apparent madness and the most logical sanity, as, in one way or another, do all of the detective stories. In innumerable ways, Poe presses against the limits of rational knowledge, testing its possibilities. In "The Thousand-and-Second Tale," Poe annotates Scheherazade's account of incredible phenomena to show his readers that even the most improbable have been confirmed by science. The king, however, believes none of it until Scheherazade tells him of "a continent of immense extent and prodigious solidity, but which, nevertheless, was supported entirely upon the back of a sky-blue cow that had no fewer than four hundred horns." Whereupon the king responds, "*That, now,* I believe . . . because I have read something of the kind before, in a book." And Poe, with devilish humor, again provides the annotation: "'The earth is upheld by a cow of a blue color, having horns four hundred in number.'—*Sale's Koran.*"[17]

Whatever Poe's religious convictions, or lack thereof, he was mesmerized by the possibilities of scientific explanations for the apparently impossible. Science was stretching the boundaries of human knowledge beyond the wildest flights of imagination and, thereby, blurring the boundaries between fiction and truth. But where did the vast expansion of knowledge leave the human mind? And where did it leave God? Poe began "A Descent into the Maelström" with a quote from Joseph Glanville:

> The ways of God in Nature, as in Providence, are not as *our* ways; nor are the models that we frame in any way commensurate to the vastness, profundity, and unsearchableness of His works, *which have a depth in them greater than the well of Democritus.*[18]

He concluded the tale with the acknowledgment that he did not expect his reader to believe it any more than had the merry fishermen of Lofoden.

Rubin reminds us that Poe, like all authors, projected a storytelling personality. More than others, Poe created "a literary aesthetic *presence*, a performance," so that the author "is more than an artist; he is a mesmerist" (p. 145). But Rubin does not take that artfully constructed, pervasive presence as evidence that Poe is toying with or tricking his readers. To the contrary, he insists that Poe "*is engaged in baring his soul*" (p. 145). And frequently, Rubin believes, that authorial personality, for whom the first person narrator is merely a device for conveying what happens, "seems in danger of giving in to unreason, so irrational and hopeless is the situation he has been imagining" (p. 145).

The situation, Rubin insists, is that of the modern *déraciné*, the urban isolate—as far from freedom in nature as possible. Caught in a world without meaning and connection, Poe's authorial presence presages the modern sense of the absurd. Small wonder, Rubin reflects, that Baudelaire, Mallarmé, and Dostoievski appreciated him. He was writing out of their own condition of anomie and despair. Rubin is at his best in evoking this aspect of Poe's work, although somewhat less successful in explaining it. His biographical and psychological explanations are plausible, but vaguely unsatisfying. No doubt Poe's life abounded with a sense of malaise and rootlessness; no doubt he never felt at home in the world; no doubt he had sufficient experience of the modern metropolis to embrace it as the symbol of his own psychological condition. But his relation to the South in these explanations becomes tenuous indeed.

Poe probably neither felt nor aspired to be sufficiently at home in the Old South to attempt to celebrate it in the manner of Simms. But it is at least permissible to wonder if he ever identified strongly enough with the North or western Europe to write of their dangers as an insider. Rubin himself argues that the Northern Romantics drew from their immediate experience an ideal of mythic freedom that counterbalanced and provided perspective on the engulfing development of industrialization. The difference for Poe may well have been that he, like many other Southerners, viewed the unfolding of Northern and western European individualism and industrialization as of a piece—as the enemy that threatened everything Southerners cherished. From this perspective, Poe can be seen as articulating the very core of the slaveholding world view—its tension-fraught ambivalence about modernity, its genuine horror at the desolate prospects that thorough modernity boded for the human condition.

Rubin clearly does not much admire Poe's poetry, which he barely discusses, asserting that "to sophisticated readers" Poe's verse "with its singsong, overwrought, melodramatic stanzas and its reliance upon lurid, stagy technical effects at the expense of poetic meaning, has been suspect" (p. 134). And admittedly, the poetry has not worn as well as the prose. But it remains enough of a piece with the prose to invite some attention. For one thing, the versification frequently moves beyond the singsong, suggesting something of the quality that is now so much appreciated in Emily Dickinson, notably a covert internal struggle against patterned rhyme and meter. Set against Longfellow's verse, Poe's seems genuinely innovative.

More to the point, Poe's verse occasionally provides an instructive gloss on his tales. "The Conqueror Worm," for example, evokes the theater, which Rubin uses, in his discussion of "Hop-Frog," to link Poe's attitudes toward his mother's death to his fear of slave insurrection. In this instance, the theater is given over to a "play of hopes and fears," and the audience is "An angel throng, bewinged, bedight / In veils, and drowned in tears" (*Tales,* p. 960). The "motley drama," Poe writes, contains "much of Madness, and more of Sin, / And Horror the soul of the plot" (*Tales,* p. 961). Amidst this "mimic rout," the angels witness "A crawling shape intrude!" And the "Mimes in the form of God on high" who have composed the motley drama "become its food."

> Out—out are the lights—out all!
> And, over each quivering form,
> The curtain, a funeral pall,
> Comes down with the rush of a storm,
> And the angels, all pallid and wan,
> Uprising, unveiling, affirm
> That the play is the tragedy "Man,"
> And its hero the Conqueror Worm.[19]

"The Conqueror Worm," like all of Poe's work, permits multiple readings. But, among other possibilities, it suggests that Poe did indeed see the ideal of Man being supplanted by the reality of the worm. Such a reading is easily compatible with the view of innumerable other Southerners that the mindless, faceless individualism of modernity was threatening the essence of humanity in general and of manhood in particular. According to this view, Man would stand for the Southern ideal of manhood and the Conqueror Worm for the industrial hordes. But the reading is also compatible with the view of Southerners like Augusta Evans, who blamed Northern intellectuals for substituting man for God, and argued that man, by deifying himself and forgetting his duty, was bringing the world to ruin. According to this view, Man would stand for the inflated pretensions of bourgeois individualism and the Conqueror Worm for his inevitable chastisement.

The main difference between these two views, neither of which is necessarily correct, much less exhaustive, lies in whether one reads Poe as openly defending the proslavery world view or simply as castigating human presumption. We need not settle for one or the other, for, however much Poe refrained from celebrating Southern values in the manner of Simms, his "imagination of disaster" (p. 154) did not simply take the urban wasteland as given. Buried in his mind, and even in his words, lay the conviction that something had caused it and that there did exist a standard against which it must be measured.

Withal, as Rubin insists, Poe's relation to his region remained oblique. "Like it or not, the genius of a Poe seems to have been required to overcome the barriers that prevented the region's authors from successfully grounding the literary imagination in the meaningful details of community experience" (p. 190). But Rubin also finds much that is worthy of admiration in the work of Henry Timrod, the younger Charleston contemporary of Simms and eventually the poet-laureate of the Confederacy. In Rubin's judgment, the war itself prompted Timrod's best and most enduring poetry. For the war moved Timrod to an explicit identification with the values of his community. It is, Rubin muses, as if identification with Southern political aspirations leads him, "for the first time," to relinquish "the notion of the poet as being outside of and above the concerns of the everyday world" (p. 198), to forsake elevated poetic abstractions in favor of the ordinary language of the community itself.

In a succession of sensitive readings of Timrod's war poetry, Rubin underscores the new concreteness and specificity of that language. The transformation, he argues, first appeared in "Ethnogenesis," initially published, on the occasion of the establishment of the provisional government, in the Charleston *Daily Courier* as an "Ode on Occasion of the Meeting of the Southern Congress" (p. 196).

> Hath not the morning dawned with added light?
> And shall not evening call another star
> Out of the infinite reaches of the night,
> To mark this day in heaven? At last, we are
> A nation among nations; and the world
> Shall soon behold in many a distant port
>   Another flag unfurled!
> Now, come what may, whose favor need we court?
> And, under God, whose thunder need we fear?[20]

The remainder of the poem, Rubin argues, demonstrates that Timrod's newly concrete language especially associates the destiny of the Confederacy with material prosperity. References to cotton as "the snow of Southern summers," as "fleeces warm and soft," reinforce the message that the economic power of cotton will protect the Confederacy from attack. The result, Rubin notes, is "surprisingly materialistic." He acknowledges that Timrod repudiates the view that money is to be worshipped for its own sake, but nonetheless insists that "depiction of the South's virtues, as opposed to those of the North, contains its own kind of capitalistic satisfaction" (p. 197).

For Timrod, the South's virtue rests upon "Faith, justice, reverence, charitable wealth, / And for the poor and humble, laws which give, / Not the mean right to buy the right to live."[21] For Rubin, this means that "it is ethically desirable . . . to provide full employment, a comfortable home, and to possess 'charitable wealth'" (p. 197). Southern ambition is one with which a Rockefeller or a Carnegie would have been perfectly comfortable.

> For, to give labor to the poor,
> The whole sad planet o'er,
> And save from want and crime the humblest door,
> Is one among the many ends for which
> God makes us great and rich![22]

Timrod now has access to "a vocabulary and an idiom that will allow him to document his experience in the language, however intensified, in which as a middle-class American he normally thinks" (p. 198).

Here, I fear, Rubin is indulging in a sleight of hand. Rubin's appreciation of Timrod's new language could not be improved upon; his respect for the quality of the poetry could not be faulted; his sympathy for the man could not be warmer. Yet his interpretation of Timrod's meaning must be questioned. Timrod may well have intended the Confederate South to provide labor for the poor throughout the world. He may well have believed that his new nation's manifest destiny included saving the poor from want and crime. But he also expected that nation to protect the laboring classes from "the mean right to buy the right to live"—in plain English, he was advocating the enslavement of the laboring classes for their own good. And if that aspiration identifies him as just another middle-class American, then it is hard to understand why so many Northern middle-class Americans made such a fuss about slavery.

For Lewis Simpson, "Ethnogenesis" above all testifies to the fissure between the Old South and modern history. Simpson reads Timrod as urging the South, at its moment of destiny, "to make an image of itself and of its meaning in history."[23] There is, in fact, nothing in Rubin's subtle and illuminating readings of Timrod's poetry that could not be assimilated to Simpson's point of view, although it would be impossible to assimilate Rubin's general argument to Simpson's. And in the end, Rubin, in attempting to fit his own discrete interpretations of antebellum Southern literature into a mainstream, middle-class mold, does violence to his own best work.

Southern historians have reason to be grateful that, in *At the Edge of the Swamp,* Rubin turns seriously to history for an explanation for the failure of the literary imagination in the antebellum South. His quest results in a book that is as important for its weaknesses as for its considerable strengths—and even for the strengths of the weaknesses. Throughout his impressive life's work, Rubin has been determined to set limits to how different the South has been and to underscore its fundamental similarities to the middle-class

American mainstream. This determination leads him, in this instance, to reproach most antebellum Southern writers, here represented by Simms, for their inability to participate in the Romantic image of the freedom of man in nature.

To make his case Rubin has to assume that Southerners did not really mean all that nonsense they prattled about slavery. That they were racist, he has no doubt. That they were seriously proslavery, he will not countenance. That being proslavery, they rejected the fundamental premises of the trans-Atlantic Romantic image of freedom he does not consider. And to take their proslavery views seriously would indeed present problems. For the dream of absolute freedom that cast slavery as its unacceptable contradiction could not be assimilated to the view that slavery represented only a special case of the hierarchical relations that constituted the cement and sinews of a viable society.

Perhaps it would be more useful to ponder the failure of most antebellum Southern writers to create the greatest literature—for good literature they surely produced—out of their vision of human freedom as rooted in time and place. Commitment to such a vision does not necessarily dictate the shape of its artistic expression, which can, as Poe demonstrated, take complex, indirect forms. If the idiosyncrasies of individual biography suffice to explain Poe, what becomes of history? Serfdom and autocracy do not seem to have fettered the imaginations of Tolstoy and Dostoievski.

In the end the problem is not so much that the Old South did not produce more "great" writers. Given the size of the slave states' population, the existence of one Poe compares well enough, in quantitative terms, to the existence of one Melville and one Hawthorne in the more numerous and more populous free states. There was, as many from antebellum times to our own have insisted, a problem of adequate material support for a regional literature—reading public, publishing houses, literary community. The more important problem, which directly concerns the entire cultural and intellectual life of the region, remains the failure of Southern writers and intellectuals to fashion artistically compelling representations of their distinct world view.

Notes

1. He especially engages the arguments developed by Lewis P. Simpson, in *The Man of Letters in New England and the South* (Baton Rouge, 1973), *The Brazen Face of History: Studies in the Literary Consciousness in America* (Baton Rouge, 1980), and *The Dispossessed Garden: Pastoral and History in Southern Literature* (Athens, Ga., 1975); by Allen Tate in *Essays of Four Decades* (Chicago, 1968); and by Eugene D. Genovese in *The Political Economy of Slavery* (New York, 1967) and *The World the Slaveholders Made: Two Essays in Interpretation* (New York, 1969).

2. William R. Taylor, *Cavalier and Yankee: The Old South and American National Character* (New York, 1961).

3. See my *Within the Plantation Household: Black and White Women of the Old South* (Chapel Hill, 1988), chapt. 1, for a discussion of the ways in which the social and economic structure of the South differed from that of the North and the dangers of using "middle class" to describe the middling groups of both.

4. See, for example, Eugene D. Genovese, "The Southern Slaveholders' View of the Middle Ages," in B. Rosenthal and P. E. Szarmach, eds., *Medievalism in American Culture* (Albany, N.Y., 1989).

5. For a preliminary discussion of the complexities of Southern Romanticism from a somewhat different perspective than my own, see Michael O'Brien, "The Lineaments of Antebellum Southern Romanticism," in his *Rethinking the South: Essays in Intellectual History* (Baltimore, 1988).

6. See especially Rubin's discussion of Grayson in *Edge of the Swamp*, 124.

7. Mary Ann Wimsatt, *The Major Fiction of William Gilmore Simms: Cultural Traditions and Literary Form* (Baton Rouge, 1989). A student of Rubin, Wimsatt is clearly building upon his work and, indeed, shares much of his sensibility about the Old South. Her fine book, the only modern comprehensive study of Simms's fiction, makes a valuable, fresh contribution in its careful consideration of Simms's literary strategies and deserves careful attention.

8. William Gilmore Simms, *The Yemassee: A Romance of Carolina*, 2 vols. (New York, 1935), 1: vi–vii, cited by Wimsatt, *Major Fiction*, 35.

9. Jan Bakker, *The Pastoral in Antebellum Southern Literature* (Baton Rouge, 1989). Michael Kreyling, *Figures of the Hero in Southern Narrative* (Baton Rouge, 1987), esp. 30–51, offers an illuminating discussion of the special Southern conception of the hero.

10. See, for example, John Pendleton Kennedy, *Swallow Barn or, A Sojourn in the Old Dominion* (Baton Rouge, 1986, c1853); William Alexander Caruthers, *The Kentuckian in New York: or the Adventures of Three Southerners* (Ridgewood, N.J., 1968, c1834); John Esten Cooke, *The Last of the Forresters; or, Humors on the Border: A Story of the Old Virginia Frontier* (New York, 1856). See also Mary Ann Wimsatt, "Antebellum Fiction," in *The History of Southern Literature*, edited by Louis D. Rubin, Jr., et al. (Baton Rouge, 1985), 92–107.

11. Frederick Porcher, "Southern and Northern Civilization Contrasted," *Russell's Magazine* 1 (May 1857): 97–107.

12. Eugene D. Genovese and Elizabeth Fox-Genovese, "Slavery, Economic Development, and the Law: The Dilemma of the Southern Political Economist, 1800–1860," *Washington and Lee Law Review* 41 (Winter 1984): 1–29.

13. Mark Tushnet, *The American Law of Slavery, 1810–1860: Considerations of Humanity and Interest* (Princeton, 1981).

14. Edgar Allan Poe, *Collected Works*, 3 vols., edited by Thomas Ollive Mabbott (Cambridge, Mass., 1978): *Volume 2, Tales and Sketches, 1831–1842*, 807; *Volume 3, Tales and Sketches, 1843–49*.

15. Poe, *Collected Works*, 3: 812.

16. Ibid., 843.

17. Ibid., 1165. The Koran, of course, contains no mention of a blue cow with four hundred horns that holds up the earth. Poe was referring to the translation of the Koran by George Sale, which appeared in 1734. Sale undertook his translation to promote an

The Fettered Mind   123

accurate understanding of Islam among Protestants, whom he believed uniquely qualified to overthrow it. The conversion of "Mohammedans," he insisted, required that the Protestants avoid compulsion and avoid "teaching doctrines against commonsense; the Mohammedans not being such fools (whatever we may think of them) as to be gained with ease." *The Koran: Alcoran of Mohammed; with Explanatory Notes; and Readings from Savary's Version; also Preliminary Discourse by George Sale* (London and New York, 1891), ix. There have been various editions of Sale's Koran. The 1891 edition is the fullest and most elaborate that I have seen. In the 132-page "Preliminary Discourse" and the very extensive notes, Sale discusses pre-Islamic religions in the Middle East and compares Islam to other faiths. I have found no blue cows—although many cattle. In any event, the king, as represented by Poe, would hardly have read the Koran in English translation. The issue, accordingly, concerns the multiple layers of Poe's ironic meaning: What credence should be placed in what is (purportedly) written in books? It is safe to assume that similar ironies run through his footnotes. In fact, Poe may have been putting his readers, notably the sophisticated New York intellectuals, to a test by an invention they ought to have spotted. I am very much indebted to my friend and colleague, Jane McAuliffe, for assistance with and discussion of *Sale's Koran*.

18. Poe, *Collected Works*, 2: 577.

19. Edgar Allan Poe, *The Complete Tales and Poems* (New York, 1975), 961.

20. Henry Timrod, "Ethnogenesis," in *Poems of Henry Timrod* (Boston and New York, 1899), 150.

21. Ibid., 153.

22. Ibid., 154.

23. Simpson, *Brazen Face of History*, 78.

Nine

The Anxiety of History
The Southern Confrontation with Modernity

With virtually each passing year, the South's representation in the humanities becomes more elusive. To be sure, programs in "Southern studies" abound, and some scholars continue to specialize in Southern history or literature. But the South that figures in their pages looks more and more like a regional variant of the rest of the country. Indeed, "regionalism" is increasingly replacing everything else as the principal justification for Southern studies. No doubt the centrality of race relations, the special patterns of labor relations, and the persistence of rural character endow Southern history with distinct features. But more often than not, these features are seen as no different from the peculiarities of any other group in an ever-more-ethnically varied United States. The tendency to view the South as one region among many thus corresponds nicely to a growing interest in "difference" in general. Nothing could be further from my mind than to quarrel with the intrinsic interest of various folk cultures and folkways, not least because they assuredly do enrich our national culture. But the South cannot be understood only as one region among many.

Since the Civil War, the primary difference between the South and the rest of the nation has been its anguished, and occasionally violent, struggle with the consequences of its history. Before the war, Southern distinctiveness was grounded in slavery as a social system. That we all now recognize slavery as abhorrent has understandably tended to discourage historians

"The Anxiety of History: The Southern Confrontation with Modernity." *Southern Cultures*, inaugural issue (1993): 65–82. Copyright 1993 by the Center for the Study of the American South. Used by permission of the University of North Carolina Press. www.uncpress.unc.edu

in particular and students of the humanities in general from linking Southern regional identity to it. There is an almost irresistible tendency to want the true story of the South to have been antislavery, and even secretly "progressive"—simply more rural and more biracial than that of the rest of the country. But in order to understand the distinctiveness of the South, we have to acknowledge that even the present story of the South is grounded in its past defenses of slavery and in resistance to modernity.

The Distinctiveness of Southern Conservativism

The distinctive aspects of the Southern tradition have always been conservative. Modern Southern conservatism stands virtually alone in the spectrum of conservatisms of our time, primarily because of two key tenets: (1) its insistence upon the centrality of personal and local histories in the self-definitions of individuals and communities; and (2) its abiding discomfort with the solvent effects of rampant capitalism and individualism. These two tenets are closely bound together, even intertwined, in Southern conservative thought.

In an age in which the national political triumph of conservatism has been linked above all to the defense of minimal restrictions upon the free play of the market and the proliferation of consumer goods, Southern conservatives have resolutely insisted upon the importance of "remembering who we are."[1] They are proudly and self-consciously heir to what may well be the most sustained critique of the excesses of capitalism that this country has known. But unlike socialists, Southern conservatives have largely avoided grounding their thought in abstract universal truths and international movements. On the contrary, they have resolutely defended the right of specific households, churches, communities, and regions to order their own affairs. From the start, Southern conservatism has preferred confederation to consolidation as a model for national government and has mounted a sustained critique of that systematic individualism, and its attendant claims of universal equality which have especially defined American ideology.[2]

The Southern critique of systematic individualism merits attention, if only because so many Southern conservatives have also passionately defended their own interpretation of individualism.[3] Indeed, from the antebellum period on, it would be hard to find more enthusiastic proponents of the independence of the individual—normally understood to mean the male head of household. But the same men who insisted upon their rights as heads of households and families, who passionately defended their right to carry guns, who vehemently opposed the intrusion of the federal government into the life of their communities, no less forcefully rejected the notion that all members of society had equal claim to the status of individual. They thus rejected the view of individualism as a universal ideology, frequently on the grounds that, by leveling all social differentiation, systematic individualism eroded the boundaries of households and communities, leaving everyone equally prey to the domination of a consolidated, centralized government.

At least since the early nineteenth century, when universal equality became imaginable (however remotely), the dominant tendency in Southern conservative thought has insisted that there were other worthy gods—has insisted, that is, that equality is an unattainable dream that masks the destruction of valuable particularities, undermines the mutual responsibilities of different human beings, and threatens all forms of social cohesion. Even today, when the vision of Dr. Martin Luther King, Jr., has brought equality to the center of Southern consciousness, there remain black and white Southerners who, although committed to equality between the races, recognize inequalities among individuals and cherish the self-determination of families, churches, and communities. Thus M. E. Bradford can insist even in the 1980s that he sees "no contradiction between an organic conception of society, profoundly anti-egalitarian yet still dependent upon popular validation, and a restricted view of the state and federal power."[4]

Antebellum Southern men and women of letters, watching the unfolding of industrial capitalism in the North and in western Europe, developed a searing critique of its degradations. What self-respecting society, they regularly asked, could in good conscience leave working people entirely to their own devices, leave babies to wither from disease and malnutrition, drive women and children to brutal factory labor, leave working men and women to languish in alcoholism and despair, leave old people to perish in want? If these were the consequences of the freedom of labor, then they would have none of it.[5]

Today, the words of the antebellum Southern conservatives ring surprisingly modern. Much of what they dreaded has come to pass, although it has been accompanied by a material prosperity of which they could never have dreamed. But their critique did not consist in a romantic Luddism or a mindless celebration of rural life. It was grounded in a defense of chattel slavery as the necessary foundation for a decent, God-fearing, orderly society. And when slavery was outlawed as an option, Southern conservatives were left without a clear alternative to a social order grounded in free labor. Southern employers turned to tenancy, sharecropping, and a variety of labor controls to thwart the independence of agricultural and industrial workers, but their efforts were always attempts to intervene into the free labor system, never to create an alternative to it. Similarly, white Southerners' moves to racism and segregation were at best weak substitutes for the discredited proslavery ideology, and at worst evidence of massive bad faith.

Southern proslavery ideology rested upon a vision of social inequality within as well as between races, which it accepted as natural. It also included a genuine commitment to a network of rights and responsibilities that bound people of different social stations. Racism and segregation, in contrast, substituted a crude defense of racial privilege for the older notion of social interdependence and responsibility. By tacitly accepting that working people should be left to their own devices, this notion repudiated the corporatist strand in proslavery thought and represented an unacknowledged acceptance of the principles of individualism, which, in the North as in the South, proved conveniently compatible with racism.

The abolition of slavery severed Southern conservative thought from its moorings. It did not destroy Southern conservatives' commitment to an alternate vision of society, but it did deprive that vision of a distinct social foundation. No less portentously, it also risked depriving it of that history on which it claimed to be grounded.

Southern Literature, Modernity, and Modernism

The now commonplace recognition of Southern culture, notably literature, as somehow distinctive was initially fostered by Southern writers themselves and has been endlessly elaborated by their critics. But beyond their acceptance of the mere fact of difference, critics of Southern letters are more likely to disagree than to agree. And their disagreements inevitably lead back to their interpretation of that burden of Southern history which has weighed so heavily on the most gifted twentieth-century Southern writers—the burden that, in its clearest rendition, drove Quentin Compson to his suicide and sent Sutpen's Hundred up in flames.[6]

Lewis P. Simpson, a masterful critic of Southern letters, says that Allen Tate inaugurated "the historical study of the literature of the South by the modern literary intelligence" and explained the flowering of twentieth-century Southern literature by the "peculiarly historical consciousness of the Southern writer."[7] For Tate, that historical consciousness resulted from a struggle between the forces of traditionalism and those of modernism. Tate especially sought to identify Southern traditionalism with the European feudalism from which he claimed it derived; modernism, in contrast, embodied the anomie, rootlessness, and sinister centralized power of unfettered industrialism.[8] Simpson, however, insists that Tate's formulation obscures rather than illuminates the central reality of Southern history and, accordingly, misses the real mainspring of Southern culture.

In Simpson's view, antebellum Southerners never re-created feudalism; they created a modern slave society born of the capitalist market and grounded in the relations of chattel slavery. Simpson's point is that Southern nostalgia for a pastoral harmony could never be realized because in the American South the relations between laborer and lord were those of owner and owned, not of common members in a "great chain of being." Thus, to the extent that Southerners attempted to create a distinct Southern literature that would embody their distinct values, they cut themselves off from the struggle between traditionalism and modernism that was coming to dominate Northern (and western European) literature. "The cost," Simpson insists, "of making the man of letters into the *Southern* man of letters was the loss of contact with the shape and substance of modern literary history: the great drama involving the reaction of traditionalism against modernism that commenced in the early nineteenth century."[9] So, from Simpson's perspective, Tate is rereading the antebellum South through the prism of modernism, not on its own terms.

Ironically, Simpson's argument, in this form, resembles that of Louis D. Rubin, his principal sparring partner in contemporary Southern letters. For Rubin, although flatly rejecting Simpson's insistence upon the centrality of slavery in Southern history and culture, also views Southern literature as severed from the central dynamic of the American Romantic mind, which he sees as the opposition between the solitary man in nature and man in society.[10] Like Simpson, Rubin rejects a view of the South as traditional in the sense of feudal. Very much unlike Simpson, Rubin simply views the South as much like the rest of the nation, but decisively more rural.

Given the sharp differences in interpretation that have divided Professors Simpson and Rubin—all conducted with the utmost traditional Southern good manners—their inadvertent and perhaps unwitting agreement on a central point is, for my purposes, instructive. For they do agree, and agree in regretting, that the South, for whatever reasons, cut itself off from the main life of the American mind. Indeed, it could be argued that their definitions of "the main life of the American mind" are compatible, for both see modern culture as primarily at war with itself, as focused on the identity and purpose of the individual who has been cut adrift from historical, social, and natural moorings. And both see Southern culture as having failed to confront those defining questions of modernity.

Let it be clear from the outset that the South, whether viewed as a slave society or a rural backwater, never rejected modernity outright. As Eugene D. Genovese has recently argued, the Southern intelligentsia fully grasped the promise of progress, especially material progress. Many Southern intellectuals even cautiously nourished the hope of moral progress.[11] But, whatever their enthusiasm for railroads or the improved social position of women or other manifestations of the (admittedly gradual) improvement of the quality of human life and even the human spirit, they remained deeply ambivalent about what we might call the substance of modernity. In this perspective, Simpson's insistence upon the modernity of their conception of slave society is at once breathtakingly accurate and seriously misleading. For, if Southern slave society was born of the capitalist market and hence of the first impulse of economic modernity, it mustered all of its resources to forestall the erosion of its values and institutions by the currents of modernity that were inundating the North and fueling the progress of antislavery. At issue is the meaning of modernity and how, if at all, it may be distinguished from modernism.

Modernity has generally been associated with three main developments: the vast acceleration of material progress that has accompanied industrial capitalism, the triumph of political democracy, and the emergence of "autonomous" individuals. These three attributes of modernity have, historically, been closely intertwined—and closely associated with a general conception of progress. Taken together, they amount to a massive revolution in the conception of the nature and purpose of society, based upon a distinct conception of individualism—what I shall call bourgeois or systematic individualism—that envisions the individual as prior to society. In essential ways, modernism can be understood as the cultural articulation of modernity (although it remains debatable whether the two arose in tandem). For modernism embodies a special form of the triumph of individual subjectivity.

Elements of subjectivity characterized western European and Northern bourgeois literature from the first stirrings of Romanticism on. But during most of the nineteenth century, those elements remained tied to preoccupations first with realism and subsequently with naturalism. Only toward the end of the century was there a sustained revolt against realism, a revolt that triumphed during the early decades of the twentieth century in the self-conscious complexity of form that preeminently characterized literary and artistic modernism.

Southern society and culture had been born of the initial triumph of modernity—notably the world capitalist market and the forces it unleashed—the full consequences of which they strove to forestall. Southern modernism, notably the Southern renaissance, embodied the distinct Southern response to literary modernism and to the new forces of modernity in the cultural and economic surge following World War I. Especially during the decades between the two world wars, Southern literature bore the strong imprint of such characteristic modernist preoccupations as disruption of chronology, complexity of motivation, and multiple perspectives on events and personal relations. According to Daniel Singal, these developments embodied Southern writers' revolt against the lingering Victorianism of their society.[12]

But the legacy of slavery and defeat had ensured that Southern Victorianism was no simple recapitulation of its western European and Northern prototypes. Singal's version of the origins of Southern modernism takes little or no account of the attempt of antebellum Southern writers to create a distinct Southern literature that could rival the literature of the North. They especially sought to develop versions of the pastoral and the romance that would faithfully represent what they took to be the core of their values. For complex reasons, including their ambivalent feelings about bourgeois culture, they never realized their dream. It has, accordingly, been too easy for critics to dismiss antebellum Southern literature as an inferior version of Northern literature, distinguished from its rival only in its tendency to dwell on plantation themes.[13] But if we wish to understand the distinctiveness of the South and of Southern literature, we must take this antebellum literature more seriously than previous critics have, rather than taking the easier course of dismissing it because of its unpleasant philosophical basis in the defense of slavery as a social system.

Antebellum Southern Literature and the Rejection of Individualism

The Victorianism that Singal identifies as the backdrop for Southern modernism emerged only after the Civil War had effectively repressed, or driven underground, antebellum Southern literary culture. Southern Victorianism thus rests upon a kind of collective amnesia, and the postbellum Southern writers who perpetrated it are vulnerable to the charge of having wedded bourgeois realism to nostalgic plantation themes. In this respect, the Civil War indeed defeated what was distinct in the Southern literary imagination, leaving nothing but a sentimentalized attempt to wrap the shreds of plantation fiction around the harsh realities of poverty, racism, and segregation.[14] Southern modernism, epitomized by William Faulkner, thus takes shape as a rejection of the South's repression of its own history.

The slave South never completely severed its ties to the modernity of its day. Antebellum Southern men and women of letters, like their Northern counterparts, were heirs to the great political and cultural revolutions of the eighteenth century—notably the American, French, and Haitian—as they intertwined with the Enlightenment and the emergence of Romanticism.[15] Tremendous differences notwithstanding, those revolutions all embodied a commitment to individualism—to the view that political sovereignty and cognition originated in the individual rather than in God or the collectivity. But whereas Northerners rapidly interpreted the consequences of those revolutions to dictate the abolition of slavery, Southerners insisted that the defense of slavery provided the surest, indeed the only reliable, foundation for a worthy civilization.

For those who condemn the Southern defense of slavery, it is worth noting that, in that time and place, antislavery, not slavery, constituted the radical departure from accepted norms. Throughout world history, countless societies in different parts of the globe had assumed that social stratification and some form of unfree labor constituted the norm. Although serfdom had largely disappeared from eighteenth-century France, for example, its vestiges, notably in the form of restrictions upon the mobility of labor and land, persisted. Serfdom was not abolished in central and eastern Europe until the nineteenth century, and then only in spurts, with much of the peasantry left in one or another kind of dependence. And the Africa that Europeans plundered in their quest for human chattel featured its own forms of slavery, which persisted in some regions well into the twentieth century. The vulnerability in the antebellum Southern defense of slavery lay not in the arguments for the ubiquity of unfree labor, but in the uniquely modern cast of the slavery that the South itself practiced.[16]

The proslavery argument that, in its innumerable formulations, permeated antebellum Southern culture betrayed traces of this vulnerability. George Fitzhugh, for example, unflinchingly insisted that the defense of Southern values might require outright repudiation of capitalism (which had permitted the development of the South in the first place) and even of capitalism's attendant lure of material progress. If the South had to be an economic backwater in order to sustain its organic social relations and distinct worldview, so be it.[17] Fitzhugh was not, as so many have argued, an eccentric aberration, although he did pose the problems for Southern thought more starkly than most.

Mrs. Henry Schoolcraft of South Carolina put the matter somewhat differently, but could not have agreed more fully on the basic points. In *The Black Gauntlet,* Schoolcraft insisted that the scriptural and historical cases for slavery were as one. She argued that history demonstrates that slavery "has been the efficient cause of civilization and refinement among nations."[18] For South Carolinians in particular, the "exemption from *manual* labor" afforded by slaves was "at the foundation of a class of elevation and refinement, which could not, under any other system, have been created," and which provided the slaves with the personal care and "moral" instruction from their owners that far exceeded anything provided to Northern "free" workers.[19] The abolitionists should look to "perfecting the morals of those poor, degraded pale-faces, that surround the doors of their own State," who suffered an oppression so intense "that negro slavery [was] far preferable."[20]

Writing in the midst of mounting sectional crisis, Schoolcraft, along with other Southern women writers such as Mary Eastman and Caroline Lee Hentz, was in part responding to the abolitionists, but more than the others, she was frontally challenging the abolitionists' worldview. South Carolinians, she approvingly avowed, were "old fogies" who, unlike the abolitionists, did not believe "that *God* is a progressive being; but that throughout eternity *He* has been the same; perfect in wisdom, perfect in justice, perfect in love to all his creatures." From this perspective, she found it impossible to credit "the new-light doctrine, 'That slavery is a sin.'"[21] Mrs. Stowe's vision of a world in which "all are born equal" was nothing but a millennial fantasy. Even Thomas Jefferson's celebrated words in the Declaration of Independence defied six thousand years of historical experience, not to mention scripture, and had caused nothing but mischief.[22]

For Schoolcraft, as for Fitzhugh, modernity wore a Northern face and came trailing the degradations of free labor and free thought. Augusta Jane Evans, arguably Margaret Fuller's peer among antebellum American women intellectuals, concurred, but presented a more nuanced argument. Evans's novel, *Beulah*, published in New York and a national bestseller, took up the war against modernity from that most hallowed ground—the religious faith of women. With what some have berated as excruciating and exhibitionistic learning, *Beulah* details the crisis of a young woman's faith. Seduced by Edgar Allan Poe into paths that led inexorably to skeptical European philosophy and back to Emerson, Evans's protagonist, Beulah Benton, slips to the brink of atheism. Fear not. She catches herself on the sands of agnosticism and makes her way back to the solid ground of Protestant Christianity, Methodism to be precise. But her travail exposes her to the nadir of doubt and to the height of modernity's presumption that she could ultimately become one with the divinity and that all truth is relative.

For understandable reasons, most antebellum Southern novelists did not, like Evans, attempt to grapple directly with the problems of individual identity and destiny that increasingly shaped the most compelling and dynamic Northern and European fiction. They never flinched from excoriating the social implications of bourgeois individualism, but its subjective dimension caused them problems they generally failed to acknowledge. It was one thing to reject the social chaos attendant upon the emerging free labor system, with its ubiquitous threat of political unrest. It was another to deny the heroes and heroines of Southern literature the introspective complexity that increasingly characterized their Northern and European counterparts. In this, I think, lay the apparent impoverishment of antebellum Southern literature: Southern authors neither developed a distinct alternative to the angst-ridden characters whose stories consisted primarily in the shaping of their own destinies, nor successfully formulated a master plot that could dispense with the drama of portentous individual choices. The great power of bourgeois literature lay in the underlying assumption that individuals in essential ways shaped their own destinies, that the individual's choices did not simply conform, or fail to conform, to a prewritten script, but helped to write a new script about the possibilities of being.

Southern proslavery ideology was grounded in a repudiation of individualism as an adequate foundation for civilized society. In letters, as in so many other aspects of Southern culture, commitment to that ideology coexisted with a commitment to what Southerners saw as best and healthiest in bourgeois culture. Many Southerners seem indeed to have believed that their proslavery ideology was the logical heir to centuries of European culture. In this spirit, they espoused their own version of individualism.

To be sure, Southern notions of individualism remained exceptionally complex, including such diverse elements as a conception of responsible Christian freedom and accountability and a deep distrust of restraints upon the independent action of the white male individual. In large measure because of the continuity of the vocabulary of individualism and freedom, notably in the language of republicanism, it did not immediately become apparent that the individualism that was unfolding in bourgeois societies represented the absolute antithesis of slavery, although the slaves grasped that message rapidly enough.[23] The mounting clash between Northern and Southern cultures in the decades following the revolutionary watershed, can, in this perspective, be recognized as a battle over history. Was slave society or free society the legitimate heir to centuries of Western culture?

The Distinctiveness of Southern Narrative Literature

Numerous critics and historians of Southern literature have perceptively discussed Southern writers' fondness for their own versions of the pastoral and the romance. Identifying an emerging tradition, best exemplified in the works of John Pendleton Kennedy and especially those of William Gilmore Simms, they have called attention to the ways in which Southern authors turned to the slave plantation as the locus of Southern values and elaborated plots that primarily served to reinforce its order.[24] Moving beyond this work, Michael Kreyling has developed an arresting discussion of figures of the hero in Southern narrative, arguing that "he is the linchpin of a powerful social, historical, and psychological myth, which supports the unanalyzed structures of individual and group awareness and behavior."[25] Kreyling especially insists upon the importance of form:

> A cultural group accepts its narrative form, and rejects others, because that form alone embodies the group's nearest image of itself as its most truthful and accessible scripture. The group defines and recreates itself in the repetition of its form, confirms its understanding of the nature of

things in the ritual of retelling, and advances its cause against a host of enemies and aliens in the promulgation of its story.[26]

To see the Southern hero—for example, Captain Porgy of Simms's *Woodcraft*—through the prism of bourgeois realism is to miss the point entirely. Simms was not writing some local color variant on the realistic novel. He was self-consciously attempting to create a distinct narrative genre that would embody "the self-remembering and self-creating drama of the Southern consciousness of literature and history." Unlike Hawthorne's protagonists, who struggle with the legacy of the Puritan American consciousness and "generate the moral allegory," Southern heroes generate the heroic narrative.[27] Or, as Simpson would surely caution, they generate the distinctly modern heroic narrative of modern slave society. In so doing, they do not, however, wrestle with the classic problems of bourgeois fiction as defined by Simpson and Rubin: the struggle between tradition and modernism or the struggle between the solitary individual in nature and the individual in society.

Southern writers, with Simms in the lead, were set upon creating a distinct Southern literature that would represent the values of their region. To the extent that subsequent critics have treated their project with anything more than disdain, they have concluded that the crude attempt to write an ideologically freighted proslavery literature interfered with literary accomplishment. And it is child's play to point to blatant proslavery manifestos in antebellum Southern literature. Porgy's conversations with his servant Tom offer favorite examples: when Porgy says that, obviously, Tom would not want to live without him; and when Tom says that Porgy belongs to him as much as he belongs to Porgy. Other examples abound, notably in such proslavery women's answers to Harriet Beecher Stowe as Caroline Lee Hentz's *The Planter's Northern Bride* and Mary Eastman's *Aunt Phyllis's Cabin*. Here indeed is Southern paternalism as it would be celebrated by postbellum nostalgia for the world that was lost.

A moonlight and magnolias view of slavery does not, however, account for the substance of antebellum Southerners' confrontation with modernity. Indeed, the true moonlight and magnolias narrative emerged after the Civil War and modernity's bloody triumph. The core of the antebellum Southern struggle lay elsewhere, namely in the quest for a narrative that would represent the values of legitimate authority, hierarchy, and particularism, which most proslavery Southern intellectuals saw as the true substance of their distinct culture. It is singularly instructive that a woman—Augusta Jane Evans—produced the most successful rendition of this narrative. As discussed earlier, in *Beulah* Evans attacks the perils of individualism—the besetting temptations of pride and independence. That Beulah spends most of the novel struggling to realize qualities that would have been deemed admirable in a bourgeois male hero, only to repudiate them in the end, has led feminist critics to view the novel as yet another instance of the suppression of female intellect and ambition in a formulaic marriage. This interpretation fails to acknowledge that Beulah's ultimate submission is not to man, but to God, much less that in the end her greatest triumph is over misguided men—the male intellectuals who have led her astray.

Beulah represents the Southern triumph over the seductions of modernity through an acceptance of faith, limits, and ordained social roles. The temptation to see her victory as a defeat arises primarily from the ease with which Evans was able to cast her story in the conventions of domestic fiction. *Beulah* sold widely in the North, where its success was in large measure due to its resemblance to a familiar genre. There is, however, no reason to doubt that, if we allow for variations in male and female roles, Evans intended her larger moral to apply as much to Southern men as to Southern women. Confusion results because no one succeeded in telling the story from a male point of view. Antebellum Southern literature does not offer stories of heroes wracked by anxiety or beset by existential dilemmas. The function of the Southern hero is to embody a special kind of socially grounded individual excellence, the very antithesis of the rootlessness of bourgeois individualism.

Typically, the Southern hero owes his identity to his identification with society, rather than his struggles against it. He embodies in his person what Kreyling calls the figure of the hero: a resolution of conflict and tension, and a realization of history. He belongs to others as much as they belong to him. The triumph of bourgeois individualism has been such that it has colored our deepest perceptions of literature—of exemplary stories. Yet Southern writers like Simms were groping toward an alternate story, the telling of which presupposed an alternate view of the necessary and appropriate relations of the individual to society. The attempt to anchor their ideology and imaginations in slavery fostered a special historical consciousness, although not initially the one that Tate had in mind. In particular, Simms's historical consciousness embodied an insistence upon continuity. His constant return in his novels to the settlement of South Carolina, and especially to the Revolution and its immediate aftermath, signals his determination to claim American history as the direct origin of Southern slave society. *Woodcraft* thus represents the immediately post-Revolutionary period as one of restoration, notably the restoration of plantation households. The heroic struggle for freedom had been waged to defend slavery, not to inaugurate its abolition. Above all, it was waged to ensure the freedom of an ordered society against the depredations of commercial avarice. Capital might be necessary to sustain the life of the slaveholding household—as Simms knew all too well—but the pursuit of capital accumulation for its own sake was another matter entirely. Down that road to modernity lay the dissolution of all social bonds.

In this respect, the antebellum Southern hero converges with the mainstream of proslavery thought, although not on the basis of narrow proslavery rhetoric. Much like Beulah, although noticeably less introspectively, the Southern hero represents the human and social values of a particularistic and hierarchical community, which he is obligated to lead, protect, and defend. His quest, in this respect, consists precisely in a direct confrontation with modernity and with the tortured heroes that the literature of modernism was generating. The resolution of his story requires his triumph over rapacious or fanatical representatives of unbridled individualism. Whatever the predilection of antebellum Southerners for Sir Walter Scott and the trappings of chivalry, serious thinkers harbored few illusions about feudalism or the Middle Ages.[28] But unlike many British Victorians and other nineteenth-century bourgeois intellectuals, they did not see the struggle between modernity and tradition as internal to their own society. Whereas British men and women of letters tended to emphasize the rapid and decisive change attendant upon the triumph of individualism and capitalism within their own society, Southern men and women of letters attributed the most dramatic changes to other societies and tried to forestall their intrusion into their own.[29]

On this matter, antebellum Southern men and women of letters may fairly be charged with sleight-of-hand. For if they correctly referred to slavery as having been ubiquitous in human history, they also knew that their particular form of slavery, embedded as it was in a world capitalist economy, was something new under the sun. They nonetheless legitimated it on the grounds that it embodied the last best chance to preserve the accumulated values of Western civilization. This project helps to account for both the Southern determination to claim the American Revolution as uniquely its own and Simms's commitment to the historical romance. Historical novels helped to legitimate present views and, yet more importantly, to claim a specific interpretation of history. Simms and others intended to demonstrate that historical progress, such as it was, pointed toward their distinct proslavery conservatism, not toward fanatical abolitionism, which they viewed as the logical and disastrous outcome of individualism.

The Distortion and Repression of Southern History

In a deep sense, antebellum Southerners' use of history betrayed symptoms of their ambivalence towards progress and their complex attitudes towards individualism. But, on balance, it reflected their confidence that their society served and protected the best values of Western civilization. It took defeat in the Civil War and the emancipation of the slaves to turn history into a source of anxiety. After the war, countless Southerners turned to history as a consolation for present ills. Their craving for justification and solace led directly to the fantasy of ladies and cavaliers presiding over happy darkies amidst lush foliage and endlessly sunny skies. Their cause had been just, their defeat brutal. And with their defeat had come the destruction of all that was good and bold and gracious in a mindless, faceless, gray world.

Like all fantasies, this one, captured in the flood of lost cause and plantation novels, testified to deep-seated, literally repressed anxieties. The South of Reconstruction and Jim Crow, the South in which the clergy joined and even led the Ku Klux Klan, could not readily confront its tragedy. The economic ruin of families caused deep and sometimes shrilly voiced distress. The military defeat and economic collapse of the region caused anger and shame that easily turned to bitter resentment, normally directed against carpetbaggers, scalawags, and emancipated blacks. But those palpable woes effectively masked the drastic undermining of the Southern conservative ideal of a Christian slaveholding society. For beneath the distress, anger, and shame percolated a new engagement with modernity. The destruction of slavery as a social system with a distinct ideology that openly defended natural inequalities and theoretically countenanced the enslavement of whites as well as of blacks unleashed a "scientific" racism that reduced the conception of social order to individualistic convenience—an advantage of some individuals over others, however much a whole race of individuals might be placed beyond the pale.

The rhetoric and vestiges of Southern conservatism persisted, occasionally coalescing, as with Tate and the Agrarians, in a renewed broadside against capitalism. But the growing tendency to conflate slavery and racism led to a growing determination to divorce Southern conservatism from slavery. Ironically, racism and segregation, however vehemently defended and brutally enforced, introduced a note of bad faith into Southern conservatism that merged with and exacerbated the anxieties born of defeat. To be sure, racism had infected Southern attitudes from the start. Yet slavery had, however paradoxically, contained its most sinister features. The antebellum South included black slaveholders, whose class position effectively overrode their color. The postbellum South precluded such anomalies, drawing an unbridgeable color line along purportedly biological lines. The gradual emergence of a "new" South even permitted the emergence of indigenous Southern protests against the excesses of racism. In this climate, it became ever more difficult to remember, much less to acknowledge, that those "who we have been" were slaveholders. Margaret Mitchell's *Gone with the Wind*, which, along with its considerable virtues, provided a palatable rendition of Thomas Dixon's *The Clansman*, set the seal. Yes, Mitchell admitted, we Southerners are racists—and in this respect no different from any other Americans.[30]

Tate and the Agrarians implicitly rejected Mitchell's urban, New South individualism out of hand. No, they insisted, we are not like other Americans. We are, or we should aspire to be, the last true Europeans, the self-appointed custodians of traditional anticapitalist, anti-urban values. But even Tate's attempt to forge a modern Southern conservatism grounded in the celebration of rural communities was itself infected with the virus of modernity. For Tate's vision embodied precisely what Simpson and Rubin reproach the antebellum Southern literati for lacking, namely concern with the struggle of traditionalism against modernism, with the solitary individual in nature against the individual in society.[31]

Tellingly, Tate's version of the Southern tradition included virtually no slaveholders and assuredly did not emphasize slaveholding as the foundation of the conservatism he sought to resurrect. Rather, he focused on the household of the independent rural yeoman as the embodiment of anticapitalist values. In *The Fathers*, he even suggests that an internally crumbling slaveholding order could be reinvigorated by an infusion of capital.[32] More important than his specific representations, however, is his saturation in the essence of individualism, as manifest in his commitment to modernism in art and literature. Unlike Katharine DuPre Lumpkin, who openly acknowledged her slaveholding legacy because she had committed herself to combating it, Tate ignored that slaveholding legacy in order to create a sense of quasi-timeless conservative virtues. In this respect, he helped to sever conservative thought from its grounding in history.

As for Tate, so for Faulkner and the other Southern modernists, only more so. Faulkner, as has frequently been noted, found the burden of history especially heavy and especially anxiety-producing. Any brief generalization about Faulkner lays itself open to the charge of hopeless superficiality, but, with full recognition of the complexities and necessary qualifications, I shall hazard one: Faulkner, for all his obsession with Southern history, ultimately collapsed it into the personal history of individuals. In his rendition, the Southern past becomes the ghosts that haunt Quentin Compson; access to that past becomes the stories of individuals. In this respect, Faulkner's embrace and brilliant development of modernism in form decisively shaped his attitude toward content. And, in the case of Quentin Compson, the anxiety of that history, its repression and the personal efforts to reclaim it, became the anxiety that kills. "You can't understand it. You would have to have been born there," Quentin tells Shreve, his Harvard roommate in *Absalom, Absalom!* "Remembering who we are" becomes in Faulkner a personal matter—the very antithesis of a collective identity.

At the close of the twentieth century, most critics find it insurmountably difficult not to see the distinctiveness of Southern culture in the context of the recent struggles against segregation and racism, and therefore they too frequently condemn it out of hand. The Southern confrontation with modernity becomes in this view the reactionary wing of modernity itself, not an alternate vision. Today, our commitment to individual freedom has made the very thought of slavery unacceptable. At the same time, many of us have become acutely aware of the perils of unfettered individualism—the ruthless competition of the self-revolutionizing capitalist market. Antebellum Southern men and women of letters also doubted the benefits of individualism unbound, warning that it could lead only to social dissolution. Understanding the seductions and concrete benefits of modernity, they nonetheless insisted that it was coming at too high a price. They grounded their alternate vision of responsible social order in modern slavery as a social system. We can no longer do the same. But it might behoove us to remember that the struggle against the excesses of modernity cannot easily be waged on the basis of modernity's own premises. Denied and repressed, a people's history inevitably returns as personal anxiety.

It's all right, Shreve tells Quentin at the end of *Absalom, Absalom!*, that it "takes two niggers to get rid of one Sutpen." "It's fine; it clears the whole ledger, you can take the pages out and burn them, except for one thing." And when Quentin does not answer what that thing might be, Shreve continues, "You've got one nigger left. . . . Of course you can't catch him and you don't even always see him and you never will be able to use him"—but from him will spring in some few thousand years, a mixed race. So why, Shreve asks Quentin, "do you hate the South?" Quentin, "quickly, at once, immediately," responds "I dont [*sic*] hate it." And then, "panting in the cold air, the iron New England dark," thought, "I dont. I dont! I dont hate it! I dont hate it!"

In one brilliant stroke, Faulkner has conflated the South and its history, permitting no doubt that the South is its history. But with the same stroke, he has collapsed slavery into race, leaving a legacy of miscegenation, but no ground from which to criticize modernity. For Quentin's crippling—ultimately suicidal—anxiety offers an inadequate ground from which to criticize modernity. It is, indeed, the very essence of modernity that views history as little more than a collection of ghosts, the troubling stories that haunt individual minds. In such a view, history becomes something to be buried so as to get on with life. That Quentin cannot do so confirms that history retains its claim. And it confirms that in the modern Southern imagination racism survived emancipation at the expense of the more complex values of the antebellum slaveholding South.

The abolition of slavery—the recognition of human bondage as morally and politically unacceptable—together with the military defeat of the Confederacy eroded Southerners' confidence in their traditional critique of modernity. The racism deepened by the bitterness of defeat was a grudging acceptance of modernity, never a critique of it. The distinct Southern contribution to a critique of the modern—increasingly the postmodern—world must begin, although it cannot end, with a reclamation of the tragedy and nobility of Southern history.

Notes

1. The phrase is that of M. E. Bradford, *Remembering Who We Are: Observations of a Southern Conservative* (University of Georgia Press, 1985).

2. See, for example, Richard Weaver, *The Southern Tradition at Bay: A History of Postbellum Thought*, ed. George Core and M. E. Bradford (Arlington House, 1968). For a discussion of individualism, see Elizabeth Fox-Genovese, *Feminism without Illusions: A Critique of Individualism* (University of North Carolina Press, 1991).

3. For an excellent discussion of the problem of Southern individualism, see John Shelton Reed, "The Same Old Stand?" in *Why the South Will Survive: Fifteen Southerners Look at Their Region a Half Century after "I'll Take My Stand"* (University of Georgia Press, 1981), 13–34.

4. Bradford, *Remembering Who We Are*, 70.

5. For a fuller development of this interpretation of the antebellum South, see Elizabeth Fox-Genovese, *Within the Plantation Household: Black and White Women of the Old South* (University of North Carolina Press, 1989); Eugene D. Genovese, *The Slaveholders' Dilemma: Freedom and Progress in Southern Conservative Thought, 1820–1860* (University of South Carolina Press, 1992); and Elizabeth Fox-Genovese and Eugene D. Genovese, "The Divine Sanction of Social Order: The Religious Foundations of the Southern Slaveholders' World View," *Journal of the American Academy of Religion* (Fall 1987). These attitudes reached the status of a literary convention among antebellum Southern women novelists (see Caroline Lee Hentz, *The Planter's Northern Bride* [1854; repr. University of North Carolina Press, 1970]).

6. The reference to Quentin Compson comes from William Faulkner, *Absalom, Absalom! The Corrected Text* (Random House, 1968). On the cost of the burden of Southern history for Quentin Compson, see also *The Sound and the Fury: The Corrected Text* (Random House, 1984).

7. Lewis P. Simpson, *The Brazen Face of History: Studies in the Literary Consciousness in America* (Louisiana State University Press, 1980), 67; and Allen Tate, *Essays of Four Decades* (Swallow Press, Inc., 1968), 533.

8. *Who Owns America? A New Declaration of Independence*, ed. Herbert Agar and Allen Tate (Houghton Mifflin, 1936).

9. Simpson, *Brazen Face of History*, 79.

10. Louis D. Rubin, *The Edge of the Swamp: Literature and Society in the Old South* (Louisiana State University Press, 1989), 50. For a fuller discussion of Rubin's position

in particular and antebellum Southern literature in general, see Elizabeth Fox-Genovese, "The Fettered Mind: Time, Place, and the Literary Imagination of the Old South," *Georgia Historical Quarterly* (Winter 1990): 622–50 [reprinted in this volume, pp. 102–23].

11. See Genovese, *Slaveholders' Dilemma*.

12. See Daniel Singal, *The War Within: From Victorian to Modernist Thought in the South* (University of North Carolina Press, 1984).

13. See Rubin, *Edge of the Swamp*, and Fox-Genovese, "Fettered Mind."

14. Lewis P. Simpson, in *Mind and the American Civil War: A Meditation on Lost Causes* (Louisiana State University Press, 1989), develops a similar argument.

15. Obviously many, with Southern slaveholders in the lead, reacted with frightened horror to the revolution in Haiti, but that revolution nonetheless contributed decisively to the general understanding of the full implications of individualism.

16. Lewis P. Simpson, in *Dispossessed Garden: Pastoral and History in Southern Literature* (University of Georgia Press, 1975), is especially strong in underscoring that Southern slavery was no mere continuation of older forms of dependency, but genuinely something new under the sun. See also Elizabeth Fox-Genovese and Eugene D. Genovese, *Fruits of Merchant Capital: Slavery and Bourgeois Property in the Rise and Expansion of Capitalism* (Oxford University Press, 1983).

17. George Fitzhugh, *Sociology for the South, or, The Failure of Free Society* (1854; repr. Burt Franklin, 1967). On Fitzhugh's proslavery argument, see Eugene D. Genovese, *The World the Slaveholders Made: Two Essays in Interpretation* (Wesleyan University Press, 1988).

18. Mrs. Henry Schoolcraft, *The Black Gauntlet*, in *Plantation Life: The Narratives of Mrs. Henry Rowe Schoolcraft* (1852–60; repr. Negro Universities Press, 1969), 93.

19. Ibid., 227.

20. Ibid., 306–7.

21. Ibid., iv.

22. Ibid., v.

23. See Eugene D. Genovese, *From Rebellion to Revolution: Afro-American Slave Revolts in the Making of the Modern World* (Louisiana State University Press, 1979).

24. See Mary Ann Wimsatt, *The Major Fiction of William Gilmore Simms: Cultural Traditions and Literary Form* (Louisiana State University Press, 1989); Lucinda Hardwick MacKethan, *The Dream of Arcady: Place and Time in Southern Literature* (Louisiana State University Press, 1980); and Francis Pendleton Gaines, *The Southern Plantation: A Study in the Development and Accuracy of a Tradition* (Columbia University Press, 1924).

25. Michael Kreyling, *Figures of the Hero in Southern Narrative* (Louisiana State University Press, 1987), 11.

26. Ibid., 10–11.

27. Ibid., 50–51.

28. Eugene D. Genovese, "The Southern Slaveholders' View of the Middle Ages," in *Medievalism in American Culture: Papers of the Eighteenth Annual Conference of the Center for Medieval and Early Renaissance Studies,* ed. Bernard Rosenthal and Paul E. Szarmach (Medieval and Renaissance Texts and Studies, 1989), 31–52.

29. See Walter E. Houghton, *The Victorian Frame of Mind, 1830–1870* (Yale University Press, 1957).

30. Margaret Mitchell, *Gone with the Wind* (Macmillan, 1936); and Thomas Dixon, Jr., *The Clansman* (Grosset & Dunlap, 1905).

31. Donald Davidson et al., *I'll Take My Stand: The South and the Agrarian Tradition, by Twelve Southerners* (1930; repr. Harper & Brothers, 1962); also Tate's *Essays of Four Decades* and his *Collected Essays* (Alan Swallow, 1959).

32. Allen Tate, *The Fathers and Other Fiction* (Louisiana State University Press, 1977). On the Agrarians in general and *The Fathers* in particular, see Mark G. Malvasi, "Risen from the Bloody Sod: Recovering the Southern Tradition" (Ph.D. diss., University of Rochester, 1991), published as *The Unregenerate South: The Agrarian Thought of John Crowe Ransom, Allen Tate, and Donald Davidson* (Louisiana State University Press, 1997).

Part Two

Challenging and Deploying Cultural Analysis

Ten

The Claims of a Common Culture
Gender, Race, Class, and the Canon

Frantz Fanon, psychologist and theorist of revolution, once wrote movingly of the feelings of black children on the island of Martinique who opened their textbooks to read: "Our ancestors the Gauls. . . ." Such indeed is the toll of imperialism and colonization. They appropriate the history and the culture of those they dominate and replace them with metropolitan histories and culture. To be worthy, to advance, is to think oneself white (or male)— to accept a new identity, the identity of your conquerors. Fanon, who went on from his Martiniquais beginnings to a French medical education and immersion in Existentialist philosophy, came to believe that colonized peoples must throw off European social, political, and, perhaps especially, cultural domination through a purging violence. To be free—more, to be liberated— the human spirit must rid itself of the shackles and manacles of other peoples' traditions, histories, patterns of reasoning, languages. The canon, including its epistemologies and standards of excellence, must be destroyed, or at least uprooted from the minds of the colonized.

Imperialism and colonization, as I think Robert Scholes might agree, nicely capture the relations between many students and the official culture that is taken to constitute a liberal education. He nonetheless rejects the idea that liberal education is—as the conservatives, or reactionaries, would have it—in crisis. Apparently, he sees no crisis because he distrusts the role of any canon in a liberal education. Yet surely he would not deny that from the

"The Claims of a Common Culture: Gender, Race, Class, and the Canon." *Salmagundi* 72 (Fall 1986): 131–43. Copyright 1986 by *Salmagundi*. All rights reserved. Used by permission of *Salmagundi*.

    This essay originally appeared as part of a forum responding to Robert Scholes, "Aiming a Canon at the Curriculum," *Salmagundi* 72 (Fall 1986): 101–17.

perspective of liberal education as the transmission of a canon—a common culture—crisis indeed there is, if only in the sense of fundamental change. Our culture as a whole suffers from a gap between words and things, between official discourses and the world. That gap has opened the space for the questions and revisions of those like Mr. Scholes who are challenging the status of the canon. The gap strengthens the case of those who view the canon as arbitrary, artificial, and politically biased. Perhaps more alarming, the gap strengthens the case of those who would abolish the canon, the idea of the canon, any canon at all.

The canon, in fact, has never been the true canon, never been the immutable body of sacred texts, that both its defenders and its detractors like to claim. Subject to "vision and revision," it has been modified by successive generations. Moreover, the canon we have inherited, and against which so many are warring, did not always appear so reactionary and repressive. It took shape as a body of privileged texts that encoded the rise and progress of the individual mind as the custodian of knowledge and of standards of excellence. It was closely tied to the notions of individual responsibility in politics. It encoded the triumph of rationality over superstition, of opportunity over acquired status, of universalism over particularism. It provided the common currency of what some called "the republic of letters." Its fashioners and contributors also assumed that membership in the republic would be restricted by gender, race, and class. The few who gained admission on the basis of individual talent were expected to embrace, so to speak, their "ancestors the Gauls."

These days, it does not require any special intellectual or political commitments to take pot shots at the canon. They are coming from all quarters. I do not count myself among those who would destroy it outright, although I do favor substantive revisions both in the canon and in the various survey courses that are intended to transmit it. But I also favor the defense of the idea of the canon, which is to say both the revision of its contents and the transformation of its teaching. For however narrow and exclusive the canon we have inherited, the existence of some canon offers our best guarantee of some common culture. In fact, the teaching of the canon probably offers the best possible way to expose the limitations of the ideals of individualism on which so much of our public life is based, and the best possible way to introduce some notion of collective standards and values.

There is no small irony here. The attacks on the canon derive primarily from the perception that it does not adequately represent the experience and identities of most of those who are expected to study it. The received notion of the responsible, autonomous, elite male individual seems alien to most white middle-class young men. What have Cicero, St. Thomas Aquinas,

Machiavelli, Descartes, John Locke, Voltaire, Dr. Johnson, Goethe, Cardinal Newman, and all the rest to do with J. R. Ewing and Sonny Crockett? And how much more alien to Afro-American and Hispanic-American men, not to mention to women of all classes, races, and ethnic groups? The attack on the canon owes much to the quest for relevance that has its roots not merely in the liberation movements of the nineteen sixties, but perhaps even more in the cynical instrumentalism that accompanied the political conservatism of the nineteen fifties which gave us Holden Caulfield as the alter ego of the man in the grey flannel suit long before we got Mike Nichols' and Dustin Hoffman's graduate.

On the face of it, the demand for relevance in education has its merits. After all, the initial function of the canon was to provide selected individuals with a collective history, culture, and epistemology so that they could run the world effectively. The canon emerged as the privileged texts of what functioned as a collective autobiography, as the foundation for identity. Individuals do require histories, cultures, and epistemologies to make informed choices and to act politically. But at some point the attack on the received canon shifted ground. Increasingly, the attack has been waged in the name of the individual's right to education as a personal history, a parochial culture, and a private epistemology. The worst of it is that the "radical" critics of the purportedly irrelevant canon have sacrificed the ideal of collective identity that constituted its most laudable feature. To settle for education as personal autobiography or identity is tacitly to accept the worst forms of political domination. Fanon was criticizing the substitution of French history for Martiniquais history, the substitution of the history of the imperialist power for that of the colonized people. He was invoking the right of colonized children to their own collective history.

In revising the survey courses in the Humanities, we face a delicate problem. The motivation for revision stems in large part from the alienation of students from the elite culture whose relevance to their own concerns seems obscure. Unless I am much mistaken, we succeed in engaging their imaginations by invoking their own experience. That first step is normally essential to establish any student's relation to the Humanities. But it is not enough. The Humanities, as a curriculum, must also offer the student perspective on his or her personal experience. The primary failure of the canon lies in its no longer appearing to offer that perspective.

Let me proceed by a detour through the problem of cultural crisis. There are those who bemoan the crisis in the interest of restoring lost forms of domination, in particular the public and private cultural domination of elite white men. This nostalgia especially plagues certain kinds of liberal male academics who formed their own sense of self respect from their identification with a particular canon. Others, less wedded to the specific forms, are rejecting the explicitly anthropomorphic form of the dominant culture and are pressing to substitute a higher level of abstraction and depersonalization. These developments encompass a multitude of specific tactics: quantification, analytic philosophy, deconstruction. They share an explicit distaste for "bourgeois humanism" and for the personal subject or author. They are offering us society as text and text as society and both as process or system. They are contributing to the disillusionment with values that had been tailored to the measure of man. Yet they have done little or nothing to reestablish the accountability of the Humanities to a pluralistic society. In truth, they resemble nothing so much as the spoiled child who refuses to play at all if he cannot win. From the perspective of those previously excluded from the cultural elite, the death of the subject or the death of the author seems somewhat premature. Surely it is no coincidence that the Western white male elite proclaimed the death of the subject at precisely the moment at which it might have had to share that status with the women and peoples of other races and classes who were beginning to challenge its supremacy.

The point for those who wish to revise the canon to take greater account of gender, race, and class is that the foundations of the canon they wish to revise are about as solid as quicksand. Conceivably William Bennett and his colleagues will succeed in restoring the traditional surveys in something near their pristine form, but the resistance even from within their own camp will be strong. And they will find little agreement about which texts incontrovertibly belong to the canon. Growing numbers of humanists appear to find the surveys more problematic than the claims of those the surveys have excluded. But they seem primarily to wish to attack the very concept of a legitimate canon. In its place, they would prefer to see a thousand flowers bloom.

Yet unless we agree that there is a place for some canon, the apparent issue of whether or not to introduce gender, race, and class is no issue at all. We just do it, or refuse to do it—and our decision reflects our personal whim, or perhaps our character or politics, but little else. Let me offer you a paradox: It may well be those who reject the narrowness of the established canon, but who remain committed to the validity of some canon, of some collection of texts that reflects a common culture, who are the true custodians of liberal education or of the humanities. For those who insist on expanding the canon and transforming the surveys take seriously the political function of a humanistic education. They also probably believe that such an education must be accountable to its constituents.

Myths serve poorly as foundations for identity, much less political action. We do our students no favor by pretending that the past consisted in the popular cultures of laboring people or the personal writings of elite women.

The Claims of a Common Culture 149

We do them no favor by ignoring kings and presidents and famous philosophers and those who earned reputations as great writers. A return to the metaphor and the reality of colonization will illustrate the point.

Fanon's emphasis on purging violence derived at least in part from his understanding of the compelling hold of European ideas and institutions on the minds of the colonized. As a psychologist, he believed that an outpouring of anger would help to restore the colonized's possession of their own minds—would exorcise the demons of centuries of domination and dependency. Mao Tse Tung acted on a similar insight when he encouraged the Chinese peasants to kill their former landlords. We could debate the value of such strategies for revolutionaries, but our conclusions would not necessarily apply to the teaching of surveys. And, in any event, developments around the world, notably in China, clearly demonstrate that social revolutionaries and ex-colonial peoples above all need control of Western, that is capitalist, technology and science. The challenge remains to appropriate those techniques, or that technical knowledge, without becoming mired in the social values with which they were initially entwined. However elusive the connections, Western society did engender the scientific and industrial revolutions: They did not, as has been argued for some other inventions, originate by spontaneous combustion in different parts of the globe.

Very likely, our students feel colonized in relation to that elite Western culture that has constituted the backbone of our humanistic education. Female and minority students in particular are, as it were, being asked to look at someone else's picture and acknowledge it as their own mirror image. To throw out the canon does not solve their problem any more than expurgating all traces of Western technology solves the problems of colonial peoples. From one perspective, throwing out the received histories and culture only makes things worse. For, if you do not include a heavy dose of the history of elite males, how do you explain why women and members of minorities are not running the world? One of the more difficult tasks facing those who have been excluded from the corridors of political and intellectual power is to accept the history of their oppression or exclusion and to transform it into a base for future action. In other words, to transform the canon and the surveys in response to changing constituencies has less to do with rewriting the story than with reinterpreting it.

All of the humanities address problems of values and human relations, problems of authority and freedom in society. The humanities as a canon, or a body of key texts, has taken shape in conjunction with the rising commitment to humanism as a form of individualism. The texts that have dominated the canon for at least the past century have privileged the ideals of responsible individualism, rationalism, and universalism. The emphasis on generalization and universalism are decisive. They betray the extent to which the canon was developed as a weapon in the struggle against hierarchy, dependence, and particularism—the extent to which the canon we have inherited has been associated with the history of Western notions of individualism.

The texts that constitute the canon, like the narratives that structure the surveys, owe their status to a process of selection. Although discriminations remain difficult, the criteria for selection seem to involve some uneasy mix of assessment of quality, theme, and representativeness. Those who defend and oppose changing the inherited canon would doubtless insist primarily on the standards of quality. The texts, or at least the authors, included enjoy their position as a result of their incontestable superiority of craft, reasoning, and execution. They are the best. Next, they develop central themes in Western culture. Finally, they can be seen as representative of that culture.

In deep ways, these claims are untrue or at best only partially true. The problem of quality remains the most difficult, and should not be dismissed as trivial. But even if one accepts that there may be reasons of quality for reading Cervantes or Lope de Vega or Shakespeare or Kant, one should recognize that those standards of quality are not absolute, [but] result from cultural and social values. The problems of theme and representativeness are more socially corrupted yet. Theme probably offers the best avenue to the transformation of both the canon and the narrative. For if the rise of individualism does constitute a central theme in the development of both capitalism and modern culture, it hardly constitutes the only one. For openers, the theme of individualism invites a skeptical rereading. And with respect to representativeness, the canon fails woefully. It represented a small, sometimes minute, portion of the elite, which itself constituted a statistical minority of the population.

I agree entirely with Mr. Scholes' insistence on teaching the Humanities in historical context. Indeed, that context offers the best—indispensable—way to introduce students to the tension between the tradition and the society that engendered it. Some recent tendencies in scholarship, and not merely on the right, have frowned upon the reduction of texts to the putative influences that shaped them, and have favored a return to something resembling the new criticism that viewed texts as irreducible entities that should be taken on their own terms. But there is a broad ground between the purist view of the text and the reduction of text to the life of its author. Texts can, legitimately, be taught as articulations of the societies that produced them. The strategy rests on the assumption that all authors are, in some sense, hostage to the society and culture in which they live. In this respect, authors work with the images and questions that lie to hand. Consequently, it becomes legitimate to probe a text for what it does not say as well as for what it does say. It also becomes legitimate to query the functions of the text in its broader context. Texts vary in their explicit indications of their own contexts and silences. In instances in which the familiar texts present a seamless front, in which they fiercely resist their own deconstruction, other texts can be substituted.

Take a couple of familiar texts: Thomas Hobbes' *Leviathan* and John Locke's *Second Treatise on Government*. Both explicitly address the notion of sovereignty during the period of the English Revolution. Both rank as classics of political theory. On the simplest level, Hobbes can be taught as an apostle of authority, John Locke as an apostle of reasonable freedom. Centuries of commentary have swathed the texts in conflicting readings, including conflicts about their authors' possible relations to specific political parties. Commentaries notwithstanding, both can be rendered compelling and even relevant to students. On the assumption that both Hobbes and Locke accepted the essentials of what C. B. Macpherson has called "possessive individualism," both can be shown to have responded differently to its implications. For Hobbes, the growth of individualism warranted an increase in centralized authority. Individuals sacrificed their sovereignty upon entering society in order to enjoy the benefits of peace. Locke saw individualism as grounded in labor, including the congealed labor of absolute private property, and, therefore, as presocial. In his reading, sovereignty resided in the individual and his property, which government could only represent. These familiar outlines acquire new meaning when subjected to an analysis of gender. Both Hobbes and Locke assumed that the individual was male. Both also openly discussed the relation of women to that individual and, perhaps more interesting, to individualism in general.

Both Hobbes and Locke repudiated the venerable notion that woman's inferiority to man derived from Eve's curse. To accept that religious justification for women's subordination would have been to accept the religious foundations for political sovereignty, as propounded by Sir Robert Filmer. Both also rejected the related argument from patriarchy. Hobbes pointed out that according to his model of the state of nature as the "warre of all against all," women, like weak men, could kill strong men through cunning. This argument for equality between the genders in nature did not lead him to advocate their equality in political society, although he came close to advocating a kind of equality in submission to absolute authority. But in addition to that submission, he suggested that women contractually subordinate themselves to men in the interests of protecting their children. Locke was less generous. Having also admitted an original equality of women with men, he rapidly passed to the assertion that "law and the customs of the country" had, in practice, instituted women's political subordination to individual men.

Hobbes' and Locke's texts on government meet every standard of quality. Their place in the most conventional version of the canon would hardly be contested. Yet, these texts lend themselves to a serious discussion of the relations between gender and political theory. It is not even necessary to stretch the intentions of the authors, since both Hobbes and Locke clearly viewed the relations between the genders as a cornerstone of any polity. More important, in contributing to a revolutionary bourgeois political theory, both thinkers found it necessary to postulate the theoretical equality of women to men—however rapidly they brushed that theoretical equality aside. To read their texts in the light of that theoretical necessity is to open up innumerable questions about the relations between gender relations and political relations. In effect, Hobbes and Locke were precociously attacking the time-honored notion of female inferiority. They did not repudiate the political and social necessity for the subordination of women, but they justified it on new grounds and, in so doing, opened the way to subsequent notions of female individualism and equality.

The case of Hobbes and Locke demonstrates that canonical texts frequently dealt with gender. But how representative were their concerns? Furious arguments have been waged over their specific political affiliations, but, however interesting, those potential affiliations do not exhaust the subject. For Hobbes and Locke probably did articulate important tendencies within their society. And the significance of those tendencies should not be reduced simply to how many others held their views. Hobbes and Locke both had an intuitive grasp of the nature and implications of emerging capitalism. They brilliantly perceived the erosion of traditional social and political relations and the pressing need for some new form of analysis. No, peasant men and women doubtless did not share their views, doubtless had not even heard of them, frequently were not even literate. Assuredly peasant and even artisanal men remained deeply attached to notions of female inferiority and subordination. The case of the Levellers during the Civil War further suggests that solid laboring people did not even believe that servants should be allowed to vote. But in their case too, changing discourses opened opportunities for discussion. For the Levellers did not tolerate outmoded notions of deference and hierarchy. They did not cotton to divinely or humanly ordained structures of social inferiority. They did believe that to be a responsible member of the community an individual must have a direct stake in it, must not depend upon the will of another man. The critique of dependence would have a long career and culminate in the campaign for the abolition of slavery. Hobbes' and Locke's ideas of individualism lay at the core of that ideological current. If Hobbes and Locke did not directly represent the thought of the common man or woman, they assuredly did both respond to the social and political changes of their era and formulate the ideological currents in the name of which successive struggles for fuller social and political participation would be waged.

The representativeness of canonical texts can be addressed on various levels. We can adopt a version of the techniques of reader-oriented criticism and ask whom the authors of the texts thought they were addressing. An overwhelming percentage of our canonical texts have a polemical edge. Their authors are arguing in favor of one or another position. So what did authors argue for, whom did authors argue against, and who was likely to compose their readership? The next step concerns the more general relation of authors' ideas to the ideas of their epoch. Here, we can turn to an (admittedly less than precise) analysis of correspondence: Specific formulations of ideas relate to other formulations of ideas. We cannot establish a causal relation between the two but we can identify the correspondences and frequently even the likely paths of dissemination.

In this perspective, it may be rash to insist on too sharp a distinction between high and popular culture. The canonical texts of much of the Western tradition took shape against the backdrop of a predominantly oral popular culture. Indisputably, some intellectuals wrote only for other intellectuals—or clerics. But they did not write in isolation from the culture of the people amongst whom they lived.

The possible correspondences between the texts of the canon and the broader culture at best suggest only that elite culture had something to do with the society from which it derived. Elite culture did not express the intentions, feelings, or perceptions of laboring people and rarely those of women, even elite women. Especially from the Renaissance on, elite culture tended to generalize from the experience of a very small group of men whom it identified with humanity, or "man." Yet we can teach elite culture from the perspective of gender, race, and class if we are prepared to accept attention to issues of gender, race, and class as proxies for the subjective testimony of those excluded from the most exalted cultural roles. For some, that is a big "if." For some would, understandably, prefer to abolish the status of elite culture entirely.

Yet that elite culture functioned in relation to women, the lower classes, and some non-white races analogously to the way in which imperialism functioned for colonized peoples. At worst, it denied the values and perceptions of all others and imposed itself as an absolute standard. It also exercised a powerful hegemony. Since those who developed it spoke in the name of power, progress, and, increasingly, rationalism, it commanded emulation or excited envy merely by virtue of that power. Even those who most intransigently opposed the individuals or classes for which it spoke frequently sought to claim its benefits for themselves. It is at least possible that significant numbers of intellectual women sought to "think like a man" because men had successfully identified themselves with the most sophisticated and compelling modes of thought. The successful identification is the point.

The canon, however we constitute it, can best be taught if it is recognized at least in part as a kind of political spoil. The canon, or the power to speak in the name of the collectivity, results from social and gender relations and struggles, not from nature. Those who fashioned our collective elite tradition were the victors of history. Their ability to write as authorities derived from their social and political position—not so much as individuals but as members of a gender, a class, a race. Their victory constitutes an important feature of all our histories. If we remain bound to their accomplishment, they remain bound to our subordination. Hegel's discussion of the master and the slave hits the mark.

No definition of the canon could fail to include authors who did not produce texts that can appropriately be subjected to the analysis of gender, class, and race. Gender remains the easiest to decode, for gender constituted a primary category of social and cognitive organization for most peoples. Class and race pose greater, but hardly insurmountable, challenges. We can, with little difficulty, select texts by standard canonical authors that address issues of gender, race, and class. We can, in the spirit of contemporary theory, view teaching as an exercise in hermeneutics: We reread our texts from the perspective of contemporary concerns. In addition, we can transform the entire focus of conventional courses by the themes we select. If one rejects all the pieties about the rise and triumph of the individual as the manifestation of progress and civilization, one can, for example, look closely at the tension between freedom and authority for society at large; one can focus on the shift from particularism to universalism; in short, one can present the individual as the problem rather than the solution.

In addition to reinterpreting or thematically reorganizing the canon, we can also expand it, although not necessarily by substituting, say, popular ballads for elite texts. Because access to literacy was so frequently limited by gender and class, we do not have a large pool of women, working people, and members of non-white races to draw upon. Furthermore, the case of lower class white men proves that the elite had enormous powers of absorption. To the extent that women were excluded from the organizations that engendered various professional discourses, especially philosophy, they were unlikely to have written much that could compete with the professionals. Or, to be blunt, women's opportunities more often than not led them to write in the margins of, when not in outright opposition to, the dominant culture. And when opportunity permitted them to write within it, they were very likely to preach, as Queen Elizabeth I did, women's necessary subordination to their husbands—if not to ignore women and gender entirely. But the rare exceptions to these general trends deserve a general recognition that they too infrequently receive. Christine de Pizan, Mary Wollstonecraft, and Harriet Taylor Mill, to name only the most obvious, belong in the canon. As we move beyond 1850, the choices become more numerous. Virginia Woolf is a current favorite, and legitimately so. But we also have Harriet Jacobs, George Eliot, Charlotte Perkins Gilman, Simone de Beauvoir, and Rosa Luxemburg. And I am only picking at random. We also have Frederick Douglass, Richard Wright, Sembene, and Fanon.

Excluded and oppressed groups are, by definition, largely excluded from membership in the republic of letters. The excellence on which that republic has so prided itself remains profoundly bound by gender, race, and class. Its honorary members have normally been asked to leave their origins at the door. But it is in the nature of a vibrant culture to offer more than it intends. Modern criticism reminds us that even a reactionary text may raise contradictions that it imperfectly resolves.

Mr. Scholes, in a spirit that is hard to fault, concludes with an impassioned plea for the intrinsic interest of all forms of "human expressiveness" and for the claims of local conditions in determining the selection of texts. But if the spirit is touching, the politics are misguided. Mr. Bennett is, in this respect, correct. The status of the canon is of large political significance. The canon has faltered, in large measure, as a consequence of the unprecedented expansion of higher education in our time. The unpleasant implications of Mr. Bennett's proposals lie not in his attempt to shore up the canon, but in his related—and thinly veiled—determination to reverse that expansion and restrict access to higher education. To defend the claims of personal experience and local culture in the face of that attack is to fall victim to his sophisticated strategy. The challenge is not to condemn quality as anti-democratic (a sure formula for defeat), but to reclaim it for a reinvigorated national democracy.

Eleven

The Great Tradition and Its Orphans, or, Why the Defense of the Traditional Curriculum Requires the Restoration of Those It Excluded

Gnashing of teeth, beating of breasts, and righteous indignation variously distinguish discussions of our curriculum—or lack thereof. What has happened to our standards? What has happened to our culture? What are we teaching and why? Whom are we teaching and for what purpose? Can we justify spending the money of taxpayers and parents on the humanities, or on what was once known as a "liberal education"? Can we justify our claims as educators if we do not offer a liberal education? Perhaps above all, what has happened to the Great Tradition?

Even to talk these days of the Great Tradition invites confusion. For some of us, the phrase means little more than the history of Western civilization. For others it means more specifically the history of great ideas, or great books. For most, it probably means some combination of political and intellectual history—great men and great books. But it is probably safe to say that those who defend the importance of the Great Tradition to the curriculum

"The Great Tradition and Its Orphans, or, Why the Defense of the Traditional Curriculum Requires the Restoration of Those It Excluded." In *The Rights of Memory: Essays on History, Science, and American Culture*, edited by Taylor Littleton, 185–213. University: University of Alabama Press, 1986. Copyright 1986 by the University of Alabama Press. All rights reserved. Used by permission of the University of Alabama Press.

This essay was originally delivered as part of the Franklin Lecture Series at Auburn University. The Franklin Lectures seek to address broad topical themes that highlight interdisciplinary connections between the sciences and the humanities.

view it as, in some way, central to our collective identity and collective sense of purpose. It is this commitment to the function of the history of Western civilization in our contemporary consciousness that makes its place in the curriculum so hotly contested. Unless I am very much mistaken, those who seek to restore the Great Tradition to its rightful place do not intend it to take its place as one "option" among many. They intend it to anchor the revitalization of our national cultural and intellectual and political life. And those who oppose its restoration in original form do not oppose a curriculum's including a history of Western civilization as one option among many; they oppose the claim that the Great Tradition constitutes the foundation of our identity, and they deny that it offers an adequate map for our collective future.

Anyone who has ever confronted a resentful beginning college student who, having been instructed to take one's survey course, responds "I hate history" has had to wonder why we teachers of history subject ourselves to this misery. The short answer is "to earn our salaries." The longer answer may vary from person to person, but is likely to include a love of history and a vague—probably ill-formulated—commitment to its importance. But whether we try to tell the resistant student that to know history is to love it, or that history is good for the character or the soul or the future paycheck, we have started the discussion on the defensive. Most of us, that is, tacitly accept the premise that education must justify its utility to the student, especially its economic utility but also, because the 1960s still cast a long shadow over our lives, its psychological relevance.

The recent bugle call of our new secretary of education, William Bennett, demonstrates that the arguments from utility and relevance will not go unchallenged. A growing number of educational leaders are publicly insisting that the "Great Tradition" can stand on its merits and, more to the point, can be forced down the throats of unwilling students as a condition of their access to the lucrative jobs they covet. The history survey can be restored to its proper place by fiat: It can be made a requirement.

I, being something of a cultural conservative and perhaps a bit authoritarian by temperament, am not opposed to requirements. I am especially not opposed to requiring one or more history surveys, for I both passionately love history and believe that it is good for the character, the soul, and our political life. But the arguments of those who would restore some putative "traditional survey" or "Great Tradition" make me uncomfortable. For they rest on the assumption that the SURVEY, in caps, has been graven in stone, sanctified by the generations, and, having been temporarily neglected, can be restored to its rightful place in pristine condition. Maybe it would be nice if it could, and I am no longer even sure of that; but it cannot.

By temperament an intellectual and cultural, though by no means political, conservative, I grew up on the comforting narrative of the Great Tradition as it was until very recently conceived. There is a pleasure in knowing the succession of kings, the rise of the bourgeoisie and the liberal tradition, the growth and triumph of humanism. There is another and related pleasure in knowing—preferably by heart—the uncontested great texts of our tradition. And I find those pleasures have been shared by others in conditions you might find improbable. For the past few months, I have been immersed in the diaries of antebellum Southern women, many of whom spelled imperfectly and punctuated yet more imperfectly. Yet many of these women sprinkled their private writings with unacknowledged quotations from Shakespeare: "slings and arrows," for example, abounds. And antebellum Southern men who went to college appear to have received a version of the history of Western civilization—notably, as formulated by Thomas Roderick Dew, president of William and Mary—that did not differ radically from what I was taught in the late 1950s and early 1960s—certainly differed little at all from what was taught at Harvard or the University of Wisconsin or the University of Virginia, or, for that matter, Smith or Vassar or Tuskegee in the 1890s or the 1930s.

That tradition, as embodied in the history surveys, began to collapse during the 1950s in the face of the insurgent instrumentalism displayed by American educators who rushed, after World War II, to get their share of the goodies that accompanied America's sudden position as the world's great, and, for a while, only, superpower. Matters worsened in the late 1950s, when the Soviets beat us into space and set off a panicky race to turn every red-blooded American boy into a nuclear scientist, or at least an engineer. The *denouement* came with excruciating irony during the 1960s, when a politically naive, culturally radical generation declared war on the "academic establishment" by demanding "relevance"—that is, another form of the same instrumentalism. The student and faculty rebels, in effect, did the establishment's work for it: They completed the burial of the Great Tradition, along with the humanities in general. The quest for relevance and the revolt against authority in all forms, however, contained a more positive note: a broadening of the constituency for higher education—the unprecedented, if still inadequate, admission of women, blacks, Hispanic Americans, and others into the hallowed halls and sacred discourses of the academy. But the visible "radicalism" of the 1960s still shrouds their "invisible" contribution to the conservatism of the 1980s. The radicalism of the sixties, however shocking and painful to some at the time, lubricated the potentially painful changes in our society and culture—the advent of the age of the video, the Walkman, and the computer—that had been brewing since the Second

The Great Tradition and Its Orphans

World War. The common denominator—at the risk of oversimplification—must be sought in the personalism of both. But before I pursue that far-from-simple topic—too frequently cast as an accusation—permit me to reconsider the survey we have lost.

Unless I seriously misjudge, the sanctity of the survey, or the Great Tradition that it transmitted, derived from the assumption that it embodied the collective identity of civilized men and the collective values of civilized people. It assumed that members of the true polity and the republic of letters, who were overwhelmingly elite, white men, would acquire from the survey a sense of their proper identity and aspirations. They would learn not so much of cabbages as of kings, of the qualities of leadership and the perils of fortune, of statesmanship and character, of power and its corruptions, of civic duty and moral responsibility. The Great Tradition was fashioned by and for those who were to inherit the earth—not the meek, but the mighty. At its best, the Great Tradition introduced its heirs to a powerful set of values and to the perils of falling from those values. It offered a model of excellence and insisted that excellence comes at a price—and that, in the words of the record about Prince Valiant I listened to as a child, "freedom also has its responsibilities." The actors in the Great Tradition were a restricted group: Othello and Shylock paid the tragic prices of their race and their religion, respectively; Portia, who pleaded in fidelity to her modest woman's mission, but triumphed because of her outsider's ability to push the letter of the law to its logical extreme, [yet] in her triumph reaped her reward by reassuming her subservient woman's role. Those excluded from the cast were invited to identify with its values, each according to its kind. That identification rested largely on submission to the proper order, to the dominance of others in matters political and moral.

I do not wish to take cheap shots, although the political and critical movements of the last couple of decades have generated the motives and skills for doing so. The Great Tradition sits like a duck on a pond, to be peppered by the buckshot of deconstruction and its votaries. Our skills have become those of cynicism, and we are rapidly losing the will or the ability to remember. But those who are asking us to celebrate and to honor mock us by their inability to remember and their refusal to understand anything. The Great Tradition cannot be restored as a blueprint for life in the fast lane. In all fairness, I do not think that Mr. Bennett intends it to be, but I fear that many of those who are rushing to support his initiative will. In the late twentieth century, it cannot be restored as a simple narrative of the triumph of truth and justice. It has more to offer as a record of the triumph of some people over others, of the cultivation of collective values at the price of many individual lives, and of the ways in which those privileged enough to do so wrestled with their angels, their demons, their honor and power in this world, and their salvation in the next.

The point is twofold: First, the Great Tradition that we have inherited was itself the product of a history; was made, not born—much less divinely ordained; and is, accordingly, open to visions and revisions. Second, that tradition was constructed by particular groups to serve their particular needs. It embodies one of the many possible narratives of our collective past—not all of them, not the only possible one. We have two elements to consider: the moment of vision and the viewers; the historical context in which the story was written and the tellers of the story.

Here, recent developments in philosophy and literary criticism have something to offer. And I must, in advance, beg the indulgence of the philosophers and critics for I am about to bowdlerize, or at least vulgarize, their sophisticated work beyond their recognition. In my own defense against their probable reactions, however, I must insist that their work in its original sophistication frequently defies the recognition of others. More's the pity, for they have something important to teach. Crudely put, they insist, in this echoing common sense, that no story (they would prefer "narrative," but "story" will do) is either innocent or transcendent. No story, that is, can be told without some intervention on the part of its teller, without the teller's intentions shaping the choice of characters, the sequence of events, or the ending—or, what amounts to the same thing, without a heavy dose of implicit or explicit interpretation. No more than the camera faithfully and directly records reality do storytellers "tell it like it really was." And no story—we can, for purposes of this discussion, grant exception to the fundamental religious texts—tells it like it always will be, presents human affairs from the perspective of eternity. Stories belong to the living, to communities, to nations—yes, to civilizations, with all their tensions, imperfections, needs, and aspirations. They constitute compromises between things as they are and things as they ideally should be. Master—and, we might add, "mistress"—stories figure among the most important aspects of any individual's or group's consciousness. They order past experience to permit future action. They are indispensable. And the privilege of telling "official" stories ranks among the most important prerogatives that a community can afford any of its members.

The Great Tradition figured as one of, if not *the*, premier story of our civilization from roughly the end of the eighteenth century until the Second World War. And even when presented in the form of "Western Civilization" it carries a special importance for citizens of the United States, for it has provided the contours of a key official story throughout most of the life of our republic. We, collectively, embody its most privileged aspirations. We, collectively, represent the first great triumph of "progress," "individualism," and "democracy" over feudalism, barbarism, bigotry, and all the other forces of darkness against which the Great Tradition was forged. But its special resonance for us makes us specially vulnerable both to its prestige and to its distortions as collective autobiography. It is as if the developments of the 1960s had taught us that its claims to the status of official autobiography constituted a tissue of lies, consisted in the claims of the few rather than of the many. We, the people of democracy!

We feel betrayed. We do not, of course, put it that way. But we seem prepared to toss off any attempts to teach the Great Tradition as the remaining shred of that European authoritarianism and artifice that we began our national career by rebelling against. (I do not, by the way, mean to suggest that the Western European countries are not experiencing their own version of our present crisis, but it is their own, differs in significant ways from ours, and cannot concern us directly here.) Or, perhaps even worse, to reduce the survey to one option among many, to the kind of pre-tour lectures that alumni associations are wont to offer those whom they can persuade to travel in groups to Europe. Our attitude suggests that, for whatever reasons, we have dismissed what was once our official story as irrelevant, although whether irrelevant to most of us individually or irrelevant to the collective business of our republic remains unclear. And our attitude also suggests that we had been mesmerized by the story's claims to official status—that we too uncritically embraced it as either innocent or transcendent. As the product of a specific historical moment and a specific group, the story permits—some would say requires—revision. But its inadequacies for our present purposes do not cancel out our need for some story of our collective past.

I grew up on history. No surprise, if you consider that my father was a professional historian who was uncommonly interested in the mind and education of his oldest child, and who, long before "shared parenting," was named as such, took charge of me for the long hours between 4:00 and 8:00 in the morning. We were early risers; my mother was not. We began, when I was about two, with simple stories. As the years progressed, we went on to more complicated ones, introduced maps, charts, and classic texts. Before I had finished college, we had started to work on Arnold J. Toynbee's *Reconsiderations*. Heady stuff for a mere girl, but I loved it. It did not, in those days, occur to me that my identification with the people and events that were unfolding before my imagination was of primary concern. Although I did harbor a special fondness for Queen Elizabeth I and even a sneaking ambition to be the first woman President.

But I uncritically accepted the terms of the discourse as it was presented to me: The name of the game was power, the exciting story concerned who rules whom, how, and why. I was entranced by the Capetian kings, who managed simply to have surviving sons, to crown them in their lifetimes, and thus to secure the succession to the throne—in short, to build a state. I found the intrigues of the popes delightful. I marveled at the development of the canon law, which I certainly did not understand. I trembled vicariously at the wrath of the Hebrew prophets. I pondered the vicissitudes and fanaticisms of the religious wars. I cheered the victors of the French Revolution, never suspecting that in those days when the modern world was a-borning some women also tried to claim their rights. I never heard of Mary Wollstonecraft, which was a great loss. I shivered at the intrigues of Bismarck, torn between outrage at his insolence and admiration for his success. And more.

In retrospect, I can see that I was torn by contradictions that I had no words to express. When my younger brother and I began to share reading and to act out the stories we read, the only question in the assignment of roles was who would be the bigger boss: Who would play King Arthur and who Launcelot; who Athos, Porthos, Aramis, or d'Artagnan; who Robin Hood and who Little John?—although I did occasionally persuade him to play Maid Marian. Guinevere was not on my list, and I did not know enough about Morgana LaFey to understand what her special powers might be. A young friend of mine now writes her own stories, finding those available entirely unsatisfactory, and her hero, Princess Taraveev, leaves her husband the prince at home while she goes out to slay dragons, monsters, and wicked kings. But this is a new generation. I did not give much conscious thought to women's having been excluded from the roles that I admired, even less to what the implications of their exclusion might be for me. I suspended my disbelief and identified with the causes, the values, the characteristics of my heroes—claimed, in some measure, the tradition as my own. But then, I took great delight in simply knowing the story, in understanding how we had come to be what we were. The structure of the events and my ability to grasp it alike pleased me. I appropriated the tradition in some sense as my own, even if I could not face that my own kind, in the direct sense, had been largely excluded from it.

I also grew up on another kind of history, on what we might today call variously "oral" or "women's history." For that history, I am indebted to my grandmother, with whom I spent roughly a month of every year. Born in 1880, she was the repository not merely of the fascinating events of her own life, but of many previous generations of family lore. With her, I explored and settled in the Cumberland country and Shenandoah Valley, crossed the prairie, scaled the passes at Pike's Peak, witnessed the premature deaths of children in a large family, hemmed sheets by stretching them the

The Great Tradition and Its Orphans

length of a staircase, made bread, taught in a one-room schoolhouse, joined women's clubs, fought precociously for recreation facilities in a Middle America community, taught immigrant children to read, and more. Her history functioned in a direct sense as an extension of my autobiography. I felt myself especially heir to her struggles and her values.

It came as a great shock to me to learn, when somewhat older, that she voted Republican. I knew by then that some of her family had been staunch Free Soilers and abolitionists. I did not know that the party of Lincoln had become the party of Dwight D. Eisenhower, had opposed the party of Roosevelt and Truman. Still less did I suspect that an occasional social prejudice, such as anti-Catholicism, might accompany her upstanding and otherwise generous values. Nor did I know that on one occasion she had sorrowfully defied my grandfather—at the time chairman of the local Republican party—to vote for Franklin Roosevelt.

Today, many history teachers find that students who otherwise "hate history" respond enthusiastically to the opportunity to write a family history or an autobiography; find that students "come alive" when invited to construct an oral history. Suddenly, history acquires that personal dimension, comes home to them, takes on meaning. History in the personal mode becomes relevant. And it is true that I could not easily relate my grandmother to the Great Tradition, although, had I been more knowledgeable or wiser, I might have, since a particular strand of Protestant Christianity lay at the core of her identity. At her funeral, we read from Proverbs, chapter 31: "Who can find a virtuous woman? for her price is far above rubies . . . ," and sang the "Battle Hymn of the Republic." These choices correctly reflected her sense of herself, how she located herself in the world. The choices also reflected the public values encoded in the Great Tradition.

Two sets of stories thus presided over my initiation as a historian. In the beginning, I did not insist that they meet, but more or less easily tolerated their coexistence in my imagination and intellectual life. Of such coexistence, you may shrewdly observe, is schizophrenia made. And the recent disenchantment on the part of many with the Great Tradition derives in no small measure from their recognition of the schizophrenia. "Who needs it?" as they say. The recent developments in black, feminist, and ethnic scholarship have sharply—I should say irreversibly—challenged the Great Tradition's claims to be "everybody's autobiography." Clearly it is not. You can get to the middle of the nineteenth century (depending on the course), even until the final quarter of the twentieth, without being offered a woman, a black, or a Jew worthy of serious emulation or who speaks for the tradition as a whole. Oh, you can get your odd Joan of Arc, your Queen Elizabeth, your Hebrew prophet (providing that the course includes the Judeo part of the

Judeo-Christian tradition). But how many surveys of the Great Tradition seriously propose such figures as embodiments of a distinct gender, or of minority groups? How many acknowledge that the tradition itself resulted from a clash of values and that the losers, or the excluded, might have had their own perspective on the story?

Frequently it is said—or perhaps worse assumed, not said—that the Great Tradition has been established on the basis of quality. Elite men just happened to produce the best and most serious work; elite men just happened to secure the leadership of states, movements, religions. There is no bias here, only recognition of quality—and the way things were. This position rests on a partial truth. Elite men did their best to monopolize the sword and the pen, and to secure that monopoly they threw in the right to tell the story as well. The right to tell the story proved decisive, for it permitted the victors of history to present their spoils as the desserts of individual skills and excellence. This is the quality part, and it emphasizes individual talent. The part about the way things were is more problematic. For in focusing on the individual, the tellers of the tale dropped the bit about the very few individuals who were permitted to enter the lists at all.

Let me be blunt. The Great Tradition, in its various guises, takes for granted that the pool of potential heroes was restricted to white, normally elite, males. If the tradition considers the reasons why some failed and others succeeded, it does so within the framework of individual ability and character, not within the framework of group membership. It includes the occasional improbable success story—the odd peasant lad who rises to the position of advising kings or popes, who produces a splendid text—but never so much as admits that some groups of individuals suffered systematic exclusion from exemplary roles. This, if I understand what is happening, is at the core of the many's rejection of the tradition as their own. On one level, the proponents of ethnic and women's studies have a point: in its official guise it is not their own.

Mr. Bennett proposes that we "reclaim the legacy," but does not explain how we persuade our people to recognize the legacy as their own. Professor (and Rabbi) Jacob Neusner, a conservative whom President Reagan appointed to the National Arts Council and who, as a Carter appointee, served on the National Endowment for the Humanities, recently wrote in William Buckley's *National Review* of the compelling claims of ethnic studies, notably black and Jewish, upon our national attention. Professor Neusner can hardly be charged with a radical quest for relevance, much less with a willingness to undermine high intellectual standards. A distinguished scholar, his commitment to intellectual rigor brooks no challenge. A convinced conservative, his commitment to society's collective moral and political responsibility defies question. I am loath to put words in Professor Neusner's mouth, but think I can fairly translate his remarks as a plea that we recognize that our legacy is plural, not singular, a plea that we accord proper weight to the contributions of various traditions to our collective tradition. But let me leave his forceful case in his own hands and suggest that you read it for yourselves. Instead, let me turn to the case of gender—the necessary place of women in any reconstruction of our collective legacy.

Women's studies, like various forms of ethnic studies, and indeed like the social history of the common people, have developed in large measure as a revolt against the claims of the Great Tradition to reflect the values and legacy of society as a whole. During the past decades, scholars, especially women scholars, have uncovered a vast amount of information on women. Although much remains to be done, we are beginning to have the rudiments of a history of women, and the hard truth is that history bears little immediate resemblance to the history that has been taught as the Great Tradition. The gap resembles the gap between the histories that I learned from my father and from my grandmother. In the first place, much of women's history does concern private, or at least mundane, matters: the bearing and raising of children, the cooking of food, the carrying of water, tilling of the soil—a great deal of hard work and the ubiquitous risk of death in childbearing. In other words, much of women's experience has not been of much concern to those who have written history. And if many women have demonstrated deep commitment to the religious values of their society—and to its churches, which is not precisely the same thing—those values and those churches offered negative, or at least passive and subservient, views of themselves as women and precious few opportunities for leadership.

In the second place, and more surprising, women's history has also addressed public as well as private affairs, and has revealed that women have engaged in the most dangerous employments, including military action. They have participated in, and even led, a variety of riots and protests; have exercised political power; and have attempted to participate in the most advanced culture of their societies. No woman has ever been pope, but short of that, women have done almost everything that men have done, albeit not as regularly. And "regularly" may be the key, for if individual women have proved their abilities to accomplish almost anything, women as a group have not been viewed as capable of such accomplishments. Worse, women as a group have been, to the extent possible, excluded from the opportunity to prove their excellence according to their society's most prestigious definitions of excellence.

The harsh lessons about women's place in society as women, about Western civilization's prevailing attitudes toward women, have convinced a significant group of feminist scholars that the Great Tradition has nothing to offer them. Mr. Bennett has asked us to reclaim our tradition's struggle for the ideal of justice, a plea to which some feminist scholars would doubtless respond that the project deserves their attention—but must inevitably result in women's rejection of previous ideals of justice. In this respect, the defenders of the Great Tradition are reaping the whirlwind their predecessors sowed. For if the Great Tradition has been less than hospitable to women, much of the scholarship on women that has developed in recent years has been resolutely hostile in return. In extreme form, the argument runs that the Great Tradition has always been militantly male and that it has silenced, even brutalized, women—"Women of Ideas and What Men Have Done to Them," to borrow the title of an encyclopedic history of women's intellectual work. But this extreme view does not merely dissect the "misogyny" of the tradition, it explicitly challenges the standards of quality on which it has been based. According to the logic, men began by controlling women's bodies and went on to control their minds, silence their voices, and trample upon their values. The very ideals of quality that the tradition embodies result from the struggle between men and women, or from men's determination to control women. The standards are neither innocent nor transcendent. They result from history itself: They are indeed the spoils of the victor.

This line of reasoning, which I in part follow and in part reject, leads, in its extreme form, to affirmation of an entirely distinct women's tradition. Women, so it is argued, speak "in a different voice." The generalizations concerning women's "difference" cloak a host of specific claims. Let me give you some examples. Women—this is the most common example—devote their lives to nurturing life and, accordingly, hate war. Either innately or socially given to so-called "maternal thinking," women are explicitly or implicitly pacifists. Women identify primarily with other women, rather than with men. Women are less likely than men to engage in the violation of nature: since the early glimmerings of industrialization in the sixteenth century, there has been a natural affinity between women and what we now call "ecology." Men, not women, have burrowed into the bowels of (Mother) earth, have turned waterways from their natural courses, have raped the land. Women write differently than men, not merely about different things, but in a different voice. Women have been less attuned than men to the modes of self-assertive individualism, in part because its privileges have been denied them. But leave the causes aside for the moment: Women have been less likely than men to say or write "I" with conviction, much less with anger. Women shroud their judgments in "silences." In political action, women are more likely than men to defend the needs and claims of communities, including small children, and less likely to embark on conquest either personal or collective.

This line of thought, at its most sophisticated, say in the mind of an Elizabeth Janeway, leads to a systematic critique of power as it has been used and abused by the great political figures of the Western tradition. It argues that women have specialized in the "powers of the weak." In sum, the attempts to identify a specific women's tradition have, by and large, resulted in the identification of women with the values of nurture, pacifism, collective life—the diametric opposites of what are taken to be the values of men, especially as encoded in the Great Tradition. Therefore, many women are tempted to retort to the plea that we reclaim that legacy with a defiant charge that since men have forged it, let them keep it if they choose. It has nothing to offer women. Indeed, it may have nothing to offer humanity, which it has brought to the brink of a nuclear holocaust.

There is an irony in this view of women's collective identity and collective dissent from the reigning truths encoded in the Great Tradition. For the women who oppose the tradition are, in large measure, espousing the view of themselves that it propounds. Shakespeare portrays Portia as triumphing, in the name of mercy, in a situation in which the unmediated claims of justice would have required delivering up the pound of flesh. Sophocles depicts Antigone as championing the principles of family religion—of clan and kin and their gods—against those of the state. And he carefully identifies the conflict of laws with a conflict between genders: if Antigone can thus "flout authority / Unpunished, I [Creon] am woman, she the man." And again: "No woman shall be master while I live." In the event, Creon's victory—the victory of the *male state* as the preserve of order—proves Pyrrhic indeed. Yet Sophocles casts the tale of Antigone's rebellion against that order as a tragedy, because of the legitimacy of both sets of claims. She lost because the claims she represented were archaic, impeded the progress of civilization. Creon also lost because he could not find a place for them in the new order he was trying to build.

But there is a second irony as well, for many of the women about whom we have the most information did not fit the mold at all. All that Queen Elizabeth I had in common with the myth of womanhood was her virginity—which itself was surely a myth. Catherine de Medici, Catherine the Great, Rosa Luxemburg, Dolores Ibarruri (the "Pasionaria" of the Spanish Civil War) were pacifists? Hardly. And they are only a few exemplars of a venerable tradition of battling women that includes poor women who have rioted for bread and against taxes since time immemorial. Social history abounds with women, not all of them patient Griseldas.

Here is the rub. The events that have produced the feminist critique of our prevailing attitudes toward power have also produced a resurgent interest in social history: "history from the bottom up" or "the history of the common people" as it is variously known. To be sure, much of the new social history has been developed by men on the same male-centered principles that govern the Great Tradition, but social history has incontestably proved more hospitable to women than its high-culture, high-politics counterpart. And social history shares with women's history the temptation to dismiss the Great Tradition as irrelevant. Social history also suffers from the same problems of interpretation and of establishing significance as the Great Tradition. Suffice it to say that were one to substitute the new social history for the Great Tradition, one would be able to include considerable information on those whom the Great Tradition has excluded. But in my opinion, the substitution of social history for the Great Tradition would not solve the problems—would probably only defer them. We inevitably return to the problems of interpretation and point of view: to the problems of who is telling the story for what purpose. And unless we propose to give up on some meaningful political life entirely—unless, that is, we propose to leave our future in the hands of malevolent fates—we are condemned to take the function of the Great Tradition—of our collective intellectual and political legacy—seriously.

For the past few years I have been directing a large project "to restore women to history" by introducing materials on women into the basic American and European survey courses, and, by any normal standard, the project has been successful. It has also taught those who have worked on it a great deal about the difficulty of the problems and the choices. And, as in selecting illustrations for a story, the preeminent problem is choice. At the simplest level, the choices concern which parts of the "material" the instructor chooses to "cover." You can, for example, decide to include, or to exclude, information on women's participation in the English Civil War—just as you can include information on the members of the Model Army but exclude the Levellers, include information on the Levellers but exclude the Fifth Monarchy radicals, and so forth. The story of the French Revolution can and has been told with only passing reference, or none, to the women who played such an important role in its unfolding. You can also argue that a survey course—the Great Tradition—leaves little time for discussion of every little radical sect that happened along. What we want, after all, is a sense of the logic of events, of the outcome, of the abiding legacy. And I can counter that the stock figures of the story—the "great leaders," if you prefer—took account of those radical sects, and assuredly took account of the disorderly women who plagued their political lives, in making the decisions that we are told are worth remembering. To consider the decisions independently of the context in which they were made is to denigrate the great figures themselves, by ignoring the stern challenges they had to master. Worse, it is to obscure the important causes of actions in time and place. It is—and I trust you will pardon my incursion onto a sensitive contemporary terrain—to discuss the pros and cons of bombing abortion clinics without reference to religion, or politics, or capital punishment, or the lives of women. I am decidedly not taking a position on abortion, which I regard as one of the most agonizing issues in our society; I am merely pointing out that all positions on issues reflect the complexity of the societies in which the issues emerge.

The choice of whom to include in the story is difficult but soluble. Neither stalwarts of the Great Tradition nor extreme feminists may like the results, but it can be done. And it yields a refreshingly complex story. For women figure dramatically in the history of Western civilization, albeit not always in the ways any of us might have thought or wished.

In the French Revolution, women participated in, and frequently launched, some of the most portentous popular uprisings; women organized the *salons* in which many of the liberal ideas of the day were developed and disseminated; a woman, Charlotte Corday, killed the popular leader Marat; another woman, Mme. Roland, prodded, poked, loved, and otherwise shaped the members of the party of the Girondins; yet another, Marie Antoinette, embodied everything that different people most opposed or most wanted to defend; and yet another, Olympe de Gouges, drafted a statement on the rights of women that earned her the scaffold from those spearheads of revolution, the Jacobins. Different revolutionary groups held very different positions on the "woman question," the disposition of which played an important role in the ultimate outcome of the Revolution. Almost all the revolutionaries, with the possible exception of that quintessential *roué* Danton, had strong views about the proper place of women in society and the importance of that place to any society worth living in. Almost all of them also agreed on the necessity of women's subservience to men, but they disagreed mightily on the nature of the subservience and to which men it should be due. To teach the French Revolution as an exclusively male story is not merely unfair to women, it distorts the French Revolution. And the same obtains for almost every topic normally covered in any survey of the Great Tradition.

The exclusion of women from the Great Tradition has been a matter of choice. Their restoration to it is long overdue. The perplexing questions pertain not to exclusion or inclusion, but to the terms of inclusion. If we are to retain some semblance of the Great Tradition as our collective legacy, as the cornerstone of our identity—all the more if we are to insist that the tradition reflect what we consider the highpoints of that legacy, and that it must consist in something more than a random sample of autobiographies or family histories—then we must revise our story. I am by no means suggesting that we simply substitute social history for political and intellectual history, although I believe that politics and intellectual life can only be understood within their social context. I am suggesting that we restore gender to its rightful place as one of the basic categories through which we understand our experience and evaluate our past. I also fear that gender constitutes a good deal more than stalwarts of the tradition want to deal with and a good deal less than many feminists think is women's due.

By "gender," I mean, quite simply, what a society presents as the way to be a man and the way to be a woman—and the proper relation between the two. Gender is nothing more nor less than a social—or, if you prefer, cognitive or epistemological—category. Gender tells us little, if anything, about individual perceptions or feelings. Gender belongs in the realm of language. It offers a structure for personal experience. The structure may be social, economic, political, intellectual, even, perhaps, psychological.

Gender organizes experience from the perspective first of society and second of the observer of society. To introduce gender as one of the essential ways of telling the story of the past will not distort the past. It will not substitute a problematic women's culture for what we have been taught to regard as high culture. It will not create more women generals and popes than we know there to have been. It also will not transform bellicose women princesses into closet pacifists and maternal thinkers. It will not, in short, radically transform the past we have inherited. But it will radically revise our view of that past—radically revise what we accept as innate or natural, how we assess different groups' opportunities to display excellence. Above all, it will revise our view of what was necessary and why. And our attitudes toward historical necessity determine our attitudes toward our own possibilities for creating a good society.

Make no mistake. To introduce gender into our reading of great texts and great political events is to increase, rather than decrease, our fidelity to the experience of our predecessors. Being closer than we are to societies in which gender constituted the fundamental principle of social organization, they were, if anything, more aware than we of the ways in which it impinged on any attempt to conceive the good society. With the passage of centuries, those who made the Great Tradition came more and more to define the polity and the republic of letters—those monuments of the good society—as male. They also tended to associate the forms of worship and organization that they were leaving behind—Antigone's clans and gods—with women. The tradition contains a good deal about the triumph of male rationality over female disorder. I warned you that we might not always like the story. My point is that we need to know it.

As a child, I now recognize, I was guilty of a horrible failure of imagination. I could not understand the fuss about adopted children's wanting to know who their real parents were. From my perspective, anyone who had parents, adopted or not, and a good home should be smart enough to let a good thing be. The existential question, "Who am I?" moved me not at all. It was difficult enough to work with the world you had been given—why bother about the worlds "we know not of"? You will recall, from the beginning of these remarks, that I also did not want to know that I could not realistically aspire to the roles, all male, with which I tended to identify. I think I have learned that I was wrong on both counts. And, further, learned that both kinds of being wrong are related, and are related to the future of any justification for teaching the Great Tradition.

The Great Tradition earned its place in our education on two grounds: its creators and exponents presented it simultaneously as our collective history and as our autobiography. The political and social changes of the recent past have exposed its claims to be our autobiography as outrageous and fraudulent. And the erosion of those claims has reduced its claims as collective history to frivolity. Much of the revolt against the Great Tradition has been fueled by the refusal to accept someone else's autobiography as our own, and by the insistence that—whatever the world may say—our *own* autobiography matters. Both these responses command respect: The orphan—even the secure, adopted child—*does* need to know who he or she is. However painful the knowledge, orphans need to know—at least must try to know—who their parents were, and what their special legacy is. One can only admire the courage that can face those anxieties squarely, especially when the coveted knowledge is likely to demonstrate not that the real parents were dukes or counts, but that they were unfortunates who had a drinking problem, or not enough money to get married, or worse.

Similarly, those who have been excluded by the Great Tradition—and here I refer particularly to women, but they are not alone—need to know why. They need to know why they did not win, why they lacked the power or the resources to impose their views, why their kind did not tell the story. Here, as with real-life orphans, I am suspicious of the romantic answers. I doubt, for example, that all women shared a distinctive culture and opposed the reigning values of their societies in a consistent and programmatic fashion. But my real point lies elsewhere.

I am deeply committed to the recovery of women's past. I also believe that the recovery of that past will illuminate and transform our reading of the Great Tradition. It will not substitute for it. No one's autobiography can substitute for our collective history. Nor can any of us hope to reconstruct our autobiographies without such a history. We cannot reclaim the legacy of the Great Tradition unless we understand and revise the purposes for which it was constructed. It is neither innocent nor transcendent—above all, not graven in stone—but rather, as Rousseau said of the Constitution, engraved in the hearts of men (and women). And if it addresses many of the problems that plague all peoples who attempt to live together in societies, it does so on the terms of those who were able to cast the autobiography of the male individual as the collective history of humanity. The old truths about the importance of history still obtain: history *does* constitute a kind of collective memory and memory *does* provide the only foundation for identity, informed choice, and, yes, freedom. Our age has proved itself uneasy with history, has permitted itself to wonder whether history still has a bearing. Perhaps things have changed so much and so fast that the wisdom of the past is dead—or merely no longer relevant.

History is not the main problem, however out of fashion its virtues may be. We know—and here I am speaking as a historian and a woman—however little we like to acknowledge, that the individual and collective life of peoples inescapably throws up the intractable problems of mortality, morality, and politics. No, the problem lies in the relation between history and autobiography. For a long time, many of us had accepted the constraint of interpreting our personal stories through the prism of an official story, and official standards of excellence. We did so because we accepted the story as objective. In recent decades, two things have changed. First, we have been encouraged to place a greater premium on our personal story than that of anyone else, however prestigious. Second, we have learned that most stories that purport to be objective are in fact someone else's story.

We can no longer restore the original version of the Great Tradition as everybody's autobiography. We know that it was not. Nor can we afford to surrender to the anarchy of an infinite number of personal autobiographies. Our Great Tradition has a different purpose: It constitutes the collective history without which none of our individual stories makes sense. We now face the challenge of rewriting it as a collective history that is not the monopoly of a single group, a single perspective. The orphans of the Great Tradition must reclaim it for themselves, for only they, and those who accept their just claims, can revitalize it for us all.

Twelve

The Empress's New Clothes
The Politics of Fashion

Fashion is all the rage. Clothing designers figure among the inner circle at Reagan's White House. The public fascination with fashion as style continues to dominate *Miami Vice* and the MTV offerings with which it and a variety of commercials intersect. Nancy Reagan apparently seeks to claim glamor for the White House circle. Princess Di is doing her bit for Britain. A couple of years ago, NBC reported on the thefts and murders perpetrated to obtain German eyeglasses. The reporter interviewed a number of young men in Harlem who sported pairs of the glasses; they insisted that wearing the glasses fully justified the risk of being murdered by others who coveted them. The glasses were fashion, were they not? They were it.

In recent years, even intellectuals have turned their attention to fashion. Roland Barthes discovered a system in the apparently random manifestations of fashion.[1] Alison Lurie, in a popularization of Barthes, has introduced Americans to "the language of clothes."[2] Indeed most of those who currently write on fashion concur in presenting it as a language—as, in Barthes's formulation, a system of representation. Some, to be sure, also recognize fashion for the very big business it has become.[3] But those who write of its distinctive sartorial or cultural features remain entranced by the idea of fashion as a language. This intellectual fashion has its own sinister, or at least complacent, cast, for it projects a deceptive notion of language as innocent communication. And, despite the legitimacy of fashion as a system of communication, which it indisputably is, innocent it is not. History records the

"The Empress's New Clothes: The Politics of Fashion." *Socialist Review* 17 (January/February 1987): 7–30. Copyright 1987 by *Socialist Review*. All rights reserved. Used by permission of the Radical Society, Ltd.

ubiquitous propensity of men—and women—to kill for ideas, or for the words that encode ideas, but not normally for language as a system. When we kill for words, we are killing for their referents, for what they signify. The propensity of youths to kill for a pair of eyeglasses brutally exposes the limits of viewing fashion as a closed system—a self-referential language. Killing for eyeglasses reveals the language of fashion to be anything but innocent, reveals it to point inexorably beyond itself to the ways in which individuals locate themselves in the world and in relation to others. Killing for eyeglasses challenges us to recognize fashion as politics, even if an especially distorted and corrupted politics.

In truth, to call fashion a politics—or perhaps a language of politics—does not necessarily challenge the fatuous view of fashion as innocent. To link the two realms in a common discourse can, after all, provide solace to those who would also trivialize politics. The rage for fashion has its counterpart, at least in some circles, in a rage for politics. The various movements for personal liberation have been offering us a veritable smorgasbord of politics for the past two decades. Pre-eminently, they are offering us what might be called the politics of everyday life. And there are good reasons to mine the political implications of daily life and mundane rituals.

But in connecting the personal and the political—an early dictum of the women's movement—we must remember that politics ultimately consists in the formal and informal relations of domination and subordination that govern the distribution of resources, opportunities, and respect within a society— i.e., the distribution and ends of power.[4] Fashion constitutes an important dimension of politics in this precise sense. It also constitutes a representation of the social relations and values that some are imposing and others are accepting, or at least failing to challenge.

The apparently autonomous contribution of rebellious and "punk" youth to our fashion does not, from this perspective, amount to a serious challenge to the aid and comfort that fashion as a system offers our politics, political economy, or class relations. For the diversion of social protest into the realm of fashion only confirms the political impotence of youthful protest against closing opportunities and social despair. When Michael Jackson, Madonna, or Annie Lennox make it as representations of style and thereby modify the language of fashion, they do nothing for their brothers and sisters—except perhaps reconvert them to the possibilities of the prevailing class system and make them feel more at home within it. The movie *Saturday Night Fever* provides a fine example of the dead-end of fashion—or dance—for working-class youth.

Punk has indisputably constituted the most visible popular influence on recent fashion. Stylistically, it has made its mark in the colors that dominate the scene: harsh, bright colors that have little relation to the muted tones normally associated with discrete—and discreet—femininity; painted, rather than made-up, faces. Even fashionable haircuts bear its mark: short, angular cuts. And some critics cogently argue that Punk represents a serious critique of our society, an angry rejection of its values. I am not about to argue the interpretation here, especially since I think it contains some truth. But the marriage of Punk and the fashion endorsed by Nancy Reagan should make us thoughtful.

The practitioners of Punk seem to direct their anger and rebellion as much, if not more, against themselves and each other—against society's victims—as against the society itself, which they purport to loathe. More important for immediate purposes, Punk has been inescapably co-opted through its embodiment in fashionable commodities. You can now buy the signs of Punk, and in very expensive, if slightly transposed, forms. And there is a kind of escalation in matters of style: the better something is made, the better it looks. There is a painful irony in social rebels' having to view the signs of their rebellion sported in exquisite materials by those they thought they were rebelling against. It is only human to want to be able to buy the superior version. An Annie Lennox may brilliantly press the style to its limits and beyond, but fashion is already catching up with her, already identifying her as merely an especially dramatic version of itself. She has lost her power to shock, and is losing her power to command attention. For what fashion can always co-opt is the outrageous. Since its business is novelty, in its always having to be replaced, shocks constitute one of the tools of its trade.

Fashion, Class, and Capitalist Development

The politics of fashion are multiple. These days, we tend to be especially conscious of its politics of gender, but fashion has always played an important role in the politics of class. So far as we can determine, fashion has existed as long as human societies have existed. From the first string of shells and the first paint on the face or skin, people have sought to identify with others, and differentiate among themselves, by the use of clothing and decoration. Early European history offers evidence of distinctive costumes for different groups, and evidence of fashion, at least in cities and at courts. The distinction between costume and fashion, although difficult to draw with any precision, indicates significantly different tendencies. The most important difference probably consists in the element of change, especially the rate of change. Costume changes slowly, and normally likes to pretend that it does not change at all. It serves to articulate specific differences among members of groups that prefer to think of themselves as stable, as embodying tradition. The most important distinctions drawn by costumes differentiate members of genders, and sometimes age groups as well. Costume permits variation according to wealth and status, but in principle, certain basic elements, say cut of clothing and dominant colors, are supposed to be constant, even if people express their personalities, or their sense of their own standing, through variations in embroidery or ribbons or other decorations. The point is to emphasize membership in a group and the membership of groups in a community.[5]

European costume sank its roots in the very early Middle Ages among agricultural peoples who were attempting to carve out or to defend communities in a very unsettled world. It remains difficult to pinpoint precisely the moment at which regional peasant costumes emerged, but it is safe enough to assume that their emergence corresponded, however roughly, to the establishment of village councils, the early presence of the Catholic church, and the consolidation of feudal lordship. Indeed, in some cases costume was invented late, in response to the commercialization of the bourgeois era, and as a nostalgic effort to create a sense of community mores or identity in the face of the community's erosion by expanding capitalism.[6] Whatever the date, the origins lie in that oral culture so cogently invoked by Marc Bloch in which tradition was taken as permanent precisely because each generation could modify received wisdom and rules without having to acknowledge that it was changing anything.[7] In that world, costume served to delineate boundaries.

Fashion, in contrast, derives an important part of its very existence as fashion from change. Even today, one of the first criteria for fashion is newness, or nowness. Precapitalist societies normally did not have the possibilities for subsidizing rapid changes in fashion by our standards. So the new could remain new for a longer period of time than it can today. In addition, the proportions of newness in a total garment may have been smaller than they are today. A new decoration, a new headdress, a new piece of ivory might suffice.

The mention of ivory underscores the usefulness of a touch of the exotic in creating the illusion of fashion. To wear something that others can only procure for themselves with expense and difficulty is to identify oneself as someone of significance. Which raises the matter of expense. Fashion has always been costly, although the cost has varied wildly. Thorstein Veblen, who contributed one of the most penetrating discussions of fashion, specifically linked it to conspicuous consumption—not just cost, but exhibitionistically non-utilitarian cost.[8] The complex relations between fashion and sheer expenditure defy any neat analysis, and probably vary from period to period and from polity to polity. Nonetheless, the attribute of cost, of being paid for, has had an important influence on the development of fashion as a social and political phenomenon.

During the Middle Ages, most members of European society did not spend a great deal of money on clothing. They did not have the money, and the clothing was not lying around to be bought. Furthermore, clothing was proportionately more expensive than it is today, and even for those who affected fashion, it was expected to last much longer. One of fashion's principal functions in such a society was to overawe. The magnificence of the clothing of the royalty or nobility set them apart from common folk—not just a little richer, but qualitatively different. Royalty and nobility exploited to the hilt the political advantage their ability to dress afforded them. One of their most instructive strategies can be found in their eagerness to put those who served them in livery. The retainers and servants of a powerful noble were frequently expected to wear the lord's—or the lady's—colors, and possibly specific garments as well. Dressing established vertical links in the society, articulated ties of dependency as the ligaments of political order. A noble's servant (and the category encompassed many more occupations and social ranks than its pale residue does today) embodied and displayed his power. Display thus became one of the principal political obligations of service. The point was to demonstrate not merely that you belonged to someone else, were identified by being in his service, but that he was powerful. And *he* is the appropriate pronoun for this aspect of service. Fashion in this sense also demonstrated the political and personal advantages of being in some man's service. Those who were thus garbed by lords were pulled out of the common run of their fellows. Their being thus distinguished conveyed no message of individual mobility in the modern sense. Their advancement was advertised as a way of confirming social hierarchy. But it also advertised the links that could bind social groups across class lines. The expense of servants' garments was borne by the one they served.[9]

The forms of service recognized, or articulated, by the wearing of livery bore close relation to the development of political and military institutions. With the development of courtly love during the high Middle Ages, when knights affected the wearing of their ladies' colors they were confirming the beginnings of the great decline of medieval society. For, whatever honor they intended, they were effectively trivializing the visible personal bond between lord and man. They were also marking an important transition in the very concept of liveried servitude. The first servants to wear livery had not been those who fulfilled the menial tasks we associate with service today. Scullery maids, stable hands, and agricultural laborers did not wear livery. Their tasks remained essentially invisible. No one perceived the need to articulate the links that bound them to their betters, for their betters, generally speaking, were ensconced in a different order of being. The liveried status adhered primarily to those whom we would not consider servants at all: to various kinds of household managers and to fighters under conditions in which household managers effectively managed the duchy or the county or the realm. Servants thus did not normally wear women's colors, for women did not normally preside over these proto-political and proto-administrative occupations in their own right as women. On the rare occasions on which they did so preside, they did so as temporary delegates of their families—the appropriate male being dead or otherwise absent—without disrupting the larger order that deemed such positions to be normatively men's.[10]

In short, the increased circulation of money, the growth of cities and trade, and all the other early manifestations of capitalism disrupted these harmonious images. In growing numbers, first individuals, and then whole social groups, began to be able to buy fashionable clothing for themselves. Middling sorts of people on the rise correctly learned the lesson of fashion in their time: clothes made the man or woman, made social position, paved the road to power. And middling sorts of people began to procure fashionable garments, to buy what their social superiors deemed outrageous articles of display.

The social superiors initially responded with an attempt to keep the world from turning. As committed as ever to their own view of proper social and political relations, and to fashion as the natural expression of those relations, they passed legislation that would prevent social upstarts from sporting the trappings of a status they in principle did not possess. The fashionable garments of parvenus represented nothing more than money. They did not represent social standing or political power, however much they might have embodied their wearers' will to both. Money did not correctly represent social standing or political power. The proliferation of sumptuary laws merely testified to their ineffectiveness. And, in the long run of a few centuries, money had its revenge.

The great bourgeois revolutions, notably the French, and the consolidation of capitalism in industrialization transformed fashion as artifact, as language, and as politics. Dress shook free from the social structures and values that bound, or at least inhibited, it in more traditional societies.[11]

Our modern notion of fashion remains deeply hostage to the systematic fetishism of commodities that emerged with modern capitalism. Throughout the development of precapitalist class societies, fashion developed apace with the dissemination of commodities. Fashion may even have attained some coherence within the ruling strata of these societies. But precapitalist fashion, even among the ruling classes and their growing numbers of emulators, did not structurally resemble modern capitalist fashion. For precapitalist fashion did not fully engage the lower classes in its web. If such fashion powerfully contributed to the hegemony of the ruling classes it did so because of the display of opulence, not because of their changing forms of display that are taken as essential to fashion as a comprehensive system. Dress indeed articulated differences so deep as to defy bridging. The power of capitalist fashion lies precisely in the lure it extends of possible emulation. The people who watch *Dynasty* and *Miami Vice,* not to mention all those who watch television commercials and MTV, suffer under the illusion, carefully cultivated by the media, that they might participate in fashion.

With the advent of capitalism, everything that the social conservatives of the early modern period feared occurred. Status, in the form of self-presentation, became a market question. Fashion mediated that transformation, primarily by becoming the premier example of what Marx called the "fetishism of commodities." In this respect, fashion in the modern world can be understood by analogy to the emergence of labor-power as a commodity. Obviously, the two should not be seen as identical. But the analogy deserves careful attention, for it offers the best way to underscore the paradox of fashion in the modern world and to call attention to its complex politics.

In Marx's analysis, the fetishism of commodities invokes human beings' alienation from their own labor-power, and, by general implication, their alienation from themselves and others. For increasingly the market works to make social relations—one person's relations to others—appear to be the relation of a person to a thing. The commodity form disguises the human and social content. Under capitalism, commodities apparently acquire a life of their own as the actual embodiments of value. In truth, their value lies in their representing alienated and congealed labor-power, not in the qualities evoked by their external form. The move towards the expanded consumerism of the society of mass production has provoked both Marxist and non-Marxist cultural critics to underscore the growing predominance of mere things in our society, culture, and consciousness. The terms alienation and reification have been extended well beyond their original Marxist meanings to invoke a generalized sense of estrangement, the perception that in a world materially "too much with us" we are as strangers in a strange land.

The vulgarized intuitive understanding of the fetishism of commodities and its related concepts, alienation and reification, implies little other than a disgust with materialism that is shared by various conservatives and even some liberals. The insight has its place, but should not be confused with a

Marxist analysis, which justifies an article in its own right. In linking fashion to the fetishism of commodities, I am assuming that the commodities that function in, or help to create, the illusion of fashion resemble all other commodities in their economic attributes. Like other commodities, they embody the congealed labor-power which has produced their contribution to surplus value. If anything, these commodities can intuitively be recognized as diverging widely from simple use-value. In an important sense, their market value derives from their direct defiance of use-value, from their quality of luxury.

Marx's analysis of commodity fetishism lies in his understanding of historically specific relations of commodities as the products of the social relations that produce them. Bourgeois theorists grasp at the idea of fashion as ahistorical or, better yet, as transhistorical. This commitment permits them to argue that fashion obeys other laws than those of the market, that its analysis requires other sensibilities than crude economic determinism. Marxist analysis permits at least a preliminary understanding of fashion as historically specific and thus inescapably hostage to specific social relations of production and reproduction. It does not require that we present fashion as economically determined.

The emergence of modern fashion, like the rise of capitalism which it paralleled, occurred piecemeal rather than in a single cataclysmic advance. Struggles over different groups' rights to engage in fashionable display manifested one aspect of the larger struggle between an emerging bourgeois class and the traditional nobility that defined itself as an estate. During the course of the struggle, the nobility implicitly defended the tendencies toward caste that informed its own class position, whereas the bourgeoisie implicitly defended the tendencies toward individual mobility that would inform the capitalist class system. The increasingly rapid dissemination of fashion throughout the eighteenth century appeared to contemporaries—who, in this respect, saw clearly—as a dramatic solvent of traditional social bonds and, consequently, order. Much of the language of social criticism of the eighteenth century focused explicitly on fashion, which it systematically linked to the corrosion of traditional morals and politics.[12]

During the same period, the defenders of fashion, perhaps inadvertently, cogently exposed its ambiguous position as link between culture and economics—between ideology and social relations of production. The defenders, however, did not normally defend the cultural consequences of fashion directly. Rather, they defended the economic advantage of luxury consumption. But the expansion of luxury consumption did not proceed in isolation from culture and social relations; it required consumers and producers of luxury goods. Before the French Revolution consumption and production uneasily jostled traditional, or corporatist, social relations. They affected dynamic sectors within both the nobility and the bourgeoisie, which they began to bind together in a common culture despite official differences in status. They affected dynamic sectors of production, fueling the increase in various "free" trades, wage laborers especially in textiles, and merchant capitalists.[13]

The French Revolution, like other bourgeois revolutions before and after, resolved some of the more glaring contradictions, albeit while introducing some contradictions of its own. The substituting of bourgeois for feudal property as the fundamental law of the land buried the question of fashion's explicit and enforced relation to social standing. No longer would the ruling class turn to sumptuary laws to buttress its own pre-eminence. Henceforth, it relied directly on wealth, as generated by capitalist social relations, to do the job. As a general rule, its most firmly established exponents favored a certain sobriety; the parvenus, who frequently had difficulty in mastering the subtleties of affluent sobriety, continued to favor display. But the general tendency, which operated in fits and starts and with wide variation according to region and even to occupation, pointed towards the integration of various elite and upwardly mobile social groups within a single capitalist ruling class.[14]

From the period of the bourgeois revolutions on, the hegemony of that ruling class rested on different foundations. The panoply of bourgeois discourses of individual freedom and opportunity converged in repudiating legally established social distinctions. This repudiation proved consistent with the capitalist market, which included the maximum possible free mobility of commodities, including labor-power. To be sure, the old constraints on individual action and attitudes did not succumb immediately. Various restrictions continued to limit the mobility of labor and, in particular, the transformation of beliefs.[15] Nonetheless the self-revolutionizing operation of capital had been irreversibly launched.

Under these conditions, fashion as a system, which had been taking shape along the lineaments of merchant capital, came into its own. Intrinsically, the new system manifested itself in accelerating rapidity of change; extrinsically, in its growing influence over the perceptions, self-perceptions, and dress of members of the lower classes. At first, fashion unevenly penetrated general consciousness and affected individual behavior. Proximity and disposable income, however paltry, began to play as important a role as objective class standing in any individual's observance of fashion's laws.

During this period, fashion consolidated its hold on the female imagination and increasingly defined its mission as shaping female consciousness and commanding female purchasing power.[16] Men, notably the dandies of the more cosmopolitan cities, did not entirely escape its hold, but, as a general rule, it spared them its worst excesses. Male dress settled into general patterns of sobriety and efficiency that provided appropriate garb for action in the world and an appropriate backdrop for female display.

Gender and Fashion

The advent of capitalist fashion brought with it a marked division of fashionable labor by gender that would persist through the late twentieth century. This division echoed the development of bourgeois domesticity in particular and capitalist gender relations in general, complete with their own internal contradictions. It is common for many feminists to view modern fashion as a massive conspiracy against the mobility, comfort, and healthy self-perception of women. The truth probably remains more complex. Fashion did emphasize a special discourse of femininity and, in so doing, powerfully contributed to women's internalization of gender roles. Nonetheless, the women who embraced the image were neither mindless nor uniformly masochistic. The fashionable image of femininity did cost women, sometimes heavily, but it also articulated substantial gains that they had made. If today we reject the image of enforced leisure that nineteenth-century female fashion invoked, we must also recognize that in time and place some freedom from heavy domestic labor (including such delights as the lugging of gallons of water) had its appeal for women themselves. Even the images of youthfulness—the unkind would say girlishness—and contained sexuality that prevailed during the middle decades of the nineteenth century may have had some appeal to women who confronted their own premature aging and were just beginning to escape overtly misogynist attitudes towards female sexuality.

Women's subjective relation to the fashion they warmly, and sometimes compulsively, embraced remains as fraught with contradiction as every other aspect of women's identity during the early phase of capitalism. And within whatever general pattern we may discern, variations abounded. The whole issue of tight-lacing, for example, generates heated discussion.[17] There are even grounds for believing that fashion helped to direct women toward a potentially self-inhibiting narcissism. Certainly nineteenth-century feminist critics of fashion emphasized its physically and psychologically debilitating and constraining aspects. For fashion did constitute women's special form of commodity fetishism—and an all the more destructive form for its intertwining itself so intimately in women's psyches.

Fashion tightened the bonds of womanhood in other respects as well, for women functioned simultaneously as its premier producers and consumers. Fashion generated its own material culture that embraced women of very different class positions. Working girls, especially maids and seamstresses, but also textile workers, glove makers, and all the other women who worked in the fashionable trades, shared with those for whom they provided fashionable commodities a concrete knowledge of feathers, materials, the turning of seams and the fitting of collars, bodices, or bustles. These foundations in material practice endowed images of fashion with a special concreteness for women. They also afforded lower-class women their premier experience of status and wealth. It would appear that innumerable women indeed viewed their own mobility, to the extent that they considered individual mobility at all, as passing through—depending on—the ability to dress the part.[18]

The expansion of mass production and the rise of big business during the late nineteenth century vastly increased the influence of fashion on women of all classes. The accelerating accessibility of fashion as commodity, particularly in ready-to-wear clothing and standardized printed dress patterns, and at rapidly falling prices, brought at least facsimiles of fashionable dress within the means of growing numbers of women. The simultaneous loosening of social bonds through the growing penetration of the market into families and communities also began a long process of freeing young women from the hold of expected patterns of behavior. While middle-class women began to travel to Europe, attend college, or enter quasi-professional employment, working-class women entered the paid labor force. Women still tended to return to primarily domestic roles upon marriage, but growing numbers never married at all, and even those who did were more and more likely to enjoy a brief period of independence before marriage. The growth of department stores in particular and consumer culture in general further ensured that even after marriage many women would participate in a consumerism that required them to keep up with fashion.[19]

Fashion: Choice or Constraint?

Since the early nineteenth century, and at an accelerating rate in the twentieth, fashion, powered by the expansion of the capitalist market, has afforded a medium for the self-expression of the individual. The ability to buy has become an ever more important measure of success and worth. The abolition of formal, or legally guaranteed, social hierarchy opened the way to talent, initiative, and work. It opened the way to freedoms for individual advancement and self-expression undreamed in previous societies. In theory, as individuals enjoyed progressively greater freedoms, fashion should have become more individualistic. Above all, it should have become more diverse and less rigid in its claims. Fashion should, in a word, have disappeared. Since it has not, and since, paeans to liberation notwithstanding, it has shown no signs of relinquishing its grip on human imagination and behavior, its politics compel attention.

This failure of fashion to dissolve into individualistic self-expression brings us back to my suggestion that fashion displays in order to conceal. Consider the contemporary scene. At first glance, fashion appears to have collapsed into a veritable kaleidoscope of differences, of that free play of the imagination which should result from the ideal of fashion as self-expression. But precisely like the kaleidoscope, contemporary fashion operates within clearly defined boundaries. The contemporary scene offers much that is disquieting, but little that is random. In fact, the fashion with which we live is, in its own way, even more dictatorial than the fashion of a century or even a half-century ago.

Anne Hollander, the art historian, writing of the relation between clothing and art under the revealing title *Seeing Through Clothes*, has argued that our art never presents us with realistic portrayals of the human body, that even naked bodies are depicted as they would look if clothed in the garments of their time.[20] We all see each other, and especially recognize each other, through clothing. Clothing constitutes the external manifestation of the internal person. Just as it is difficult for people to know each other independent of the words in which they represent themselves, so is it difficult for most people to know each other—at least in normal social situations—independent of the clothes through which they represent themselves. For many purposes, clothing does make the woman or the man. And there is very little innocent clothing left in our world—very little clothing that clearly can be identified as costume or uniform—identified, in other words, as a neutral representation of occupation or status.

Some may applaud this development as evidence of the decline of external constraints on personal freedom. But it has another side. For the decline of costume and uniform has resulted in fashion's domination of most of the clothing that most of us wear. Every garment that we purchase implicitly represents a choice. Those choices may be governed by innumerable factors not directly related to fashion—money, opportunity, time, interest, and more. But since the clothing, independent of our intentions, will exist and represent us in a world governed by fashion, our unconcern can never be neutral. It will identify us as lacking the money, or the time, or the taste, or the interest to have bought other clothes than we did. The rules for the right thing to wear have almost entirely collapsed. Almost the only remaining rules concern men's dress at the highest levels of business and government. It should make us thoughtful about women's and less important men's so-called "liberation." For that liberation has left those of us whose public existence—in the sense of image or self-presentation—depends upon a politics of fashion that we do not directly control, hostage to a ceaseless obligation to define and redefine ourselves. The imperative to be "right," to be in fashion, is probably stronger than it has ever been: there is so little other than fashion or style left to define us.

Only this imperative can make sense of the willingness to risk being murdered for a pair of eyeglasses, of the passion and anxiety with which so many twelve- to fifteen-year-old girls, and increasingly boys, try to select the "right" pair of blue jeans or running shoes. And the tide is engulfing men as well as women. Male cosmetics have proliferated, as have styles in men's clothing. The mounting pressure that fashion is exerting on men, although not my subject here, confirms my general argument. For men, who were once understood to owe their standing in the world to their internal qualities, especially their ability and effort, are increasingly represented as owing their (precarious) position to their self-presentation.

The growing pressure of fashion on men indirectly underscores its concealed class politics. Perhaps as fashion's gender lines erode further, its class lines will become more visible. For the moment, the gender lines still provide the dominant taxonomy, notwithstanding mushrooming emphasis on sports and other kinds of unisex garb. Even the most stylish and elite fashion magazines willingly concede, indeed frequently celebrate, the contributions of the women's movement to contemporary fashion and our new diverse and casual—to invoke that fashionable barbarism and ideological swindle—"life styles." In fact, most of them have moved well beyond the early phase of what the well-dressed woman wears for success. *Glamour* or *Mademoiselle* or *Cosmopolitan* or *Savvy* or *Working Woman* still offer plenty of advice on what to wear to what kind of office or for what kind of job interview, and plenty of warnings about how you will lose or never get the job if you do not. But those magazines predominantly aim to reach young, single working women who presumably have to hustle to support themselves. They see their primary responsibility as adapting changing fashions to the needs of their clientele. *Vogue* or *Harper's Bazaar* or *Elle* tell a different story. Their pages have all but banished the world of work, except for passing glances at show business and the redecorating of country chateaux—and, naturally, the demanding world of high fashion itself.

Vogue, Bazaar, and *Elle* do, however, offer the best introduction to what might be called fashion in the raw. And what they offer offers pause for thought. The fall offerings of the past two years cluster around two main trends that give little aid and comfort to feminists. First, the trend that has been evident during the past few years toward structured, or official, dressing continues. Formal evening dresses, dinner dress, "little" dresses, afternoon suits abound. The retreat from gender equality leaps from every page. Here is the fairy-tale version of the world of the housewife, the world of the soaps and of Harlequin romances—although most of them make more concessions to women's careers, if only as pastimes. The emphasis on femininity in the conventional sense proliferates. But since even reactionaries cannot completely turn back the clock, it is a sexually liberated femininity. The shapes frequently recall those of the nineteenth century, when the cult of separate spheres was at its height, or the nineteen-fifties, when it enjoyed a resurgence—but with altogether more flesh exposed. In fact, both the shapes and the colors especially evoke nineteenth-century images of the courtesan. The images are as contradictory and confusing as the politics they evoke. Sexual license with no abortion? The stability of the family with visible female sexuality? Conservative social mores that can be bought for hard cash by any chorus girl? I do not begrudge chorus girls social mobility; I do wish they could get something better for their efforts. When the conservative values that are being evoked were in their heyday, no lady could afford to have her name, much less her picture, in the newspaper. Now we have *People* magazine and the "Lifestyles of the Rich and Famous."

The second trend superficially makes more concessions to the sensibilities of the women's movement, for it promotes loose, men's clothing for women. What more could one ask? Comfort and a hint of androgyny. But look again. The men's clothing for women is not merely loose, it is oversized. Instead of disguising female sexuality, it emphasizes it. The women who model the clothes look disconcertingly like young girls in their father's, older brother's, or big strong boyfriend's shirts and sweaters. They drown in them. The artful cut of broad, cropping shoulders makes the woman look tiny, fragile, and quintessentially female.

So what is the message? All we wanted all along was to dress up in men's clothes? This particular fashion presents the women's movement as little more than a masquerade, as does the persisting emphasis on broad, structured shoulders for jackets and dresses—shades of quarterbacks—especially when coupled with miniskirts. It should not require comment that no woman could plausibly wear such clothes to any normal job. They are not professional clothes; they are play clothes, display clothes. If they reflect the relaxation of outmoded and artificial rules, they do so only by offering leisured women something new to wear when they meet other leisured women for lunch in chic restaurants, or go to the country for the weekend. They would doubtless prove acceptable for fashion models to wear to work, but they otherwise caricature working women—reduce women's work to at best a game of play-acting, at worst a farce.

In this respect, the formal clothes and the oversized men's clothes, however disparate in appearance, belong to a single system, a single view of the world, a single politics. They both emphasize privilege based on wealth; they emphasize conventional female roles, and they harshly repudiate the notion of women's equality with men. In both instances, the cut of the clothing underscores its thematic message. Whatever the volume of material—and it can be considerable—the waists are accentuated, as are the wrists and ankles, and frequently mobility is restricted. This theme extends not only to tight waists, straight skirts, and uncomfortable shoes—although all of those abound—but even to the large sleeves of the purportedly liberating men's clothing. A sleeve that stretches directly from wrist to waist, carrying yards of material, does not encourage sharp, vigorous, or efficient use of the arms and hands. Tellingly, this sartorial emphasis on female fragility has captured the fashion scene at the very moment at which the necessary consequences of physiological difference between men and women are dramatically shrinking. Modern industry and warfare no longer require brute force. The contraceptive revolution has even freed women from the reproductive consequences of sex.

It is safe to assume that the growing number of successful, professional, upper-middle-class women are not wearing any of these clothes, although Geraldine Ferraro made a concession to them in what she wore for her acceptance speech. Tune into *Wall Street Week* some Friday evening. You will see women who have made it indeed, and if you even notice their clothes, you will not find them worthy of special attention. Growing numbers of successful, professional women are no longer doing their own shopping at all. They are hiring professional shoppers who not merely save them the time and energy required by shopping, but who limit their choices for them. These women are finding their sartorial as well as their professional path into the elites of business and government. And they have, professionally speaking, succeeded in opting out of fashion.[21] They are also exercising no influence whatsoever on fashion as a system of representation and hence no influence on the politics of fashion. The conservative professional man also may be of little concern to the world of fashion, but at least he occasionally appears as prop, or backdrop, for the fashionable woman whose skills in her métier have presumably earned her free access to his bank account and charge cards. The conservative professional woman is represented by her antitheses—the fashionable wife and the little girl dressed up in men's clothes.

The gender politics of fashion merge, almost imperceptibly, into its class politics. Fashion's tendency to conceal the independent woman by revealing everything else—the wife, the little girl, the lover, and above all the sex—intervenes decisively in the political struggles that dominate American society.

Normally those who write about fashion delight in celebrating its democratic tendencies. We have heard much since the 1960s about the influence of the street on the salons of *haute couture,* which in fact experienced a number of bad years but have rebounded forcefully in the last few years. Popular culture was said to have given us miniskirts and blue jeans and more.

Repeatedly we hear that fashion responds to the will of the people; it is democracy incarnate. In fact popular culture has exercised a recognizable influence on fashion, but only at the most superficial level. At its core fashion is not unmediated self-expression. Mediation is what fashion is all about. And the first great mediator is the market. How democratic are the politics of a fashion that borrows themes from popular culture to entertain a bored and cynical clientele and offers working people visibly inferior copies in visibly inferior materials and colors? And that is before we even raise the question of a fashion industry that feeds off the sweated labor of the women of the third world, including the third-world enclaves that our own big cities are becoming, while throwing "greedy," "overpaid" American workers out of work.

Most lower-class women do not, in fact, read *Vogue, Bazaar,* or *Elle,* or expect to own the clothes they promote; yet these magazines do influence lower-class women's relation to fashion. For they, along with *W* and, perhaps especially, *Women's Wear Daily,* constitute the general staff of the multinational fashion industry. They serve the industry by promoting its commodities in association with the looks and lives of real and imagined women. The pages flip from models to women just-like-you, the reader. Few readers are anything at all like the women whose lives are depicted, but the invitation to identify is explicit, and the success of fashion advertising depends upon it. You see the same technique at work in television ads. Here is the fetishism of commodities in action. You are what you possess, what you wear. What you possess or wear can make you what you want to be. Fashion advertising knows no mercy. It leaves us with no attributes or qualities to withstand its wares. The message is stark: without those wares we are nothing. This process extends throughout society. The upper echelons of the fashion industry do establish the styles for the rest of society. There may be brief periods during which popular currents escape its grasp, but normally the best designers co-opt those trends before they acquire a life of their own. The fashion industry dictates not merely the styles that will be available in any year, but the sizes in which they will be available. And, above all, it determines what will look "right"—the lines and the colors that will permit people to recognize each other as belonging—as okay.

At present, fashion seems to be successfully binding together the aspirations of different social classes in ways that firmly support the growing class differences in our society. The repudiation of the independent working woman is especially important here. By emphasizing the domestic and sexual and play identities—the leisure—of upper-class women, fashion is offering working-class women a distorted version of their own goals. It is confirming the purportedly natural alliance between sunbelt, high-tech money, and the traditional values of working people who still want their daughters to be virgins, their sons to have jobs, and their own women to be mothers—the values, to borrow from the reactionary ad for Miller beer, of the "American Way." In this respect, upper-class women are being invited to accept restricted roles—or at least a restricted image of their roles—in the interests of the dominance of their class as a whole. I cannot here do more than ask how the flagrant display of female sexuality that accompanies this purported upper-class domesticity can be squared with the values of people who oppose abortion on moral grounds and who desperately fear the disintegration of what once looked to them like a stable world grounded in stable values. But I do think it has something to do with the destructive combination of what a group of feminist scholars has called "the powers of desire" and that fetishism of commodities to which I keep returning.[22] It also has to do with the complex relation between the structures of order and the attributes of fantasy and change as ordinary people experience them.

Fashion and Desire

The power of fashion over human imagination and behavior derives from specific relations of class, gender, and race. Its politics reflect and articulate those complex politics as they themselves reflect and articulate the prevailing social relations of production. Fashion, as the embodiment of our interdependence through the market, designates commodities as signs of identities. As the commodities more and more replace alternate forms of mediating social relations, they become invested with all the desires with which humans are born. They surely restrict the forms or objects of our desire—multiplication of commodities notwithstanding—but they do not dull their intensity. Rather, they provide the illusion that the desires can be sated. That commodities do not, in fact, normally sate desire, but rather feed it only means that we are bound in a web of commodities, condemned to experience an escalating sense of need.[23] Many people survive and prosper without succumbing to a compulsive addiction for fashion, although most people who live and work in the world cannot afford to neglect it entirely.

Their investment of fashion—commodities—with personal desires and goals does, however, significantly shape the ways in which people think about themselves. The acceptance of commodities as the embodiment of the self, and its corollary, the acceptance of fashion as the articulation of the self, leads many women, and perhaps men, to focus their efforts on the acquisition of clothing that will somehow transform them, make their dreams come true, make them like the leisured, privileged women who represent femininity. Fashion in this sense plays a significant role in shaping women's dreams and in deflecting them from identifying with the goals of the women's movement, whose members many persist in seeing as a bunch of angry women, "bra-burners," and lesbians. It surely testifies to the power of fashion as a political language that women have had such trouble in breaking through many women's image of feminism. So long as it can be assumed that feminists do not like men, do not like pretty clothes, and are incapable of participating in loving marriages or raising decent children, we shall have millions of decent and hard-working women who will resist fighting for rights and causes that would improve their lives and strengthen the class interests of themselves and their husbands. They will continue to be mesmerized by that fantastic distortion of their own values that promises them that, if they do not question the status quo or the powers that be, some stroke of the wand may one day transform them into fashionable women who—whatever their apparent unwomanly exhibitionism—stand undisputed in their claims to represent the best of American womanhood.[24]

Fashion cannot be identified with any single group or institution, and for that reason alone the conspiracy theories of fashion do not work. We cannot point to any specific evil power that is doing this to us. Yet fashion is not simply a language, a reflection of imagination and self-expression. Fashion does articulate the way in which we interact in society, but it does not allow equal weight to all members of society and to competing social values. Because it depends so heavily on the brilliance of execution embodied in commodities, it disproportionately reflects the values and intentions of the powerful. Fashion can always borrow bright ideas wherever it finds them, but it does not integrate them merely into its own system of representation, it also integrates them into its own system of commodities. Fashion would not work, would not be fashion, if it did not correspond or refer in some way to the real world. Its themes must evoke recognition. But it does have the power to invite identification with distorted images. It can wrap its tentacles around some small part of our sense of ourselves and then convince us that the new image into which it weaves that part is in fact us. Not for nothing do the leading fashion magazines so frequently proclaim: The Real You! By claiming to be the custodian of the real us, fashion helps to shape how we see ourselves, makes us hostage to how others see us. And, despite the fantasies of utopian theories of liberation, so we are. The point is not our interdependence, but its content, forms, mediations. The fashion with which we live reinforces the worst inequalities and injustices of our society, does its best to distract us from what might be our serious purposes, and makes a mockery of what remains precious and valuable in our inherited values.

Notes

1. Roland Barthes, *The Fashion System*, trans. Matthew Ward and Richard Howard (New York: Hill & Wang, 1983).

2. Alison Lurie, *The Language of Clothes* (New York: Random House, 1981). Cf. the more focused view of the professional fashion reporter Kennedy Fraser, *The Fashionable Mind: Reflections on Fashion 1970–1981* (New York: Knopf, 1981).

3. For accounts of successful business careers in various aspects of fashion, see, e.g., Edmonde Charles-Roux, *Chanel*, trans. Nancy Amphoux (New York: Knopf, 1975); Caroline Seebohm, *The Man Who Was Vogue: The Life and Times of Condé Nast* (New York: Viking, 1982); Axel Madsen, *Living for Design: The Yves Saint-Laurent Story* (New York: Delacorte, 1979); and Carrie Donovan, "Designer Donna Karan: How a Fashion Star Is Born," *New York Times Magazine*, 4 May 1986.

4. For the implications of that dictum, see my "The Personal Is Not Political Enough," *Marxist Perspectives*, no. 8 (Winter 1979–80), pp. 94–113 [reprinted in this volume, pp. 51–68].

5. See, e.g., Petr Bogatyrev, *The Functions of Folk Costume in Moravian Slovakia*, trans. Richard G. Crum (The Hague: Mouton, 1971); Mary Ellen Roach and Joanne Bubolz Eicher, eds., *Dress, Adornment, and the Social Order* (New York: Wiley, 1965); A. L. Kroeber, *Style and Civilizations* (Ithaca, N.Y.: Cornell University Press, 1957), and his "On the Principle of Order in Civilization as Exemplified by Changes of Fashion," *American Anthropologist*, vol. 21 (1919), pp. 235–263; Ruth Benedict, "Dress," *Encyclopedia of Social Science*, vol. 5 (New York: Macmillan, 1931), pp. 235–237; Max von Boehn, *Modes and Manners*, 4 vols., trans. Joan Joshua (London: George Harrap, 1932–1936).

6. The early capitalist bourgeoisie contributed to this process in a variety of ways, notably by collecting and marketing the proverbs and songs that had been developed over the years by rural oral culture. On ballads, see Deborah Symonds, "The Reforming of Women's Work and Culture: Scotland 1750–1830," doctoral dissertation, SUNY Binghamton, 1985, and on proverbs, Martine Segalen, *Love and Power in the Peasant Family* (Chicago: University of Chicago Press, 1985).

7. Marc Bloch, *Feudal Society*, trans. L. A. Manyon (Chicago: University of Chicago Press, 1961).

8. Thorstein Veblen, *The Theory of the Leisure Class* (New York: Macmillan, 1899).

9. Françoise Pionnier, *Costume et Vie Sociale: La Cour d'Anjou, XIVe–XVe Siècle* (Paris / The Hague: Mouton, 1970).

10. The general argument derives from my own reading of medieval history. Feminist and social historians normally view courtly love as evidence of the rise of women's status in particular and the rise of civilization in general, not as a symptom of the decline of early medieval (male) society. See, e.g., Joan Kelly, "Did Women Have a Renaissance?" in her *Women, History, and Theory: The Essays of Joan Kelly* (Chicago: University of Chicago Press, 1984). On the changing nature of service at the end of the early modern period, see Sara C. Maza, *Servants and Masters in Eighteenth-Century France: The Uses of Loyalty* (Princeton, N.J.: Princeton University Press, 1983), and Cissie Fairchild, *Domestic Enemies:*

Servants and Their Masters in Eighteenth-Century France (Baltimore: Johns Hopkins University Press, 1984).

11. On the general emergence of urban civility, see Norbert Elias, *The Civilizing Process,* 2 vols., trans. Edmund Jephcott (New York: Pantheon, 1982), and his *The Court Society,* trans. Edmund Jephcott (New York: Pantheon, 1983).

12. See my "Introduction" in Samia Spencer, ed., *French Women in the Age of Enlightenment* (Bloomington: Indiana University Press, 1985). Both Mary Wollstonecraft and Adam Smith sharply criticized fashion as a form of crippling dependency, she for women, he for middle-class men.

13. See Elizabeth Fox-Genovese and Eugene Genovese, *Fruits of Merchant Capital* (New York: Oxford University Press, 1983), on the general problem. On French fashion in particular, see my "The Peasant Revolution of Yves Saint Laurent," *Marxist Perspectives,* no. 2 (Summer 1978), pp. 58–93. The article includes a preliminary bibliography of works on fashion on which I have also drawn for this essay.

14. European novels provide dramatic confirmation of the concern with dress as self-presentation and fashion as social code. See, in particular, the meticulous descriptions in the novels of Flaubert and Balzac.

15. William H. Sewell, Jr., *Work and Revolution in France: The Language of Labor from the Old Regime to 1848* (Cambridge: Cambridge University Press, 1980), and William M. Reddy, *The Rise of Market Culture: The Textile Trade and French Society, 1750–1900* (Cambridge: Cambridge University Press, 1984).

16. See, for example, Evelyne Sullerot, *Histoire de la Press Feminine en France des Origines à 1848* (Paris: A. Colin, 1966).

17. On tight-lacing, see David Kunzle, *Fashion and Fetishism* (Totowa, N.J.: Rowman & Littlefield, 1982), and his "Dress Reform as Antifeminism," *Signs,* vol. 2 (1977), pp. 570–579. See also Helene E. Roberts, "The Exquisite Slave: The Role of Clothes in the Making of the Victorian Woman," *Signs,* vol. 2 (1977), pp. 554–569, and her "Reply to David Kunzle's 'Dress Reform as Antifeminism,'" *Signs,* vol. 3 (1977), pp. 518–519. For general overviews, see Valerie Steele, *Fashion and Eroticism: Ideals of Feminine Beauty from the Victorian Era to the Jazz Age* (New York: Oxford University Press, 1985), and Lois W. Banner, *American Beauty: A Social History . . . through Two Centuries . . . of the American Idea, Ideal, Image of the Beautiful Woman* (New York: Knopf, 1983).

18. Margaret Walsh, "The Democratization of Fashion: The Emergence of the Women's Dress Pattern Industry," *Journal of American History,* vol. 66, no. 2 (September 1979), pp. 299–313.

19. For recent discussions of consumer culture, see Richard Wightman Fox and T. J. Jackson Lears, eds., *The Culture of Consumption: Critical Essays in American History, 1880–1980* (New York: Pantheon, 1983), and Stuart Ewen, *Captains of Consciousness: Advertising and the Social Roots of Consumer Culture* (New York: McGraw-Hill, 1976). See also Michael B. Miller, *The Bon Marché: Bourgeois Culture and the Department Store, 1869–1920* (Princeton, N.J.: Princeton University Press, 1981); Marylene Delbourg-Delphia, *Le Chic et Le Look* (Paris: Hachette, 1981); and Trevor Millum, *Images of Woman: Advertising in Women's Magazines* (London: Chatto & Windus, 1975).

20. Anne Hollander, *Seeing Through Clothes* (New York: Viking, 1978).

21. They seem also to be opting out of traditional female roles entirely. See Patricia A. McBroom, *The Third Sex* (New York: William Morrow, 1986).

22. Ann Snitow, Christine Stansell, and Sharon Thompson, eds., *Powers of Desire* (New York: Monthly Review Press, 1983).

23. For an ahistorical psychoanalytic analysis of fashion, see J. C. Flugel, *The Psychology of Clothes* (New York: International Universities Press, 1930). See also Frank Alvah Parsons, *The Psychology of Dress* (Garden City, N.Y.: Doubleday, 1920), and Elizabeth B. Hurlock, *The Psychology of Dress: An Analysis of Fashion and Its Motive* (New York: Ronald Press, 1929). For a more socially informed psychological analysis, see Réné Konig, *A La Mode: On the Social Psychology of Fashion,* trans. F. Bradley (New York: Seabury Press, 1973). Georg Simmel remains the premier analyst of the social psychology of fashion. See his *On Individuality and Social Forms; Selected Writings,* ed. Donald N. Levine (Chicago: University of Chicago Press, 1971).

24. Agnes Heller, *The Theory of Need in Marx* (New York: St. Martin's Press, 1976).

Thirteen

Literary Criticism and the Politics of the New Historicism

In recent years, literary critics, surfeited with the increasingly recognized excesses of post-structuralist criticism in its various guises, have discovered history. Or rather, lest one suspect them of a regression to simplicity, they have discovered "historicism." In this enterprise they have, it should in fairness be noted, been wonderfully aided and abetted by a growing number of historians who, for their part, are reveling in this new attention to their own crisis-ridden discipline. A bastard child of a history that resembles anthropological "thick description" and of a literary theory in search of its own possible significance, this "new historicism" consists in a plethora of converging, but also conflicting, tendencies within cultural studies broadly construed.[1]

This move offers an unexpected opening to call contemporary literary theory to the bar of that history on which it had (albeit building on a long formalist precedent) previously declared war. The critics' war on history had its own logic, for the history they had received did not admit of happy endings. Heirs to the whimpering collapse of bourgeois individualism, they sought to wrest victory from apparent defeat by themselves proclaiming the primacy of sign and texts and the attendant deaths of author, subject, and all extra-textual selves. Their project captured the mood of our own, and all other post-heroic, times. Like innumerable predecessors, they sought to

"Literary Criticism and the Politics of the New Historicism." In *The New Historicism*, edited by H. Aram Veeser, 213–24. New York: Routledge, Chapman & Hall, 1989. Copyright 1989 by Routledge, Chapman & Hall, Inc. All rights reserved. Used by permission of the Taylor & Francis Group.

claim for the epigones the mantles of the giants. In so doing they raised technique over substance, analysis over narrative, and critic over author. Indeed, pressing the limits of credibility for all but the votaries of fashion, they announced that technique had subsumed substance, analysis narrative, and, most important, critic author. There they were standing not, as Newton would have had it, on the shoulders of giants, but sitting, as the second Napoleon pretended—recall Marx's epigram about the second time—on the imperial throne. Yet, as those of us who recognize history as the most demanding of mistresses could have told them, history herself would sooner or later confront them with the naked recognition: The Emperor has no clothes.

History will not down easily: She never does. But her returns are protean, disguised, and no more salutary than we make them. Today's "new historicism" is clearly viewed by its proponents as a good thing. Not one to gainsay this heartening rush of enthusiasm, I cannot withal let it go unchallenged. For the proponents of the new historicism have yet fully to clarify either the "good" or the "thing" of their devotion. History, like criticism, must sooner or later answer to judgment, to discrimination, and, however unfashionable the term, to meaning.[2]

Tellingly, the diverse practitioners of the new historicism have yet to issue a manifesto or even a clear statement of their respective purposes. If the new historicism has an official organ, it would appear to be the journal *Representations*, which brings together historians and literary critics in a colorful carnival of cultural readings and thick descriptions.[3] Yet *Representations* does not begin to account for the diversity of new historicist work or even its multiple tendencies. Presumably, we should have to include under the general label of new historicism the growing interest in reader-response criticism, notably the work of such feminist critics as Jane Tompkins and Cathy Davidson.[4] Assuredly, we should have to include the work of such historical and theoretical critics as Fredric Jameson, Michael McKeon, Dominick LaCapra, Richard Terdiman, and Timothy Reiss.[5] And what of the growing numbers of literary historians who also have their own journal that explicitly addresses problems of theory and interpretation?[6] The attention to rethinking literary history reminds us, if need be, of the uncertain and contested boundaries between the literati's new historicism and intellectual history. One would look in vain in new historicist pages for references to the great cultural critic, Lewis P. Simpson, or to such younger intellectual historians of the South as Michael O'Brien or Drew Faust, much less to the conservative literary scholar M. E. Bradford.[7] One can only assume that from the new historicist perspective such literary and intellectual historians do not qualify as "new."

The newness of the new historicism derives in no small measure from its continuing affair with post-structuralist criticism—notably deconstruction, with which it is much less at war than one might think—and anthropological thick description.[8] It remains, in other words, enthusiastically embroiled in that web of contemporary intellectual fashion which none of us can hope to escape completely. Withal the emphasis on newness bespeaks the central paradox that informs the new historicism as a project: Notwithstanding some notable exceptions, it is not very historical. It is especially not self-critically or self-reflexively historical. For part of the project of any contemporary historicism must inescapably be a fresh consideration of history herself—that is, a hard look at the history of modern historicism and its conflicted relations with other critical strategies.

Today's historicism has developed in response to a series of debates within cultural studies and the human sciences broadly construed, not least to those that contest the validity of disciplinary boundaries themselves. In this climate, the new historicism understandably signifies different things to its various practitioners: to some, mere attention to the past; to others, context, which includes social relations; and to at least some few others, even change over time. Historicism has also been taken to provide an opening wedge for overdue attention to the claims of gender, class, and race—to the claims of the multiple subject and the uncanonized author. If so, it is, if not necessarily a good thing, at least a good intention. But we all know about good intentions and the road they pave.

In general, the devotees of the new historicism have proved less than self-aware about the relation between their concerns and the continuing debates among historians with which they intersect. From one perspective, the new historicism bears a strong family resemblance to the venerable model of history and literature, which, it might be noted, is under serious attack in its most developed form, namely American Studies.[9] Those debates have their own history, which defies neat summary here. But the central conflicts are instructive. They especially concern the relation between the canonized texts of high culture and the culture at large and the appropriate strategies for reading any texts. Or, to put it differently, previous generations have bequeathed to us the interlocking problems of which texts to read and of how to read them. These debates in turn intersect with those about the nature of history, notably the rise of social history in opposition to discredited elite history (especially intellectual and political history), and the related skepticism about the nature of historical "events" and "facts." The main tendency in new historicism has bravely swept over most of these debates without explicitly addressing the nature of the historicism—preeminently thick description—that it is seeking to restore to the reading of texts. But it seems safe to say that the new historicists do view their project as revitalizing the increasingly formalist project of deconstruction. They thus apparently take historicism to imply something about the social life to which texts testify and by which they are informed.

Not long ago, historicism had different meanings or, better, connotations. It signified reductionism, present-mindedness, and teleology. Historicism, in short, stood in direct opposition to history, which itself was not as clearly defined as one might have hoped. The reversals—history's own deceptions—are worth savoring. The bad historicism of the recent past was normally attributed by bien-pensant bourgeois to uncouth, deterministic Marxists. Things, as things are wont, got a little confusing during the great bourgeois declension, for during a brief period the once sanctified "whig interpretation" of history—the view that history consisted in the steady progress of the human race from barbarism towards its present enlightened state—disconcertingly began to resemble historicism. No matter. We know what happens when undesirables move into a neighborhood: property values collapse. So too with intellectual values. Bourgeois individualism a-dying relegated the whig interpretation to the old neighborhood in which it was trying to confine Marxism, never pausing for that self-analysis which would have indeed revealed Marx to have been steeped in the very Scottish Historical School that engendered the whig interpretation. Today the neighborhood is being gentrified, and historicism with it. But it remains unclear whether we are witnessing a reinvigorated attention to historical understanding or a nostalgic retro window-dressing. For, as Fredric Jameson has argued, the related questions of causation and extra-textual "reality" cannot be brushed aside.[10]

History consists in something more than "just one damn thing after another," in something more than random antiquarianism, even in something more than what happened in the past. Some of those who are turning to history to redress the excesses of contemporary literary theory are calling it a "discourse"—a label that at least has the virtue of acknowledging its claims to intellectual status, and more, of acknowledging its possible internal cohesion and rules, of beginning to recognize it as a distinct mode of understanding. But their strategy runs the risk of confusing history as accounts, narratives, or interpretations of the past, with history as the sum or interplay of human actions, notably politics. School children who first learn of history as what happened in the past may lack the intellectual sophistication to grasp that what we know of the past depends upon the records—implicit interpretations of who and what matters—and upon the ways in which subsequent human beings have written about and interpreted those records. Only later do they learn to recognize history as a genre, as one particular kind of text. We still use history to refer, however imprecisely, to what we like to think really happened in the past and to the ways in which specific authors have written about it. Contemporary critics tend to insist disproportionately on history as the ways in which authors have written about the past at the expense of what might actually have happened, insist that history consists primarily of a body of texts and a strategy of reading or interpreting them.[11] Yet history also consists, in a very old-fashioned sense, in a body of knowledge—in the sum of reliable information about the past that historians have discovered and assembled. And beyond that knowledge, history must also be recognized as what did happen in the past—of the social relations and, yes, "events," of which our records offer only imperfect clues.

History cannot simply be reduced—or elevated—to a collection, theory, and practice of reading texts. The simple objection to the subsumption of history to textual criticism lies in the varieties of evidence upon which historians draw. It is possible to classify price series or coin deposits or hog weights or railroad lines as texts—possible, but ultimately useful only as an abstraction that flattens historically and theoretically significant distinctions. If, notwithstanding occasional fantasies, the nature of history differentiates historians from "hard" social scientists, it also differentiates them from "pure" literary critics. For historians, the text exists as a function, or articulation, of context. In this sense historians work at the juncture of the symbiosis between text and context, with context understood to mean the very conditions of textual production and dissemination.

In fairness, many literary critics or theorists seem also to be working at this juncture, and their best work is opening promising new avenues. I am hardly alone among historians in being heavily indebted to the work of Antonio Gramsci and Mikhail Bakhtin in particular, although admittedly both rank more as cultural philosophers than as literary critics.[12] Thus, in important instances, the center of attention can be seen to be shifting from text to context, with a healthy emphasis on the concept of hegemony and the notion of struggle within and between discourses. But only in rare instances have new historicists embraced the full implications of this project. In most cases they have implicitly preferred to absorb history into the text or discourse without (re)considering the specific characteristics of history herself.

Such a blanket charge may appear churlish, especially since so much of the work in the new historicism has attempted to restore women, working people, and other marginal groups (although rarely, so far, black people) to the discussion of literary texts. Nor can a blanket charge pretend to do justice to the diversity of works that can be lumped under the general category of new historicism. Understandably, as with any fledgling enterprise, the new historicists, in all their diversity, have worked piecemeal, borrowing from the materials that lie to hand. And, in the vast majority of instances, they have drawn their materials from the new social history and have followed it in substituting experience for politics, consciousness for the dynamics and consequences of power. Feminist critics, to be sure, have attended to the consequences of power—from which they singlemindedly argue women to have suffered—but have tended to homogenize its dynamics under the mindlessly simplistic category of "patriarchy." The end result, despite the uncontestable value of discrete efforts, has been to take as given precisely the most pressing questions, namely the (changing) relations of power and their (multiple) consequences.[13]

History, at least good history, in contrast to antiquarianism, is inescapably structural. Not reductionist, not present-minded, not teleological: structural. Here, I am using structural in a special—or, better, a general—sense, not in the sense developed by Saussure, Lévi-Strauss, or even Roland Barthes or Lucien Goldmann. By structural, I mean that history must disclose and reconstruct the conditions of consciousness and action, with conditions understood as systems of social relations, including relations between women and men, between rich and poor, between the powerful and the powerless; among those of different faiths, different races, and different classes. I further mean that, at any given moment, systems of relations operate in relation to a dominant tendency—for example, what Marxists call a mode of production—that endows them with a structure. Both in the past and in the interpretation of the past history follows a pattern or structure, according to which some systems of relations and some events possess greater significance than others. Structure, in this sense, governs the writing and reading of texts.[14]

This use of structure requires a word of justification. Structure has lapsed in fashion in large measure because of our recognition of the multiple ties that link all forms of human activity, including thought and textual production. In other words, the preoccupation with structure has given way to the preoccupation with system. The very notion of textuality in the large sense embodies the insistence on system, interconnection, and seamlessness, and therefore leads inescapably to what Jameson calls totalization.[15] That recognition is compelling, but it rests upon a denial of boundaries. The concept of structure, not unlike that of discourse, represents a commitment to drawing at least provisional boundaries. In this respect, structure, like discourse, attempts to take account of present and past politics. For politics consists in nothing if not the drawing of boundaries. If indeed, we live in and represent ourselves through a seamless web of textuality, ultimately the spoils of our living and representing accrue to those who draw the boundaries:

boundaries of the law, of the literary canon, of superordination in all its manifestations. In this perspective, politics as the will to define and the ability to impose boundaries constitutes the irreducible core of experience, textuality, and history. Politics draws the lines that govern the production, survival, and reading of texts and textuality—of text and Text.

Here again, we have an irony of sorts. Contemporary criticism implicitly, when not explicitly, grants the text a status *sui generis*, as if it somehow defied the laws of time, mortality, history, and politics. But beneath that surface lies an implacable hostility to history as structure and to politics as the struggle to dominate others and thus to shape the structure of social relations. Thus the evocation of history reduces to history as accident (in the Aristotelian sense) of the text rather than its essence, and thus, implicitly, reduces politics to its textual embodiment.

At the core of the contemporary critical project lies the conviction that we think, exist, know, only through texts—that extratextual considerations defy proof and, accordingly, relevance. And how wonderful it is that these critics make precisely the same claims for their theory that the more reductionist, not to say vulgar, cliometricians and psychohistorians make for theirs. In this respect, contemporary criticism as a philosophical project returns through the thickets of modern philosophy to the eighteenth-century Berkeleyan dilemma: Does the falling tree make a sound if none is there to hear it? Or, to take the modern variant, does the thought exist if none is there to write it? The radical attempt to transcend this dilemma, which does command attention, proposes the text as society, culture, history, consciousness, on the grounds that it is all of them or all that we can know. And it further proposes that in addition to being all of them that we can know, it is the only form in which we can know them.

Life would be easier if we could dismiss this challenge to our commonsensical, intuitive apprehension of the solidity of things out of hand. We cannot. In the post-Einsteinian and post-Wittgensteinian universe of intellectual relativism in all spheres, in the post-capitalist world of modern technology and of a restively interdependent globe, our culture's received wisdom about order, about cause and effect, about subject and object no longer suffices. Most of us know all too well that complexity, uncertainty, and indeterminacy govern our world and have effectively shattered our abiding longing to grasp the scheme of things entire. And those who refuse to accept the evidence—notably religious fundamentalists of varying persuasions—engage in a massive effort of denial and self-deception. Bourgeois culture had bravely assumed that the scheme of things obeyed a logic that the individual mind could grasp—had rested on a commitment to what modern critics are now dismissing as "logocentrism." Bourgeois attitudes towards history, notably the whig interpretation, rested upon this commitment. We now know that what we called reality is but appearance, no more than the interplay of self-serving opinions. Historians told the stories that legitimated and served the perpetuation of the powerful's control of the weak. For some, the collapse of this illusion is taken to have opened the way to intellectual anarchism: to each his or her own history. For others, it may be opening the way to a new intellectual totalitarianism, or at least to an elitist thrust that divorces history from the perceptions of the general educated public.

The literary critics cannot absorb history piecemeal, as curiosity, landscape, or illustration. Nor can the historians restore history in all its innocence. The epistemological crisis of our times itself reflects the crisis of bourgeois society—a crisis of consciousness, certainty, hierarchy, and materially grounded social relations. I am not suggesting that we should return, if indeed we could, to an untransformed Marxism any more than to a sanctimonious whig interpretation. Not least, recent developments in history and literary studies have exposed the bankruptcy of the authoritative white male subject and pressed the claims of women, working people, and peoples of non-white races and non-Western cultures.[16] I am suggesting that a structurally informed history offers our best alternative to the prevailing literary models. For serious attention to the claims of history forces the recognition of the text as a manifestation of previous human societies. The problems of "knowing" history persist. We remain hostage not merely to the imperfection but to the impossibility of precisely recapturing the past and, in this sense, remain bound on one flank by the hermeneutic conundrum. But those constraints neither justify our abandoning the struggle nor our blindly adhering to the denial of history.

The acknowledgment of history's claims, however, confronts us with an especially delicious irony. With the collapse of the whig interpretation, Marxism has inherited the royal historical mantle.[17] This outcome would have delighted, if not entirely surprised, Marx, who studiously grounded his own political, philosophical, and historical project in the bourgeois society and ideology he was so resolutely opposing.[18] Today Marxism has, if anything, been tarred with the brush of cultural and philosophical conservatism, although the efforts of some neo-Marxists have succeeded in moving Marxism itself down the road of radical individualism and cultural pluralism. The moral is that, bourgeois pieties to the contrary notwithstanding, Marxism offers no more static a doctrine than any other vital political and intellectual current, and that Marxism is no more immune to the winds of political and intellectual change. At one extreme, neo-Marxists have succeeded in divorcing their work from its political moorings and legacy; at the other they have tied it too firmly to the vicissitudes of specific political regimes and parties.[19] But between these extremes, Marxism continues to develop as an explicitly historical and political theory, even if, as John Frow has reminded us, the "political and theoretical radicalism of Marxism can no longer be taken for granted."[20]

Marxism has, in effect, benefited from the attribute that its harshest bourgeois critics have always reproached in it: a sense—however diluted—of social, which is to say political, accountability. In the old days, the same would have been true of its bourgeois opponents. Today, however, bourgeois critics have largely abandoned the political field, or rather, they have abandoned the notion of accountability. Conservatives, however much they may be recognized as members of the bourgeois camp, have not made the same mistake. But they, even more than Marxists, have been marginalized and silenced by the academic establishment. To be sure, the popular success of Allan Bloom's *The Closing of the American Mind* should make people thoughtful. But by and large the liberal academy has responded with outraged dismissal rather than serious debate.[21] Thus, by the grace of bourgeois culture in decline, Marxism has emerged as the last bastion of historical thinking.

The philosophical problems persist, not least because of our culture's reluctance to confront the conflicted relation between what Jameson calls "freedom and necessity," and what I should prefer to call "freedom and order." But most of the practitioners of the new historicism are not addressing them at all. To the extent that they implicitly accept the view of society as text and equate history with thick description, they, if anything, implicitly perpetuate the dubious politics of what many are calling our society of information. Their considerable skills are devoted to the decoding of intertwining messages with little attention to sources or consequences.

Texts do not exist in a vacuum. They remain hostage to available language, available practice, available imagination. Language, practice, and imagination all emerge from history understood as structure, as sets or systems of relations of superordination and subordination. To write in the name of the collectivity, which is what—however narrowly and self-centeredly—all fabricators of text do, is to write as in some sense as the privileged delegate of those who constitute society and culture. Here, the concern with the links that bind different texts to each other genuinely approaches attention to history. It should prompt us to read such antebellum Northerners as Nathaniel Hawthorne and Harriet Beecher Stowe, such escaped slaves as Harriet Jacobs and Frederick Douglass, and such proslavery Southerners as William Gilmore Simms, Louisa Susanna McCord, James Henley Thornwell, and John C. Calhoun, as members of an interlocking universe. For texts, as manifestations or expressions of social and gender relations, themselves constitute sets of relations: not relations innocent of history, but essentially historical relations of time, place, and domination. And without a vital sense of the structure of those relations, the reading of texts collapses into arcane, if learned and brilliant, trivia.

With a sense of structure other possibilities open. The best recent example can be found in Michael McKeon's ambitious and compelling discussion of the origins of the English novel.[22] One need not agree with all of McKeon's formulations in order to appreciate his sensitivity to the historical location of discourses and the dynamism of their historical unfolding. For the novel did emerge in tandem with the emergence of the bourgeoisie, even if its early history also embodies a struggle between that bourgeoisie and its recalcitrant aristocratic opposition. Moreover, to take the story beyond the point at which McKeon leaves it, the ensuing history of the novel—as privileged form of bourgeois discourse—continued to enact struggles between new political positions. Bourgeois discourses, in Richard Terdiman's formulation, engendered counter-discourses.[23] And what was true for Britain and France was all the more true for the United States with its persisting division among classes, races, and world views. Antebellum Southerners, like their Northern counterparts, turned to the novel—among other genres—as a powerful weapon in defending their distinct, proslavery culture.[24]

Undeniably, an insistence on history as structure is political, although not in any narrow way. It is at once more modestly and more inclusively political than the defense of a specific political position. For texts themselves are products of and interventions in the inescapably political nature of human existence. The point is not that texts defend specific political positions, although they may, but that they derive from political relations from which they cannot be entirely abstracted.

In general, the new historicism, in failing to address these questions, has aligned itself with the post-structuralist criticism the excesses of which it is seeking to redress, and has thus positioned itself in radical opposition to history. For the new historicism is tending to restore context without exploring the boundaries between text and context. In this respect, it is modifying, but not seriously questioning, the premises that have informed post-structuralist textual analysis. And, in so doing, it is obscuring yet more thoroughly the specific character of history and historical understanding.

The defense of history as structure rests on a conviction that texts have the power to crystallize the pervasive discourses of any society and thus to shape their development. This view endows texts with considerable, although not autonomous, power. For texts enjoy a privileged position in the continuing process of fashioning and refashioning consciousness, of defining possibilities of action, of shaping identities, and of shaping visions of justice and order. But that power derives precisely from their inscription in a history reread as structured relations of superordination and subordination.

No more than the author can the text escape history, although history herself assures some texts the power to speak compellingly to more than one historical moment. No more than the author can the text claim political innocence, although a sophisticated politics invariably presents itself as comprehensive world view. The history that informs even the most abstract text is ultimately political in privileging a particular distillation of common experience. Craft and talent play their roles, as does audience response, in permitting the production and dissemination of texts and thereby in establishing their influence. But craft, talent, and audience response themselves result from history and politics. Ultimately, to insist that texts are products of and participants in history as structured social and gender relations is to reclaim them for society as a whole, reclaim them for the political scrutiny of those whom they have excluded, as much as those whom they have celebrated, for all of those in whose names they have spoken or have claimed to speak. And it is to reclaim them for our intentional political action, and ourselves for political accountability.

Notes

1. The preeminent figure associated with thick description is Clifford Geertz. See, in particular, his *Interpretation of Cultures: Selected Essays* (New York, 1973).

2. On the need to reclaim meaning, see Fredric Jameson, *The Political Unconscious: Narrative as a Socially Symbolic Act* (Ithaca, 1981).

3. *Representations* is published by the University of California Press at Berkeley and co-edited by Svetlana Alpers and Stephen Greenblatt. In fact, *Representations* does not so much stand for a philosophical movement as for a methodological one. Thus, not surprisingly, it encompasses authors of different—or undifferentiated—philosophical positions, or without philosophical concerns. Since method, however important and whatever its most devoted exponents claim, cannot stand in for philosophy, the privileging of method over philosophy understandably results in the appearance of philosophical eclecticism.

4. See especially, Jane Tompkins, *Sensational Designs: The Cultural Work of American Fiction* (New York, 1985), Cathy Davidson, *Revolution and the Word: The Rise of the Novel in America* (New York, 1987), and Janice Radway, *Reading the Romance: Women, Patriarchy, and Popular Literature* (Chapel Hill, 1984). These feminist critics are obviously building on the work of other reader-response critics, notably Wolfgang Iser. See, esp., Wolfgang Iser, *The Act of Reading: A Theory of Aesthetic Response* (Baltimore, 1978): but also for a general introduction to the work in the field, Jane Tompkins, ed., *Reader-Response Criticism: From Formalism to Post-Structuralism* (Baltimore, 1980); and Susan R. Suleiman and Inge Crosman, eds., *The Reader in the Text: Essays on Interpretation and Audience* (Princeton, 1980).

5. Jameson, *Political Unconscious*; Michael McKeon, *The Origins of the English Novel 1600–1740* (Baltimore, 1987); Dominick LaCapra, *Madame Bovary on Trial* (Ithaca, 1982); Richard Terdiman, *Discourse/Counter-Discourse: The Theory and Practice of Symbolic Resistance in Nineteenth-Century France* (Ithaca, 1985); Timothy J. Reiss, *The Discourse of Modernism* (Ithaca, 1982).

6. *New Literary History: A Journal of Theory and Interpretation* is published by the Johns Hopkins University Press and edited by Ralph Cohen. For the new developments in literary history, see Ralph Cohen, ed., *New Directions in Literary History* (Baltimore, 1974). In truth, *New Literary History* represents a catholicity and diversity that far exceed the bounds of the new historicism, however loosely drawn.

7. Among Lewis P. Simpson's extensive oeuvre, see esp., *The Dispossessed Garden* (Athens, Ga., 1975), *The Man of Letters in New England and the South* (Baton Rouge, 1973), and *The Brazen Face of History* (Baton Rouge, 1980). See also, Elizabeth Fox-Genovese and Eugene D. Genovese, "The Cultural History of the Old South: Reflections on the Work of Lewis P. Simpson," in J. Gerald Kennedy and Daniel Fogel, eds., *American Letters and the Historical Consciousness: Essays in Honor of Lewis P. Simpson* (Baton Rouge, 1987), pp. 15–41. For Michael O'Brien, see *A Character of Hugh Legaré* (Knoxville, Tenn., 1985), his edited collection, *All Clever Men Who Make Their Way* (Columbia, Mo., 1985), and his "Preface" and "Politics, Romanticism, and Hugh Legaré: The Fondness of Disappointed Love,'" in Michael O'Brien and David Moltke-Hansen, eds., *Intellectual Life in Antebellum Charleston* (Knoxville, Tenn., 1986). See also, Drew Gilpin Faust, *A Sacred Circle: The Dilemma of the Intellectual in the Old South, 1840–1860* (Baltimore, 1977). For M. E. Bradford, see, for example, *A Better Guide Than Reason: Studies in the American Revolution* (La Salle, Ill., 1979).

8 For a clear formulation of the relation between deconstruction and the new historicism, see Walter L. Reed, "Deconstruction versus the New Historicism: Recent Theories and Histories of the Novel," paper presented at the annual meeting of SAMLA, Atlanta, 1987. I am much indebted to Professor Reed for letting me read his thoughtful paper.

9. For an introduction to the debates about the nature of American Studies, see Gene Wise, guest editor, "The American Studies Movement: A Thirty Year Retrospective," *American Quarterly* XXXI, no. 3 (1979): 286–409, which includes essays by Wise and Wilcomb Washburn. For recent developments in American Studies, see, for example, Sacvan Bercovitch and Myra Jehlen, eds., *Ideology and Classic American Literature* (Cambridge and New York, 1986), and Walter Benn Michaels and Donald E. Pease, eds., *The American Renaissance Reconsidered: Selected Papers from the English Institute, 1982–83* (Baltimore, 1985).

10. Jameson, *Political Unconscious*. It should be clear from my discussion that I do not think that Jameson's work can be completely subsumed under the rubric of new historicism, if only because of his proclaimed and serious philosophical concerns.

11. See in particular, Hayden White, *Metahistory: The Historical Imagination in Nineteenth-Century Europe* (Baltimore, 1973).

12. See e.g., Antonio Gramsci, *Selections from the Prison Notebooks*, ed. and trans. Quintin Hoare and Geoffrey Nowell Smith (New York, 1971), his *Gli Intellettuali e l'organizzazione della cultura* (Torino, 1949), and his *Quaderni del Carcere*, 4 vols., ed. Valentino Gerratana (Torino, 1975); Mikhail Bakhtin, *Rabelais and His World*, trans. Helene Iswolsky (Cambridge, Mass., 1968), and Michael Holquist, ed., *The Dialogic Imagination: Four Essays by M. M. Bakhtin*, trans. Caryl Emerson and Michael Holquist (Austin, 1981).

13. See, for example, Margaret W. Ferguson, Maureen Quilligan, and Nancy J. Vickers, eds., *Rewriting the Renaissance: The Discourses of Sexual Difference in Early Modern Europe* (Chicago, 1986); Catharine Gallagher, *The Industrial Reformation of English*

Fiction (Chicago, 1985), and her "Embracing the Absolute: The Politics of the Female Subject in Seventeenth Century England," *Genders* 1 (March 1988): 24–39.

14. For a position similar to my own, see Robert Weimann, *Structure and Society: Studies in the History and Theory of Historical Criticism* (London, 1977), esp. pp. 146–87, in which he criticizes various practices of literary structuralism. In fact, the work of Roland Barthes and Lucien Goldmann, in particular, offer promising directions, even if both ultimately remain unsatisfactory on the nature of historical structures and the relations between social and literary structure. For Barthes, see, for example, Roland Barthes, *Sur Racine* (Paris, 1963); and, for Goldmann, *Le dieu caché: Etude sur la vision tragique dans les "Pensées" de Pascal et dans le théâtre de Racine* (Paris, 1955).

15. Jameson, *Political Unconscious*, p. 26.

16. For preliminary statements of my views of these matters, see my "The Great Tradition and Its Orphans: Or Why the Defense of the Traditional Curriculum Requires the Restoration of Those It Has Excluded," in Taylor Littleton, ed., *The Rights of Memory: Essays on History, Science, and American Culture* (University, Ala., 1986), and "The Claims of a Common Culture," *Salmagundi*, no. 72 (Fall 1986) [both reprinted in this volume, pp. 156–72 and pp. 145–55, respectively].

17. Jameson, *Political Unconscious*, p. 19, makes a similar point: "My position here is that only Marxism offers a philosophically coherent and ideologically compelling resolution to the dilemma of historicism evoked above."

18. For a premier example of Marx's dialogue with his bourgeois predecessors, see Karl Marx, *Theories of Surplus Value*, trans. Emile Burns, ed. S. Ryzanskaya, 2 vols. (Moscow, 1969).

19. Apolitical Marxism is best represented in the work of Edward P. Thompson and his followers. See, in particular, E. P. Thompson, *The Poverty of Theory & Other Essays* (London, 1978). Political Marxism is best represented in dominant Soviet historiography, but for Western variants, see, for example, Claude Mazauric, *Sur la revolution française: Contributions a l'histoire de la révolution bourgeoise* (Paris, 1970). For a more satisfying, yet nonetheless politically engaged Marxist history, which eschews both fashion and dogmatism, see the work of Eric Hobsbawm.

20. John Frow, *Marxism and Literary History* (Cambridge, Mass., 1986), p. 5.

21. Allan Bloom, *The Closing of the American Mind* (New York, 1987).

22. McKeon, *Origins of the English Novel*.

23. Terdiman, *Discourse/Counter-Discourse*.

24. See, for a striking example, Caroline Lee Hentz, *The Planter's Northern Bride* (Philadelphia, 1854).

Fourteen

Between Individualism and Fragmentation
American Culture and the New Literary Studies of Race and Gender

American Studies has always had to engage the problem of American identity and has even been tempted to see itself as the special custodian of our sense of ourselves as a people and a nation. (What does it mean to be an American?) Until recently, American Studies, like our culture at large, tended to answer that to be an American meant to be, or to aspire to become, white, Protestant, middle class, male, and probably from the Northeast.[1] From this perspective it naturally followed that first Longfellow, Whittier, and other representatives of the genteel tradition, and then Emerson, Hawthorne, Melville, and their successors represented the essence of American culture.

The last two decades have shattered those illusions and turned American Studies into a battleground, with the concept of American identity as the stakes. Today we know Americans to be female as well as male, black as well as white, poor as well as affluent, Catholic or Jewish as well as Protestant, and of diverse national and ethnic backgrounds. On occasion, even Southerners receive some attention, although white Southerners rarely, especially the more affluent. The last two decades have also witnessed a growing restiveness with any complacent assumptions that the culture of a privileged few

"Between Individualism and Fragmentation: American Culture and the New Literary Studies of Race and Gender." *American Quarterly* 42 (March 1990): 7–34. Copyright 1990 by the American Studies Association. All rights reserved. Used by permission of the Johns Hopkins University Press.

could adequately represent the specific beliefs and practices of the many varieties of Americans.

Our new eclecticism has included considerable soul-searching about what we mean by culture, with a general tendency to move toward a broad definition that can include the sum of any people's activities, practices, and beliefs, and it has questioned the artificial hierarchies that privilege some forms of cultural expression over others. The immediate casualty has been the willingness to accept the special place of "high" literary culture in our national self-representation.[2] The long-term casualty has been the possibility of acknowledging an American national culture.

The sharpness of the reaction against the equation of American culture with high literary culture testifies to the prior success in linking American culture with American identity. Those who reject the literary canon as the primary embodiment of American identity reject it as "not my canon or that of my people." If that canon ignores or demeans African-American women, how can an African-American woman be expected to acknowledge it as the highest expression of her identity as an American? The notion of culture as a powerful articulation of identity has thus emerged from the debates essentially unscathed, even as the battle over whose identity continues to rage. Thus, the growing numbers of postmodernists stake their conception of a transformed culture on expanding the numbers of voices to which we attend in order to let groups that have been excluded speak directly of their own experience.[3]

That battle, which pits conservatives against liberals and is, as conservatives are wont to remind us, political to its core, is leading, directly or indirectly, to the replacement of a long uncontested hegemony of white, male authors, by a plurality of women, African-Americans, and members of various minority or marginalized groups. Increasingly, previously acknowledged canonical texts are, directly or indirectly, being replaced not merely by alternate texts such as domestic fiction and slave narratives, but by films, comics, television shows, folk tales and songs, artifacts, quilts. For if many conventional courses are persisting largely untransformed, they are losing their exclusive status and being forced to compete with new courses devoted exclusively to the new scholarship. Increasingly, the conventional methods of history and literature are giving way to cultural anthropology, ethnography, oral history, the study of material culture, reader-response criticism, the sociology of literature. To its practitioners, the new American Studies embodies a welcome opening to pluralism, to its critics little more than a modern Tower of Babel. The battle for American Studies can only be understood as part of a larger struggle that encompasses all of the Humanities—our attitudes towards education, culture, texts, and criticism.[4]

Nationally, the struggle has attracted more attention than matters of cultural and educational policy normally warrant. From William Bennett's pronouncements on education to Allan Bloom's *The Closing of the American Mind* to the debate over the Stanford curriculum, and beyond, tempers have flared over the purpose and content of teaching. Hence, the special case of American Studies received careful scrutiny in the pages of *The Chronicle of Higher Education*.[5] Today the most pressing question appears to be whether any new synthesis is possible or even desirable. How, in other words, are we to weave the various cultures that we are learning to recognize and appreciate into a general view of American culture?

Much of the recent work in American Studies has been framed by the larger battle and self-consciously intended as an assault on established academic power. Thus Joan Scott, in a forum at the American Historical Association, openly conflated the introduction of new perspectives with the accession of new people.[6] In a necessary first step, this work has, above all, attempted to establish the cultural integrity of noncanonical culture. The determination to right perceived wrongs has frequently led to an identification with the excluded, but that identification has, ironically, obscured the extent to which the new perspectives have triumphed. Today, the conservatives rank as the principal, embattled defenders of an unpopular position.

The new work essentially rests on the assumption that the heretofore dominant tradition, abstracted from complex class, race, and gender relations, defended the prerogatives of a small elite to speak in the name of American culture as a whole. In so doing, that tradition marginalized or silenced outright the voices of those who did not belong to the white, male elite. To rectify that neglect, scholars have succeeded in imaginatively reclaiming the voices, representations, productions, and values of the oppressed and excluded, and they have demonstrated the cultural strength and richness of those who have been ignored. Yet the conceptual implications of this work remain, on the whole, as fragmented as the individual studies on which they are based. In other words, as Linda Kerber insisted in her keynote address to the 1988 American Studies Association meeting, American Studies scholars have been "early to widen the definition of what constitutes a text," to understand the links among Emerson's essays, Harriet Jacobs's *Our Nig*, and Campbell's soup cans, but have, withal, "remained too much a part of the complacency and status quo we deplore."[7]

The next step, in Kerber's view, which I share, must consist in understanding "difference as a series of relationships of power, involving domination and subordination, and to use our understanding of the power relations to reconceptualize both our interpretation and our teaching of American culture."[8] Some promising exceptions notwithstanding, they have given rise neither to a new synthesis nor a clear theory.[9] Thus, for example, Werner Sollors's arresting study, *Beyond Ethnicity: Consent and Descent in American Culture*, offers "consent" and "descent" as fruitful metaphors for understanding the relation of ethnic cultures to the dominant culture, but has little to say about the specific writers and texts of the dominant culture, or even about race and gender, much less class.[10] The challenge remains to understand the pattern of marginalized cultures in relation to each other as well as in relation to the canonical culture, and, especially, the relation between the canonical culture and the ideal of a national culture.

The ideas of canonical and national have largely developed in tandem, although they have potentially different implications. For the most recalcitrant defenders of canonical culture normally have in mind the Western tradition beginning with the Greeks, whereas the defenders of national culture have to wrestle with American culture's longstanding sense of itself as derivative, secondary, or "colonial" in relation to that tradition. The conservatives do not help much on this score, for they give scant attention to the new scholarship—except for occasional angry outbursts on its allegedly excessive claims and misreadings—and certainly do not propose a general theory or synthesis that would take account of its claims. The critics of the canon, for their part, normally conflate its specifics with its claim to represent all of American experience; accordingly, they dismiss the possibility of a core experience. The ghost of the canon lingers in their writing as an object of attack, but no successor has taken its place. Thus, the cultures of women, African-Americans, working people, and ethnic groups are normally considered for their specific dynamics and in relation to the canon or dominant groups that excluded, oppressed, or ignored them, but rarely in relation to other previously ignored groups. Identity in this perspective becomes primarily identity in relation to other members of the group, community primarily the community of the group itself.

In a sense, this attitude flows logically from the writings that are being rediscovered. African-Americans, Jewish-Americans, women, and others who sought to capture their distinct experience normally focused on their relations as writers and as individuals to what they accepted as "American" culture—focused on what W. E. B. DuBois captured in his memorable words,

> It is a peculiar sensation, this double-consciousness, this sense of always looking at one's self through the eyes of others, of measuring one's soul by the tape of a world that looks on in an amused contempt and pity. One ever feels his twoness—an American, a Negro; two souls, two thoughts, two unreconciled strivings; two warring ideals in one dark body, whose dogged strength alone keeps it from being torn asunder.[11]

Feminist and African-American literary studies have, perhaps, most directly and systematically explored the power of the sense of twoness among those whom they study. They have especially attacked the assumption that the quintessential American self can be represented by the solitary white male individual and have focused on the distinct experience of those whose identities that representation denied.[12] In so doing, they have primarily sought to re-create the alternate senses of self and community of women and African-Americans. These concerns have led both feminist and African-American scholarship to deploy a panoply of new methods and to address a variety of new topics in their quest to understand the dynamics of self and community among the excluded. They have especially questioned the assumption that texts may enjoy privileged status on the basis of their quality, as if they existed independent of society and history.

Frequently the new scholarship of race and gender, in insisting that the status of texts depends precisely upon society and history, appears to question whether we can appropriately speak of a unified culture at all.[13] Yet women and African-American writers were themselves pre-eminently conscious of a dominant American culture. They have fully understood that the idea of a prestigious, dominant culture was promoted by successive elites who had the political, social, and economic power to claim to speak in the name of American society as a whole. But they also took its claims seriously and did not readily jettison its standards of excellence. For us similarly to recognize the hegemony of that culture is not to slight the claims of the innumerable discrete cultures, especially those of women and African-Americans, but is merely to recognize that the elite conception of American culture was able to offer itself as the standard against which all discrete cultures had to define themselves, or at least as the standard that those who aspired to be taken seriously by it had to match.

The dominant culture, in other words, challenged women and members of other excluded groups to frame their own experience at least in part according to its norms. For many, as DuBois's words suggest, the response to that challenge required a form of bilingualism. Thus Henry Roth, in his brilliant novel, *Call It Sleep,* poignantly evoked the young Jewish boy's attempt to navigate between the language of his mother and the language of school.[14] His conundrum admitted no facile resolution. His mother's voice was that of home, love, nurture, and the traditions of his forbears; the voice of school was that of the new country and his own advancement—the voice that would eventually permit him to master and recreate the specific conflicts and wonders of his childhood.

The general case of bilingualism carried special force and poignancy for women and for African-Americans. Between them, the feminist and

African-American challenges to our inherited notion of a unified American culture largely define the main lines of the broader attacks on that culture. For if both challenge the narrow elitism of the view of culture as a privileged, white male preserve, and if both insist upon the existence and integrity of alternate cultures, namely those of women and those of African-Americans, in the end they do so on somewhat different grounds. The feminist attack on established culture understandably emphasizes gender and sexuality, arguing that to understand culture from a male perspective ignores the experience and perceptions of half of humanity. The African-American attack, in contrast, emphasizes the importance of a people's distinct cultural legacy. The most extreme separatist claims notwithstanding, feminist scholarship does not necessarily challenge the predominance of white American Protestant culture; it challenges the ways in which individuals of different genders experienced and elaborated that culture. African-American scholarship challenges precisely that predominance, although it does not necessarily challenge the predominance of men over women. However different their perspectives and implications, the literary scholarship of race and gender each delineate an encompassing attack on a white, male canon that denied the experience and identities of African-Americans and women.

Langston Hughes's "A Theme for English B" explores the complexities of that unequal bicultural or bilingual experience.[15] Hughes, representing himself as the only colored student in his class but as liking the same things as white students, wonders whether if being asked to write of himself within the context of white education does not amount to being asked to shape himself to fit the expectations of white America—to adopt white speech, a foreign tongue, as his own? How do you write your self in someone else's words? in another people's words? What can be the relation between the objective structure of our canon or tradition and the subjective experience of individuals? What can be the relation between the hallowed traditions of whites as a people and the experience of blacks as a people? "Being me, it will not be white. / But it will be / a part of you, instructor." The instructor is white, "yet a part of me, as I am a part of you. / That's American."[16]

Hughes thus raises, as a matter of personal experience and identity, the problem that Houston Baker has discussed in *Modernism and the Harlem Renaissance*.[17] How can a black student establish the links between his personal identity, what Baker calls "family history," and the language of his people's oppressors? Hughes, refusing to accept the racist implications of radical difference between the experience of his represented self and that of his white classmates, insists that he, too, likes bebop and Bach, that he is partially immersed in white culture as they are, in lesser degree, immersed in black. But writing the self presents a special challenge, for the codes of selfhood have been derived from white culture. The white modernism of Joyce and Eliot does not "sound" like the history of African-Americans. Baker's point is that the success of the Harlem Renaissance cannot fairly be measured by white, modernist criteria. Hughes's point is yet more complex and more fundamental. For Hughes, in writing his poem, does inscribe a representation of himself in the words of others and, in so doing, insists upon his independent right also to claim their tradition as his own—even as he recognizes the ways in which it denies him.

Alice Walker develops similar themes in her story "A Sudden Trip Home in Spring," poignantly exploring the response of Sarah, a black student, to the white college that has no place for the writers that represent her tradition and experience.[18] Sarah's roommate has never heard of Richard Wright, nor of any black poets—"half of America's poetry." For Sarah, Wright remains compelling especially because of his difficulty in dealing with his own father, whom, in childhood, he had seen, as children are wont to see fathers, as "Godlike," as "big, omnipotent, unpredictable and cruel," as "entirely in control of his universe"; and who, in adulthood, he had recognized as "just an old watery-eyed field hand." What, Sarah wondered with Wright, was "the duty of a son to a destroyed man?" Sarah herself could not draw black men, for she could not bear "to trace defeat onto blank pages." How could she now deal with the death of her own father, who, like Wright's, seemed to close the doors to the rooms of the mansion of this life and, by implication, the next?

Walker underscores Sarah's rootlessness and suspension between the Georgia of her people and the intellectual world of her own present and future. Where was Sarah's home? How could she claim as home a place in which she spent weeks trying "to sketch or paint a face that is unlike every other face around me?" Sarah's trip to Georgia for her father's funeral reminds her that among her people she is at home, even as it reminds her that college too has, in important ways, become her home.

So where was Sarah's home? What did she find in Georgia? And, having found it, why did she return to college? College, Walker suggests, had already given her something, if only the knowledge of Dylan Thomas that led her to wish a red coffin for her father, to wish him not to go "gentle into that good night." College, as her brother reminds her, is what her mother would have wanted for her, and her father too—the education she deserves. To spend weeks trying to draw one face is what education is about. Only when she has learned to draw that face—to represent the men of her people—will she be free to go where she chooses.

To rage, with Thomas, against the "dying of the light," Sarah had to learn to claim the history of black men, had to be able to see her grandfather in all his pride, simply as he was, "*his face turned proud and brownly against the light*." Having finally seen him that way, free from all the "*anonymous, meaningless people*," she could paint him, or, better yet, plan to make him, as he himself suggested, up in stone. For his eyes spoke to her of yes as well as no, just as her brother's courage suddenly became her "door to all the rooms."

And, with the yes and no, Walker glancingly evokes another of Sarah's debts to her white education, for her insistence on seeing both yes and no in the eyes of the men of her people shows her having made the vision of Albert Camus her own, having recognized it as also about her own life. From Camus, Sarah could borrow the fundamental insight of *The Rebel*: "What is a rebel? A man who says no. But if he refuses, he does not renounce: he is also a man who says yes, from his first movement."[19] Burying her father and planning to make her grandfather up in stone, Sarah had reclaimed the men of her own people and had thereby learned how to take from another people's education what she needed.

Langston Hughes and Alice Walker, exploring their own situations as writers between two cultures, followed in the tradition of their people.[20] For if, as Henry Louis Gates has argued in a bold theory of African-American literary criticism, African-American writers have largely learned to write by reading texts of the Western tradition, and have largely been trained "to think of the institution of literature essentially as a set of Western texts," they have also worked out of a black vernacular tradition that has provided them with the central topoi and tropes that they have shared with other African-American writers.[21] In *The Signifying Monkey*, Gates elaborates a theory for the systematic reading of the distinct African-American literary tradition and for understanding the relation between the African-American vernacular and literary traditions—primarily he seeks ways to consider the African-American tradition on its own terms, to allow it to speak in its own voice.[22]

Gates, in other words, offers an elegant and challenging theory of African-American literature as poised and constantly negotiating between a predominantly oral vernacular and a formal literary tradition. Although he avoids using "popular" as a category, he is clearly addressing its proper meaning as of the people, and thereby seeking to delineate the ties that bind a people's inherited sense of itself to its literary expression. In this respect, he is, at least in part, building upon and developing W. E. B. DuBois's notion of "twoness." But, in the end, even Gates is more interested in recovering the distinct African roots of that twoness than in exploring African-Americans' engagement with elite American culture.

There can be no doubt, as the work of Toni Morrison powerfully demonstrates, that a distinct African-American oral tradition has persisted into our own time, and informs the work and identities of innumerable African-American writers. But from the start, and especially since the mid-nineteenth century, African-American writers have also attended to the models of elite literate culture. The move from oral to written itself requires an act of translation and, as African-American writers effect it, they inescapably commit themselves to participating in some measure in a culture that is not of their own people's making. That act of translation further commits them, whatever their intentions, to viewing their people's community through the eyes of the observer. Like Zora Neale Hurston, who in *Jonah's Gourd Vine* carefully translates the more obscure words of dialect for her potential white readers, they must always think of how the vernacular should be spelled on the printed page.[23] Even if they remain direct participants in the oral culture of their youth, they necessarily do so in some measure as outsiders. The tragedy of twoness, which cannot be divorced from its potential richness, consists in that inevitable alienation.

The African-American literary tradition has developed through constant interaction with the dominant (white) culture, although the relations between African-American writers and that culture have changed in relation to changing historical conditions.[24] As Susan Willis has cogently argued, and as Toni Morrison's *Beloved* breathtakingly demonstrates, African-American women's fiction can only be understood as the product and reenactment of history, specifically the history of the South and slavery.[25] The continuing engagement with slavery testifies to African-American women writers' continuing engagement with the central myth of modern American culture—the myth of individual freedom and equality.[26] From Harriet Jacobs to Frances Ellen Watkins Harper to Pauline Hopkins and beyond, African-American women writers implicitly and explicitly confront the dominant white traditions—male and female—with their hypocrisy and bad faith.[27] But in doing so, they draw directly upon the proclaimed standards of the tradition itself, beginning with the Bible but including fiction and political theory.

Beginning with Phillis Wheatley, they have also adopted the forms of that culture, adapting them to their own visions, but also accepting most of their formal constraints and many of their cultural assumptions. These aspects of African-American women's writing have been slow to attract attention, most likely because the simple acknowledgment of their having been written required heroic efforts of demystification.[28] Not surprisingly, most of the groundbreaking work has been devoted to the sustained project of recovery that established basic facts, notably that the first African-American novel, *Our Nig*, was written by a woman, and that the most highly crafted narrative by a slave woman, *Incidents in the Life of a Slave Girl*, was, as its title page proclaimed, "written by herself."[29] On the basis of these foundations, scholars are now building a clearer picture of the accomplishments of African-American women writers, as evidenced in the splendid Schomburg Library edition.[30]

For these women writers, alienation carried special and complex meaning. For if, as Hazel Carby has argued for Nella Larsen's *Quicksand*, it was experienced as a personal state of mind, it was never only that.[31] The alienation of the African-American woman writer inevitably evoked the condition of her people and, especially, the implications of her own ties to them. Most, accordingly, intermingled sharp protests against degradation, exclusion, and oppression with direct testimony to their own ability to meet genteel social and literary standards. Harriet Wilson's *Our Nig*, which explodes with ill-contained anger, constitutes the principal exception to this tendency prior to the twentieth century when first Zora Neale Hurston and then Alice Walker turned, albeit differently than Wilson, to the recovery of African-American folk culture.[32] But, as Carby has also argued, to reduce the tradition of African-American women's writing exclusively to a romanticization of the rural folk is sorely to miss its point.[33]

In *Incidents in the Life of a Slave Girl*, Harriet Jacobs crafted a self-representation that she intended for the consumption of a white, Northeastern, middle-class, female readership. Her text simultaneously cultivates and wars with the expectations of purity and gentility that she knew she had to meet to serve the cause of abolition. Jacobs took great pains to differentiate her protagonist, Linda Brent, from the ordinary women of the slave community. Depicting Brent as speaking in flawless English, Jacobs implicitly drew a sharp contrast between her and the other slave women on the plantation whom she depicted as speaking in dialect. And although less broadly educated than her contemporary, Charlotte Forten, like Forten, she evokes Anglo-American high culture as a means of locating her text within that general discourse and locating herself as author as a potential member of the republic of letters.

Those who came after, from Frances Ellen Watkins Harper and Pauline Hopkins to Nella Larsen and Jessie Fausset, more often than not similarly wrote in "standard" English for an educated middle-class audience. The consolidation of the African-American bourgeoisie influenced their concerns as well as their style, especially their determination to demonstrate their social and literary respectability. That concern with respectability did not undercut their concern for their people, nor did the larger society permit them to sever their identification with even the least polished members of it, but they also refused to relinquish their own aspirations to respect and excellence as writers. For these women, first slavery and then the plight of the African-American rural and urban working classes constituted an undeniable aspect of their own identity as African-Americans—a moral responsibility that they could never forsake—but never an alternative to elite culture.

Literate African-Americans have always engaged the dominant culture. They have not necessarily accepted its premises about themselves nor countenanced its neglect of the vernaculars of their own kind, but engage it they have. And how could we expect them to have done otherwise? For the dominant culture advanced the prevailing standards of excellence and embodied the values of that republic of letters from which most writers have sought acceptance and respect. No less important, it enjoyed disproportionate control of the production and distribution of books.[34] Much of the tension and conflict that characterize powerful writing derive from the need to mediate between the writer's "mother" tongue and the language of formal culture. If written culture bears witness to the experience of the particular experience of the individual, it also aspires to that measure of universality or, yes, abstraction, that will make the individual's experience accessible to others.

The dominant culture has in truth exhibited an arrogant disdain for the contributions of women, African-Americans, and others to their particular cultures; worse, it has been blind and deaf to their explorations of the human condition. But if the particularity of such writers is scorned, how could their universality be recognized? The bigotry of the dominant culture has thus made a mockery of its greatest strength, namely its insistence that the representation of individual experience illuminate our understanding of what it is to be human. In response to this denial, leading scholars of African-American culture have increasingly insisted on the divorce between it and the dominant culture. However understandable their impulse, it sadly denies an important dimension of African-American writers' aspirations and ironically reinforces the current postmodernist and fragmentary tendencies of the dominant culture itself.

More sharply than any other ethnic culture, the African-American tradition exposes the tensions that bind discrete American peoples to the dominant culture. For more than any other ethnic group, African-Americans have been individually and collectively stigmatized first by the experience of slavery and then by race. Indeed African-American women writers have consistently wrestled with both questions, without ever feeling free to distance themselves as individuals or as members of the middle class from the condition of their people in general. In this respect, the power of the dominant culture to mask the reality and significance of class divisions while simultaneously denying the legitimacy of black nationalism has reinforced the notion of racial identity as the primary determinant of individual status. And the recent literary studies of race have tended to follow that lead, albeit in reversing its values. Yet most African-American women writers did not see their purpose as the celebration of oral culture, much less as the divorce of their own work from the dominant culture.

Feminist scholars have similarly castigated the dominant culture, in their case for its denial and silencing of women—for its pretensions that elite, white, male culture properly represents American identity. In Nina Baym's strong formulation, American critics have resolutely and purposefully misread our literary past in their determination literally to recreate it as a literature of beset manhood, or, as I should prefer to call it, of anxious male autobiography.[35] Following this lead, Jane Tompkins has demonstrated that Hawthorne's reputation derived in no small measure from the concerted efforts of his friends and relatives, from his position as a well-connected, white, Northeastern male.[36] Tompkins juxtaposes the case of Hawthorne's fabricated reputation to that of Harriet Beecher Stowe, who, although she enjoyed remarkable popularity and even respect in her day, has been marginalized by literary posterity as one of those "scribbling women" whom Hawthorne jealously deplored.[37]

One feminist scholar after another has seconded Tompkins's view, insisting that the picture of a uniform American tradition or national destiny rests upon ideological choices, upon a willful simplification of complex realities and relations. They are, that is, arguing that the principle of "to the victor belongs the spoils" has dominated culture and imagination as well as politics and economics. The prevailing view of what is worth reading primarily depends upon some people's vision of Americans as a people, on some people's ability to impose their views on others.[38] American Studies based on the reading of Emerson, Hawthorne, Melville, Poe, and their successors amounts to little more than a usable past for a white, Northeastern, male elite. Thus the new literary studies of gender, in labeling this received notion of a usable past as a self-serving deception that has deprived most of us of our true culture, has complemented the new literary studies of race in contesting its claim to centrality.

In reaction to the excessive claims for the representativeness of the canon, feminist critics have sought to identify and explicate a distinct female literary tradition and its relation to women's distinct experience. In an impressively thoughtful and learned study, Mary Kelley adopted the rubric "literary domestics" to capture the spirit of women writers caught between their commitment to the privacy of women's nature and mission and their participation in the public world as successful writers. Annette Kolodny, also emphasizing women's domestic vision, has argued that women developed their own fantasies of the West that differed significantly from those of men.

Between Individualism and Fragmentation

Judith Fryer has traced the theme of women's perceptions of private and public—self and world—through Edith Wharton's and Willa Cather's "imaginative structures," their representations of space.[39] Although these scholars do not argue explicitly that women were negotiating between a vernacular and the literary culture in which they sought to inscribe themselves, they do draw heavily upon women's private, as well as published, writings to reconstruct the women's lives and values, which they view as radically different from those of men. Overwhelmingly, they emphasize what women shared as women as the mainspring of women's writing and imaginations.[40] They thus reinforce the general tendency in feminist theory to see the pressing intellectual problem of our time as recognizing and understanding difference and marginalization, as recuperating the voices that the dominant culture has silenced.[41]

Women, according to many of these critics, have developed a distinct perspective on American society and, implicitly and explicitly, have held dominant male values to account. Mindful of the stringent conditions that have governed their possibilities for happiness and security, women have normally refrained from open revolt against prevailing values, but nonetheless found innumerable subtle ways of criticizing them. This view, however, as some feminist critics are beginning to understand, risks submerging the experience of different groups of women under a single homogenizing model.[42] In effect, the dominant tendency in literary studies of gender inadvertently tends towards countering the dominant image of the elite, white male self with a complementary image of an elite, white female self. But this general model of the female self does not even account for the experience and perceptions of elite, white Southern women who, like their men, normally opposed the very premises of white, Northeastern culture.[43]

Caroline Lee Hentz, a prolific and accomplished novelist, directly countered Harriet Beecher Stowe's influential *Uncle Tom's Cabin* with *The Planter's Northern Bride*. Feminist scholars have devoted considerable effort to demonstrating the ways in which Harriet Beecher Stowe engaged the necessity of abolition from a distinct female perspective. Yet a comparison with *The Planter's Northern Bride* clearly reveals that, however much Stowe spoke in the female voice, she spoke in the female voice of her class, race, and region. She never, moreover, decisively repudiated the values of the men of her community. For if she chastised their mistakes and their excesses, she nonetheless shared with them an immersion in a specific form of white, Protestant, individualistic culture. Certainly Caroline Lee Hentz, a Northeasterner by birth, purposefully echoed the elite, male culture of her region in condemning the oppression and tragedy engendered by wage labor and in celebrating the superior qualities of the beneficent slaveholder.[44]

Throughout a career that extended from the 1850s until the early twentieth century, Augusta Jane Evans yet more dramatically engaged the high (male) culture of her day. In her first three novels, *Inez* (1854), *Beulah* (1859), and *Macaria* (1863), she systematically and successively explored the problems of Catholicism which she abhorred, of faith which she believed essential, and the legitimacy of the Southern cause in the Civil War which she unequivocally supported.[45] In each of these novels, especially *Beulah*, she also explored the related problems of women's identity and independence. Evans never questioned the importance of female strength, nor the importance, within acceptable bounds, of female initiative and self-accountability. But she sharply rejected the Northeastern model of individualism and celebrated woman's acceptance of her proper role within marriage and, above all, her willing subordination to God who guaranteed any worthy social order. Although *Beulah* includes some of the themes that were appearing in Northeastern women's fiction, notably a critique of the prevailing obsession with fashionable values and hypocritical religious observance, in essential ways it departs radically from conventional domestic fiction. And although it seriously engages the implications of individualism for women, it endorses the distinct Southern values of hierarchy and particularism. The novel can profitably be read as a gloss on early nineteenth-century high culture, especially Coleridge and Carlyle, whom Evans deeply admired. Unabashedly learned, Evans used her fiction to explore the most serious intellectual issues of her day.

Hentz and Evans can no more be fit neatly into any general model of nineteenth-century womanhood than can Harriet Jacobs, however much they, like she, might occasionally borrow its rhetoric for their own purposes. After the war, as before, Southern white women, like African-American women, found themselves frequently at odds with the prevailing models of womanhood and might as easily turn for ideas and interchange to the writings of men as to those of other women. Women who took their own literary aspirations seriously especially turned to men, or possibly to Charlotte Brontë or George Eliot, because they sought recognition by what they viewed as the literary elite. For them, the canon that we are trying to dismantle enjoyed genuine literary and intellectual prestige. Their acceptance of its general merits did not, in their minds, include acceptance of all of its specific attitudes, but they did see it as legitimately representing the pinnacle of national culture.

Women and African-Americans, including African-American women, have developed their own ways of criticizing the attitudes and institutions that hedged them in. Confronted with rigidly class-, race-, and gender-specific models of acceptability, they have manipulated the language to speak in a

Between Individualism and Fragmentation

double tongue, simultaneously associating themselves with and distancing themselves from the dominant models of respectability. Their continuous negotiation with the possibilities that the culture has afforded them has had nothing to do with a mindless acceptance of themselves as lesser. It has had everything to do with their determination to translate the traditions and values of their own communities into a language that would make them visible to others—and with their own determination to participate in American culture.

As conservatives insist, the central questions are political. In general, the new literary studies of race and gender have positioned themselves resolutely on the left end of the liberal spectrum, even as they have—for whatever reasons—sharply distanced themselves from Marxism. Since Marxist thought had, until very recently, paid little attention to race, gender, and ethnicity *per se*, scholars who are primarily concerned with African-American, women's, and ethnic culture have some grounds for believing that Marxism does not directly or adequately address the issues that most interest them.[46] But the real problem seems to lie with the general view of Marxism as at least as authoritarian and mechanical as the earlier elitist consensus.[47] For, in general, the new literary studies in race and gender have focused on recovering personal experience rather than a systematic view of the central dynamics of American society and culture.[48] The haste to dismiss Marxism thus merges with a general disinclination to engage general theories of social and cultural relations and leaves many of the new studies hostage to the models that they are attacking.

Rather than engaging the battle for American culture as a whole, many of the new studies have, if anything, enthusiastically embraced fragmentation, variously described as diversity or pluralism. They, accordingly, risk settling for a one-sided reading. At issue is not the importance of recuperating previously excluded voices, and assuredly not the importance of demonstrating the integrity of African-American or women's cultures. African-American writers read and built upon other African-American writers just as women writers read and built upon other women writers. As Gates, himself building upon a tradition of African-American scholarship, has argued, African-American writers have retained strong ties to the vernacular cultures of their people. Similarly, women writers have retained close ties to the everyday lives of women. Neither African-Americans nor women unquestioningly accepted the negative views of themselves engendered by elite white men, even if those views occasionally caused some pain and anxiety. But these discrete cultures developed within a larger society and polity with which, in some measure, they identified. To sacrifice that context is to abandon the attempt to understand the ways in which African-Americans, women, and others related to each other and, especially, to those who wielded cultural as well as social and political power. It is, in effect, to lose the national dimension of the American in American Studies.

Any concept or notion of identity and culture as the articulation of community forces us to confront the problem squarely, for the cultures and communities that constitute America have notoriously permeable boundaries. If African-American and women writers understood their identities to derive, in important ways, from the communities to which they belonged, as writers they did not readily accept that they should have access only to the communities to which they were assigned. They did not accept the view that they should be defined solely in terms of their race or gender. African-American writers did not read only other African-American writers; women writers did not read only other women writers. And if they drew upon their own experience to fashion narratives and visions, they also sought to link that experience to the accepted central traditions of American—and beyond it Western— culture as a whole. The vast majority of African-American and women writers have not belonged to homogeneous communities. Literate African-Americans have never been able to avoid regular interaction with whites; literate women have never been able to avoid interaction with men. Whatever we may view as the boundaries of their immediate, affective communities, both African-Americans and women have lived in and belonged to more than one community—frequently to several interlocking social or cultural communities.

Werner Sollors's model of consent and descent begins to engage the central issues, but does not exhaust them, especially in the cases of race and gender in which both consent and descent remained problematic. He has argued that we have overemphasized and actually misrepresented the significance of ethnicity in American culture, for ethnicity, far from being a distinct cultural identity based on community identification, is the product of precisely that objectifying elite gaze which scholars of ethnic cultures have warred against. He can thus be read to suggest that mainstream American culture has created "ethnic" as a category for its own ends, in order to explain American diversity to itself and, perhaps even—Sollors does not put it this way—to ensure the marginalization or compartmentalization of subordinate cultural communities. If we push Sollors's insight to its logical conclusion, we should be forced to recognize that the very commitment of the new scholarship to acknowledging, naming, and appreciating ethnic—and I should add racial and gender—diversity risks confirming the exclusion of those groups from the cultural mainstream. The celebration of ethnicity amounts to a reinforcement of marginalization—a reinforcement of the idea that those who consent to join the dominant culture leave their culture of origin behind them.[49]

Between Individualism and Fragmentation

T. S. Eliot insisted that we cannot hope to understand culture if we thoughtlessly identify it with individual experience. Culture, he might have said, cannot be reduced to autobiography. Instead, he said:

> that the culture of the individual is dependent upon the culture of a group or class, and that the culture of the group or class is dependent upon the culture of the whole society to which that group or class belongs. Therefore it is the culture of the society that is fundamental. . . .[50]

Culture must be understood as a manifestation of interlocking and hierarchically related communities. Relations of power inescapably color the ways in which we perceive ourselves in relation to others, ourselves in relation to the past, ourselves in relation to humanity. To put it differently, we know ourselves through the languages available to us and the languages that we know inescapably influence what we perceive ourselves to be. Individual perception is not prior to or separate from collective identity; individual perception is a function of collective identity.

Some scholars of the American literary tradition are beginning to explore its relation to prevailing social and economic relations, notably T. Michael Gilmore, Walter Benn Michaels, and others who share their perspective. This work is revealing the ways in which American literature implicitly or explicitly testified to the contradictions that undergirded the celebration of the autonomous individual.[51] Sacvan Bercovitch has compellingly insisted on the relation between the American self and the history of American culture.[52] Bercovitch, together with Myra Jehlen and others, has also insisted that we recognize the ideological dimension of even the texts we most value.[53] Recently, Jeffrey Steele has offered a close investigation of the concept of the self in the American Renaissance.[54] For more than a decade, Carroll Smith-Rosenberg has been exploring the ways in which gender structured American identity and social relations.[55] Amy Lang has charted the ways in which changing social and political preoccupations influenced the ways in which men (re)constructed Anne Hutchinson to embody their visions of gender and dissent.[56] And Gillian Brown has demonstrated that the language of domesticity pervaded nineteenth-century American cultural consciousness, affecting even elite men's representation of their society.[57] Separately and together, these and similar undertakings, specific disagreements notwithstanding, point toward a new synthesis in literary studies.

At its best, this scholarship is teaching us to recognize even the most revered texts as the products of society—covertly, if not openly—as witnesses to its struggles. Thus, as David Reynolds has recently reminded us, even so-called canonical texts betray their deep engagement with the tensions of the world in which they were produced. Elements of popular culture, preoccupations with economic change, anxieties about social status and class position all figure in texts that may not explicitly acknowledge either their debts or their anxieties.[58] Similarly, David Leverenz insists that the "vital relation between classic American writers and history" should be sought "in the broad pressures of class and gender ideologies." But even Leverenz takes pains to distance himself from the (presumably old-fashioned) view that the connection might also be sought in "the specific links between texts and political or cultural contexts"—as if ideologies could be separated from the political and cultural systems within which they develop and which they articulate.[59]

In general even the most exciting new scholarship has not fully answered the most pressing concerns voiced in the new literary studies of race and gender, particularly the determination to recover the subjective experience of those whom the dominant culture marginalized and silenced. It is as if they were moving from the preoccupation captured in William Andrews's title, *To Tell a Free Story*, to the preoccupation to "tell my own story," on the conviction that "free" embodies the values of the dominant society and thus distorts the individual's self-perception. But to abandon "free" as the product of collective experience is to abandon the cultural, social, and political context that gives meaning to the individual story. It is to lose precisely what most concerned Langston Hughes and Alice Walker—the possibility of bridging "twoness."

Under the expanding influence of postmodernism and poststructuralism, the new literary studies of race and gender are increasingly extending the notion of text to cover all social relations. Adopting from literary criticism the idea that language is all of society or "reality" that we can hope to know, they are insisting that we attend to a plurality of voices on equal terms—that we introduce genuine "democracy" into our appreciation of diverse cultures.[60] This position embodies a commitment to the equal value of human beings in their particularity and diversity. But in rejecting the notion of a hierarchy of intrinsic worth, it also rejects the attempt to understand the structures of domination and subordination within which cultures are elaborated and articulated.[61] The new literary studies of race and gender are thus repudiating the dual focus of text and context that traditionally characterized American Studies. Leverenz's opposition of "ideologies" to "political and cultural contexts" is, in this perspective, sobering. For Leverenz admirably prides himself on writing "about something" in contrast to engaging in sterile exercises. He is not, disclaimers notwithstanding, repudiating context, he is renaming it under the pressure of postmodernist and poststructuralist currents.

Between Individualism and Fragmentation 225

Significantly, the most compelling results of the new literary studies of race and gender point back, albeit in new terms, towards the older paradigm of American Studies as some combination of history and literature. Yet too often they make the case for the value of the cultures of previously marginalized groups as if those cultures should be understood on their own terms, which in part is to say in isolation. Too often they appear to be seeking to replace the very idea of an American culture—and especially an American self—with a multiplicity of unrelated cultures and selves. Too often they seem to assume that if it could be demonstrated that our dominant culture has resulted from the privilege and power of some then that culture must be repudiated entirely. These conclusions do not follow from those premises.

The new literary studies of race and gender have, in general, insisted upon the claims of a myriad of subjective experiences and upon the cultural distinctiveness of marginalized or oppressed communities. Yet for all their insistence on community, they have not decisively challenged the commitment to individualism advanced by the dominant culture.[62] In effect, these studies are proposing that we study new individuals, not that we study differently the ways in which individuals interact—their conflicts, but also their accommodations, and the ways in which the dominant discourses have obscured those interactions.

The most compelling lesson of this work should be the insistence that our inherited notion of American culture is the product of historical struggles that have been won by some and lost by others.[63] Such are the consequences of power. Yet they have, in large measure, repudiated the very notion of power in favor of a radical democratization. If our dominant culture has indeed resulted from the silencing of those who lacked the power, prestige, or connections to ensure that their views would prevail, then it behooves us to understand it as the product of conflict it has been. It also behooves us to understand that the very power which facilitated its triumph endowed it with an undeniable prestige in the eyes of those it excluded, and especially with the power to set the terms of any criticisms of it.

The American self of our tradition has been white and male, normally Northeastern although occasionally western, normally elite, although occasionally poor but upwardly mobile. That self has functioned as a collective self-representation, even as it has also functioned as the implicit autobiography of the men of the dominant class and race. Today we no longer accept it as an adequate self-representation. Those of us who are not members of a white, male, Northeastern elite need to understand the conditions that have permitted it to prevail. To do so, we must recognize that, in essential respects, it has prevailed. The new literary studies of race and gender scholarship suggest that we should reexamine that national image from the perspective of those whose lives it did not reflect. Perhaps the most sobering lesson of such an examination will be the hegemony enjoyed by that image in which so many did not share. However sobering, that lesson could help to instruct us in the inescapable relations between culture and power and remind us that American identities, like American culture, have always been shaped by the (conflicted) relations of class as well as gender and race.

Race and gender should enjoy privileged positions in our understanding of American culture, for race and gender lie at the core of any sense of self. The incalculable advantage of the dominant culture has been its ability to deny their significance, to define the individual as not black and not female. Yet that very negative betrays the centrality of race and gender to any conception of the American self. American culture has developed as a celebration of freedom and individualism, as a repudiation of inequality. The measure of its success—its hegemony—can be seen in its ability to promote the ideal of American exceptionalism, to deny the existence of systematic or structural inequalities. Above all, its success has consisted in its ability to conflate the subjective notion of the self with the objective notion of national identity and thereby to exclude those who do not fit the subjective model from its objective corollary.

Understood as collective rather than strictly personal expression, our culture can permit different individuals to claim it as their own—not necessarily as an expression of their immediate personal experience, but as an affirmation of their national identity. Our culture, like all cultures, has always been subject to change. To recognize its national and inherently political character is to understand that to be an American means something more than to belong to a specific group of Americans. To be an American is forthrightly to acknowledge a collective identity that simultaneously transcends and encompasses our disparate identities and communities. Unless we acknowledge our diversity, we allow the silences of the received tradition to become our own. Unless we sustain some ideal of a common culture, we reduce culture to personal experience and sacrifice the very concept of American.

Notes

1. The similarity of the response never meant that American identity as embodied in American culture was not subject to contest, but that even as the favored authors shifted from those of the genteel tradition to those of Matthiessen's *American Renaissance* the chosen continued to belong to the Northeastern, WASP tradition. See, for example, Eric Cheyfitz, "Matthiessen's *American Renaissance*: Circumscribing the Revolution," *American Quarterly* 41 (1989): 341–61.

2. Gene Wise, "'Paradigm Dramas' in American Studies: A Cultural and Institutional History of the Movement," *American Quarterly* 23 (Bibliography Issue 1979): 293–337.

3. See, among many, Patricia Hill Collins, "The Social Construction of Black Feminist Thought," *Signs* 14 (Summer 1989): 745–73, esp. 770, "Living life as an African-American woman is a necessary prerequisite for producing black feminist thought because within black women's communities thought is validated and produced with reference to a particular set of historical, material, and epistemological conditions." See also Joan Wallach Scott, *Gender and the Politics of History* (New York, 1988), and Jane Flax, "Postmodernism and Gender Relations in Feminist Theory," *Signs* 12 (Summer 1987): 621–43. For an extended development of my position, see Elizabeth Fox-Genovese, *Feminism Without Illusions: A Critique of Individualism* (Chapel Hill, 1990).

4. For a thoughtful assessment of the general problem, see, esp., William E. Cain, *The Crisis in Criticism: Theory, Literature, and Reform in English Studies* (Baltimore, 1984), and, for the sharpest formulation of the conservative position, Allan Bloom, *The Closing of the American Mind* (New York, 1987). For overviews of the status and mission of American Studies, see, e.g., Gene Wise, "'Paradigm Dramas'"; Michael Cowan, "Boundary as Center: Inventing an American Studies Culture," *Prospects* 12 (1987): 1–20; Guenter H. Lenz, "American Studies and the Radical Tradition: From the 1930s to the 1960s," *Prospects* 12 (1987): 21–58; Kay Mussell, "*The Social Construction of Reality* and American Studies: Notes Toward Consensus," *Prospects* 9 (1984): 1–16; Thomas J. Schlereth, "American Studies and Students of American Things," *American Quarterly* 35 (Bibliography 1983): 236–41; Dell Upton, "The Power of Things: Recent Studies in American Vernacular Architecture," *American Quarterly* 35 (Bibliography 1983): 262–79.

5. William Bennett, "To Reclaim a Legacy," *Chronicle of Higher Education*, 28 Nov. 1984, and his "Why the West?" *National Review* 40 (27 May 1988): 37–39; Bloom, *Closing of the American Mind*; and on the Stanford controversy, see *New York Times*, 19 Apr. 1988, A18, and *Chronicle of Higher Education*, 27 Apr. 1988, A2.

6. Joan Wallach Scott, "History in Crisis? The Others' Side of the Story," *American Historical Review* 94 (June 1989): 680–92. Discussions of this confusion between points of view and the professional promotion of those who advance them are proliferating. See, for example, Jonathan M. Wiener, "Radical Historians and the Crisis in American History, 1959–1980," *Journal of American History* 76 (Sept. 1989): 399–434; John D'Emilio, "Not a Simple Matter: Gay History and Gay Historians," *Journal of American History* 76 (Sept. 1989): 435–42; Peter Novick, *That Noble Dream: The "Objectivity Question" and the American Historical Profession* (Cambridge, 1988).

7. Linda K. Kerber, "Diversity and the Transformation of American Studies," *American Quarterly* 41 (Sept. 1989): 424.

8. Kerber, "Diversity and the Transformation of American Studies," 429.

9. Many of the most promising exceptions to the tendency are strongly rooted in history, notably, Christine Stansell, *City of Women: Sex and Class in New York, 1789–1860* (New York, 1986); David Leverenz, *Manhood and the American Renaissance* (Ithaca, N.Y., 1989); Sacvan Bercovitch, *The Puritan Origins of the American Self* (New Haven, 1975), and his *The American Jeremiad* (Madison, Wisc., 1978); Carroll Smith-Rosenberg, *Disorderly Conduct: Visions of Gender in Victorian America* (New York, 1985); Werner Sollors, *Beyond Ethnicity: Consent and Descent in American Culture* (New York, 1986);

Allan Trachtenberg, *The Incorporation of America: Culture and Society in the Gilded Age* (New York, 1982).

10. Sollors, *Beyond Ethnicity*. I do not wish to slight the significance of Sollors's general argument, but am struck at how little attention he gives to Hawthorne, Emerson, Poe, Melville, Whitman, and company. For random examples, Theodore Dreiser, Edith Wharton, Harriet Jacobs, Pauline Hopkins, Susan Warner, Fanny Fern (Ruth Hall), Augusta Evans Wilson, and William Gilmore Simms do not appear in his index. Nor do gender or women.

11. W. E. Burghardt DuBois, *The Souls of Black Folk* (1953; reprint, Millwood, N.Y., 1973), 1.

12. Leslie Fiedler, *Love and Death in the American Novel* (1960; reprint, New York, 1966), and his *The Return of the Vanishing American* (New York, 1968).

13. Henry Louis Gates does address the question in his comments on my paper, and I am very much indebted to him for forcing me to address it.

14. Henry Roth, *Call It Sleep* (New York, 1934).

15. Langston Hughes, "A Theme for English B," in *The Langston Hughes Reader: The Selected Writings of Langston Hughes* (New York, 1958), 108–109.

16. Hughes, "A Theme for English B," 109.

17. Houston A. Baker, Jr., *Modernism and the Harlem Renaissance* (Chicago, 1987).

18. The story is included in Alice Walker, *You Can't Keep a Good Woman Down* (New York, 1981).

19. Albert Camus, *L'homme revolte* (Paris, 1956), 25.

20. Harriet A. Jacobs, *Incidents in the Life of a Slave Girl. Written by Herself*, ed. Jean Fagan Yellin (Cambridge, Mass., 1987); Elizabeth Fox-Genovese, *Within the Plantation Household: Black and White Women of the Old South* (Chapel Hill, 1988), Epilogue. And many of her black, female successors did the same.

21. Henry Louis Gates, Jr., *The Signifying Monkey: A Theory of Afro-American Literary Criticism* (New York, 1988), xxii.

22. Gates, *Signifying Monkey*.

23. Zora Neale Hurston, *Jonah's Gourd Vine* (1934; reprint, Philadelphia, 1971).

24. Among the works in history and culture, see, esp., Eugene D. Genovese, *Roll, Jordan, Roll: The World the Slaves Made* (New York, 1975); Lawrence Levine, *Black Culture and Black Consciousness: Afro-American Folk Thought From Slavery to Freedom* (New York, 1977); Alfred J. Raboteau, *Slave Religion: The "Invisible Institution" in the Antebellum South* (New York, 1978); Deborah G. White, *Ar'n't I a Woman? Female Slaves in the Plantation South* (New York, 1985); Norman R. Yetman, "Ex-Slave Interviews and the Historiography of Slavery," *American Quarterly* 36 (Summer 1984): 181–210; Fox-Genovese, *Within the Plantation Household*. On slave narratives and African-American autobiographies, see, esp., William Andrews, *To Tell a Free Story: The First Century of Afro-American Autobiography, 1760–1865* (Urbana, Ill., 1986); William E. Cain, "Forms of Self-Representation in Booker T. Washington's *Up From Slavery*," *Prospects* 12 (Cambridge, 1987): 201–22; Charles T. Davis and Henry Louis Gates, Jr., eds., *The Slave's Narrative* (New York, 1985); Frances Smith Foster, *Witnessing Slavery: The Development of Ante-Bellum Slave Narratives* (Westport, Conn., 1979); Elizabeth Fox-Genovese, "My Statue, My Self: Autobiographical Writings of Afro-American Women," in Shari Benstock, ed., *The Private Self: Theory and Practice of Women's Autobiographical Writings* (Chapel Hill, 1988); Waldo E. Martin, Jr., *The Mind of Frederick Douglass* (Chapel Hill, 1984); John Sekora and Darwin T. Turner, eds., *The Art of Slave Narrative: Original*

Between Individualism and Fragmentation 229

Essays in Criticism and Theory (n. p., 1982); Sidonie Smith, *Where I'm Bound: Patterns of Slavery and Freedom in Black American Autobiography* (Westport, Conn., 1974); Robert B. Stepto, *From Behind the Veil: A Study of Afro-American Narrative* (Urbana, Ill., 1979). For recent work in African-American literary criticism, see, esp., Henry Louis Gates, Jr., *Figures in Black: Words, Signs, and the "Racial" Self* (New York, 1987) and his *Signifying Monkey*; Houston A. Baker, Jr., *The Journey Back: Issues in Black Literature and Criticism* (Chicago, 1980), and his *Modernism and the Harlem Renaissance*; Hazel Carby, *Reconstructing Womanhood: The Emergence of the Afro-American Woman Novelist* (New York, 1987); Barbara Christian, *Black Feminist Criticism: Perspectives on Black Women Writers* (New York, 1985); Trudier Harris, *Exorcising Blackness: Historical and Literary Lynching and Burning Rituals* (Bloomington, 1984); Gloria T. Hull, *Color, Sex, and Poetry: Three Women Writers of the Harlem Renaissance* (Bloomington, 1987); Barbara Ann McCaskill, "To Rise Above Race: Black Women Writers and Their Readers, 1859–1939," Ph.D. diss., Emory University, 1988; Marjorie Pryse and Hortense J. Spillers, eds., *Conjuring: Black Women, Fiction, and Literary Tradition* (Bloomington, 1985); Valerie Smith, *Self-Discovery and Authority in Afro-American Narrative* (Cambridge, Mass., 1987); Susan Willis, *Specifying: Black Women Writing the American Experience* (Madison, Wisc., 1987); Gloria Wade-Gayles, *No Crystal Stair: Visions of Race and Sex in Black Women's Fiction* (New York, 1984).

25. Willis, *Specifying*, 10.

26. From the Revolution on, individual freedom and equality began to emerge as the dominant myth of American culture, but it long coexisted with older visions of the primacy of community and with the Southern defense of hierarchy and particularism.

27. For the relevant texts see the wonderful *Schomburg Library of Nineteenth-Century Black Women Writers*, gen. ed., Henry Louis Gates, Jr., 30 vols. (New York, 1988). In some ways the most challenging and disturbing text of all is Harriet Wilson's *Our Nig*.

28. Reasons of space preclude my doing full—or indeed any—justice to the work on specific ethnic groups, although the work on Hispanic Americans and Native Americans in particular justifies serious treatment.

29. Harriet E. Wilson, *Our Nig: Or, Sketches from the Life of a Free Black*, ed. Henry Louis Gates, Jr., (New York, 1983); Jacobs, *Incidents in the Life of a Slave Girl*. See also, "Texts and Contexts of Harriet Jacobs's *Incidents in the Life of a Slave Girl*: Written by Herself," in *The Slave's Narrative*, ed. Davis and Gates, 262–82, and her "Written by Herself: Harriet Jacobs's Slave Narrative," *American Literature* 53 (Nov. 1981): 479–86.

30. *The Schomburg Library of Nineteenth-Century Black Women Writers*. Each volume in the library contains an introduction to the specific work by a scholar in the field.

31. Carby, *Reconstructing Womanhood*, esp. 169–73.

32. On the difficulties of *Our Nig* in particular and the tradition of nineteenth-century African-American women's writing in general, see Barbara McCaskill, "To Rise Above Race."

33. Carby, *Reconstructing Womanhood*, 174–75.

34. Alexander Saxton, "Problems of Class and Race in the Origins of the Mass Circulation Press," *American Quarterly* 36 (Summer 1984): 211–34; Ronald J. Zboray, "The Transportation Revolution and Antebellum Book Distribution Reconsidered," *American Quarterly* 38 (Spring 1986): 53–71, and his "Antebellum Reading and the Ironies of Technological Innovation," *American Quarterly* 40 (Mar. 1988): 65–110.

35. Nina Baym, "Melodramas of Beset Manhood: How Theories of American Fiction Exclude Women Authors," *American Quarterly* 33 (Summer 1981): 123–39.

36. Jane Tompkins, *Sensational Designs: The Cultural Work of American Fiction, 1790–1860* (New York, 1985). That Hawthorne's reputation was largely fabricated does not mean, at least in my judgment, that his work was not as good as advertised. That is another question. It is also, in large measure, another question that Hawthorne's work was ideologically charged. For a discussion of his hostile treatment of Margaret Fuller, see, Bell Gale Chevigny, "To the Edges of Ideology: Margaret Fuller's Centrifugal Evolution," *American Quarterly* 38 (Summer 1986): 173–201. For an insightful discussion of the reception of Stowe's *Uncle Tom's Cabin* in time and place, see, Nina Baym, *Novels, Readers, and Reviewers: Responses to Fiction in Antebellum America* (Ithaca, 1984); and, for new readings of the novel, Eric J. Sundquist, ed., *New Essays on Uncle Tom's Cabin* (New York, 1986).

37. On the scribbling women, see Ann Douglas, *The Feminization of American Culture* (New York, 1977). Most feminist critics have been more sympathetic to antebellum women writers than Douglas. See, e.g. Tompkins, *Sensational Designs*; Baym, *Women's Fiction: A Guide to Novels by and about Women in America, 1820–1870* (Ithaca, 1978); Mary Kelley, *Private Woman, Public Stage: Literary Domesticity in Nineteenth-Century America* (New York, 1984).

38. Annette Kolodny, "The Integrity of Memory: Creating a New Literary History of the United States," *American Literature* 57 (May 1985): 291–307, and her *The Land Before Her: Fantasy and Experience of American Frontiers, 1630–1860* (Chapel Hill, 1984); Cathy Davidson, *Revolution and the Word: The Rise of the Novel in America* (New York, 1986), and her "Introduction: Towards A History of Books and Readers," to the special issue, "Reading America," that she edited of *American Quarterly* 40 (Mar. 1988): 7–17; and references to Tompkins and Baym in note 34 *supra*.

39. Kelley, *Private Woman, Public Stage*; Kolodny, *Land Before Her*; Judith Fryer, *Felicitous Space: The Imaginative Structures of Edith Wharton and Willa Cather* (Chapel Hill, 1986).

40. For other examples of this position, see also, Judith Fetterley, "Introduction," to *Provisions: A Reader from 19th-Century American Women* (Bloomington, 1985), 1–40; Elizabeth A. Meese, *Crossing the Double-Cross: The Practice of Feminist Criticism* (Chapel Hill, 1986); Vivian R. Pollak, *Dickinson: The Anxiety of Gender* (Ithaca, 1984); Janice Radway, *Reading the Romance: Women, Patriarchy, and Popular Literature* (Chapel Hill, 1984); Joanne Dobson, "The Hidden Hand: Subversion of Cultural Ideology in Three Mid Nineteenth-Century Women's Novels," *American Quarterly* 38 (Summer 1986): 233–42; Shirley Samuels, "The Family, the State, and the Novel in the Early Republic," *American Quarterly* 38 (Bibliography 1983): 236–41.

41. For an extreme formulation of the theoretical implications of the tendency to identify a distinct women's discourse, see Margaret Homans, *Bearing the Word: Language and Female Experience in Nineteenth-Century Women's Writing* (Chicago, 1986), esp. 4–15 and 28–29.

42. For a thoughtful discussion of the limits of the Northeastern model of woman's sphere, see, Jeanne Boydston, Mary Kelley, and Anne Margolis, *The Limits of Sisterhood: The Beecher Sisters on Women's Rights and Woman's Sphere* (Chapel Hill, 1988), and Linda K. Kerber, "Separate Spheres, Female Worlds, Woman's Place: The Rhetoric of History," *Journal of American History* 75 (June 1988): 9–39.

43. See, e.g., Fox-Genovese, *Within the Plantation Household*.

44. Harriet Beecher Stowe, *Uncle Tom's Cabin*, ed. Ann Douglas (1854; reprint, New York, 1981); Caroline Lee Hentz, *The Planter's Northern Bride* (1854; reprint, Chapel

Hill, 1970). See also, Ann Douglas, *The Feminization of American Culture* (New York, 1977); Gillian Brown, "Getting in the Kitchen With Dinah: Domestic Politics in *Uncle Tom's Cabin*," *American Quarterly* 36 (Fall 1984): 503–23; Sundquist, ed., *New Essays*.

45. On Wilson, see, William Perry Fiddler, *Augusta Evans Wilson: A Biography* (University, Ala., 1951), and Anne Goodwyn Jones, *Tomorrow Is Another Day: The Woman Writer in the South, 1859–1936* (Baton Rouge, 1981).

46. Obviously, Marxists have paid considerable attention to the political rights of blacks and women, but they have normally attempted to incorporate them within their established theoretical framework. See, e.g., the pathbreaking work of Herbert Aptheker, esp., *American Negro Slave Revolts*, 40th anniversary edition (New York, 1983); his "Resistance and Afro-American History: Some Notes on Contemporary Historiography and Suggestions for Further Research," in *In Resistance: Studies in African, Caribbean, and Afro-American History*, ed. Gary Y. Okihiro (Amherst, Mass., 1980), 10–20; and his "American Negro Slave Revolts: Fifty Years Gone," *Science and Society* 51 (Spring 1987): 68–72.

47. Michael Denning, "'The Special American Conditions': Marxism and American Studies," *American Quarterly* 38 (Bibliography 1986): 356–80. The distancing has been of a very special kind for, as Michael Denning has argued, much of the most innovative recent work in American Studies is heavily indebted to Marxist thought, even when it offers itself as a substitute for Marxism. In general even those scholars who are working with Marxist concepts have refrained either from calling themselves Marxists or from accepting an integrated Marxist theory.

48. See esp., David Brion Davis, *The Problem of Slavery in the Age of Revolution, 1770–1823* (Ithaca, 1975). Thus, although references to "hegemony" have become fairly common, and although references to the consciousness of working people abound, they are not normally linked—Davis and a precious few others excepted—to economics and politics.

49. Sollors, *Beyond Ethnicity*. See also, his "Region, Ethnic Group, and American Writers: From 'Non-Southern' and 'Non-Ethnic' to Ludwig Lewisohn; or the Ethics of Wholesome Provincialism," *Prospects* 9 (1984): 441–62, and, esp., "Theory of American Ethnicity, Or: '? S Ethnic?/Ti and American/Ti, De or United (W) States S S1 and Theor?,'" *American Quarterly* 33 (Bibliography 1981): 257–83, e.g., the discussion of ethnicity and class on 263–66. Here, Gates's observations on the relations of African-American writers to the Western and vernacular traditions respectively (in *Signifying Monkey*) requires development. For a thoughtful treatment of a specific instance in the relations between white and black culture, see, William J. Mahar, "Black English in Early Blackface Minstrelsy: A New Interpretation of the Sources of Minstrel Show Dialect," *American Quarterly* 37 (Summer 1985): 260–85.

50. T. S. Eliot, *Christianity and Culture: The Idea of a Christian Society & Notes Toward the Definition of Culture* (New York, 1960).

51. Michael T. Gilmore, *American Romanticism and the Market Place* (Chicago, 1985); Walter Benn Michaels, *The Gold Standard and the Logic of Naturalism: American Literature at the Turn of the Century* (Berkeley and Los Angeles, 1987).

52. Bercovitch, *Puritan Origins of the American Self*.

53. Sacvan Bercovitch and Myra Jehlen, eds., *Ideology and Classic American Literature* (New York, 1986).

54. Jeffrey Steele, *The Representation of the Self in the American Renaissance* (Chapel Hill, 1987); Gillian Brown, *Domestic Individualism: [Imaging Self in Nineteenth-Century America* (Berkeley: University of California Press, 1990)].

55. Smith-Rosenberg, *Disorderly Conduct*.

56. Amy Schrager Lang, *Prophetic Woman: Anne Hutchinson and the Problem of Dissent in the Literature of New England* (Berkeley and Los Angeles, 1987).

57. Brown, *Domestic Individualism*.

58. David S. Reynolds, *Beneath the American Renaissance: The Subversive Imagination in the Age of Emerson and Melville* (New York, 1988). See also, e.g., Michaels, *Gold Standard*; Walter Benn Michaels and Donald E. Pease, eds., *The American Renaissance Reconsidered: Selected Papers from the English Institute, 1982–83* (Baltimore, 1985).

59. Leverenz, *Manhood and the American Renaissance*, 3.

60. Scott, "History in Crisis?"

61. For a sharp critique of the growing hold of postmodernism, see Bryan D. Palmer, *Descent into Discourse: The Reification of Language and the Writing of Social History* (Philadelphia, 1989).

62. For a fuller development of this argument, see my *Feminism Without Illusions*.

63. It should, parenthetically, be noted that what applies to blacks and women also applies to Southern culture, which has been shamefully neglected.

Fifteen

Beyond Transgression
Toward a Free Market in Morality

With his special gift for contrariety, Judge Richard Posner places his ambitious investigation of the vicissitudes of sex under the aegis of a quote from Aristotle's *Nicomachean Ethics*: "Pleasures are an impediment to rational deliberation, and the more so the more pleasurable they are, such as the pleasures of sex—it is impossible to think about anything while absorbed in them." Posner then devotes the ensuing 442 dense pages to challenging Aristotle's assertion. That sex and reason normally make incompatible bedfellows should not be taken as evidence that it is impossible to subject sex to the rigors of reason. Sex, Posner suggests throughout the book, must be considered as one form of behavior among many, no more nor less immune to the operations of the rational mind.

Posner's commitment to the power of rationality, as he understands it, constitutes the great strength and ultimate weakness of his work. And it is easy to imagine that many readers will find his rational foray into sex infuriating. He has no patience for the facile confusion of sex with passion, much less of sex with desire, which so mesmerizes contemporary critics. Posner's discussion of sex has more to do with theories of animal behavior than with the feelings of individuals. In this respect the great strength of Posner's book overlaps with its most disturbing weakness, namely, his determination to organize complex human behavior in predictable—and largely determined—patterns.

"Beyond Transgression: Toward a Free Market in Morality." *Yale Journal of Law and the Humanities* 5, no. 1 (1993): 243–64. Copyright 1993 by the *Yale Journal of Law and Humanities*. All rights reserved. Used by permission of the *Yale Journal of Law and the Humanities*.

Throughout *Sex and Reason* Posner sails against the tide of recent political attitudes that emphasize the claims of subjectivity and personal experience and cluster together in what is loosely known as the "politics of identity." Personalism, Posner forcefully argues, does not preclude flagrant efforts to impose normative judgments upon others. So he turns to a combination of economics and sociobiology to place contemporary passions in perspective. In this sense *Sex and Reason* embodies the mind of an unflinching skeptic who is willing to question anything and to be bound by little or nothing. Human history and contemporary challenges alike emerge from Posner's pages as manifestations of structural—he prefers "functional"— patterns. To see ourselves from his perspective is to see ourselves as just another colony of ants. The experience is humbling and, up to a point, salutary. It assuredly provides a welcome corrective to the imperialistic personalism that leads people of various political positions to attempt to impose their "values" upon others. Up to a point, the perspective is admirable, reminding us that we are manifestations of life rather than its essence. It was, notwithstanding differences, the perspective of the great theologians (e.g., Thomas Aquinas).

My reservations about Posner's view of sex derive less from his attempt to locate our immediate debates in a broad, agnostic perspective than from his underlying assumptions about rationality, which he unflinchingly identifies with the rationality of free-market, neoclassical economics. That this rationality must, in the measure possible, abstract from passion is not the issue. Posner's insistence upon the legitimate claims of rationality implicitly aligns him against those—notably feminists and critical legal theorists—who so insistently proclaim that any claim of rationality or, heaven forbid, impartiality in the law mocks and masks the domination of some over others. It is this domination which the law serves, pretenses to the contrary notwithstanding. The issue, however, is the basis upon which one defends abstraction from the play of individual passions and interests.

Here, in my judgment, Posner takes something less than the neutral ground he claims. The defense of rationality in intellect and impartiality in the law does not require a grounding in free-market economics and may even be weakened by it. Not all societies, indeed precious few, have shared our predilection for the freedom of commodities and transactions as proxy for justice among individuals. Indeed, to turn Posner's tactics upon him, one could argue that across history and cultures, societies have been more likely to privilege the reproduction of the community than the private economic gain of individuals. Anticipating this kind of objection, Posner counters that his model does not depend upon the transhistorical projection of economic relations, but upon economic reasoning, which he equates with rational choice and which, in his view, does apply across history and culture (pp. 86–87).

Defending his economic theory and method as an attempt to find "unity in diversity," Posner dismisses the predictable objections that his perspective is "dehumanizing, ideological, complacent, imperialistic, reactionary" (p. 86). He insists fairly that the point of any theory is to organize seemingly disparate phenomena into categories that permit meaningful analysis. Here and throughout, Posner identifies his primary enemies as those who claim priority for the immediacy and irreducibility of personal experience. But personalism does not constitute the strongest, nor even a good, ground from which to criticize him. I have no serious quarrel with Posner's interest in identifying general patterns in human behavior. My quarrels are, first, with his tendency to return in each instance to what he sees as unchanging patterns of behavior and, therefore, to neglect the historical development of specific human communities and societies; and, second, with his tendency to attribute modern individualist reasoning to societies in which the primacy of the individual was entirely foreign.[1]

In a crude way it is safe to assume that human societies, in contradistinction to their individual members, do tend to follow broad productive and reproductive strategies and tend to develop norms and taboos to justify and enforce them. As they become more entrenched and more complex, societies may well develop internal conflicts, initially, over norms and eventually, as in our case, even over taboos. Over time the politics of societies also tend increasingly to articulate their growing divisions by class and even, eventually, by gender, race, and ethnicity. Over time the history of the justification and enforcement of the norms and taboos acquires its own force. As a result, societies' pursuit of what might seem to an impartial observer to be their "objective," rational strategies is mediated by the history of how they have become themselves. As the paleontologist Loren Eiseley has pointed out, human evolution proceeds within a human, not a "natural" environment and human beings mature to a world that has been shaped by other human beings.[2] Notwithstanding the considerable virtues of Posner's model, it does not take adequate account of the complex social and cultural environment in which the current debates about sexuality are occurring.

Within living memory sex has moved from behind the veil of propriety—some would say hypocrisy—with which bourgeois societies sought to shroud it, into the glare of public and frequently acrimonious discussion. At an accelerating rate since the late 1960s, sexual issues have become the most visible signs of political and cultural contention in a vigorously contentious society. The list includes abortion, homosexuality, pornography, rape, sexual harassment, surrogate motherhood, incest and other forms of sexual abuse, exploitation, and exhibitionism. If nothing else, the extent and intensity of the discussions confirm that sex is anything but a private matter, although according to Posner, knowledge about sex remains sketchy and imprecise.

The sex wars pit those who seek to shore up what they regard as traditional family values against those who seek to defend the maximum individual autonomy in experience and expression. This is the familiar war between those who defend the fetus's right to life and those who defend a woman's right to choose to have an abortion, between those who oppose and those who defend the extension of homosexual rights, between those who oppose and those who defend the allocation of federal support for an exhibit of Mapplethorpe's photographs. Innumerable guerrilla wars, in which the alignment of parties becomes murky, cut across this great divide. Thus feminists, who normally support a woman's right to choose to have an abortion, split over the question of surrogate motherhood and over restrictions upon the dissemination of pornography.[3]

As suggested by the language of rights, in which so many of the issues are cast, the sex wars are primarily being fought on the terrain of law. In *Sex and Reason* Posner proposes to bring some order into the debates, first by summarizing the vast literature on sex for the benefit of his fellow judges who, he wittily suggests, tend "to know next to nothing about the subject beyond their own personal experience"—which may be even more limited than that of ordinary citizens because of the elaborate screening procedures that virtually exclude people with "irregular sex lives" from the judiciary (p. 1). Second, and more ambitiously, Posner aims to present a positive and normative theory of sexuality "that both explains the principal regularities in the practice of sex and in its social, including legal regulation and points the way toward reforms in that regulation" (pp. 2–3).

Posner, while acknowledging both the "intense emotionality of the sexual act" and the grounding of sexual desire and preference in human biology, holds that sexual behavior, like other aspects of volitional human behavior, is subject to rational choice, which, in his view, means the principles of economic analysis (p. 3). Yet he seems faintly puzzled, and even a little impatient, to find that, to date, sexuality has escaped the grasp of rationality. And to correct this inattention, he advances a "functional, secular, instrumental, utilitarian" theory that draws heavily upon what he calls "the economic theory of sexuality" (p. 3).

Posner insists upon the significance of sexuality in contradistinction to sex, which is not what his theory or its rivals are about. The term "sexuality" signals a concern with the social context and implications of sex, including attitudes and customs as well as practices. Sexuality, in this sense, is a concern of law and, by extension, of an economic theory of the law. He regards the principal—"uncompromising, truly unassimilable"—rival to the economic theory of sexuality as "a heterogeneous cluster of moral theories" (p. 3). Posner respects the moral theories of sexuality, both because of their intrinsic interest and because most members of our society subscribe to them. But they are not his primary concern. Moral and religious beliefs, by which some would judge sexuality, cannot be reduced "to genuine social interests or practical incentives," which makes them incompatible with the broadly scientific outlook that informs his own economic theory (p. 4).

History and Sexuality

Sex and Reason falls into three distinct but overlapping parts: "The History of Sexuality," "A Theory of Sexuality," and "The Regulation of Sexuality," with the first two understood as the indispensable backdrop or building blocks for the third. Posner's cavalier romp through the history of sexuality, admittedly prefaced with caveats and apologies, shows all of the disregard for complexity and ambiguity common to enthusiastic system-builders, even the most learned and insightful. In this section Posner is primarily concerned to sketch the range of variation in social attitudes toward and regulation of sexual practices and attitudes. Within a broad range, he especially seeks to demonstrate the far-reaching differences between two basic types of societies, respectively based on companionate and noncompanionate marriage.

This distinction forms the bedrock of Posner's distinction between two major groups of sexual practices and attitudes. In his view societies that practice noncompanionate marriages, including polygamy, tend to sequester women and to sustain very permissive attitudes towards various forms of extra-marital sex, thus effectively severing erotic from procreative sex. In contrast, societies that practice companionate marriage emphasize the bond between erotic and procreative sex and, accordingly, display a much lower tolerance for sexual adventures and deviations of all kinds.

Fifth-century Athens offers his clearest example of what he takes to be the consequences of noncompanionate marriage. There, he believes, men married women whom they probably did not love and with whom they were not expected to spend much time except for the occasional obligatory sexual encounters that produced offspring. The objects of their sexual interest and desire, Posner contends, were adolescent boys of their own class or accomplished, upper-class courtesans. The Greeks, Posner insists, openly accepted homosexual acts, although not between men of the same age and class and not between lesbians, but their understanding of homosexuality differed significantly from ours. Posner does not believe that the men of the Athenian citizen class were especially preoccupied with homoerotic desire: For them homosexuality was one among many possible forms of sexual release available to men who were not yet married or not emotionally tied to their wives. Many Greek men, like prison inmates today, were what he calls "opportunistic homosexuals"—men who would take the anus of an attractive young boy if the vagina of an attractive young woman were unavailable (p. 149).

Posner takes Catholic and Protestant Europe as prime examples of companionate marriage, which concerns marriage between (more or less) social equals, who are expected to treat each other with love and respect and to share a close association in running the household and raising children. Like the mores of noncompanionate marriage, those of companionate marriage place a high premium on the pre-marital virginity and marital fidelity of wives, primarily to safeguard the legitimacy of offspring. Thus the professed mutuality of companionate marriage, with its ideal of confining sex to marriage, uneasily coexists with a persisting sexual double standard. Practice, Posner allows, did not always live up to the ideal: many peasants did not bother to marry; most marriages were arranged; members of the clergy frequently kept concubines or engaged in homosexual relations; prostitution flourished. From the early medieval through the modern eras, European societies, nonetheless, tended to proclaim their intolerance of extra-marital sex, from masturbation to homosexuality.

The sharp distinction between companionate and noncompanionate marriage serves Posner's argument well but slights the complexity of the historical record. For most of world history, noncompanionate marriages of various kinds have probably been the norm, especially among ruling classes (including the citizen class of fifth-century Athens), which primarily viewed marriage as an essential element in consolidating and advancing the interests of families. While the Catholic Church espoused the idea of companionate marriage, it did so, in part, as a way of attracting pagans to the Church and, increasingly, as a way of strengthening its position against powerful families. Officially, the Church also opposed extra-marital sex, though it felt compelled to tolerate it, to some degree, in practice. Thus in some ways the early-modern (companionate) Catholic nobility behaved much as Posner describes fifth-century (noncompanionate) Athenians as having behaved. The Protestant Reformation gave new impetus to the idea of companionate marriage, but the idea in its modern form seems only to have gained broad acceptance during the eighteenth century, when modern ideas of motherhood and female sexuality also took hold.[4] Tellingly, these developments coincided closely with the rise and expansion of capitalism, including the economic, technological, and demographic changes that have so decisively shaped the changing relations of women and men during the twentieth century.

Posner's casual attitude toward historical complexity does not necessarily invalidate his argument—at least not at the abstract level at which he casts it. But that casual attitude revealingly underscores the functionalist nature of the argument. For Posner, history is more interesting as the raw material for theoretical system-building than as a process of development. Or, to put it differently, he has little interest in the specific dynamics of historical change. Brushing aside charges of reductionism, he claims that his goal is to identify central and recurring phenomena and to free them from the clutches of the specialized vocabularies beneath which their similarities are normally concealed. In this spirit he enunciates the claim "that much of the variance in sexual behavior and customs across cultures and eras is explained by a handful of factors, such as the sex ratio (which is far more variable than is usually assumed), the extent of urbanization, and, above all, the changing occupational role of women" (p. 86). In his attempt to explain the variance, he relies upon theory, which he views "as a source of testable hypotheses" (p. 86). He fails to note that his factors are not all of the same kind and, more seriously, that some, notably the occupational status of women, are not what social scientists call "independent variables"—that is, they are not, properly speaking, causative.

Theories of Sexuality

Posner's intellectual interests emerge most clearly in his section on the theory of sexuality, in which he draws upon propositions from the biology of sex and from economics. He sensibly dismisses the notion that a viable economic theory of sex must explain everything about sex, maintaining that, as an analyst of rational choice, the economist "understands that choice is constrained by circumstances that may have nothing to do with economics" (p. 87). Thus, any such economic analysis must take the sex drive itself as given. Beyond that, such a theory must recognize that the possible range of sex acts is largely determined by biological and developmental factors and that the object of the sex drive is partly a given and partly a choice. These premises, Posner asserts, should not be taken as evidence that he assigns biology to the realm of determinism and economics to the realm of freedom. He views both theories as equally deterministic, insisting that both can be reduced to an analysis of benefits and costs. The difference between them lies in biology's concern with our uniform species and economics' concern with cultural, and hence local, benefits and costs that help to explain the variety of sexual customs and attitudes.

Even Posner's most thoughtful qualifications fail to grapple directly with a central problem in the application of rational choice theory to complex human relations, namely, that although people frequently—perhaps even normally—tend to behave rationally in the aggregate, they may not do so as individuals. He also slights the significance of societies' political choices, which may prove less than rational and which may shape a society's future development, thus altering the baseline from which its future choices will be made. Rational choice theorists' obvious answer to my objection would be that even apparently irrational social choices may, upon further investigation, turn out to have been rational from a larger point of view. Thus, if you step back far enough, the Germans' election of Hitler in 1933 may have been the most rational response to a threatening situation, notwithstanding its ultimate costs. Such are the tautological pitfalls of any functionalist argument: What is had to be because it is.

Posner, who doubts that sexual preferences can be entirely explained by cultural factors, accepts most of the insights of sociobiology, notably that individuals and peoples strive to ensure maximum reproduction of their genes and that men and women pursue different sexual strategies. He especially emphasizes the biological foundation of the link between reproductive and sexual strategies. He considers fundamental the sexual distinction according to which men can inseminate countless women, whereas women, who must devote nine months to sustaining a fetus and frequently more to nursing an infant, can only receive infrequent insemination. This sexual division of labor leads women to pursue conservative sexual strategies, men to pursue aggressive ones. In his view the "over-mastering male sex drive incites a competition among men for women" that may result in a few strong men's monopoly of a disproportionate number of women (p. 99).

Although Posner acknowledges the limits of sociobiology, he takes seriously the biological foundations of human sexuality and holds that the best explanation for "real," in contradistinction to opportunistic, homosexuality is genetic (p. 296). Here, as elsewhere throughout the book, he asserts that the core of homosexuality lies not in the occasional participation in homosexual acts but in homosexual preference. He suggests that "real" homosexuals, of whom there are fewer women than men, account for roughly 2.5 percent of the population—not the 10 percent or more that homosexual activists normally claim (p. 294). Yet he views genes as influences on behavior, not determinants of it. Genes may well incline women to pursue a conservative sexual strategy, but in cultures in which women do not depend upon men, "many women resist the genetic inclination and abandon the conservative strategy" (p. 109). Similarly, real homosexual men pursue different strategies and face different problems in accordance with their social and cultural milieu. In a society of noncompanionate marriage, a homosexual can meet the minimal responsibilities of marriage and procreation while pursuing his erotic life elsewhere; in a society of companionate marriage, that strategy becomes problematic.

The problem with this argument brings us back to Posner's timing of the emergence of companionate marriage. Throughout the medieval and early modern periods, divorce remained virtually unavailable—with Henry VIII of England a notorious exception. Thus, although married men had affairs, frequented prostitutes, raped lower-class women, and engaged in sexual acts with other men, they were not significantly more likely to dissolve or escape from their marriages on that account than were ancient Athenians. Even after the ideology of companionate marriage took hold during the eighteenth century, divorce remained difficult and uncommon. And, significantly, there was no clear recognition of homosexuality as a possible expression of male identity. Although the causation remains obscure, it is clear that homosexuality emerged as a recognized identity toward the end of the nineteenth century,[5] at roughly the same time that divorce became more accessible and that mothers began to get custody of children upon the dissolution of a marriage.

In our own time, the term "homosexual" has gradually given way to the self-affirming term "gay," and even to "queer," as an explicit act of cultural reappropriation. That the period of this evolution has also been marked by the emergence of no-fault divorce and, more recently, by the public affirmation of the choice of single motherhood, should make us thoughtful. What we might call the transformation of homosexuality from one sexual practice among many to a self-proclaimed erotic identity has, above all, coincided with the modern world's unprecedented acceptance of love and personal gratification as an appropriate standard for social norms and practices. Posner does not explore the connection.

Posner develops his understanding of these changes in discussions of the theory of sexuality from the perspective of economics, optimal regulation, and morality. Drawing heavily upon comparisons with contemporary Sweden, he emphasizes the revolutionary changes in women's lives, sexuality, and gender relations that have exploded during the twentieth century. Sweden, he suggests, has effectively turned reproduction over to women by substituting the taxpayer for the husband as the source of maternity and child support. Under these conditions Swedish women, who no longer need male protection, have little reason "to surrender their freedom and share control of their children" (p. 168). And Sweden represents but a specific instance in a general trend of women's declining economic dependence upon men, which, in turn, has led women to shift their sexual strategy. With male protection of steadily diminishing importance to women, women have proven steadily less willing to "provide the commodity used to purchase that protection—female chastity" (p. 171). For Posner, this decline in female chastity constitutes "the most dramatic manifestation of the sexual revolution" (p. 171).

Morality and the Regulation of Sexuality

Posner's historical and theoretical discussions, which are richer and more extensive than this sketch can capture, lay the foundation for his exploration of and recommendations for the regulation of sexuality in the United States today. Posner advances evidence that suggests that the United States tends to punish sex crimes more heavily than do other developed nations, but to punish non-sex crimes less heavily. Significantly, the United States also seems to criminalize more forms of sexual conduct than do other developed nations. Posner openly acknowledges that his evidence, which derives from his somewhat arbitrary comparison of non-random samples, should hardly be taken as conclusive. Problems with the evidence notwithstanding, his basic argument is intuitively plausible, and all the more interesting since we do know that the United States leads the industrialized world in violent (non-sex) crime.[6]

The evidence that the United States punishes sex crimes more heavily than other industrialized nations might easily be taken to suggest that the legacy of Puritanism continues to weigh heavily on American culture, although Posner gives more credit to the Catholic Church than the Protestant denominations for attempting to enforce puritanical sexual attitudes. More interesting and important is Posner's suggestion that the true source of American public attitudes towards sex lies in the country's moral and religious diversity. We are, in effect, a nation of contested moralities and our anxieties about those differences tend to result in punitive rather than permissive attitudes. In contrast, Sweden, which is at once more religiously homogeneous and more homogeneously non-observant, is much more permissive and yet ends up with not merely fewer sex crimes but fewer abortions.

These and other considerations lead Posner to propose that rational thinking about sex requires that we sever sex from morality—that we learn to regard sex with moral indifference. According to his positive economic theory of sexual behavior, it is reasonable to attribute the type and frequency of different sexual practices—in contradistinction to the sex drive and sexual preference—to "rational responses to opportunities and constraints" (p. 111). From this perspective it logically follows that if the costs of one kind of sexual behavior become too high, rational individuals will substitute another that costs less. When heterosexual male prisoners lack access to women, they will turn to men. When the costs of infanticide skyrocket, women who wish to terminate pregnancies will turn to abortion. And so forth. If we learn to regard sex with moral indifference, we will accept only such limitations of sexual freedom as are "required by economic or other utilitarian conditions" (p. 180).

Posner's main quarrel with the moral theory of sex lies in his conviction that it has lost its hegemony. If all, or even most, Americans accepted Christian sexual morality, if such offenses against that morality as prostitution, adultery, homosexuality, or fornication "evoked as wide and deep an antipathy as infanticide, gladiatorial contests, or suicide, those offenses would be immoral. Period" (p. 232). Demonstrably they do not. And since unanimity of feeling on such matters has dissipated, "their morality is contestable" and the invocation of moral traditions will prove ineffectual (p. 232). Argument will not suffice to convince someone that infanticide is a bad thing. And anyone who seriously demands that you provide an argument against infanticide "inhabits a different moral universe" (p. 230).

Posner passes lightly over the ubiquitous conflicts among those who inhabit different moral universes, leaving the reader to wonder if he believes that such conflicts will yield to the commanding logic of economic rationality. Had he paid more attention to history, he might have noticed that if history teaches anything, it assuredly teaches that inhabitants of different moral universes frequently have great difficulty in coexisting peacefully. He does acknowledge that the United States today combines an extraordinarily high level of allegiance to Christian beliefs with an extraordinarily high rate of crime, but does not dwell upon possible explanations.

More to the point, and independent of specific crimes, the varied moral universes of different Americans are resulting in ferocious disputes, most dramatically over abortion, but also over homosexuality, pornography, and more. In the spirit of economic rationality, Posner valiantly attempts to maintain neutrality with respect to these struggles, steadfastly refusing to credit the validity of moral claims on one side or the other. From time to time, however, he betrays his impatience with the sexual radicals, most notably Marcuse, who, he contends, remain passionately committed to their own version of a moral conception of sex, notwithstanding its apparent reversal of the traditional religious conceptions. As Posner shrewdly remarks, "the idea that polymorphous perversity is the road to Utopia has been shown to be no more convincing than the contrary idea" (p. 240). He might well have added that the defenders of various forms of sexual liberation yield nothing to their adversaries in the sanctimonious passion with which they defend their views.

The tendency emerges most clearly from the debates over abortion, in which the practical issue of the availability of abortion must be separated from the terms in which that availability is defended. Increasingly, proponents of available abortion have cast their position in the argument of individual rights.[7] Arguments abound that, for women, access to abortion constitutes a fundamental, constitutional right. Underlying these arguments, and occasionally surfacing within them, lies the moral premise that pregnancy constrains women's equality in relation to men. Since men cannot be burdened by pregnancy, respect for equality demands that women not be burdened either. Proponents of this view believe their cause to be one of the most rudimentary fairness and morality.

As Posner suggests in his discussion of abortion, the clashes that rend American culture are not simply over ideology, however much they are those, but clashes over material interests as well, for example, child support payments. He rightly argues that many of the women who oppose abortion are attempting to defend the frayed remnants of a world in which men were held to protect and support women.[8] The virtual disappearance of female virginity as a commodity to be traded for male protection and support has left them vulnerable, especially since it has already been encoded in no-fault divorce. Many women do understand, however, that the public acceptance of abortion would indeed release men from virtually all responsibility for procreation and thus deliver the death blow to marriage as we have known it.

Toward a Functional View of Sexuality

Posner is at his best in such passing observations—and the book abounds with them—which demonstrate his capacity for empathy and humane understanding. He displays, throughout, an acute grasp of the monumental—I am tempted to say revolutionary—significance of the changes in women's situation in the late twentieth century. Yet he resolutely eschews the least trace of sentimentality. His own primary interest obviously lies in the possibility of scientific understanding—the ability of the human mind to grasp the scheme of things entire. Such an enterprise leaves scant room for sentimentality or *parti pris* of any kind. It is difficult, if not impossible, fairly to charge Posner with taking sides, although one can imagine a Christian theologian who charges him with hubris. For Posner, above all, wants passionately to understand how it works. This passion for functionalism leads him to speculate whether, in the end, "a moral conception of sex . . . is vital to civilization" (p. 240). Obviously, he thinks not. In his view, only by divorcing sex from morality can we hope to construct a rational system of regulation, although he falls cautiously and uncharacteristically silent on how the divorce is to be effected. Yet it defies credulity to suggest that those who will go to the wall to defend their own moral position will suddenly decide that sexual issues have no moral consequences at all.

In his third section Posner brings to bear on the specific problems of regulation his general emphasis "on seeking functional explanations for rules and practices often thought to be based unreflectively on tradition, superstition, or misogyny" (p. 243). He displays, throughout, a commendably judicious and thoughtful tone, as well as considerable sensitivity to the emotionally and ideologically charged positions of others. His proposals for regulation embody a radical break with the attitudes and practices of the past, albeit a radicalism expressed in the sober tones of reason. Here the significance of his "scientific" functionalism finally becomes clear: rather than arguing that the only response to our current crisis over the appropriate limits, if any, to sexual self-expression is to embrace functionalism, he elides the present with the past by asserting that regulations of sexuality have never been anything but functional. Thus, however reasonable and possibly constructive his specific suggestions, we would miss the larger significance of his bold project were we to divorce them from the more comprehensive judicial philosophy from which they derive and which they articulate.

Consider marriage. Stripped to its functional essentials, marriage has served as the cornerstone of the regulation of sex and reproduction. Across history and cultures, "marriage-related laws regulating sex have been on the whole efficient adaptations to social conditions" (p. 266). Posner allows that even polygamy and the prohibition of divorce have, in time and place, served important social purposes, notably forms of protection for women and children. In a similar spirit he insists that all societies have manifested an inverse relation between restrictions on marriage and nonmarital sex. In a regime of noncompanionate marriage, nonmarital sex of all kinds will abound; in a regime of companionate marriage, nonmarital sex will diminish. By this logic, if we abolished all restrictions on marriage, we would, by the same token, abolish all distinctions between marital and nonmarital sex.

In Posner's judgment, the growing economic power and personal independence of women, together with the disappearance of the legal status of illegitimacy, have brought us remarkably close to this situation. Western nations have effectively laid the groundwork for "the replacement of marriage [as] a status relationship—that is a relationship imposing rights and duties that cannot be altered by contract—by contractual cohabitation, the relationship at issue in 'palimony' cases" (p. 264). As contract continues to erode the status of marriage, it will become increasingly difficult for "society to withhold legal recognition of unconventional forms of voluntary sexual relationships, including polygamous and homosexual relationships," even if it refuses to call them marriages (p. 266). And if the law continues to develop in this direction, cohabitation contracts and marriages are likely to become increasingly indistinguishable, so that, eventually, all such relations will be marriages or there will be no marriages at all. Why not then conclude that, with marriage reduced to a voluntary contract between any two individuals who chose to enter into it for any duration they wish, an hour with a prostitute would be one among many forms of marriage rather than an instance of nonmarital sex?

Posner returns to marriage in his discussion of policies toward homosexuality. Could it not, he queries, plausibly be argued that as "heterosexual marriage becomes ever more unstable, temporary, and childless," it becomes more and more difficult to distinguish it from homosexual relations? But might that growing similarity not, he continues, be less a point in favor of homosexual marriage than one in favor of chucking marriage as a distinct institution and explicitly recognizing it as a contract? The real problem, Posner allows, lies in the entitlements that accompany marriage. Should homosexual couples enjoy marital benefits in inheritance, social security, income tax, welfare payments, adoption, medical benefits, life insurance, immigration, and the rest? Should they have the same rights of adoption and custody as heterosexual couples? Posner believes that we would do best to treat each of the entitlements separately, rather than as a group; he also believes that none alone and maybe not all together justify a decisive rejection of homosexual marriage. The salient issue should be whether the costs outweigh the benefits. For the moment, however, he avers, public hostility to homosexuality forces the conclusion that homosexual marriage is not a feasible option.

Many readers will doubtless find it significant—and even sinister—that Posner so easily defers to a presumed public opinion with respect to homosexual marriage. But in accepting the unlikelihood of public support for homosexual marriage, he artfully dodges the more serious questions concerning the allocation of social resources. The entitlements that accompany marriage as a relation and a status embody some residual public concern about the conditions under which children live and mature. The United States, with its customary preference for private rather than public support of children, has, much more than other industrialized nations, entrusted almost the entire economic responsibility for children to their parents. Had we an extensive network of family support, we probably would not face the issues that Posner raises. We have, in effect, identified marriage as the core of family life, as the privileged locus of social transfer payments. No wonder that, under these conditions, we face an escalating battle about who has a right to enjoy those benefits. But, by the same token, we have tied a cultural—for some, a moral—preference to have children reared in a heterosexual setting to economic benefits for individuals. In this sense our delinquency with respect to public support for reproduction has fueled an acrimonious debate about the putative morality of limiting marriage (economic advantages for specific individuals) to those who profess one form of sexual preference rather than another.

Posner brings his special combination of logic and social realism to bear upon all of the other difficult and contested issues of sexual regulation: homosexuals as teachers, homosexuals in the military, contraception, abortion, sodomy, pornography, nudity, and coercive sex. The logic of his position remains fundamentally hostile to any regulation that curtails the personal autonomy of adults, but time and again he backs off the extreme position out of respect for what he takes to be strong community sensibility. Thus he presents us with a paradox: He unilaterally rejects the alternate theories of sexuality, notably Christian morality, as adequate justifications for regulation, but frequently accepts other people's adherence to them. He shows altogether less patience with the sensibilities of radicals, notably some feminists, who seek new justifications for regulation. If, he impatiently observes, we cannot distinguish between a Reubens and a Playboy centerfold because both embody patriarchy and misogyny, then we cannot regulate the dissemination of either. As ideologies, both patriarchy and misogyny are protected by the First Amendment.

Posner reserves his greatest impatience for the liberal Supreme Court of 1965 to 1977, which, in his judgment, effected its own sexual revolution. In a succession of decisions, notably in *Roe v. Wade,* the Court's "curious appropriation of the word privacy to describe what is not privacy in the ordinary sense but rather freedom is an attempt by semantic legerdemain to make sexual liberty appear to occupy a different plane of social value from economic liberty. It does not" (p. 335). The problem does not lie in the description of a prohibition against abortion as "a deprivation of a pregnant woman's liberty"; the problem lies in the description of it "as a denial of due process of law" (p. 336). By its reasoning and rhetoric, the Court opened itself to the suspicion that the justices were following their own values and politics, which seemed, however oddly, "aligned with those of the student radicals of the 1960s, for whom sexual liberty and political liberty were . . . two sides of the same coin, while economic liberty they considered a mask for exploitation" (p. 338).

Posner reproaches the Court for having combined the deregulation of sexuality with the regulation of the economy, for having reduced liberty to sexual liberty while hampering the beneficent effects of economic liberty. He further reproaches it for having taken sides, on the basis of inadequate and even faulty legal reasoning, in the war between competing cultural and social values. The principal opposition to abortion, he reminds us, comes not from macho types and Don Juans, who probably favor it because it relieves them of responsibility, but from women and men who genuinely believe in the sanctity of fetal life. For many of those who support abortion, he continues, abortion constitutes the very symbol of feminism. "Should the Supreme Court take sides between feminism and antifeminism" (p. 340)? Should it take sides between the differing economic interests represented by the different groups of women? Do not such battles appropriately belong in the legislatures rather than in the courts? And finally, "Can we rightly call antiabortion laws even prima facie discriminatory against women if in fact they help some women and hurt others" (p. 341)?

Make no mistake. Posner does not oppose abortion, at least not during the early months of a pregnancy. He bitterly opposes the grounds upon which *Roe v. Wade* was decided. Above all he reproaches the Court for having failed to formulate "a coherent body of constitutional doctrine to decide issues of sexual autonomy" (p. 350). Firmly convinced that any responsible policy must be resolutely secular and must be grounded in utilitarian, pragmatic, and scientific arguments, he believes that the Court of the late 1960s and early 1970s simply substituted one system of "morality" for another, thus seriously jeopardizing the long-range prospects for a responsible, rational policy in keeping with the changing economic conditions of our society.

Unlike many conservatives, Posner does not count himself among those who revere "original intent" and has no interest in retarding or distorting the progress of economic development, even if that development forces us to rethink or conceivably jettison our most cherished beliefs. In keeping with a truly secular and pragmatic attitude, justices, in his view, must be willing to "invalidate state or federal laws on constitutional grounds without insisting that the invalidation be firmly grounded in the text of the Constitution" (p. 350). For those who are not prepared to do so will probably end by rejecting "the very idea of a constitutional right of sexual autonomy, or at the very least refuse to extend it beyond the existing precedents, narrowly interpreted" (p. 350).

The Age of Sexual Autonomy

Posner clearly believes that the age of sexual autonomy has arrived, although we have not yet figured out how to deal with it. He drives the point home in a discussion of reproduction, from adoption to surrogate motherhood, arguing that modern technology has opened the prospect of the separation of reproduction from sex. Modern reproductive technologies have provoked mixed reactions from feminists, although Posner expresses bemusement that feminists should worry about the decline in mothering since feminism has so aggressively sought to liberate women from traditional roles. But then, he notes, with a deadpan twist of the knife, "Fertility is just another asset, like a professional degree or other job-market human capital" (p. 425). Should men ever succeed, through cloning or artificial wombs, in completely freeing reproduction from women, women who are no longer needed as mothers probably would experience a reduction in their income. For the foreseeable future, however, artificial reproduction strengthens the bargaining position of women in relation to men, increases women's full income relative to that of men, and, accordingly, "presages a further shift in sexual attitudes and behavior toward the Swedish model" (p. 432).

The Swedish model fascinates Posner, although he does not entirely approve of it. Sweden, he believes, has largely succeeded in freeing sexuality from the manacles of morality and reproduction from the control of men. Sweden has also gone a long way toward the assimilation of marriage as status to marriage as contract, offering couples who wish to cohabit but not to undertake the commitment of marriage a cohabitation contract, which also provides homosexuals with a facsimile of marriage. Posner especially approves Sweden's extensive program in sex education and easy access to contraception, which, in his judgment, help to account for the comparatively low level of unplanned teenage pregnancies and abortions. The Swedish nonmarital birth rate nonetheless remains very high "because marriage confers relatively few benefits on Swedish women" (p. 166). Hence the paradox that although Sweden is, in most respects, "a more socialistic society than the United States," as evident in its extensive system of child welfare, "it may in matters related to sex more nearly approximate a free-market society than the United States does" (p. 167).

Notwithstanding Posner's deep reservations about Sweden's regulated economic system, he clearly believes that other Western societies are living through changes that should bring them closer to the Swedish free market in sex. He believes, in other words, that we will not respond adequately to the changes of our times unless we succeed in separating sex, morality, and reproduction from one another and in thinking dispassionately—scientifically— about each on its intrinsic merits. However contradictory it may seem, the various forms of artificial reproduction do simultaneously emancipate women from dependence upon men and men from dependence upon women, "for anything that severs reproduction from sexual intercourse reduces the dependence of each sex on the other" (p. 425).

Posner is too cautious, or perhaps too much of a gentleman, openly to celebrate the changes that are engulfing us. He even demonstrates guarded respect and sympathy for the proponents of traditional morality, who are losing the cultural war. He is much harder on liberal justices, radical feminists, and assorted other radicals, possibly because he recognizes them as dangerous opponents in the battle to shape the future. But it is hard not to believe that, at least on some level, Posner does welcome their projected brave new world of sexual autonomy. After all, as he assuredly understands, the mutual dependence of women and men upon each other, and of children upon both, anchored the dense fabric of beliefs and practices that have made up civilization and that, not incidentally, offered the most durable barrier to the unfettered progress of the market.

Rational Choice Jurisprudence

The rise and triumph of sexual autonomy bring personal life completely in line with the workings of the market, which Posner regards as the most reliable standard for human relations and social policies. The rapidity and novelty of the changes through which we are living seem to sever us from traditional moorings. Sex offers Posner an unparalleled opportunity to press the merits of his preferred vision of jurisprudence. In this respect *Sex and Reason* can profitably be read as a gloss on and case study for his theoretical treatise, *The Problems of Jurisprudence,* in which he elaborates his judicial philosophy—although, hostile to metaphysics, he would probably prefer a word like attitudes—and identifies himself as, above all, a libertarian and a pragmatist.

> The brand of pragmatism that I like emphasizes the scientific virtues (open-minded, no-nonsense inquiry), elevates the process of inquiry over the results of inquiry, prefers ferment to stasis, dislikes distinctions that make no practical difference—in other words, dislikes "metaphysics"—is doubtful of finding "objective truth" in any area of inquiry, is uninterested in creating an adequate philosophical foundation for its thought and action, likes experimentation, likes to kick sacred cows, and—within the bounds of prudence—prefers shaping the future to maintaining continuity with the past.[9]

Posner elaborates his distaste for blind devotion to continuity with the past in his rejection of the claims of natural law. Attacking Ronald Dworkin, he dismisses the concept, arguing that to confuse law with morality is first to strip it of its distinctiveness and subsequently to confuse it with politics, a confusion which ultimately leads to its own negation—no law.

> Without social, cultural, and political homogeneity, a legal system is not able to generate demonstrably right, or even professionally compelling, answers to difficult legal questions, whether from within the legal culture or by reference to moral or other extralegal norms—the traditional province of natural law. For without either nature, or a political, social, and moral community so monolithic that the prevailing legal norms are

"natural" in the sense of taken for granted, natural law can be but a shadow of its former self—can be but a name for the considerations that influence law even though not prescribed by a legislature or other official body.[10]

In *Sex and Reason* Posner relies upon the collapse of moral consensus in the United States to justify his "pragmatic" and skeptical investigation of sexual practices and norms. His investigation of sexuality thus manifests his conviction that the responsibility of a judge must always be to substitute "the humble, fact-bound, policy-soaked, instrumental concept of 'reasonableness' for both legal and moral rightness."[11]

Posner apparently equates his attack on natural law and other illusions of moral rectitude with an attack on bigotry, superstition, and irrationality. In directing his attack on natural law against Dworkin, he cleverly, if perversely, associates the defense of moral certainty and natural law with liberals and radicals. In this spirit he contemptuously associates Marcuse's permissive notion that polymorphous perversity paves the road to Utopia with the repressive ideas of Catholic and Victorian sexual theorists, arguing that there is nothing to choose between them. All of those who support one or another moral theory of sexuality fall into the same trap, namely, the assumption that a moral conception of sex "is vital to civilization" (p. 240). For Posner, it is not.

The breathtaking assertion that civilization does not require a moral conception of sex exposes the full measure of Posner's own kind of radicalism, which is grounded in his repudiation of the claims of history. By associating the moral theory of sex with permissive radicals on the one hand and repressive reactionaries on the other, Posner engages in a skillful sleight of hand that, whatever his intentions, leans toward nihilism. By categorically defining his opponents, he is attempting to structure the entire debate, excluding a broad group from traditional conservatives to moderate leftists who, differences among them notwithstanding, might not oppose all of his specific policy recommendations but would seriously question his libertarian premises.

Morality of Sex or Morality of Reproduction?

Throughout *Sex and Reason* Posner plausibly argues that the most momentous change of modern times lies in the changing situation of women, who increasingly enjoy the prospect of economic independence and who have effectively lost the protections and the constraints of marriage. Posner argues that as women have gained access to the status of autonomous economic agents they have, by the same token, claimed control of their own sexuality and with it of reproduction. In his judgment these developments have virtually exploded previous sexual norms, moral as well as institutional. They thus invite—or dictate—the acceptance of "morally indifferent sex" (p. 85).

Posner appears to be advocating a world in which the only bonds among individuals result from their market relations. Many feminists, with some reason, would counter that women do not yet enjoy equality in the market with men and cannot expect to in the near future. They would further argue that the only way to protect women against male brutality and competition is to enlist a strong state in their cause. Posner, of course, has no use for the welfare state, much less for socialism. Yet it is far from clear that, left to its own devices, the market will provide adequately for women, much less for children. In this respect the world of poor, single teenage mothers in the United States probably offers a more faithful picture of the market at work than the comfortably situated single mothers of Sweden.

This contrast suggests that Sweden's sexual freedom may not be as morally indifferent as Posner would have us believe. Sweden does provide for women and children, and not merely by disseminating sex education in the schools. Indeed, in an extraordinary concession, Posner admits that Swedish sex education seems to prove most effective when it is grounded in instruction by parents (note the plural) in the home. Posner also recognizes that Swedish—and even the more permissive Danish—cohabitation contracts for homosexuals do not include children. Thus Posner's emphasis on the freedom of adults to engage in various sexual relations in various situations obscures the extent to which provision for children remains inescapably tied to a conception of sexual morality in the full sense.

Posner notes, without comment, that in Sweden the taxpayer has assumed the role of the husband in providing for women and children. In the United States, where the free market enjoys much greater latitude than in Sweden, the taxpayer assuredly has not. Indeed, it is permissible to speculate that male taxpayers, who frequently cannot be induced to pay private child support, may long resist assuming those responsibilities. Doubtless Posner is correct that our particular situation, with its appalling rates of teen pregnancy, unwanted pregnancy, violence, and all the rest, owes much to our moral and ideological diversity. Doubtless he is also correct that the prospects for a complete victory by one or another morality are slight. But it does not follow from those premises that we should expect to sustain some facsimile of civilization with no moral concept of sex, nor does it follow that our accelerating collapse into an aggregation of autonomous (and, as Hobbes said, warring) individuals will produce any kind of civilization.

As it happens, I have no special difficulty with any of Posner's specific proposals for sexual policy, not because I agree with all of them, but because they are, on the whole, admirably thoughtful and respectful of what community sentiment is likely to tolerate. My difficulties concern Posner's premises about the divorce of sex from morality and reproduction, with their embedded disdain for the abiding consequences of history. The indisputable advantage of Posner's economic and sociobiological method lies in putting our personal parochialisms in a healthy, skeptical perspective. Sexual customs and moralities have varied tremendously across time and space. There is a dangerous arrogance in assuming that the assumptions of one society or time period necessarily hold for another.

Posner argues that the primary variations in sexuality cluster around two main types of marriage (companionate and noncompanionate), but in abstracting marriage from political systems, religions, and the rearing of children, he abstracts from the social fabric in which sexual moralities are elaborated, experienced, and transgressed. In the United States today, the level of transgression seems extraordinarily high relative to the Judeo-Christian norms in which so many Americans of different ethnicities were reared. And it is clear that prolonged public tolerance of transgression seriously erodes inherited beliefs, which are increasingly seen not to be about people's lives.

Sex and sexuality, however paradoxically, afford Posner an invaluable weapon in the justification of his libertarian commitment to the market as the ultimate arbiter of social differences. He seems to be arguing that since we have no hope of resolving our moral differences about sexuality, we might just as well leave them to the workings of the market. But his apparently forthright realism in this regard merely serves to repress another, and for him altogether more serious, topic—economics itself. For in Posner's mental universe, the sanctity of economics—understood as the minimally restricted capitalist free market—must be accepted as given. But since reproduction is as much a matter of economics as of sexuality, we are left with an uncomfortable message. For if we agree to divorce sex from morality and to divorce sex from reproduction, are we not thereby ominously agreeing to divorce reproduction from morality?

Sexual moralities have always coexisted with economic systems, which they variously shape and are shaped by. In that delicate balance, most people see economic systems as an embodiment and mirror of predictable human greed and jockeying for advantage. Sexual moralities, in contrast, even when they are not scrupulously observed, tend to be viewed as normative stories about what it means to be civilized. Above all they embody the taboos that define the essence of human communities—the conditions of their reproduction. In the end, the sanctity and sense of responsibility with which we regard reproduction may be more important to a people's moral theory of sexuality than the specific acts in which consenting adults engage. And history suggests that markets alone cannot be trusted to fulfill that function.

Notes

1. For an elaboration, see my *Feminism Without Illusions: A Critique of Individualism* (Chapel Hill: University of North Carolina Press, 1991); and on my views on the complexity of economic reasoning, see my *The Origins of Physiocracy: Economic Revolution and Social Order in Eighteenth-Century France* (Ithaca: Cornell University Press, 1976).

2. Loren Eiseley, *The Immense Journey* (New York: Random House, 1957).

3. For a recent example, see Tamar Lewin, "Furor on Exhibit at Law School Splits Feminists," *New York Times*, Friday, 13 Nov. 1992, B9.

4. We know less about the beliefs and behavior of various peasant populations, although it is possible that, having less reason to be concerned with dynastic politics and more reason to be concerned with the smooth functioning of small agricultural households, they hewed closer to the practices, if not the ideology, of companionate marriage than did their social superiors. See my "Women and Work," *French Women in the Age of Enlightenment*, ed. Samia Spencer (Bloomington, Ind.: Indiana University Press, 1984), 111–27; Elizabeth Fox-Genovese and Eugene D. Genovese, *Fruits of Merchant Capital: Slavery and Bourgeois Property in the Rise and Expansion of Europe* (New York: Oxford University Press, 1983), ch. 11; Natalie Zemon Davis, "Ghosts, Kin, and Progeny: Some Features of Family Life in Early Modern France," *Daedalus* 106, no. 2 (1977): 87–114; Lawrence Stone, *The Family, Sex, and Marriage in England, 1500–1800* (New York: Harper & Row, 1977).

5. Michel Foucault, *The History of Sexuality, Volume 1, An Introduction*, trans. Robert Hurley (New York: Vintage Books, 1990), 43.

6. On the prevalence of violent crime, see, for example, Deborah Prothrow-Stith with Michaele Weissman, *Deadly Consequences* (New York: HarperCollins, 1991).

7. For a fuller development of this argument, see Elizabeth Fox-Genovese, "Feminism and the Rhetoric of Individual Rights, Parts I & II," *Common Knowledge*, nos. 1 & 2 (1992). Similar arguments can also be found in Mary Ann Glendon, *Abortion and Divorce in Western Law* (Cambridge: Harvard University Press, 1987); and her *Rights Talk: The Impoverishment of Political Discourse* (New York: Free Press, 1991).

8. For confirmation of this position, see, for example, Kristin Luker, *Abortion and the Politics of Motherhood* (Berkeley: University of California Press, 1984); and Faye D. Ginsburg, *Contested Lives: The Abortion Debate in an American Community* (Berkeley: University of California Press, 1989).

9. Richard A. Posner, *The Problems of Jurisprudence* (Cambridge: Harvard University Press, 1990), 28.

10. Posner, *Problems of Jurisprudence*, 23.

11. Posner, *Problems of Jurisprudence*, 130.

Sixteen

Between Elitism and Populism
Whither Comparative Literature?

There is little or no disagreement about where comparative literature began, only about where it should go. Nor is there much disagreement about the challenges it faces in the American academy, only about how appropriately to respond to them. As the differences about the future of comparative literature in a postmodern, global environment take shape, they seem, like so many other disagreements about our difficult and contested world, to be falling into two principal camps which, for lack of more nuanced terms, might be called the elitists and the populists. For the former, comparative literature should remain true to its initial mission as a demanding discipline grounded in the mastery of high literature in its original languages. For the latter, comparative literature should expand in the direction of cultural studies by steadily increasing the kinds of texts it considers and by relaxing the requirement that works be read in the original.

Obviously, this crude simplification does something less than justice to the complexities of the myriad overlapping positions that do not fall neatly into one or another camp. Yet elitists and populists do represent respectively the main tendencies in the discussion, and, like magnetic poles, they tend inexorably to draw the innumerable variations into their orbit. Thus do the discussions, sooner or later, tend to reduce to the implacable choice: Are you with us or against us? More's the pity. Not because the polarization is out of step with the times, but because it so perfectly mirrors them.

"Between Elitism and Populism: Whither Comparative Literature?" In *Comparative Literature in the Age of Multiculturalism*, edited by Charles Bernheimer, 134–42. Baltimore: Johns Hopkins University Press, 1995. Copyright 1995 by the Johns Hopkins University Press. All rights reserved. Used by permission of the Johns Hopkins University Press.

Like all wars, the culture wars that have erupted on our campuses tolerate neither neutrals nor independents. Thriving on polarization, the wars are increasingly classifying all of us as either reactionaries or revolutionaries no matter how strenuously we resist. And when you consider the stakes, the pressure to polarization makes a certain depressing sense. Yet as the case of comparative literature makes abundantly clear, polarization tends to obscure precisely the questions that really matter. Does it, for example, necessarily follow that recognition of the emergence of a global culture requires one to defend a focus on "popular" rather than "high" culture, or requires one to defend instruction in translation rather than in the original? And what about history? Does an appreciation of historical context sentence the scholar or instructor to defend "historicism"?

If nothing else, these invidious choices testify to a pervasive anxiety among comparatists about how our discipline should position itself on the shifting sands that the academic terrain has become. Having initially positioned itself as uncompromisingly elitist in the sense of intellectually demanding, comparative literature now faces daunting challenges, including the changing preparation of students, the pressures of administrations, the proliferation of theory in English and the modern languages, the emergence of cultural studies, and the general infatuation with multiculturalism, diversity, and identity politics. Each of these challenges merits a discrete response, yet the general tendency is to lump rather than separate them, thus conflating ends and means. At the heart of the matter lies one set of disagreements over what comparative literature is and should be and another over how best to defend what it is and should be.

Those who defend the legitimacy of instruction in translation justify their position on a variety of grounds, notably the acknowledged inability of most students to read texts in the original and the moral claims of literatures that few, if any, of us, much less our students, can read in the original. To begin with the moral claims, who are we to exclude Polish, Finnish, or Hungarian, much less Thai, literature from comparative literature just because we are too limited (read imperialist) to appreciate it in the original? And what about the claims of cultures that have produced little or no literate culture? Are we entitled to dismiss them as unworthy of our attention? But these moral claims are overdetermined by our unhappy knowledge that many of the students we should like to reach—or at least to enroll in our classes—probably could not read a play, novel, or poem in French or Spanish, much less Thai or Swahili, and some may even have an inadequate command of English. This overdetermination has tempted some to see the claims of ill-prepared students as morally analogous to the claims of neglected cultures. They are not. Moral claims the students may have, but they are those of remedying their defective preparation, not pretending that it has no significance.

I do not wish to slight the possible value of teaching some texts in translation. Most students, especially undergraduates but too frequently graduate students as well, cannot read enough languages to permit a broad comparative perspective on the basis of texts in the original. But to cast the matter as an all-or-nothing proposition is not the appropriate solution. We must ask ourselves whether professors should be teaching texts that they themselves cannot read in the original, even if they teach translations. And we must ask ourselves if we should try to make comparative literature accessible to students who can read no language other than their own well enough to appreciate a literary text in it. If we answer no to both questions, as I do, then we must develop new strategies. We might, for example, simply insist that professors teach only (or primarily) texts they can read in the original and that students in comparative literature classes be able to read one of the relevant languages in the original. Under these conditions, we would not have to insist that in a specific course all students be able to read all of the texts in the original, although presumably the professor would. One of the benefits of this strategy would be explicitly to open comparative literature to professors in various cultures that comparative literature has not always included, perhaps because professors who know Thai have not usually taught literature classes.

It is easy to imagine the objections, beginning with the insistence that a specialist in Southeast Asia more often than not knows nothing about the theories and methods upon which comparative literature draws. But these objections bear reconsideration. Ironically, those who might most vociferously object might well be those who favor comparative literature's move toward cultural studies and who doubt the ability of traditional specialists to grasp the theoretical innovation that they believe binds comparative literature and cultural studies. Yet those who favor comparative literature's move toward cultural studies tend to be those who are most suspicious of its claims to concern itself primarily with high culture. These discussions might, accordingly, expose the lurking tendency within comparative literature to associate the discipline's traditional European focus with its traditional high-literary focus—as if *The Tale of Genji* were not every bit as much an elite text as *Madame Bovary*.

Eurocentrism versus globalism and high versus popular culture are not the same discussion, and their conflation barely masks an agenda that is no less ideological than comparative literature's original agenda is charged with having been. The main obstacles to comparative literature's adopting a global perspective on high culture lie less in the elitism of the relevant texts (although popular literature did develop primarily as a European phenomenon, largely because Europe had the technology to produce and distribute it) than in their difficulty and, for some, unpalatability. Most non-European countries were long more socially stratified than European countries, and they were much more likely to reserve literate culture for a circumscribed elite. Not surprisingly, under these conditions, their literatures were more likely than not to celebrate inequality among social classes and between women and men, or at least take those inequalities for granted. It is hard, in other words, to turn to non-Western literatures for a "progressive" message.

The popular cultures of non-European cultures frequently contain messages of protest against the status quo, although even they may manifest a disconcerting conservatism. But the main problem in teaching them within the context of comparative literature lies in the likelihood that until the twentieth century, and sometimes well into it, they were as likely as not to have been oral. And it is in the nature of oral cultures constantly to revise themselves without ever admitting to the revisions. Thus each generation will pass on "traditional" accounts of how things have always been, but will alter those accounts to reflect contemporaneous concerns. Not for nothing have Terence Ranger and Eric Hobsbawm written of the "invention of tradition." Social historians and cultural anthropologists have methods for dealing with these problems, although even they remain imperfect. But the tendency of literary methods to focus on texts (oral as well as written) as texts is not ideally suited to solving them, even with the assistance of deconstruction.

Some, to be sure, would take these caveats as justification for broadening comparative literature to include the methods of history and anthropology on the grounds that all texts must be contextualized and that to treat written texts as in some way privileged is to perpetuate illegitimate social inequalities and cultural hierarchies. Such arguments woefully distort the appropriate—and valuable—place of history in comparative literature. Indeed, the more broadly comparative literature casts its cultural net, the more valuable history becomes, precisely as a means of contextualization. It is difficult not to dismiss as irresponsible the presumption that we may select texts from around the world and teach them as unmediated expressions of human experience, although at some point we must also teach them in this way. But in order to do so responsibly, we must understand something of the social, political, moral, and religious values out of which their authors were writing.

Tellingly, the globalization of comparative literature has proved most effective with respect to twentieth-century texts. The experience of two world wars, decolonization, and the electronic revolution has indeed transformed a vast world into a global village. Increasingly, peoples throughout the world share at least the rudiments of common values, notably freedom and economic prosperity. But they remain deeply divided by their histories and even by the referents they attach to the privileged signs of freedom and prosperity. And the writers who attempt to capture their experience and aspirations themselves remain torn between a particularist past and a universal present and future. Think of Frantz Fanon's condemnation of the Martiniquais textbooks that offered the descendants of African slaves "our ancestors the Gauls." Yet Fanon wrote through the prism of the existentialism that had characterized his own European education. Countless twentieth-century African and Caribbean writers have shared the essentials of Fanon's experience. And we may readily assume that by the time they wrote for publication they were primarily writing for other literate people who shared enough of that bicultural experience to recognize European as well as indigenous themes and influences.

To contextualize such writing, comparatists themselves need to recognize both influences and to know enough about both cultures to recognize the themes, tropes, and conventions that the writers chose to emphasize. We may, in other words, safely assume that for the most accomplished African and Caribbean writers, writing invariably entailed a process of selection and emphasis. We are quick to grasp what Baudelaire, Dickens, or Tolstoy chose not to write—what they repressed or silenced. We need to be able to do the same with Ousmane Sembène or Buchi Emecheta. We especially need to be able to evaluate the significance of the former's falling within the French orbit and the latter's within the British. And, above all, we need to appreciate their properly literary aspirations. For we pay them scant respect if we treat them only as cries of protest or voices of liberation. And we treat them with still less respect if we uncritically assimilate their distinct protests to our own assumptions. I still recall with disquiet hearing a respected comparatist cheerfully avow that the many pleasures of teaching postcolonial literature included the sense of spontaneity she experienced at reading the book for the first time and at the same time as the students. Presumably, under those conditions, one does not normally have time to refresh one's memory about the salient differences between Martinique, Nigeria, and Senegal. But then what are we offering our students except perhaps the comfortable notion that people around the globe feel much as we do? And suppose they do not?

History has an important place in comparative literature, especially as it expands its scope. For history affords the inestimable value of helping us to appreciate the context within which, and the audience for which, various authors wrote. And even as it necessarily calls attention to the differences between various authors (and texts), it also advances the work of genuine comparison by permitting us to identify elements that seem to make apples apples and oranges oranges. Historical reading in this sense must necessarily begin with appreciation of the context of meaning. The historicism that indiscriminately exposes the purported classism, racism, or sexism of various texts will not serve. Yes, the warriors of the *Iliad* were more likely than not to treat women as the spoils of war. And then what? Do we read the *Iliad* to savor the objectification of women or refuse to read it because it objectifies women? Not if we are sane. But then we must think about why we do read it—about what makes it an enduring text neither because of nor in spite of many of the attitudes and assumptions it embodies. The willingness to appreciate the *Iliad*—our own and our students' openness to it—depends in part upon a fitting sense of history which sifts the ways in which the world of the *Iliad* is different from and similar to our own. More often than not, especially in the case of texts that were produced in societies radically different from our own, the differences will emerge as a complex of social and political values, the similarities as some fundamental sense of what it means to be human—the ways in which it is possible to be human.

That modern authors still draw upon ancient texts for models of human possibilities should make us thoughtful. How do Antigone, Persephone, and Medea continue to figure as sources of significant meaning for such authors as Jean Anouilh, Maya Angelou, and Toni Morrison? How may we appreciate the power that Sophocles' Oedipus held for Freud and simultaneously appreciate Giles Deleuze and Félix Guattari's insistence that Freud's use of the figure of Oedipus must also be understood as specific to the rise of capitalism? These questions and others like them remind us of the significance of theory for comparative literature. They should also remind us of the simultaneous significance of history and of myth, which itself is best understood as history's antithesis. Above all, they should remind us that comparisons, especially literary comparisons, are inherently difficult and demanding.

Much clattering of computer keyboards has been enlisted to attack and defend theory in general and specific theories in particular. Once again, we would seem to be falling into false dilemmas. It would, frankly, be difficult to imagine comparative literature without theory, not least since the mere posing of the comparative problem is inherently theoretical. What do we seek to compare and why? Thus to take up arms against the theoretical project must raise the possibility of bad faith—or at least lack of candor. The issue is not theory or no theory, but which theory and, above all, toward what end. The war over theory seems to have emerged from the implicit assumption, fed by both sides, that theory itself is at war with learning or at least attempts to substitute itself for it. The charge may not fairly be leveled at the leading theorists—a Deleuze, a Derrida, or a Bakhtin. It may more plausibly be leveled at their epigones, especially novices who grab on to theory as a panacea for the inherent difficulties of literary understanding. How comforting, especially when one is making one's way through the shoals of academic competition, to have a simple—or, even better, complex—formula that explains everything.

Those who most appreciate the challenges of theoretical work are understandably loath to concede its reductionist comforts and possibilities. But one need only scan a random sample of dissertations or first books to know they exist. The comparative study of literature is not mathematics, which is to say its stars are rarely to be found among the young. For better or worse, the comparative study of literature, like fine wine, improves with age. The reading of many texts is an advantage, even if the quantity of that reading does not itself substitute for the intelligence and sophistication with which the reading is practiced. But comparative study of literature rapidly becomes sterile and boring without learning, if only because it lacks the texture that evokes resonances and invites further (or other) comparisons.

The intertextuality that has emerged as essential to the thick understanding of comparative literature and to the texts it considers requires textual density and breadth. It is all very well to scan a group of heterogeneous texts for the sign of woman or the feminine. But in the measure that most texts contain such signs, the gesture becomes so abstract as rapidly to become meaningless. Refinement of the sign, as in woman as wife, mother, mistress, daughter, virgin, or whore, helps, but only modestly. Beyond that, the possibilities are endless. And this is where learning, history, myth, and theory all come into play. For the sign of woman acquires its meaning in relation to other signs, and the other signs in relation to which that of woman is taken to acquire meaning or salience vary according to text, culture, and historical context. They also vary in relation to the systems of signs—the texts—with which the author is familiar which have preceded them. They may especially and most complexly vary in the work of authors who draw simultaneously on oral and literate traditions or who write on the cusp of literacy.

In attending to this myriad of possibilities, comparative literature aspires to be comprehensive—to include within its purview the essence and summit of literary studies and perhaps the humanities as well. For comparative literature does aspire to elucidate and enrich the literary representation of the human condition in all its variations. In this respect, intertextuality lies at the center of its sense of itself, even when that sense is most contested as it is today. But intertextuality poses its own problems, beginning with the relation between the intertextuality of texts which, however separated in origin and purpose, resemble one another and texts that explicitly converse with one another. Differentiation between the two groups requires knowledge of the cultures or societies from which they emerged as well as knowledge of their authors' literary universe. In instances in which there are no grounds for assuming that specific authors had any familiarity with texts the themes of which they appear to be echoing, we may begin to argue for universal or archetypal patterns in human experience and imagination or for recurring narratives of what it means to be human. In instances in which it is reasonably clear that specific authors from different societies and cultures had access to the texts of others whose situation differed decisively from their own, we may be dealing with a literary history that transcends specific social, economic, and political influences. Once again, the point is the difficulty and complexity of the analysis—and the importance of learning and experience to it.

Such questions have given rise to a growing concern with the relation between popular and high culture. For intertextuality almost always sinks its deepest roots into the everyday conversations and attitudes that shape any author's earliest experience and continue to impinge upon the experience of the adult. Thus, some would argue that popular books of piety, folk songs, television shows, or rap music may influence a writer's imagination more powerfully than anything Homer, Shakespeare, or Joyce ever wrote. Perhaps. Perhaps not. Most likely every writer uniquely combines influences from disparate sources. But the recognition of the significance of popular culture in the imagination of writers does not logically justify a repudiation of the discrete claims of self-conscious literary craft. Rather, it justifies broadening our understanding of the popular influences upon discrete writers or the role of popular culture in the high-cultural imagination, on the firm understanding that the uses of popular influences will be eminently idiosyncratic.

Cultural studies aims to erase the boundaries between elite and popular culture in the name of democratization. On what grounds may we justify holding "The Love Song of J. Alfred Prufrock" or the *Iliad* in higher regard than the latest release of Ice Cube or 2 Live Crew? The impulse to democratization has been fueled by the legitimate claims that high-literary studies have notoriously tended to exclude women, Afro-American, and non-Western writers, thus promoting the impression that the only human experiences or literary expressions considered worthy of serious study are those of elite white men. Forget, for the moment, that surprisingly few of the male writers who have traditionally commanded the greatest prestige were themselves born into the elite of their respective societies. The truth remains that the academic study of literature was unpardonably delinquent in its recognition of literary merit in unfamiliar guise. Elite academics did not normally take female or Afro-American writers seriously and probably had not heard of the most accomplished non-Western writers. Rectification of that unpardonable neglect does not justify the substitution of popular for high culture.

We know that the boundaries between high and popular culture are notoriously and unmanageably permeable, and it would be foolhardy to pretend to draw them rigidly. We also know that some works of literature better justify and repay sustained attention and rereading than others. Sexism alone cannot explain why *The Scarlet Letter* fared better in literary studies than *The Wide, Wide World*, even though the latter outsold the former in time and place. However imperfect, the criteria of complexity and depth which help to justify the literary reputation of *The Scarlet Letter* are the same as those that would accord Toni Morrison's *Beloved* greater literary prestige than Frances Ellen Watkins Harper's *Iola Leroy*, even though *Iola Leroy* is a better novel than its longstanding neglect would suggest. Indeed, one of the most important missions of comparative literature is precisely to delineate those imperfect boundaries without regard to sex, race, class, or place of national origin.

Comparative literature is and should remain an intellectually elitist enterprise, on the proud conviction that intellectual elitism may not be taken as a proxy for social elitism. Make no mistake: the "democratization" of comparative literature through an expansion into cultural studies will not ensure one iota of social democratization. Social democratization occurs when we ensure the openness of our self-consciously difficult and demanding discipline to practitioners of all backgrounds. If we aspire to secure our own position in the academy by easing our intellectual requirements so as to attract ever larger numbers of students, we will get what we deserve: first and foremost the dubious blessing of teaching students who have little interest in what we do and less ability to do it.

Seventeen

Of Sin and Horses
The Compelling World of Dick Francis's Mysteries

In the fall of 1997, the British mystery writer Dick Francis published his thirty-seventh mystery novel, *10-Lb. Penalty,* which, like many of its predecessors, was selected as a Book-of-the-Month Club main selection and a *Reader's Digest* condensed book and quickly made its way onto the *New York Times* best-seller list. As it happens, *10-Lb. Penalty* differs in some significant respects from its predecessors, and I shall return to those differences. In many other respects, however, it manifests the essential features that have stamped all of Francis's work with a unique and haunting quality.

Unlike many leading mystery writers, Francis does not use a single sleuth or team of sleuths (Miss Marple, Hercule Poirot, Inspector Morse) to establish continuity from one novel to the next. Rather, he writes each in the first person voice of its main protagonist, and only three of the 37 share a common hero, the former jockey Sid Halley, whom Francis was persuaded to bring back by the demands of his readers. The diversity of protagonists, however does not compromise the reader's sense that each new Francis mystery returns us to a familiar universe.

This sense of continuity owes much to the unity of Francis's narrative voice, and the forthright directness and immediacy of that voice swiftly engages the reader's confidence, which it sustains throughout, drawing us into the comfortable sense that the narrator is a man we should like to know and even, for regular Francis readers, someone we have met before. All of the

---

"Of Sin and Horses: The Compelling World of Dick Francis's Mysteries." *Books and Culture: A Christian Review,* January/February 1998, 42–43. Copyright 1998 by *Books and Culture.* All rights reserved. Used by permission of *Books and Culture.*

Of Sin and Horses

Francis narrators are men, and most are not investigators by profession. Almost all have a direct connection to horses, and many are jockeys, former jockeys, or aspiring jockeys. A former steeplechase jockey himself, Francis knows the world of British racing inside out and, in his mysteries, brings it vividly to life. It is impossible to read more than a few without acquiring a nodding acquaintance with British racecourses, jockeys' unabating struggles to keep their weight down, the respective roles of trainers and owners, the intricacy and magnitude of betting, and the responsibilities of racetrack and Jockey Club officials.

This profusion of concrete information about the world of racing also adds to the sense of continuity from one Francis mystery to another, although not all of them take place within that world. That some do not concern racing, or concern it only indirectly, nonetheless suggests that something more than a familiar setting accounts for the underlying sense of unity among them. Francis does, properly and understandably, write primarily about people and a world he knows preeminently well, and his depiction of both assuredly engages readers' interest and imagination. But, in the end, it is not so much the world of racing itself that engages us, although it does, as it is the way in which Francis represents it. We care about steeplechasing or the ways in which it is possible maliciously and surreptitiously to prevent a horse from running to full capacity because Francis's masterful evocation brings us directly into the inner workings of racing and introduces us to its mechanics. In other words, Francis's real gift lies in his rare ability to present readers with a concrete understanding of the specific details that professionals would take for granted. When in *10-Lb. Penalty*, he turns to politics and a local election, the effect is the same.

What holds for Francis's use of detail to bring a specific world to life also holds for his ability to evoke the character of his narrator-protagonist. Both literary tasks are accomplished with a breathtaking terseness and economy. One would be hard pressed to find an extra word in a Francis mystery, much less an extraneous paragraph, and yet the reader always has enough information to understand the narrator, the action, and the relevant attributes of the main characters. We always know enough, never too much. Francis never lulls us into complicity with a flow of chat or a soothing, if extraneous, description, and his bare-bones, stripped-down prose wonderfully enhances the taut suspense that informs most of his plots.

The tone is set from the opening line in *10-Lb. Penalty*.

> I'd never sniffed glue in my life.
>
> All the same, I stood before the man whose horses I rode and listened to him telling me he had no further use for my services. He sat

behind his large antique paper-covered desk fidgeting with his clean fingernails. His hands were a yellowish white, very smooth.

A few lines later, we learn that "I was not yet eighteen," and, a few lines beyond, that the man whose horses he has ridden calls him Benedict.

Later in this first chapter, we learn that Benedict's surname is Julliard, that his father, George Julliard, calls him Ben, and that he has "dark curly hair (impervious to straightening by water)," "brown eyes, thin face, lean frame," and stands "five foot eleven (or thereabouts)."

Thereafter, relevant information about Ben appears, as we need it to follow the plot. At no point, however, does Francis break into the central narrative to give us a full account of Ben's childhood and schooling. Only in bits and pieces do we learn that, while at school, he has become an expert skier and marksman as well as a talented apprentice jockey. What we do, however, learn, almost immediately, is that more than anything Ben loves horses and racing and has set his heart on becoming a professional jockey. The opening scene shatters those dreams, freeing Ben for the action of the novel, which turns on his role in his father's run for a seat in Parliament. Indeed, as we rapidly learn, Ben's father, having ascertained that Ben would be too large ever to be a top jockey, engineered the scene, instructing the trainer, Sir Vivian Derridge, for whom Ben was riding, to fire him in a way that brooked no discussion. Thus does the scene draw us into Francis's real subject, Ben's coming of age and the evolving relations between father and son.

Francis's heroes typically live on the edge of dangers that would reduce most of us to jelly—dangers to which they are likely to respond with a rare combination of cool wits and sangfroid. And in Francis's fictional universe the opportunities to display their self-effacing, understated heroism abound. A typical Francis mystery unfolds under the shadow of menace and frequently includes one or more scenes of heart-stopping violence. For Francis's view of our world unquestionably includes a disquieting dose of genuine evil. This recognition of evil and of the havoc it wreaks upon bodies and souls testifies directly to what I take to be Francis's deeper concerns, and they amply justify our serious attention.

Evil casts an ominous shadow of danger over most of Francis's mysteries, and the sense of its lurking presence weighs equally upon the hero and the reader. Francis never hesitates to name evil and clearly wants his readers to grasp its true horror. At the same time, he never suggests that the evil, which percolates beneath so many ordinary, apparently peaceful situations, is normal. Pervasive it may sometimes be, but even at its most insidiously pervasive, true evil remains unambiguously aberrant.

Of Sin and Horses

None could be less naïve than Francis about human vulnerability to temptation and propensity to sin. His novels abound with characters who rarely pass up a near occasion of sin. But he never confuses the ubiquitous manifestations of our fallen condition with genuine evil, and it is striking how often he endows run-of-the-mill hired thugs or petty cheats with some marginally redeeming feature that locates them within the pale of predictable human frailty. Typically, such characters agree to provide information to the hero in return for a payment or inadvertently let drop something about the nature of their bullying assignment that helps the hero to identify their employer, the real villain.

Thus, in *Whip Hand*, the second Sid Halley novel, the Scottish thugs who have been imported to rough up Sid and his man Friday, Chico, resist the command of a secondary villain to kill Sid and Chico. "Kill him yourself," one retorts, "we're not doing it." And, when Peter Rammileese, the secondary villain, repeats the command, the hired thug continues, "Grow up mon. . . . We'd be gassed inside five minutes. We've been down here too long. Too many people've seen us. And this laddie, he's won money for every punter in Scotland. We'd be inside in a week." The Scots have enthusiastically showered Sid and Chico with punishing blows, but they draw the line at killing. And, in the end, the passing remark about having been down here too long proves an indispensable link in the chain of information that Sid is piecing together, and that finally enables him to identify the shadowy figure who has set the events in motion.

Time and again, Francis encompasses such figures within the predictable limits of ordinary human nature, which he never romanticizes. True evil, in contrast, exceeds the predictable, which it mocks and threatens. An important feature of Francis's special talent consists in the ability to discriminate between the ordinary and the aberrant, and it is precisely his gift for evoking the ordinary that ultimately permits readers to recognize the full aberrance of evil. Francis's heroes serve as a lens to focus our attention on evil, for, in Francis's fictional universe, evil is always experienced in its full human dimension. It is, in other words, always represented as a deeply disordered personality that commits or orders the commission of actions against others, frequently against the hero himself, although almost as frequently against horses, who represent a moving combination of power and vulnerability.

In *Bolt* (1986), the ruthless villain kills a succession of racehorses to warn their wealthy, aristocratic owner of her vulnerability—her inability to protect the animals and humans she loves against predatory aggression—and she and Kit, her jockey and the novel's hero, grieve for them as for friends. Kit thinks to himself that, on the scale of world terrorism, the killing of three great horses is a small matter, "but rooted in the same wicked conviction that the path to attaining one's end lay in slaughtering the innocent." In *Come to Grief* (1995), the third Sid Halley novel, a recklessly ambitious amateur-jockey-turned-talk-show-host fatally maims horses to recover the sense of thrilling speed that he experienced during races. In these crimes we see a cold, intelligent form of violence, worlds removed from the pummeling of the Scottish thugs—and even further removed from the calm accepting intelligence of the victimized horses. In *Come to Grief,* Sid dashes to Berkshire to help a woman whose colt has just been maimed. When he arrives, everyone but the colt is breathing worry and impatience.

> The young horse watched me with calm, bright eyes, unafraid. I stroked my hand down his nose, talking to him quietly. He moved his head upward against the pressure and down again as if nodding, saying hello. I let him wiffle his black lips across my knuckles.

The calm nobility and intelligence of horses runs like a thread through Francis's mysteries. In many, individual horses figure as minor characters in their own right, and each of those we come to know by name has his or her own personality, sometimes willful, sometimes courageous, always distinct. Their palpable reality confirms the essential goodness of God's creation, which evil is ultimately powerless to negate.

The delicate contrast and tension between tenderness and violence marks all of Francis's novels, not simply as a Manichaeism that pits good guys against bad but also as the conflicting tendencies in the human soul. The very heroes who dispatch threatening villains and push themselves and their horses to the limit in pursuit of victory evince a moving sensitivity to the women they love, who themselves embody fierceness as well as warmth. A web of nuanced human relations weaves through each of the novels, but Francis clearly ascribes a special importance to those between fathers and sons. *Hot Money* (1987), for example, places the relations between Ian Pembroke and his father, Malcolm, stage center, and *10-Lb. Penalty* returns to this theme, which dominates the plot.

Indeed, compared to previous Francis novels, *10-Lb. Penalty* is remarkably free of mystery, danger, and suspense. To be sure, there are several attempts upon George Julliard's life and several ominous attempts to destroy his rapidly rising political career, but we are rarely in much doubt about who lies behind them and are rarely frightened that they will succeed. Even the novel's representatives of pure evil, A. L. Wyvern and the loathsome, malicious journalist Usher Rudd, never assume the terrifyingly sinister proportions of earlier Francis villains. The true action of *10-Lb. Penalty* lies in Ben and George Julliard's coming to know and trust one another and in Ben's growing from a boy into a talented, resourceful, and self-assured man—every inch, if in different guise, his brilliant father's natural heir.

10-Lb. Penalty exudes a gentleness that has been latent throughout Francis's novels, surfacing in specific scenes. It is a mellow book and one that the supercilious might well find too close to the sentimental. But such sentimentality as it contains is tough, not maudlin, and it wonderfully calls attention to the aspects of life Francis demonstrably values. Ben Julliard takes second place to none of Francis's heroes in courage or intelligence, but he is younger and, unlike Sid, who has come up the hard way, he has always had the backing of his father's money. What he has not had is his father's presence, and this permits Francis, in highlighting the arresting similarities between the powerful, successful father and the unfinished son, to emphasize the importance of nature and genes in what any of us become. Without ever suggesting that nature will triumph over outright abuse and extreme deprivation (Ben has always been emotionally and financially cared for), Francis does firmly suggest that character and talent are not gifts that the world bestows. And, although the word never appears in Francis's pages, it is hard for a Christian not to sense that his understanding of nature has as much to do with grace as with mere material life.

Nowhere in his novels does Dick Francis suggest he is a Christian, and indeed there are reasons to suspect that he may not consider himself a believer. Toward the end of *Whip Hand,* Charles Roland and Sid sit in the library at Aynsford, mulling over the events of the novel. Musing on Sid's victory over the forces of evil, Charles asks Sid if he feels any temptation to gloat. Sid responds with astonishment. What did you do, he asks Charles, when during the war at sea, you saw your enemy drowning. "Gloat? Push him under?" Charles answers that he took the enemy prisoner, to which Sid rejoins that the life of the corrupt racetrack official he has exposed will be prison enough. But then, Charles asks, "And do you forgive him as well?" Sid tells him not to ask such difficult questions and thinks to himself, "Love thine enemy. Forgive, Forget. I was no sort of Christian. I thought I could manage not to hate Lucas himself. I didn't think I could forgive, and I would never forget."

But the conclusion of *10-Lb. Penalty* does offer a surprisingly Christian image of manliness. Ben, now in his twenties and successful in his own work, simultaneously saves his father from Wyvern's attempt to shoot him and exposes Wyvern's malevolence that has been percolating since his father's first election to Parliament, thereby clearing the way for George Julliard to become prime minister. Father and son stand together "The next prime minister held my hand. I gripped his tight, as if he would give me comfort and security when I needed them badly. I gripped his hand as if I'd been a little boy."

Readers may choose for themselves how much to read into Francis's words, never sure how much he intends us to read into them. But it seems difficult to doubt that a writer of his consummate skill has offered us all of these possibilities without knowing he was doing so. At the very least, we may know that his novels repeatedly and with increasing forthrightness touch upon the central themes of Christianity, and, at the most, we may fairly view them through the lens of Flannery O'Connor's thoughts about writing.

> Art is not anything that goes on "among" people, not the art of the novel anyway. It is something that one experiences alone and for the purpose of realizing in a fresh way, through the senses, the mystery of existence. Part of the mystery of existence is sin. When we think about the Crucifixion, we miss the point of it if we don't think about sin.[1]

Note

1. Letter to Eileen Hall, March 10, 1956. From *A Habit of Being: Letters of Flannery O'Connor*, edited by Sally Fitzgerald (Farrar, Straus and Giroux, 1979).

Eighteen

Multiculturalism in History
Ideologies and Realities

Increasingly, I wonder if any of us knows what multiculturalism means. Surely one of the sadder aspects of the recent history of academic culture wars must be the tendency for some to transform the term multiculturalism into an automatic epithet of opprobrium and for others to transform it into an automatic seal of approval. For critics, an endorsement of multiculturalism necessarily signals a nefarious political agenda; for supporters, it necessarily signals a certificate of good intentions. Those on both sides who allow themselves to be drawn into these self-serving characterizations are effectively capitulating to the premises of "reader response" criticism, or standpoint theory, according to which the meaning of a term such as multiculturalism depends exclusively upon the perspective of the individual. To be sure, the participants do not see it this way, but they are too deeply invested in defending their positions to appreciate a dispassionate view. In this respect, at least, the contending parties implicitly accede to the conviction that multiculturalism refers to an ideology rather than to a society, form of government, economy, coherent religious or intellectual system, or even a culture.

There is nothing surprising here. The nature and purpose of an "ism" are precisely ideological. But if an ideology is what we are dealing with, then we need to reflect briefly on the nature and purpose of ideology in general. Given the importance of ideological conflict in the modern world, it is hardly

"Multiculturalism in History: Ideologies and Realities." *Orbis: A Journal of World Affairs* 43 (Fall 1999): 531–39. Copyright 1999 by *Orbis*. All rights reserved. Used by permission of *Orbis*.

surprising that many people understand the term in the narrow sense influentially expounded by Karl Mannheim. In this sense, ideology figures as the battle cry or wartime propaganda of a specific group, party, or sect that seeks to shape an explanation of specific contested issues in such a way as to mobilize people to fight for or against them. Analyzing the process, Mannheim linked ideology to utopia and urged his readers to recognize ideologies as preeminently partisan manipulations of attitudes and beliefs. Notwithstanding the emergence of more sophisticated analyses of ideology, Mannheim's view continues to shape many people's attitudes, with the result that many still regard ideology as a deviation from, if not an outright opponent of, the truth. Ideology, in this perspective, becomes something that you—whoever you may be—"have," but I do not. This understanding reinforces the pejorative connotations of the term. Perhaps more important, it leaves the immutability and impartiality of the "truth" unscathed.

Alternate understandings of ideology nonetheless merit serious attention, if only to help us place prevailing understandings of the meaning of multiculturalism in perspective. The key figures here are Antonio Gramsci and Mikhail Bakhtin. During the early twentieth century, both Gramsci, an Italian, and Bakhtin, a Russian, focused their singular intellects upon the problem of ideology, which seemed to offer privileged access to an understanding of the role of culture in the life of peoples and nations. Notwithstanding Gramsci's primary focus upon political theory and Bakhtin's primary focus upon literary criticism, their projects converged at many points.[1]

At the risk of gross simplification, permit me to suggest that both Gramsci and Bakhtin understood ideology as a matter of participation rather than one of domination or manipulation. They further understood ideology in the broad sense as worldview rather than as partisan propaganda. Thus, ideology figures as a comprehensive system of beliefs to which different social groups adhere, often for different reasons. By the same token, ideology in their sense embodies the contributions of different groups. Thus, in a discussion of sixteenth-century France in *The World of Rabelais*, Bakhtin emphasizes the role of the common people in setting limits to the unilateral authority of the king and in shaping the prevailing view of legitimate authority. No utopian populist, Bakhtin never fudges the unequal distribution of power between king and people, but he insists that the king could only represent, justify, and exercise his power within limits set by the people. By encompassing the values of both monarch and people, the ideology that resulted from their interactions and, yes, struggles rose to the status of a comprehensive worldview that offered to all participants an acceptable picture of their relations.

Multiculturalism in History

Neither the critics nor the supporters of multiculturalism have shown much interest in Gramsci and Bakhtin's capacious understanding of ideology. Indeed, both have so single-mindedly focused upon their specific political, cultural, and educational agenda as to permit the suspicion that they either are not familiar with it or do not understand it. And their failure in this regard has made negotiation, or even conversation, between them increasingly difficult. Another of the main casualties of this failure has been the ability of either side to acknowledge the murky relations between multiculturalism as ideology and the multicultural reality of our increasingly interdependent and intertwined global society.

Independent of our attitudes toward multiculturalism, multicultural society is a fact—a fact that challenges both our presuppositions and our aspirations. But, above all, it is a fact that challenges our institutions and our culture. It requires little imagination to grasp that the increasing intermingling of peoples throughout the world places considerable pressure upon established governments, educational systems, and economies. The current crisis in the Balkans offers an especially dramatic enactment of the conflicts to which those pressures can lead, but its drama does not decisively exceed that of the conflicts that have torn apart Rwanda, Chechnya, and Afghanistan, to mention only a few.

We in the United States have been taught to see ourselves as a nation of immigrants and to take pride in the wealth of national cultures that our country has embraced. Western Europeans, however, have until recently tended to think of themselves as homogeneous peoples, although their more distant past featured a veritable olio of ethnic and national intermingling. Differences in historical experience and national memory notwithstanding, Europeans and Americans alike confront today a tide of immigration that is challenging their institutions and national cultures. The issues at stake range from the availability of jobs and the adequacy of funding for social services to the fundamental understanding of the balance between the rights of individuals and the cultural autonomy of groups. In a much-publicized case, the French government clashed with Islamic immigrants over the permissibility of veiling for schoolgirls from Islamic families. Yet more ominously, both France and Germany now confront unprecedented rates of unemployment, which predictably exacerbate tensions, and the fraying of their social welfare programs threatens citizens with what they regard as an unacceptable reduction in benefits. In other words, more than enough combustible material has accumulated to ignite a serious social and political conflagration.

Solutions, however makeshift, may be found, and the conflagration may never occur. But its non-occurrence would not alleviate this grave situation, much less guarantee a harmonious future. Skirmishes will almost certainly continue to proliferate, and loyalties to specific ethnic and national identities will almost certainly continue to harden. To complicate matters further, the European authorities in Brussels may be expected to press forward with their transnational agenda, which includes a heavy component of rules and regulations to enforce prescribed forms of personal relations and behavior— what some are wont to call "political correctness." Always and everywhere, bureaucrats seem inexorably drawn to Benthamite solutions, and the continuing expansion of the global economy seems guaranteed to expand their reach over smaller national and ethnic groups.

All current indications suggest that the continuing growth of transnational institutions that are determined to "manage diversity" will not assuage multicultural sensibilities but aggravate them. At the same time, the continuing expansion of the global economy will assuredly produce a steady increase in mobility and immigration. The developed nations underwrite a standard of living and offer an array of social services that the developing nations cannot hope to match. Unless the developed nations attempt to seal their borders—and it seems unlikely that the attempt would succeed—we may confidently predict a steady progression in the multicultural character of their populations and hence an intensification of multiculturalist passions.

Such are the contours of the fact of multicultural society. Increasingly, the world's inhabitants are living in close proximity to and interspersed among people of different ethnic and national backgrounds, and frequently at some distance from the land of their birth. For those of us who believe in original sin, it strains credulity to expect such a mixture naturally to produce a peaceable kingdom. But even those who believe that all of us are born innately good are likely to concede that sharp disparity in culture, resources, and expectations may well result in dissatisfaction and social conflict. And when differences in nationality, ethnicity, and race appear to coincide with differences in social and economic position, the potential for resentment reaches the boiling point.

As this scenario has unfolded, the West, which includes the majority of the developed nations, has become the privileged focus of resentment. The West's economic and technological success accounts for a good share of this resentment, but not all. Since the scientific revolution and the beginning of the expansion of capitalism, but especially since the eighteenth century, when both were harnessed to a specific conception of individualism, Western economic success and technological superiority have undergirded an accelerating campaign to hold other nations to "modern" Western standards. The reach and variety of this campaign defy even a minimal summary, but it included such varied features as instruction in domesticity for Native American women, introduction of Western forms of absolute property into West Africa, opposition to veiling and clitoridectomy among Islamic and African women, and widespread defense of a variety of "human rights."

Throughout the nineteenth and early twentieth centuries, the West did tend to take pride in its difference from—and often its superiority to—other cultures. From the perspective of non-Westerners, the attitude found expression in missionaries' attempts to convert "heathens" to Christianity, in intellectuals' attempts to substitute science and rationality for traditional forms of thought, and in Western colonial administrators' and visitors' defense of the superiority of their political, social, and familial institutions. Many of the salient bones of contention emerge from a long-standing debate over Orientalism. Orientalism, according to its critics, most flamboyantly Edward Said, should be understood as "a Western style for dominating, restructuring, and having authority over the Orient."[2] Although Said popularized the arguments, he did not invent them. A number of Arab scholars had long resented the Western proclivity for what we might call intellectual colonization, namely, the appropriation and reinterpretation of Arab intellectual traditions in the interest of judging and objectifying them.

Said's sweeping assimilation of all Western Orientalists, as scholars of Arabic culture were known, into a single category reflected the multiculturalist sensibility that unilaterally condemned the West for casting members of all other cultures as "the other." Among other things, he purposed to demonstrate Westerners' unwillingness to respect any culture that differed from their own and any people who did not adopt their culture. The core of the charge, however, lay in something other than a mere critique of cultural chauvinism. As Said perfectly understands, that is a crime in which countless peoples have participated. But Said had no interest in leveling the playing field by reminding Western readers of such instances of Arab disdain for Western "barbarism" as flourished at the time of the Crusades. Rather, he sought to isolate the West as uniquely guilty and to challenge Westerners to atone for their sin by confession, penance, and fitting reparation.

Unlike most American academic multiculturalists, Said, whatever his failings, is a serious political man and a knowledgeable player on the world stage. It is, accordingly, reasonable to surmise that his attack on Orientalism was primarily intended as an intervention in the persisting campaign for a Palestinian state. In this case, fitting atonement might well include Western diplomatic support for the establishment of such a state. If a flurry of collective guilt over Orientalist prejudices resulted in multiculturalist gains within the American academy, so much the better, but his true purpose lay elsewhere. Most academic multiculturalists, however, lack Said's political sophistication and, in particular, his understanding of or dedication to the international stakes. For them, the stakes lie closer to hand, notably in control over the curriculum and the hiring and firing of professors.

Here again, the contrast with Said may help to clarify the issues. I do not know Edward Said personally, which means that I may entirely misjudge him. With some temerity, let me nonetheless suggest that Said, perhaps because of the substance of his political and diplomatic concerns, seems to have resisted casting himself as the representative of the Palestinians in the American academy. Thus, while he is more than willing to use his academic position to advance his political cause, he does not seem to be using his political cause to advance his academic position. Unfortunately, the same cannot be said of many of his colleagues.

One of the salient and arguably more disturbing aspects of multiculturalism has been the tendency of many academic multiculturalists to view their own advancement as a proxy for the advancement of their people. Thus, Joan Scott has argued that contemporary academic politics are a proxy for the political struggles of the past. She thereby implies that the academic success of a woman—or a member of some other "oppressed" group—constitutes an ex post facto gain for all women, today and in the past. This attitude exposes the intimate link between multiculturalism as an ideology and the identity politics that pervade so many of our schools and colleges. The question nonetheless remains whether identity politics simply figures as a weapon of multiculturalists, or whether multiculturalism is being debased into a weapon of identity politics. Merely to raise this question is to return us to the attempt to understand the relations between multiculturalism as ideology and multicultural society as fact. And we might take a preliminary step toward unraveling these relations by considering multiculturalists' attitude toward the West.

The critique of Orientalism focuses upon the injury that Westerners inflict upon others by assigning them the role of "the other." In this view, Westerners culturally exploit other peoples in order to establish their own superiority. Westerners are the informed observers, and their complacent gaze reduces other peoples to the observed—to mere curiosities, if you will. In this perspective, the first demand of those who are observed is to receive equal respect as thinking, observing subjects. This quest for respect figured prominently in the indigenous Arab critique of Orientalism, but the history of recent decades suggests that many Islamic peoples also seek something more. For Islamic societies, more than most, are inclined to oppose everything which they—with considerable justification—believe the West represents. The Iranians, to take the most dramatic example, do not, in the normal sense, seek to be accepted by the West on equal terms. To the contrary, they consciously reject Western values, which they—again not incorrectly—credit with the destruction of religious piety, organic bonds among individuals, and respect for tradition. As Bernard Lewis has cogently argued, Islamic fundamentalists believe that they represent the last bulwark against Western materialism, decadence, and nihilism, and they envisage their relations with the West as a holy war that must end in the destruction of one side or the other. The measure of their conviction may be appreciated in the number of them who unflinchingly die for the cause.

Few, if any, other peoples have ever declared a holy war on the West, although prudence and experience suggest that it would be rash to take the Chinese lightly. But I leave that consideration for the experts. Here, my point is simply that most developing nations are more than willing to benefit from at least some of the features of Western modernization, mainly economic development, but also such Western cultural tendencies as rock music, blue jeans, and television. And increasing numbers of non-Westerners are drawn to Europe, Canada, and the United States in quest of political freedom, education, employment, a higher standard of living, and improved prospects for their families. These people are less likely to see the West as evil incarnate than to see it as the custodian of riches they covet. In this respect, their goal is less to destroy it than to stake a claim to its resources. Evidence suggests that many immigrants value highly both the opportunities available and the prevailing political freedom.

Recent events confirm that rabid anti-Western sentiment may crop up in Serbia or Somalia or the Sudan or any other country that gets a first-hand taste of Western military power, but one may plausibly argue that after the Islamic fundamentalists the most pervasive hostility to the West does not lie beyond its borders but within them. A full exploration of the reasons for this hostility would exceed the time available here, but a few main points command attention. In part, the multiculturalists' hostility to the West reflects a revolt against rationalism and science and what some sneeringly call logocentrism. In part, their hostility reflects a fixation upon personal experience and subjective perception, which you will recognize as the flip side of their anti-rationalism. Neither sensibility is new to the West, which has frequently spawned its own harshest critics. Both nonetheless embody new elements, most significantly a systematic hostility to legitimate authority, expressed as a multi-front war against reason, nature, and God.

On the face of it, the link between multiculturalism and this radical personalism and nominalism seems less than obvious. Most of us would find the core rationale for multiculturalism in loyalty to, and identification with, a specific ethnic or national group with deep cultural traditions. Since it is in the nature of such groups and traditions to value the authority of the collectivity and the past over the claims of the individual, it is difficult to understand how membership in, or identification with, the group could be taken to justify hostility to authority. But that logic ignores the extent to which the multiculturalists embody the very *Western* traditions they claim to deplore. Multiculturalism as ideology owes more to Western individualism than it does to non-Western traditionalism, and the evocation of specific cultures has more to do with self-representation than with immersion in a traditional culture.

Critics have noted that American academic multiculturalists show little interest in learning the languages of other cultures, much less in respecting their hierarchical principles and traditions. What has received less attention is the extent to which multiculturalism embodies an assault upon history itself. Multiculturalists do not much like the encumbrance of unpleasant facts, especially about the culture with which they identify. Rarely, for example, do they dwell upon the prevalence of slavery throughout the non-Western world, especially among Islamic and African peoples. In their orthodoxy, slavery was a uniquely Western crime perpetrated upon non-Western peoples. And the attempt to convince them that until the late eighteenth century few people of any culture viewed slavery as a moral evil invariably shipwrecks upon the shoals of their unyielding presentism. If we may trust the evidence of recent experience, multiculturalists cannot conceive of a culture that was not grounded in, and did not celebrate the rights of, the imperial individual.

Some might expect that these individualistic convictions would naturally lead to a renewed celebration of the Western tradition, but they would be deceived. Indeed, multiculturalists regularly assail Western individualism, which they charge with the oppression and marginalization of all of those whom elite white men have cast as "the other." African Americans, Native Americans, and women regularly top the list of those whom white male Western individualism has injured, but as members of other groups claim their place at the table of the colonized and the oppressed, the list expands. The main criterion for inclusion appears to be a subjective sense of injury, and the preferred means of redress appears to lie in establishing one's personal right to protection, preference, or reparation. And thus do we return, once again, to the Western conception of the individual. At times, it is difficult not to see the entire struggle as the perennial revolt of the sons against the father or, in this instance, the children against the parents.

The criteria for inclusion within the embrace of multiculturalism provide grounds for confusion. Why women? Why those who proclaim assorted varieties of sexual preference? If one hews to a narrow understanding of culture as the system of beliefs and practices that unites a people of a specific ethnicity or nationality, then the inclusion of people of a specific sex or sexual preference seems difficult to justify. If, however, one adopts a broad understanding of culture as the beliefs and practices shared by people of similar tastes and "lifestyles," the inclusion makes more sense. But then we lose the meaning of culture as the articulation of the beliefs and practices of a historically grounded, self-reproducing community or people. Culture in this sense is something you are born into, not something you choose. What makes less sense is the pretense that relations among the embodiments of different cultures should be harmonious. History provides little reassurance on this score. Some of you may recall that ethnic and national difference apparently supplied the original rationale for slavery. This was the spirit in which Aristotle pronounced some men "naturally" fit to be slaves, since those whom he deemed natural slaves were those whom the Greeks called barbarians, by which they meant non-Greek.

Sad as it may seem, history also provides scant reason to assume that cultural pluralism and democracy are natural bedfellows. To the contrary, the coexistence of different cultures within a single territory or society has generally resulted in the triumph of an administrative or authoritarian government or in the enslavement of the members of one culture by those of another. The United States ranks as the primary example of a democratic multicultural society, and it has owed its success to distinctly Western values and institutions, including individualism and democracy. It would be a cruel irony if zeal to push those values and institutions to their radical extreme were to engender a quasi totalitarianism and the progressive undermining of respect for the individual.

Nowhere is it decreed that a multicultural society cannot sustain democratic institutions and respect for the individual. But history and common sense alike confirm that the attempt to level all distinctions of talent, accomplishment, and inheritance is more than likely to require draconian methods and end in tyranny. Consider the history of socialism in the twentieth century. By the same token, it is nowhere guaranteed that unyielding defense of the values and institutions of the past against the onslaught of those who are viewed as the modern barbarians will safeguard the core of the Western tradition. Consider the history of Rome from the third to the fifth centuries.

Rome, you will recall, was undermined from within as much as toppled from without. Edward Gibbon, the greatest historian to write in English, blamed Rome's fall upon Christians and barbarians, although their success owed much to the Roman elite's inability or disinclination to renew and reinvigorate its inherited culture. We would do well to recognize Rome's fate as a cautionary tale for our times, not because history inevitably repeats itself, for it usually does not, but because history leaves no doubt that the unthinkable can—and sometimes does—happen.

The multicultural reality of our world is here to stay and will likely intensify. The more interesting question concerns our adaptation to it. Neither multiculturalism nor anti-multiculturalism is serving us well. What we need is a capacious worldview that invites respect for the cultures of others and loyalty to one's own. Above all, any compelling understanding of the multicultural present requires attention to the past, because all cultures are essentially historical.

Notes

1. It is worth noting that the convergence is so great as to raise the question of the two men's possible influence upon one another, which is not implausible since Gramsci lived in the Soviet Union for several years.

2 Edward Said, *Orientalism: Western Conceptions of the Orient* (London: Penguin, 1991), p. 3. On the larger debate, see Ulrike Freitag, "The Critique of Orientalism," in *Companion to Historiography*, ed. Michael Bentley (New York: Routledge, 1997), pp. 620–38.

Selected Bibliography of Works by Elizabeth Fox-Genovese

Compiled by Ehren K. Foley

This bibliography provides a listing of those works written by Elizabeth Fox-Genovese that deal substantially with the themes of this volume. It is divided into books, coauthored books, edited and coedited works, and articles, including contributed chapters and review essays. Items in each section are listed chronologically by date of original publication. Included are items in this volume, related items in other volumes of this series, and those items that were excluded from this volume by constraints on space or by editorial decision. While the bibliography does strive for comprehensive coverage, it doubtless falls short of that goal. Several conscious omissions are worth noting. The bibliography does not include the many short book reviews and articles that Fox-Genovese authored during her career. It also omits those items that deal with themes addressed in the other volumes of this series, though there is some overlap between volumes. A full sense of the breadth of Fox-Genovese's work therefore requires perusal of each of the first four volumes of the selected edition of Elizabeth Fox-Genovese's writings and its accompanying bibliography.

Books

1976
The Origins of Physiocracy: Economic Revolution and Social Order in Eighteenth-Century France. Ithaca, N.Y.: Cornell University Press, 1976.

Coauthored Books

1983
With Eugene D. Genovese. *Fruits of Merchant Capital: Slavery and Bourgeois Property in the Rise and Expansion of Capitalism.* New York: Oxford University Press, 1983.

1985
With David Burner, Eugene D. Genovese, and Forrest McDonald. *An American Portrait: A History of the United States.* New York: Macmillan, 1985.

1991
With Virginia Bernhard and David Burner. *Firsthand America: A History of the United States.* 2 vols. St. James, N.Y.: Brandywine, 1991. Revised and expanded version of *An American Portrait.*

2005
With Eugene D. Genovese. *The Mind of the Master Class: History and Faith in the Southern Slaveholders' Worldview.* New York: Cambridge University Press, 2005.

2008
With Eugene D. Genovese. *Slavery in White and Black: Class and Race in the Southern Slaveholders' New World Order.* New York: Cambridge University Press, 2008.

Edited and Coedited works

1984
Editor and translator. *The Autobiography of Pierre Samuel DuPont de Nemours.* Wilmington, Del.: Scholarly Resources, 1984.

1999
With Elisabeth Lasch-Quinn. *Reconstructing History: The Emergence of a New Historical Society.* New York: Routledge, 1999.

Journal Articles and Sections of Books

1973
"The Many Faces of Moral Economy: A Contribution to a Debate." *Past and Present* 58 (February 1973): 161–68.

1974
Review of *France and the Chesapeake: A History of the French Tobacco Monopoly, 1674–1791, and Its Relationship to the British and American Tobacco Trades,* by Jacob Price. *Journal of Modern History* 46, no. 4 (1974): 691–701.

1975
"The Physiocratic Model and the Transition from Feudalism to Capitalism." *Journal of European Economic History* 4, no. 3 (1975): 725–37.
"Poor Richard at Work in the Cotton Fields: A Critique of the Psychological and Ideological Presuppositions of 'Time on the Cross.'" *Review of Radical Political Economics* 7, no. 3 (1975): 67–83.
"Psychohistory versus Psychodeterminism: The Case of Rogin's Jackson." *Reviews in American History* 3, no. 4 (1975): 407–18.

1976
"Physiocracy and the Overthrow of the Ancien Régime." In *Proceedings of the Third Annual Meeting of the Western Society for French History,* edited by Brison D. Gooch, 156–64. N.p.: Western Society for French History, 1976.

1977
"Property and Patriarchy in Classical Bourgeois Political Theory." *Radical History Review* 4, nos. 2–3 (1977): 36–59.

1978
"Yves Saint Laurent's Peasant Revolution." *Marxist Perspectives* 1 (Summer 1978): 58–92.

Selected Bibliography of Works by Elizabeth Fox-Genovese

1979
"The Crisis of Our Culture and the Teaching of History." *History Teacher* 13 (November 1979): 89–101.
"The Personal Is Not Political Enough." *Marxist Perspectives* 2 (Winter 1979): 94–113.
"Rethinking the Bourgeois Revolution." *Proceedings of the Consortium on Revolutionary Europe* 8 (1979): 31–36.

1982
"Gender, Class, and Power: Some Theoretical Considerations." *History Teacher* 15 (February 1982): 255–76.

1984
Introduction to *The Autobiography of Du Pont de Nemours*, translated and edited by Elizabeth Fox-Genovese, 1–74. Wilmington, Del.: Scholarly Resources, 1984.

1986
"The Claims of a Common Culture: Gender, Race, Class, and the Canon." *Salmagundi* 72 (Fall 1986): 131–43.
"The Great Tradition and Its Orphans, or, Why the Defense of the Traditional Curriculum Requires the Restoration of Those It Excluded." In *The Rights of Memory: Essays on History, Science, and American Culture*, edited by Taylor Littleton, 185–213. University: University of Alabama Press, 1986.

1987
"The Empress's New Clothes: The Politics of Fashion." *Socialist Review* 17 (January/February 1987): 7–30.

1988
"Communities of Discourse, Relations of Power: Thoughts on Culture and Society." *Historical Methods* 21, no. 4 (1988): 169–72.
"History as Collective Autobiography." In *Role of the Liberal Arts in Teacher Education: Proceedings of the First Regional Meeting of the Southeastern Holmes Group in Atlanta, Georgia, October 11–13, 1987*, by the Southeastern Holmes Group, 57–63. East Lansing, Mich.: Holmes Group, 1988.

1989
"Literary Criticism and the Politics of the New Historicism." In *The New Historicism*, edited by H. Aram Veeser, 213–24. New York: Routledge, Chapman & Hall, 1989.

1990
"Between Individualism and Fragmentation: American Culture and the New Literary Studies of Race and Gender." *American Quarterly* 42 (March 1990): 7–34.
"The Fettered Mind: Time, Place, and the Literary Imagination of the Old South." *Georgia Historical Quarterly* 76 (Winter 1990): 621–51.

1992
"Race and Crime." *World and I*, September 1992, 558.

1993
"The Anxiety of History: The Southern Confrontation with Modernity." *Southern Cultures*, inaugural issue (1993): 65–82.
"Beyond Transgression: Toward a Free Market in Morality." *Yale Journal of Law and the Humanities* 5, no. 1 (1993): 243–64.

1994
"Save the Males?" *National Review*, August 1, 1994, 49–52.

1995
"Between Elitism and Populism: Whither Comparative Literature?" In *Comparative Literature in the Age of Multiculturalism*, edited by Charles Bernheimer, 134–42. Baltimore: Johns Hopkins University Press, 1995.
"Debating Political Correctness: A Kafkaesque Trap." *Academe* 81, no. 3 (1995): 8–15.
"A New World for Women and Blacks?" *World and I*, June 1995, 44–53.

1996
"Confession versus Criticism, or, What's the Critic Got to Do with It?" In *Confessions of the Critics*, edited by H. Aram Veeser, 68–75. London: Routledge, 1996.

1998
Foreword to *The Diversity Myth: Multiculturalism and Political Intolerance on Campus*, by David O. Sacks and Peter A. Thiel, xi–xiv. Oakland, Calif.: Independent Institute, 1998.
"Of Sin and Horses: The Compelling World of Dick Francis's Mysteries." *Books and Culture: A Christian Review*, January/February 1998, 42–43.
"'Ways of Thinking,' or, The Curriculum without Content." *Academic Questions* 11, no. 4 (1998): 20–24.

1999
"Diversity and the Scholarly Task." Unpublished, 1999.
"History in a Postmodern World." In *Reconstructing History: The Emergence of a New Historical Society*, edited by Elizabeth Fox-Genovese and Elisabeth Lasch-Quinn, 40–55. New York: Routledge, 1999.
"Multiculturalism in History: Ideologies and Realities." *Orbis: A Journal of World Affairs* 43 (Fall 1999): 531–39.
"'What Oft Was Thought, but Ne'er So Well Expressed': From Oral Culture to the Written Text, Again." In *Literature as a Unifying Cultural Force*, edited by Anne Paolucci, 22–32. Wilmington, Del.: Council on National Literatures, 1999.

2001
"Faith, Reason, and the Liberal Arts." *Cresset: A Review of Literature, the Arts, and Public Affairs*, October 2001, 7–14.
"Profits and Prophets." In *The Global Economy: Changing Politics, Family, and Society*, edited by Lee Edwards, 139–48. St. Paul, Minn.: Professors World Peace Academy, 2001.

2002
"Liberal Education in the University: Prospects and Pitfalls." *Journal of Education* 183, no. 3 (2002): 39–48.

2004
"Liberté! Egalité! Académie!" *Touchstone*, December 2004, 15–18.

Coauthored Articles and Sections of Books

1976
With Eugene D. Genovese. "The Political Crisis of Social History: A Marxian Perspective." *Journal of Social History* 10, no. 2 (1976): 205–20.

1979
With Eugene D. Genovese. "The Slave Economies in Political Perspective." *Journal of American History* 66, no. 1 (1979): 7–23.

1982
With Eugene D. Genovese. Foreword to *Capitalism, Slavery, and Republican Values: Antebellum Political Economists, 1819–1848*, by Allen Kaufman, ix–xx. Austin: University of Texas Press, 1982.

1986
With Eugene D. Genovese. "The Religious Ideals of Southern Slave Society." *Georgia Historical Quarterly* 70 (Spring 1986): 1–16.

1987
With Eugene D. Genovese. "The Cultural History of Southern Slave Society: Reflections on the Work of Lewis P. Simpson." In *American Letters and the Historical Consciousness: Essays in Honor of Lewis P. Simpson*, edited by J. Gerald Kennedy and Daniel Mark Fogel, 15–38. Baton Rouge: Louisiana State University Press, 1987.

With Eugene D. Genovese. "The Divine Sanction of the Social Order: Religious Foundations of the Southern Slaveholders' World View." *Journal of the American Academy of Religion* 55, no. 2 (1987): 211–33.

Index

This index includes only names, titles, and places, as they appear in the text.

Absalom, Absalom! (Faulkner), 112, 139
Addison, Joseph, xxii, xxiv
Afghanistan, 273
African Americans, 48, 66, 75, 79, 158, 163, 198, 210, 212–13, 217, 221, 278; literary studies, 211, 214–15, 222, 262; slavery, 113, 215–16, 259; women, xx, 208, 216, 218, 220. *See also* Black Studies
Age of Jackson, 38
Agrarians, 137, 138
All the President's Men (Bernstein and Woodward), 73
Althusser, Louis, xvi
American Historical Association, 209
American Psychiatric Association, xxxii
American Renaissance, 103, 223
American Revolution, 43, 135, 136
American South, xxvi, xix, 63, 128. *See also* Confederacy; New South; Old South
American Studies, 196, 207–9, 218, 222, 224–25, 231n47
American Studies Association, 209
Andrews, William, 224
Angelou, Maya, 260
Anouilh, Jean, 260
Aquinas, Saint Thomas, xviii, 146, 234
Aristotle, xvi, 42
Assembly of the Notables, 26
Aunt Phyllis's Cabin (Eastman), 134
Averroës, xvi

Bacon, Francis, xvi

Baker, Houston, 212
Bakhtin, Mikhail, xxvi, 198, 260, 272, 273
Balkans, 273
Baltimore, Md., 114
Barthes, Roland, 173, 199, 206n14
Baudelaire, Charles, 117, 259
Baym, Nina, 218
Beauvoir, Simone de, 155
Beloved (Morrison), 215, 263
Bennett, William, 148, 155, 157, 159, 164, 166, 209
Bercovitch, Sacvan, 223
Beulah (Evans), xvii, 113, 132, 134–35, 136, 220
Beyond Ethnicity: Consent and Descent in American Culture (Sollors), 210
Bible, the, 215
Bibliothèque de l'Arsenal, 12
Bismarck, Otto von, 162
Black Gauntlet, The (Schoolcraft), 131
Black Studies, 76, 79
Blackstone, William, 42
Bledsoe, Alfred, 103
Bloch, Marc, 176
Bloom, Allan, xi, 202, 209
Bodin, Jean, 31, 42
Bolt (Francis), 267–68
Book of Orders, 5
Book-of-the-Month Club, 264
Boston, Mass., 114
Bradford, M. E., 126, 195
Brandist, Craig, xxvi
Bronte, Charlotte, 220

Brougham, Henry, xxiii, xxiv
Brown, Gillian, 223
Brussels, 274
Bryant, Anita, 73
Buckley, William F., Jr., 164
Burden of Southern History, The (Woodward), xx
Burke, Kenneth, 26

Calhoun, John C., 40, 46–47, 48, 103, 202
Call It Sleep (Roth), 211
Camus, Albert, 214
Canada, 277
Canning, George, xxiv
Cantillon, Richard, 15, 20, 24n11
Carby, Hazel, 216
Cardozo, Jacob, 112
Carter, Jimmy, 164
Caruthers, William, 111
Cather, Willa, 219
Catherine de Medici, 167
Catherine the Great, 167
Cavalier and Yankee (Taylor), 105
Cervantes, Miguel de, 150
Chambers, Ephraim, xxiii
Charleston, S.C., 46
Chechnya, 273
China, 88, 147
Chodorow, Nancy, 60
Christianity, xvi, xviii, 90, 132–33, 137, 163, 243, 244, 247, 253, 275; in Dick Francis's books, 269–70. *See also* Roman Catholicism
Chronicle of Higher Education, 209
Cicero, xvi, 146
Civil War, 63, 106, 124, 130, 134, 220
Clansman, The (Dixon), 138
Clive, John, 45
Closing of the American Mind, The (Bloom), xi, 202, 209
Coats, A. W., 3, 6, 7, 8, 9n2
Cobb, Thomas R. R., 103, 112–13
Coleridge, Samuel Taylor, 220
College of William and Mary, 158
Come to Grief (Francis), 268
Communism, xxx
Communist Party, xii

Confederacy, 119, 140
Conn, Jules, 12
Constable, Archibald, xxiii
Cooke, John Esten, 111
Cooper, James Fenimore, 108
Cooper, Thomas, 112
Corday, Charlotte, 169
Cosmopolitan, 185
Cott, Nancy, 58
Crusades, 275
Cyclopaedia, or Universal Dictionary of Arts and Letters (Chambers), xxiii

Daily Courier (Charleston), 119
Danton, Georges Jacques, 169
Darnton, Robert, 26
Davidson, Cathy, 195
Davis, David Brion, 50
Davy Crockett Manuals, 96
Declaration of Independence, 132
Declaration of the Rights of Man and the Citizen, 27
Defoe, Daniel, xxiv
Deleuze, Giles, 260
Denning, Michael, 231n47
Derrida, Jacques, 260
Descartes, Rene, 147
Dew, T. R., 112
Dew, Thomas Roderick, 103, 158
Diana (princess of Wales), 173
Dickens, Charles, 259
Dickinson, Emily, 117
Diderot, Denis, xxiii, 30, 31
Dinnerstein, Dorothy, 60
Dixon, Thomas, 138
Dostoievski, Fyodor, 117, 121
Douglass, Frederick, 155, 202
Dow Chemical Company, 72
DuBois, Ellen, 64
DuBois, W. E. B., 210, 211, 214
Dworkin, Ronald, 251
Dynasty, 179

Eastman, Mary, 131, 134
Eaton, Peggy, 46
Edge of the Swamp: A Study in the Literature and Society of the Old South (Rubin), 102, 103, 120

Index

Edinburgh Review, xxiii, xxiv
Eiseley, Loren, 235
Eisenhower, Dwight D., 163
Elbert, Sara, 58
Eliot, George, 155, 220
Eliot, T. S., 213, 223. *See also* "Love Song of J. Alfred Prufrock, The"
Elizabeth I, 155, 161, 163, 167
Elle, 185, 188
Emecheta, Buchi, 259
Emerson, Ralph Waldo, 132, 207, 209, 218, 228n10
Emory University, xxi
Encyclopedia Britannica, xxiii
Encyclopédie (Diderot), xxiii
Engels, Friedrich, xii, xvi, xxvi, 13
England, 4–6, 42, 63, 91, 241
English Civil War, 168
English Revolution, 151
Enlightenment, xxiii, 25, 47, 130
Equal Rights Amendment (ERA), 55, 66
Essai sur l'amélioration des terres (Patullo), 12
Essai sur le commerce (Cantillon), 20
Essais (Montaigne), xxi–xxii
Euclid, 42
Evans, Augusta Jane, xvii, 113, 118, 132, 134–35, 220
Explication du Tableau économique (Mirabeau), 12

Fanon, Frantz, 145, 147, 155, 259
Farabi, Abu Nasr al-, xvi
Fathers, The (Tate), 138
Fathers and Children (Rogin), 36–50
Faulkner, William, xiii, 112, 130, 138–39
Fausset, Jessie, 216
Faust, Drew Gilpin, 195
Ferraro, Geraldine, 187
Filmer, Robert, 151
First Amendment, 247
Fitzhugh, George, 131, 132
Forbonnais, François Veron de, 12
Ford, Gerald, 73
Forten, Charlotte, 216
Foucault, Michel, 83–86, 88, 95, 96
Fox-Genovese, Elizabeth, 7, 18, 22, 29, 32, 40–41, 48, 120, 129, 132,

146–47, 150, 175, 186, 189, 198–99, 201–2, 218, 222; "Beyond Transgression," xxx; comparative literature, 257, 259; "The Empress's New Clothes: The Politics of Fashion," xiii–xiv; Great Tradition, 157–71; history pedagogy, 69–81; "The Many Faces of Moral Economy," xxv; multiculturalism, 271, 276, 277; "The Personal Is Not Political Enough," xxviii; "The "The Political Crisis of Social History," 71; sexuality views, 234–35, 252–53; "Of Sin and Horses," xvii; women's movement, 52–54, 57, 60–62, 64
France, xxvi, 8, 18, 29, 42, 63, 92, 94, 131, 203, 272–73; Brittany, 31. *See also* French Revolution
Francis, Dick, xxxii, 264–70
Frankfurt School, xvi
Free Soilers, 163
Freehling, William, 43
French Revolution, 25–26, 30, 32–33, 43, 162, 168, 169, 180, 181
Freud, Sigmund, xviii, 37, 48, 49, 50; criticisms of, 84–85; Oedipal complex, 59–60; sexual power struggle, 83
Freudianism, 45
Frow, John, 202
Fruits of Merchant Capital: Slavery and Bourgeois Property in the Rise and Expansion of Capitalism (Fox-Genovese and Genovese), xx
Fryer, Judith, 219
Fuller, Margaret, 132

Galiani, Ferdinando, 18, 30
Gambetta, Léon, 31
Gates, Henry Louis, Jr., 214, 221
Geertz, Clifford, 26
Genovese, Eugene D., xx, xxix, 104–5, 107, 128; "The Political Crisis of Social History," 71
Georgia, 213
German Ideology, The (Marx and Engels), 13
Germany, 240, 273
Gibbon, Edward, 279
Gifford, William, xxiv

Gilman, Charlotte Perkins, 155
Gilmore, T. Michael, 223
Girondins, 169
Glamour, 185
Glanville, Joseph, 116
Goethe, 147
Goldmann, Lucien, 199, 206n14
Goldsmith, Oliver, xxii
Goldwater, Barry, xxxii
Goldwater Rule, xxxii
Gone with the Wind (Mitchell), 138
Gordon, Linda, 58
Goubert, Pierre, 13
Gouges, Olympe de, 169
Gramsci, Antonio, ix, xxvi, xviii, 39, 198, 272, 273
Great Tradition, 156–72
Greeks, 237–38, 279
Guattari, Félix, 260

Haiti, 141n15
Hammond, James Henry, 107, 108, 111
Harlem Renaissance, 213
Harper, Frances Ellen Watkins, 215–16, 263
Harper's Bazaar, 185, 188
Hartz, Louis, 44
Harvard University, 158
Hawthorne, Nathaniel, 103, 108, 121, 134, 202, 207, 218, 228n10, 230n36. See also *Scarlet Letter, The*
Hecht, Jacqueline, 12
Hegel, G. W. F., xvi, 154
Henry VIII, 241
Hentz, Caroline Lee, 131, 134, 219
Hispanic Americans, 158, 229n28
Historical Society (Boston), xxi
History of Sexuality, The (Foucault), 83
Hitler, Adolf, 240
Hobbes, Thomas, 42, 96, 151, 152, 252
Hobsbawm, Eric, 258
Hofstadter, Richard J., 47
Hollander, Anne, 184
Homer, 262. See also *Iliad*
Hopkins, Pauline, 215–16
Hot Money (Francis), 268
Hughes, Langston, 212, 213, 214, 224
Hume, David, 12

Hurston, Zora Neale, 215, 216
Hutchinson, Anne, 223

Ibarruri, Dolores, 167
Ice Cube, 262
Ida Leroy (Harper), 263
Ideology and Utopia (Mannheim), xxv
Iliad (Homer), 260
Incidents in the Life of a Slave Girl (Jacobs), 215, 216
India, 88
Indians, 37–38, 39, 40, 47, 48, 49
Inez (Evans), 220
Islam, 122–23n17, 273, 275–78

Jackson, Andrew, xxxii, 37, 40, 41, 43, 44–48
Jackson, Michael, 174
Jackson, Rachel, 46
Jacobins, 169
Jacobs, Harriet, 155, 202, 209, 215, 220
Jameson, Fredric, 195, 197, 199, 202
Janeway, Elizabeth, 167
Jefferson, Thomas, 132
Jeffrey, Francis, xxiii, xxiv
Jehlen, Myra, 223
Jews, 163, 210, 211
Jim Crow, 137
Joan of Arc, 163
Johnson, Samuel, xxii, xxiv, 107, 147
Jonah's Gourd Vine (Hurston), 215
Joyce, James, 213, 262

Kant, Immanuel, 150
Kelley, Mary, 218
Kelly-Gadol, Joan, 52
Kennedy, John Pendleton, 103, 111, 133
Kerber, Linda, 94, 209
Kerridge, Eric, 4, 6
Keynes, John M., 17
King, Martin Luther, Jr., 126
Kolodny, Annette, 218
Koran, the, 122–23n17
Kreyling, Michael, 133–34, 135
Ku Klux Klan, 137
Kuczynski, Marguerite, xii, 11–14, 16–19, 21, 22

LaCapra, Dominick, 195
L'ami des hommes (Mirabeau), 12
Lang, Amy, 223
Larsen, Nella, 216
Lasch, Christopher, 73
Law Enforcement Assistance Administration, 68
Le Blanc, 12
Leach, William, 56
Lennox, Annie, 174, 175
Levellers, 152, 168
Leverenz, David, 224
Leviathan (Hobbes), 151
Lévi-Strauss, Claude, 199
Lewis, Bernard, 277
liberalism, 8
Lincoln, Abraham, 163
Locke, John, 41, 42, 43, 47, 147, 151, 152
Longfellow, Henry Wadsworth, 117, 207
Longstreet, Augustus Baldwin, 103
Lorin, Félix, 12
"Love Song of J. Alfred Prufrock, The" (Eliot), 262
Lukacs, Georg, xii, xvi
Lumpkin, Katharine DuPre, 138
Lurie, Alison, 173
Luther, Martin, 47
Luxemburg, Rosa, 155, 167

Macaria (Evans), 220
Macaulay, Thomas B., 38, 39
Macfarlane, Alan, 91
Machiavelli, 42, 147
Mackrell, John, 26
Macpherson, C. B., xvi, 151
Madame Bovary (Flaubert), 257
Mademoiselle, 185
Madonna, 174
Major Fiction of William Gilmore Simms, The (Wimsatt), 108
Mallarmé, Stéphane, 117
Mannheim, Karl, ix, xxv, 272
Mannoni, Octave, 59
Mao Tse Tung, 147
Mapplethorpe, Robert, 236
Marat, Jean-Paul, 169
Marcuse, Herbert, 243, 251

Marie Antoinette, 169
Martinique, 145, 259
Marx, Karl, x, xii, xiii, xvi, xviii, xxiv, xxx, 11, 13–15, 17, 19, 22, 37–38, 50, 195; alienation, 68; class, 82; "fetishism of commodities," 179–80; Scottish Historical School, 197
Marxism, ix–x, xi, xv, xviii, xx, xxix, 44, 201–2, 221; feminism, 53–54; physiocratic studies, 11; political struggles of others, 231n46, 231n47; politics, 52; theory vs. practice, 68
Marxist Perspectives, xxi
Maryland, 114
Massachusetts, 114
McCord, Louisa Susanna, 202
McKeon, Michael, 195, 203
Medici, Catherine de, 167
Meek, Ronald, 11, 13
Melder, Keith, 58
Melville, Herman, 103, 108, 121, 207, 218, 228n10
Miami Vice, 173, 179
Michaels, Walter Benn, 223
Middle Ages, 136, 176, 177
Mill, Harriet Taylor, 155
Mirabeau, xii, 12, 20, 22, 28, 32
Mitchell, Juliet, 52
Mitchell, Margaret, 138
Model Army, 168
Modernism and the Harlem Renaissance (Baker), 212
Montaigne, xxi
More, Thomas, xvi
Morgan, Robin, 59
Morrison, Toni, 214–15, 260, 263
MTV, 173, 179

Napoleon, xxiv
Napoleon II, 195
Nashville, Tenn., 46
National Arts Council, 164
National Endowment for the Humanities, xxi, 164
National Organization of Women (NOW), 55
National Review, 164
Native Americans, 229n28, 274, 278

Necker, Jacques, 30
Neusner, Jacob, 164–65
New Left Review, xxvi
New Right, 73
New South, 138
New Testament, xvi
New York (city), 114
New York Times, 264
Newman, John Henry, 147
Newton, Isaac, 195
Nietzsche, Friedrich, xvi
Nigeria, 259
Nixon, Richard, 72–73
NOW (National Organization of Women), 55

O'Brien, Michael, 195
O'Connor, Flannery, 270
Ökonomische Schriften (Quesnay), 11
Old South, xiii, 104, 105, 112, 114, 117, 120, 121, 122n7, 135, 203
Onken, Werner, 14
Organization of American Historians, xxi
Orientalism, 275–76
Our Nig (Wilson), 209, 215, 216

Past and Present, 3
Patullo, Henry, 12
Pennsylvania, 37; Philadelphia, 114
People, 186
Philadelphia, Pa., 114
Physiocrats, xii, xxiv–xxv
Pizan, Christine de, 155
Planter's Northern Bride, The (Hentz), 134, 219
Plato, xvi
Playboy, 247
Pocock, J. G. A., 26
Poe, Edgar Allan, 103, 113–16, 118, 121, 122–23n17, 132, 218, 228n10
Polanyi, Karl, 15, 93
Pope, Alexander, 107
Porcher, Frederick, 112
Posner, Richard, 233–53
Prelude to Civil War (Freehling), 43
Problem of Slavery in the Age of Revolution, The (Davis), 50

Problems of Jurisprudence, The (Posner), 250
Prospero and Caliban (Mannoni), 59
Protestant Reformation, 238
Protestantism, 122–23n17
Punk, 175
Puritanism, 242

Quarterly Review, xxiv
Quesnay, François, xii, xiii, xvii, 11–12, 17, 20, 22, 32; agriculture theories, 19; capitalist production theories, 14; economic thought, 13, 16–17, 23, 27–29; individualism, 15, 17, 18, 22; materialism, 13; theory of value, 16
Quicksand (Larsen), 216

Ranger, Terence, 258
Reagan, Nancy, 173, 175
Reagan, Ronald, 164, 173
Rebel, The (Camus), 214
Reconsiderations (Toynbee), 161
Reconstruction, 137
Redskins, Ruffleshirts, and Rednecks (Young), 38
Reiss, Timothy, 195
Renaissance, 153
Representations, 195, 204
Republican Party, 163
Reynolds, David, 223
Richet, Denis, 26
Richmond, Va., 114
Riqueti, Victor. *See* Mirabeau
Robertson, Dennis, 38
Roche, Daniel, 26
Roe v. Wade (1973), 247–48
Rogin, Michael Paul, xxxii, 36–50
Roman Catholicism, xviii, xx, xxix, xxx, xxxii, 176, 220, 238, 242
Romanticism, 107, 111, 114, 117, 128, 129, 130
Roosevelt, Franklin D., 163
Roots (Haley), 76
Roots II (Haley), 76
Roth, Henry, 211
Rousseau, Jean-Jacques, xvi, 30, 172. See also *Social Contract, The*
Rubens, Peter Paul, 247

Index

Rubin, Gayle, 86
Rubin, Louis D., xiii, 102, 103–8, 111–17, 119–21, 128, 134, 138
Ruffin, Edmund, 103
Ruffin, Thomas, 103, 112
Rwanda, 273

Said, Edward, 275–76
St. George Tucker Society, xxi
Sale, George, 122–23n17
Salic Law, 100n12
Sartre, Jean-Paul, xvi
Saturday Night Fever, 174
Saussure, Ferdinand de, 199
Savvy, 185
Scarlet Letter, The (Hawthorne), 263
Schlafly, Phyllis, 73
Scholes, Robert, 145–46, 150, 155
Schoolcraft, Mrs. Henry, 131, 132
Schumpeter, Joseph A., 17
Scott, Joan, 209, 276
Scott, Sir Walter, 108, 109, 136
Scottish Enlightenment, xxxi
Scottish Historical School, xxiv–xxv, xviii
Second Treatise on Government (Locke), 151
Seeing Through Clothes (Hollander), 184
Sembène, Ousmane, 155, 259
Senegal, 259
Serbia, 277
Sex and Reason (Posner), 234, 236–37, 250–51
Shakespeare, William, 150, 158, 167, 262
Signifying Monkey, The (Gates), 214
Simms, William Gilmore, 103, 107–13, 117, 119, 121, 133–34, 135–36, 202
Simpson, Lewis P., 103–7, 120, 127–28, 138, 195
Singal, Daniel, 129–30
Smellie, William, xxiii
Smith, Adam, 7, 9n2, 21, 38, 192n12
Smith, Sidney, xxiii
Smith College, 158
Smith-Rosenberg, Carroll, 58, 95–96, 223
Social Contract, The (Rousseau), 32
Sollors, Werner, 210, 222, 228n10
Somalia, 277

Sophocles, 167, 260
South Carolina, 107, 110, 131–32, 135; Charleston, 46
Soviet Union, xii, 158
Spanish Civil War, 167
Spectator, xxii, xxxiii
Speculative Society, xxiii
Stanford University, 209
Steele, Jeffrey, 223
Steele, Richard, xxii, xxiv
Stowe, Harriet Beecher, 132, 134, 202, 218, 219
Sudan, 277
Sumer, 88
Sweden, 241, 242, 249, 252

Tableau économique (Quesnay), 11–12, 13, 16, 19, 21
Tale of Genji, The (Shikibu), 257
Tate, Allen, xiii, 103–4, 105–7, 127, 135, 137, 138
Tatler, xxii, xxxiii
Taylor, William, 105
10-Lb. Penalty (Francis), 264–70
Tennessee, 46
Terdiman, Richard, 195, 203
Thomas, Dylan, 213
Thompson, E. P., 3–8, 9n2, 9n14
Thornwell, James Henley, 103, 113, 202
Timrod, Henry, 103, 119, 120
To Tell a Free Story (Andrews), 224
Tolstoy, Leo, 121, 259
Tompkins, Jane, 195, 218
Tories, xxiv
Toynbee, Arnold J., 161
Trescot, William, 103
Truman, Harry S., 163
Tucker, George, 103, 112
Tucker, Nathaniel Beverley, 103
Tucker, St. George, 103
Turgot, Anne-Robert-Jacques, 29, 30
Tuskegee Institute, 158
2 Live Crew, 262

Uncle Tom's Cabin (Stowe), 219
United States, xv, xxvi, xxxi, 36–37, 40, 41, 42, 43, 46, 69, 95, 158, 160, 203, 273, 277, 279; class, 93;

United States (*continued*)
  individualism, 52, 54; race relations,
  124; sexuality, 242–43, 246, 249,
  251–53; women, 94. See also U.S.
  Constitution; U.S. Supreme Court
U.S. Constitution, 248
U.S. Supreme Court, 247–48
University of Virginia, 158
University of Wisconsin, 158

Vassar College, 158
Vega, Lope de, 150
Virgin Mary, 90
Virginia, 114
Vogue, 185, 188
Voltaire, 147

W, 188
Walker, Alice, 213–14, 216, 224
Wall Street Week, 187
Watergate, 72
Weber, Max, 38
Western Civilization, 69, 78
Wharton, Edith, 219
Wheatley, Phillis, 215
Whigs, xxiv

Whip Hand (Francis), 267, 269
Whitman, Walt, 228n10
Whittier, James Greenleaf, 207
Wide, Wide World, The (Warner), 263
Willis, Susan, 215
Wilson, Augusta. See Evans, Augusta Jane
Wilson, Harriet, 216
Wimsatt, Mary Ann, 108–9, 122n7
Wollstonecraft, Mary, 155, 162, 192n12
Women's Christian Temperance Union
  (WCTU), 58
Women's Studies, 76, 79, 211
Women's Wear Daily, 188
Woodcraft (Simms), 134, 135
Woodward, C. Vann, xx
Woolf, Virginia, 155
Wordsworth, William, 111
Working Woman, 185
World of Rabelais, The (Bakhtin), 272
World War I, 129
World War II, xxxiii, 72, 158, 159, 160
Wright, Richard, 155, 213

Yemassee, 111
Yemassee, The (Simms), 107, 109–10
Young, Mary, 38